Humbling Faith

HUMBLING FAITH
Brokenness, Doubt, Dialogue

What Unites Atheists, Theists, and Nontheists

Peter Admirand

CASCADE *Books* • Eugene, Oregon

HUMBLING FAITH
Brokenness, Doubt, Dialogue—What Unites Atheists, Theists, and Nontheists

Copyright © 2019 Peter Admirand. All rights reserved. Except for brief quotations in critical publications or reviews, no part of this book may be reproduced in any manner without prior written permission from the publisher. Write: Permissions, Wipf and Stock Publishers, 199 W. 8th Ave., Suite 3, Eugene, OR 97401.

Cascade Books
An Imprint of Wipf and Stock Publishers
199 W. 8th Ave., Suite 3
Eugene, OR 97401

www.wipfandstock.com

PAPERBACK ISBN: 978-1-5326-3784-1
HARDCOVER ISBN: 978-1-5326-3785-8
EBOOK ISBN: 978-1-5326-3786-5

Cataloguing-in-Publication data:

Names: Admirand, Peter, author.

Title: Humbling faith : brokenness, doubt, dialogue—what unites atheists, theists, and nontheists / Peter Admirand.

Description: Eugene, OR : Cascade Books, 2019 | Includes bibliographical references and index.

Identifiers: ISBN 978-1-5326-3784-1 (paperback) | ISBN 978-1-5326-3785-8 (hardcover) | ISBN 978-1-5326-3786-5 (ebook)

Subjects: LCSH: Humility—Religious aspects. | Humility—Religious aspects—Christianity. | Humility. | Philosophy and religion.

Classification: BV4647.H8 A36 2019 (print) | BV4647.H8 A36 (ebook)

Manufactured in the U.S.A. FEBRUARY 26, 2019

The author especially wishes to thank poet, Laura Apol, for her permission to quote from her poetry collection, *Requiem, Rwanda* (published by Michigan State University Press), © 2015 by Laura Apol.

All Gospel and Pauline Scripture quotations herein are from the New Revised Standard Version Bible: Catholic Edition copyright © 1993 and 1989 by the Division of Christian Education of the National Council of Churches of Christ in the U.S.A. Used by permission. All rights reserved.

For quotations from the Tanakh:

The author greatly acknowledges permission to reprint from the following copyrighted work: *JPS Hebrew-English Tanakh*, copyright 2000 The Jewish Publication Society.

For my dad who taught me honesty (and the pain of being a Mets fan)
&
my mom for her boundless energy (and love of ice cream)

Contents

Acknowledgment ix
Introduction: The Dream and the Dread:
  Humility Humbled, Faith Faltered 1

1. Hubris and its Modest Foe:
   Jewish, Muslim, and Christian Views 21
2. Umble Pie: Eastern and Primal Views 47
3. Many Ways or One Way?
   Religious Pluralism and Sheltering Another's Hopes 66
4. Interfaith Dialogue as Challenge and Catharsis 96
5. Linking Theist-Atheist Dialogue: Bridges and Platforms 116
6. Illuminating Past Sins: History and Memory in Dialogue 148
7. Testimonies, Witnessing, and Moral Failure 180
8. Yielding with the Other: Forgiveness, Justice, Love 225

Conclusion: Mutual Stumbling, Together:
  Embracing Brokenness, Doubt, Dialogue 269
Bibliography 275
Name Index 321
Subject Index 333

Acknowledgment

Perhaps, one should not begin an acknowledgment page late at night, when the kids are still up, and my wife, Kelly, is getting ready for her long run tomorrow morning (fifteen miles in a build-up to The Dublin City Marathon in October), and I'm sitting at the kitchen table on a very, very small wooden chair (one of the kids'). Too many things can go wrong—interruptions of one kind or another. "Daddy, I have to pee," Mary, the two-year-old announces; or "Dad, Where's my phone-charger?" Jack, the oldest at fourteen, barks; then the twelve year-old, Chris: "Netflix isn't working"; and the five-year-old, Ryan, supposed to be asleep, but pleading for water, and Kaitlyn, the ten-year old diva singing away, but ready to talk at the slightest hint so I try to avoid eye-contact; and then, the four-legged creatures, chime in: Sally, the German short-haired pointer, wants to go outside; or the cats, Oskar and Bijou, want to be fed. And then a phone call from my mother-in-law, of all people, wanting (I kid you not) to ask about this book, of all things. I knew this was a bad idea, but this is all part of the gratitude, isn't it?

Acknowledgment pages, overlooked by many, are sometimes the secret garden of a book, the El Dorado in otherwise stale, monotonous (or swamp-infested) terrain; or the only chance (especially in an academic work) to get a Facebook-glimpse into personality, into some inner-realm of the otherwise objective, professional author. As this book is about humbling, there is little point in trying to be too guarded and so this won't be the only time the laundry is exposed. Who can write as if all this chaos wasn't a daily, loved reality?

I thank (again) the lovely people at Cascade Books and Wipf and Stock. I was lucky to work with my editor, Dr. Charlie Collier, on my first book in 2012, and it was so uplifting to get his email response: "So, great to hear from you," when I emailed about this book. I always joke the best thing about my theodicy book was the cover chosen and the index—neither done by me. Similar thanks on other aspects of this book. In addition to thanking Charlie for believing in my work again, I thank Sallie Vandagrift for copyediting, Heather Carraher for typesetting, and Elizabeth Walker, the indexer. *Humbling Faith* received financial support from the Faculty of Humanities and Social Sciences Book Publication Scheme at Dublin City University: which is my official way of saying "thank you" to them, too. I also thank my colleagues in the School of Theology, Philosophy, and Music at DCU, and especially the head of school, Dr. Ethna Regan. For the audiobook version of *Humbling Faith*, I am forever in debt to Dr. Declan Tuite, my Dublin City University colleague in the School of Communications. The generosity, enthusiasm, and time he spent helping to transform this book into an audiobook cannot be adequately stated. I also want to thank Declan and the School of Communications for generously allowing me the use of one of their studios for recording (with Declan doing all the audio-expertise heavy lifting!).

The book is dedicated to my parents: third time's the charm (and so no three strikes and I'm out). Dad, don't read the page about the kids and their favorite zoo (not the Bronx Zoo). On that note, I thank Gerry Creighton, Dublin Zoo Operation Manager, for kindly agreeing to meet with me about forgiveness in elephants and primates (see chapter 8).

As I still sit on this (more comfortable than I thought) child's wooden chair, I'm reminded of a reality a few years ago that made this prospect seem so far away—neck pain that lasted for months on end, preventing me from sitting down for any stretch without agony; and I feared: "How can I write, read, do things I love?" I'm ok now (straighten back, curl your shoulders, deep breath, drink water, run each day), but so many people in the world aren't. That experience, that humbling, helped me see a bit more of others' pain. So, too, when after my PhD, the Celtic Tiger crashed, crashing me with it due to a government hiring freeze. You see your vulnerabilities, your weaknesses, the parts of you that aren't nice, that aren't kind—that are mopey, denying depression (in others, fine, but not in you). This journey, humbling in ways I would never have signed off on, but I think, I hope, has helped make me a better person, or at least shown me how to be that better person. The title is *Humbling Faith*, and is about how and why all faith and non-faith positions can be humbled. I was definitely humbled in the process; maybe you will be, too, but I think that may be a good thing, overall.

One more glimpse in the garden: to Kelly, who once again, will never, ever read anything in books I write and is in solidarity with those partners of other writers who just want to know: is it done, yet? Because now Ryan has to pee; the phone charger is still missing; Mary (she's still up?) has just climbed onto my lap and said: "You're my best friend in the whole world" (so that kid can stay up forever); Netflix is working, but Chris wants a spider killed; Jack is hungry and there's no cereal; Kaitlyn has a rehearsal tomorrow but did she ever find her black skirt? and was Sally ever fed dinner? and the cats are scratching at the door to get out.

How could I have done any of this without her? The book's finally finished: blessed humbling.

Rathfarnham, Ireland
Autumn/Fall, 2017

Introduction

The Dream and the Dread: Humility Humbled, Faith Faltered

Elephantine Knowledge

This book's boastful (or brittle) title belies a creaking dread and a deep, burgeoning, and unrealistic dream. More on that dread and dream, later—for now let me tell a story. It's a parable we're familiar with, but that doesn't dull its beauty, charm, or luster. It's the story of the elephant and the blind men, and it traverses various religious traditions: Jain, Buddhist, Hindu, Sufi, and secular tales for adults and children.

Three (or six) blind men are asked (often by a king or prince) to describe an object before them. Hands reach out to probe and graze. Some focus on the trunk and conclude a pillar or wall; another clutches the tail and believes it's rope, still more grab and grope other body parts. They render learned pronouncements. As Rumi writes of one individual: "He's proud of his description."[1] As metaphor, momentarily severed from an interpersonal and ecological ethics, the story works because we're all blind in various ways, but unlike those men, many of us do not recognize our condition. Those of a Christian bent may think of Jesus's phrase: "You will indeed listen, but never understand, and you will indeed look, but never perceive" (Matt 13:14).

The story highlights our tendency to mistake a part for the whole and opens the way for deeper intercultural and interfaith learning: "If each of us held a candle there, / and if we went in together, we could see it."[2] Mutual sharing and solidarity of knowledge will be key elements of this work—and yet. . . .

---

1. Rumi, *Essential Rumi*, 252.
2. Ibid., 252. See also Pugliese and Hwang, *Teaching Interreligious Encounters*.

What many people miss when listening to the story is the king's role. He seems omniscient, while the others flounder, sightless, but what did he know?

Actually, the unnamed and ungendered elephant is the most important individual in the story, but is treated as an object or fact to be prodded, twisted, and grasped; a puzzle to solve. There is great presumption in decreeing a mystery solved, though I cannot rebuke the blind men for trying (could they disobey the king?). We all want to solve the riddles of the Sphinx, Delphic oracle, Samson, or Gollum. It is too tempting not to try and sometimes much is at stake if we do nothing.

From the elephant's standpoint, her experiences were cruel and unpleasant. She is forgotten once revealed: a disappointment to some (only an elephant?), a riddle-trophy to others. Awareness that "it" was an elephant formed no communion or relationship. Her role done, she was forgotten save as a means, metaphor, or moral. But so what? It's only a story, only an elephant, and an imaginary elephant at that.

Like any bestial story, there's more to the tale. Seeing the unknown as the elephant was only a preliminary step, yet some departed from the encounter as if enlightened. How much remains unknown about the elephant, and ultimately, could only be known from her perspective?[3] We again confront our ignorance and powerlessness, back in the realm of not knowing and not understanding. At least we recognize this incomplete, awkward state. Call it an embrace of elephantine knowledge.

Such an embrace may be monstrous and stupendous, but is aware of its lumbering clumsiness. Some theists may have elegant syllogisms on God's existence, for example, but amid anguish and moans become hushed and bumbling. Atheists may construct godlike arguments against God's existence, but in the presence of Hindu gurus in meditation, grow awestruck, porous.

This is a book hoping to embolden doubt and sharpen unanswerable questions, all in the context of seeking and loving self and one another. Ridiculously, it believes the world can be healed through such a hope. It humbly dreams elephantine dreams.

For an academic, such is childish, even taboo. Most books are unloved and forgotten, wisps of smoke.[4] Only hubris says otherwise, and so

---

3. See Masson and McCarthy, *When Elephants Weep*; among primates, dolphins, whales, and the octopus, see de Waal, *Are We Smart Enough*; Whitehead and Rendell, *Cultural Lives of Whales and Dolphins*; and Godfrey-Smith, *Other Minds*.

4. Aurelius, *Meditations*, VII.34 (111). Also confer Ecclesiastes 4:13.

it's ironic (or fitting) in a book highlighting humility to hope to change the world. Yet, humility at its best is transparent, neither unduly deflating nor inflating. Who crafts a book envisioning no one will read it? All hope for success, but here in the context of *tikkun olam*, the Jewish term for mending the world. It is an old hope and a new hope and—let's hope—a future hope. Our world will always need mending, but will there be menders? Sadly, books like these may not be "useless" so "long as ignorance and misery exist in the world."[5] But may they strive for such uselessness.

As humility is such a central component of *Humbling Faith*, this introduction will first outline its meanings and limitations, especially what is meant by "humbling." Such will also need a foray into the tangles of faith, which like humility, is a contested, sometimes distorted and amorphous, word,[6] disavowed by some, and cuddled by others. Sparing neither theists nor atheists (and those betwixt and between), I contend why faith includes everyone and so visit the links (and divides) of science and faith.[7] My argument is not hinged on any alliance, though. Whatever you label your position, even if seeking to visit a plague upon faiths, then substitute whatever word or phrase classifies or represents your allegiances or worldviews: reason, science, will, chaos, spontaneity, serendipity, determinism.

I will then outline chapter goals and conclude by returning to the dream and the dread (or at least the dread), as I've already hinted at the dream.

"What's in a Name?"[8] Humbling

Time for a brief grammar lesson. In the title *Humbling Faith*, notice the dual grammatical possibilities of "humbling," as adjective and gerund. As an adjective, humbling can describe a faith that should be humble. What this (the state of being humble, humility) means will be the focus of the first two chapters and returned to throughout the book.

"Humbling" also acts as a gerund—and a gerund is a verb (with an added ing-ending) that expresses an action or another state of being but forms another grammatical function in a sentence. "Humbling Faith"

---

5. Hugo, *Les Misérables*, xxxvii.
6. Tillich, *Dynamics of Faith*, xxi. See also Mackintosh-Smith, *Landfalls*, 157.
7. For a historical overview, see Larson and Ruse, *Faith and Science*.
8. Shakespeare, *Romeo and Juliet*, II.ii.43.

is only a phrase, so one could add the verb "is" along with a predicate adjective. The result could be: humbling faith is immoral, pompous, self-serving, or cathartic. If using a predicate nominative, we could say humbling faith is a waste, sacrilege, or panacea. What is meant, intended, and ultimately produced can surely differ.

What of humility and humiliation?[9] This link will be repeated by some Christian thinkers in chapter 1, but repetition does not make something good or healthy.

Humiliating and humility, although close in pronunciation and spelling, and overlapping somewhat in meaning, must be vehemently severed. It can seem humiliating to be humbled, and could seem deserved, but actions meant to humiliate exceed what I call an act of humbling. Humbling should be an act of love. To humiliate has the intention of injuring, anathema to love. *Humbling Faith* aims to help lessen our inflated sense of worth, singularity, uniqueness, and power. Perhaps, more importantly, it is a (covert) paean to love, amidst all our weakness and frailty, achievements and glory, and this world's failures and flourishing; for love is the supreme humbler.[10] The hope is we come together with our complementary strengths, amidst our mutual brokenness, loving amidst, through, and in such shared brokenness. Some of us need reminders that we are broken. Others need reminders that their brokenness doesn't define them. Both reminders can be humbling.

Of humility, consider Jesus's words in the Beatitudes: "Blessed are the meek: for they will inherit the earth" (Matt 5:5). What is remarkable about the claim is the ultimate triumph of the meek; to the meek shall be given the spoils, as it were. Conquerors and blood-thirsty tyrants, let alone swanky real-estate moguls, will ultimately be evicted. The meek are "movin' on up."[11] What kind of meekness, or in our context, humility, is this? Do the meek simply play the long game?

The humility I elevate is necessarily rugged, scrappy, and stubborn. It does not cower amidst oppression and injustice. It's relentless until heard, like the prayer of the humble in the book of Sirach (35:17). Humility, at its core, is self-assessment and self-evaluation, upholding a mirror to the self and the Other. Perhaps surprisingly, the paradox of a humble pride is one way to maintain this often abused and co-opted term. John

---

9. Heft, "Ignorance," 9.
10. See chapter 8.
11. Feel free to sing along to the opening of The Jeffersons sitcom.

Dominic Crossan speaks of "humility-in-power" and "being a servant-as-leader." His context is Jesus's response to the apostles when they were bickering after James and John tried to barter for prized heavenly seats (Mark 10:37).[12]

In the Western world, humility was virtually non-existent, ignored, or disabused by the Greeks and Romans, became preeminent in Christian thought and (in theory) practice (rooted in the prophets of the Tanach), and then later was disparaged by key Western philosophers and distrusted by many feminist and third-world thinkers. It also had little value in any naturally aggressive capitalist context and in fields like law, business, and politics.[13]

More recently, humility has received a renaissance in business circles as a means for greater success and profit. Corporate culture has deemed religious people as loyal and dependable co-workers.[14] More humble people are needed in the corporate world, but real humility would be a hard sell, if it were true to its calling. Humility is very costly. Alas, humility and venture capitalism, or humility in the board room, seem like strategy and magic tricks.[15] But then, so might meekness and inheriting the earth. Part of the problem (or richness) is the proliferation of types of humility. Consider these versions.

Kantian humility[16] expresses the notion that we cannot know things in themselves, that our knowledge is partial and incomplete, similar to epistemic humility, which accentuates the limits of whether, what, and how much we can know. Democratic humility, according to Mark Button, is rooted in the reality of a pluralist democracy with competing worldviews calling for pragmatic openness and humility.[17] Tied to the thought of Martin Heidegger is what Nancy Holland calls ontological humility. Such recognizes our limitations and ignorance about our ability to know things in themselves and the cause and reasons for existence; it is

---

12. Crossan, *Power of Parable*, 167; see also Myers, *Binding the Strong Man*, 277–80.
13. Straub, *Hidden in the Rubble*, 130.
14. See Ou et al., "Humble Chief Executive," 34–72.
15. On economists and social justice, see Kishtainy, *History of Economics*, 5; on the recent partnership of Christian fundamentalism and business, see Grem, *Blessings of Business*.
16. See Langton, *Kantian Humility*.
17. Button, "Monkish Kind of Virtue?," 841 and 861.

also linked to our inability to know who we are with certainty—let alone truly knowing other manifestations of life.[18]

Intellectual humility is characterized by a disinterest in fame or recognition through one's intellectual achievements and is instead concerned with attributes that transcend our search for identity (justice, God, love, peace), seeking intrinsic knowledge and truth for its greater good towards others.[19] It acknowledges limitations and ignorance.[20]

In the first two chapters, humility will be further stretched and investigated across religious and philosophical systems. Interfaith and interdisciplinary crossings will be necessary, both to form a thick conception of humility, and preposterously, to humble all faiths. Key questions about humility include:

1. Is humility a virtue for all?
2. Should humility be for the successful, not the marginalized?
3. Does humility trample the already trampled? Does it impede legitimate success and happiness?
4. Is any self-conscious attempt to be humble self-defeating?
5. How is humility foundational for identity and self-worth and so for treatment of others?
6. How do you humble others in humility?
7. Is pride not needed to balance humility, and vice-versa?

Such questions will be examined in subsequent chapters, but let's now humble, if not unintentionally humiliate, humility—for it comes with a mixed pedigree, and perhaps should be as resisted in some circles as it needs to be restored in others.

Downgraded, Despised, or Deficient: Against Humility

To its critics, humility pummels those already struggling. It also has a checkered and humble past. For Alasdair MacIntyre, humility "could appear in *no* Greek lists of the virtues."[21] The Homeric worlds of Odysseus

---

18. See Holland, *Ontological Humility*.

19. See Signer, "'Seeing the Sounds,'" 56; and Cornille, *Im-Possibility of Interreligious Dialogue*, 4.

20. Harari, *Sapiens*, 279.

21. MacIntyre, *After Virtue*, 136.

and Achilles are generally not hospitable to humility, though death and the battlefield humble all. While pride is valued, the poets censure hubris,[22] whether of Achilles, Agamemnon, or Paris. In the tragedies of Aeschylus, Sophocles, and Euripides, no heroic[23] embodiment of humility shines. In the Theban Plays, we don't associate humility with Oedipus, Creon, Antigone, Polynices, or Eteocles. Main characters do have virtuous qualities, whether fortitude, wisdom, or loyalty, but they are not humble, and are ultimately humbled too late.

Socrates's quest for truth, meanwhile, emphasized admitting ignorance and testing apparent knowledge (the Socratic Method), but humility seems neither fully applicable to Socrates nor Plato. In *The Apology*, Socrates's claim that he is no clever speaker, unless by that one means "someone who speaks the truth,"[24] is disingenuous at best. If we consider Plato's *Republic*, Socrates is obviously more humble than Thrasymachus[25] but the despotic world Socrates advocates isn't infused with humility. There are too many hierarchical divisions (the Guardians) or blatant totalitarian tactics, as advocated against the poets.[26]

Awareness of our ignorance, though, is crucial to what I advocate. Even if Socrates expects he knows more than his interlocutor (because he knows more of what he does not know)—feigning ignorance as strategy—is still praiseworthy, so long as he yields to another's potentially more successful argument.[27] Intellectual ignorance[28] complements similar unknowing in other areas, involving practical, social, religious, spiritual, and emotional knowledge.

For Aristotle (see chapter 1), humility is usually deemed "mistaken" or a vice.[29] While Cicero advises humility or praises the humble,[30] we don't connect humility with him, especially in his self-congratulatory Ca-

22. Kalimtzis, *Inquiry*, 8.

23. In regards to heroism, see Young, *Frank Miller's Daredevil*; and Phillips and Strobl, *Comic Book Crime*.

24. Plato, "Apology," 21.

25. Plato refers to being surprised by Thrasymachus's verbal attack on him, *Republic*, I.336d (16).

26. Ibid., 607b (277), but see Plato, *Laws*, 129 (716a). See also Ryan, *On Politics*, 59–60.

27. See Plato, "Euthyphro," 6 (1–20); and Plato, *Meno*, 24.

28. In *Meno*, Plato admits he knows "nothing about virtue" (23).

29. MacIntyre, *After Virtue*, 177. See also ibid., 182.

30. Cicero, *On Duties*, 136.

tiline Speeches.³¹ Overall, it seems MacIntyre is correct: humility is not a pre-eminent ancient virtue.

Is Augustine right when, in *The City of God,* he contrasts pagans' pride with the humility founded in Christ? Any satisfactory answer must start with Jewish conceptions of humility, but whether justly, fortuitously, or ironically (perhaps all three), Christianity became religions' spokesperson for humility. When Western thinkers rebuked Christianity, humility became collateral damage or deemed a complicit enemy. Consider some of these anti-humility highlights.

Montaigne remarks: "a man may be humble through vainglory."³² Benjamin Franklin penned something similar: "for, even if I could conceive that I had completely overcome [pride], I should probably be proud of my humility."³³ Once Christianity's most pervasive virtue is deemed hypocritical and specious, what remains of it?³⁴

Spinoza, meanwhile, wrote that humility is a passion, not a virtue, and that "Self-esteem is opposed to humility."³⁵ To be fair, he also conceded that humility has advantages,³⁶ and rebuked pride as "thinking more highly of oneself than is just."³⁷

For David Hume, humility "and the whole train of monkish virtues" are useless for gain and society, and so closer to vices.³⁸ Who would want to be intimate in society with such people?³⁹ Hume touches on the fringes of just critique, but overplays his rhetorical thrust. He misrepresents the "monkish virtues" through spurious utilitarian or quasi-capitalist catego-

---

31. See Cicero, "Against Lucius Sergius Catalina," in 71–145; see also Sallust, *Conspiracy of Catiline.*

32. Montaigne, *Essays* II:17 (479); see II:7 (274) on his thoughts echoing Aristotle's view of magnanimity; see also II:29 (359) where he says: "humility and submissiveness alone can make a good man"; and see II:12 (370), where his words resonate with a core theme of *Humbling Faith*: "To really learned men has happened what happens to ears of wheat: they rise high and lofty, heads erect and proud, as long as they are empty; but when they are full and swollen with grain in their ripeness, they begin to grow humble and lower their horns." Note how D. H. Lawrence speaks of "proud humility" in *Sons and Lovers,* 147; and see also Day, *Long Loneliness,* 255.

33. Franklin, *Autobiography,* 72.

34. Button, "'Monkish Kind of Virtue,'" 845.

35. Spinoza, *Ethics,* 108; see also 143.

36. Ibid., 144.

37. Ibid., 108.

38. Hume, *Enquiry Concerning the Principles of Morals,* 73.

39. Ibid.

ries: not advancing one's fortune or one's value to society, "nor qualify[ing one] for the entertainment of company."[40]

As an aside, who wouldn't enjoy the Dalai Lama's company, for example? He has ample monkish virtues, but that boisterous laugh alone renders him more than good cheer. When the Dalai Lama was speaking in Central Park in 2003, I tried to get as close as possible to hear him, along with 65,000 other New Yorkers. Alas, the crowds encamped were too thick; and my then seven-month-old son Jack seemed to agree with Hume's judgments about such monkish men. So off to the playground we went.

Also consider William Blake's poem, "The Human Abstract."[41] For Blake, humility springs from fear of others that leads to exclusion and hatred. Such humility is one of the three foundational roots (along with fear and cruelty) that together form a religion of mystery and deceit, concocted by human beings. We read: "He [Cruelty] sits down with holy fears / And waters the ground with tears; / then Humility takes its root / Underneath his foot."[42]

Not surprisingly, Nietzsche had no love of humility, especially for his übermensch who soars above us and our feeble gods, customs, and laws. Disgracefully, humility was a means of the lesser to exalt themselves over the greater. The humble, like other detritus, should be left to their own devices, unable to pester and claw. What ultimately happens to them is of little or no concern. For Nietzsche, humility is allied with "mendaciousness"[43] or in the image of a prudent worm feigning death to avoid further injury.[44]

While the image above may contain a potentially veiled compliment,[45] for Nietzsche, humility is a weakness that seems to enervate the potent and provide "the mill for vengeance against the strong to take root."[46] What we can glean from Nietzsche is the need to balance power and humility and to recognize where humility can be a danger to

---

40. Ibid. See also MacIntyre, *After Virtue*, 231.

41. Interpretations of Blake greatly vary: see Burdon, "William Blake," 448; and Roberts and Rowland, "William Blake," 373–82.

42. Blake, *Poems*, 126–27. See also Thoreau, *Walden*, 32.

43. Nietzsche, *Anti-Christ*, no. 44.

44. Nietzsche, *Twilight*, 26, no 31.

45. Ibid., no. 848.

46. Ibid., no. 848.

an already oppressed or humbled people.⁴⁷ This is especially a concern of marginalized women.⁴⁸ Exaltation, not humility, is sometimes required. Mennonite minister Cynthia Lapp argues that in imitating a humble Jesus who challenged the power systems of his time, women "have inspired many to overthrow their enforced humility and live in chosen humility."⁴⁹ Nevertheless, for Lapp and other feminists, the word "humility" is so tainted with hypocrisy and patriarchal control that its revaluation is too deeply compromised.⁵⁰

Feminists are not the only ones leery of humility, whose status has been invariably questioned, assessed, and reassessed. In 1985, Daniel Nelson wrote that "Contemporary scholarship in religious ethics has neglected the virtue of humility."⁵¹ Noting a "diminution in value," Button asked in 2005: "Whatever happened to humility?"⁵² In 2007, Robert C. Roberts wrote that humility "has fallen on hard times."⁵³ In 2012, Catherine Hudak Klancer remarked that "Humility is not a particularly trendy virtue"⁵⁴; in 2014 Lisa Fullam wrote that humility is "suspect,"⁵⁵ while the cover blurb in Joseph J. McInerney's 2016 book on Augustine stated that the "jury is out on humility."⁵⁶

Many contemporary thinkers argue that humility is excessively self-denying, wishy-washy, weak, passive, borderline unhealthy—and of little value in worlds that matter: finance, politics—even love.

Norvin Richards evaluates humility among the powerful and contends it isn't a virtue if requiring low self-esteem or employing the highest standards as a comparative base, concealing belief in superiority to most others.⁵⁷ Richards suggests that healthy humility requires healthy pride,⁵⁸

---

47. Lapp, "Balancing Power," 258.
48. Hooks, *Bone Black*, 138.
49. Lapp, "Balancing Power, 260.
50. Ibid., 258. For an interesting pop-culture history of feminism, see Lepore, *Wonder Woman*.
51. Nelson, "Virtue of Humility," 298.
52. Button, "'Monkish Kind of Virtue,'" 840.
53. Roberts, *Spiritual Emotions*, 78.
54. Klancer, "How Opposites (Should) Attract," 662.
55. Fullam, "Teresa of Ávila's Liberative Humility," 175.
56. McInerney, *Greatness of Humility*; see also Vainio, *Disagreeing Virtuously*, 163.
57. Richards, "Is Humility a Virtue?," 255.
58. Ibid., 255.

what leads to honest judgment, compassion, and mercy towards others.[59] In *Let Us Now Praise Famous Men,* James Agee warns against pride's most "mild, common denominator form, complacency."[60] Both observations are valuable to our inquiry. While complacency will be consistently censured, pride will resurface in the next chapter, not always under the banner of a vice. One reason pride should be praised is because of a plethora of falseness, the debauched form of humility. Can pride be more honest than humility?

Faux Humility

Usually we don't connect designer handbags with humility, but both can be knock-offs. In John Steinbeck's *East of Eden,* the narrator describes Cyrus Trask's unnamed first wife possessing "egotistical humility."[61] In *Vanity Fair,* Becky Sharp wears humility like a strategic gown to win people to her advantage.[62] R. S. Thomas warns against "a pretense at humility."[63] St. Bernard points to the pitfalls of a "prideful humility," where one can confess one's sins proudly or falsely.[64] Unduly lowering oneself is a means of false humility, or servile humility, as Nietzsche railed against.[65] Likewise, Pascal refers to absurd, or patent humility.[66] False humility, however named, disempowers and depersonalizes all those in its presence.[67] So, too, does any deification of humanity.

Combating both extremes is science, with its maturing, and deeply humbling, picture of humanity's seeming insignificance in the cosmos.

---

59. Ibid., 258.

60. Agee, *Let Us Praise,* 220.

61. Steinbeck, *East of Eden,* 16.

62. Thackeray, *Vanity Fair,* 443 and 509. See also Wiesel, *Souls on Fire,* 241. For Kant's critique of such calculated humility, see *Metaphysics of Morals,* 188. Samuel Coleridge and Robert Southy, moreover, refer to a "pride that apes humility" in their 1799 poem "The Devil's Thoughts."

63. Thomas, "Gradual," in *Selected Poems,* 151.

64. Bernard of Clairvaux, "On the Steps of Humility and Pride," 136. See also Mann, *Buddenbrooks,* 584.

65. Nietzsche, *Beyond Good and Evil,* no. 260.

66. Pascal, *Penseés,* 79.

67. See Schueler, "Why Modesty Is a Virtue," 483; Driver, "Modesty and Ignorance," 827–34; and Schueler, "Why IS Modesty a Virtue?," 835–41; for authentic humility, see the desert mothers (ammas) in Swan, *Forgotten Desert Mothers,* 52.

Stephen Jay Gould, Peter Adkins, and others have argued that all is contingency, chance, and indeterminate; that human beings were neither a necessity nor a given; and that chance variations could have easily created a world without us.[68] As Clive Finlayson comments, such requires "a large dose of humility."[69]

The deep awareness of the immensity of our universe also minimizes the self-importance often attributed to Earth.[70] The vastness of geological time without the presence of human beings, renders claims of human superiority hollow and specious.[71] Such truths are also evident when examining the fossil record, particularly the extinction of other humanoid species like Neanderthals.[72] In a book about famous scientific blunders, astrophysicist Mario Livio closes with a "plea for humility" from Charles Darwin.[73] Darwin acknowledged the noble qualities of human beings but still reminded us that "Man bears in his bodily frame the indelible stamp of his lowly origin."

Science and Faith

Vietnamese Buddhist Thich Nhat Hanh describes faith as "a kind of energy," and those without faith have no vitality, a deadness in the eyes.[74] My aim is for all of us, no matter our affiliation, label, belief, or non-belief to see how we are flawed, our systems fallible and in need of humbling. While faith is a broad word including such ideas, I mean whatever fills and frames our world, what energizes and guides us in Hanh's notion, whether reason, science, evidence, philosophy, or nationalism. The book is especially addressed to those allergic to the word "faith"[75] and to those overly confident and proud in the faith they profess or system of thought

---

68. See Gould, *Richness of Life*, 211 and 219. For theological responses, see McMullin, "Evolutionary Contingency and Cosmic Purpose," 140–61; and Delio, *Emergent Christ*, 13–31.

69. Finlayson, *Humans Who Went Extinct*, 105.

70. See Preston, *Goldilocks and the Water Bears*; Al-Khalili, *Aliens*; Comins, *Traveler's Guide to Space*; and Wohlforth and Hendrix, *Beyond Earth*.

71. Eiseley, *Firmament of Time*, 3. See also Brusatte, *Dinosaurs*, 349.

72. Finlayson, *Humans Who Went Extinct*, x.

73. Livio, *Brilliant Blunders*, 271. Interestingly, in *The Origen of Species*, Darwin adds that we should view extinction as no less surprising than sickness or death (323).

74. Hanh, *Going Home*, 83.

75. Gopnik, "Bigger then Phil."

that guides them. Again, those who loathe the word faith or insist it has no bearing on their way of life[76] are missing the point. Remove faith and substitute a better word or phrase—but the argument for humbling remains.

A secondary argument, or need for justifying, is why faith need not be constrained to a religious context, certainly not a Christian one. These arguments are particularly relevant in any discussion of science and faith. For many scientists (and atheists), faith is of no value or consequence.[77] As Carl Safina clarifies, though, science may be evidence plus logic, but we can ignore evidence and use faulty logic.[78] Although science draws a line between facts and theories, can we say faith resembles scientific theories?

Paul Tillich famously stated that "Faith is the state of being ultimately concerned."[79] For Tillich such ultimate concern includes all human beings—even in their varied and conflicting beliefs.[80] He argued that some element of faith is always present; faith as an ultimate concern of the ultimate.

According to Terry Eagleton, "If the autonomy of the universe springs from its sharing in the life of its Creator, faith is no enemy of science."[81] While Galileo and creationists may protest, religion and science have enjoyed a fairly healthy and robust dialogue, if not partnership. As astrophysicist (and atheist) Mario Gleiser comments: "both the scientist and the faithful *believe* in unexplained causation, that is, in things happening for unknown reasons, even if the nature of the cause is completely different for each."[82] As examples, Gleiser highlights how Einstein and Newton had to have faith in their theories—even as they also knew them to be "faulty and limited."[83]

Does science also need to be humbled, then, and could the spirit and practice of science gain from this book's approach—while maintaining the faith/science divide?

76. Davies, "Taking Science on Faith."
77. Ruse, *Atheism*, 243.
78. Safina, *Beyond Words*, 29 and 19.
79. Tillich, *Dynamics of Faith*, 4.
80. Ibid., 106–7.
81. Eagleton, *Culture and the Death of God*, 49.
82. Gleiser, *Island of Knowledge*, 4. See also Dworkin, *Religion without God*, 17, 19, and 65.
83. Gleiser, *Island of Knowledge*, 7.

If faith is "the assurance of things hoped for, the conviction of things not seen" (Heb 11:1), then many will scoff that they have any faith; perhaps because they do not hope (perhaps they act, instead) or their evidence is strictly verifiable and tested. The gulf between modern science and much of contemporary religious faith yawns. The use of a religious word—faith—seems biased and messy. We can hear Richard Dawkins chide: "Faith is an evil precisely because it requires no justifications and brooks no arguments."[84] Dawkins is particularly opposed to teaching children that blind, unquestioned faith is a virtue and would especially oppose any claim that he, too, has a type of faith.

Dawkins contends that non-believers like himself rely on facts, data, proof, statistics, percentages or some combination of that arsenal. As Carl Sagan wrote: "Science asks us to take nothing on faith."[85] Perhaps we can say faith in a theist can be exemplary, but not for the scientist qua scientist; either way, they both often exhibit faith, whether in moments of weakness or strength.

Life remains riddled with gaps, incongruities, fragments, ambiguity, contradiction, and mystery (or hypotheses, and so needing further tests).[86] Such demands space, hesitation, and acknowledgment of all we do not know. Science, despite major advances, remains still seeking (and testing for) ultimate answers. Barring outright any spiritual or theological possibilities for ultimate answers is to believe in one's own system of truth-claims, and so is properly called faith. Or if not faith, it certainly calls for a deep humility and profession of the unknown. As Loren Eiseley pens: "science frequently discovers that it must abandon or modify what it once believed. Sometimes it ends by accepting what it had previously scorned."[87] This is the magisterial potency of science: holding everything in question to uncover proven truths, and using ignorance and failure to do so, as Stuart Firestein writes.[88]

Science, like religious faith, must also grapple with the consequences of its actions and intentions. As Sagan added: "In too many cases we [scientists] have lacked a moral compass."[89] Here science can benefit from

---

84. Dawkins, *God Delusion*, 308.

85. Sagan, *Billions*, 166.

86. Evolutionary biologist Wallace Arthur speaks of evidence and speculation "at the heart of science" (*Life through Time and Space*, 20–21).

87. Eiseley, *Firmament of Time*, 5.

88. Firestein, *Failure*, 3. See also Gleiser, *Island of Knowledge*, 92 and 280.

89. Sagan, *Billions*, 164. See also Dalai Lama, *Universe in a Single Atom*, 208.

moral or philosophical theology, and from spiritual and religious systems that acknowledge what cannot be technologically measured: spirituality, the good, the soul, joy, interbeing (*Tien Hien*), love. It is a question of discerning and acknowledging penultimate and ultimate questions.[90]

As science and technology are symbiotic and intertwined, moreover, ponder the measured pace of scientific development and maturity while its technological means[91] develop with disproportionate celerity. Consider its ability to perform mind-bending calculations; store unfathomable amounts of data; discern movements, sounds, smells, identities, and sights beyond mere human cognition and ability; hone robotic and AI capabilities;[92] delve further into the cosmos and deeper into immemorial time for causes and contingencies, even to create and modify life, or restore species long extinct. Yet, the moral record of science reveals a mixed legacy. Science and that indispensable technology have both offered the means to prolong and improve life and to desiccate and eradicate it many times over.

Science fails to achieve its full potential when not reflecting on, and instituting, whether its means and aims are best suited to the long-term protection and viability of life. In the name of science, commitment to human dignity and the preciousness of all life have been trampled and dismissed. Science has calibrated who is human, who is not; who is worth saving, who is not; what is torture, and what is torture light. Here religion and science have little clash, sadly. Often these moral failures of science are from scientists unduly partnering with national interests or under the sway of a totalitarian and brutal dictatorship.[93] Prosaically, it is the allure of fame, lucre, or job stability. While genocide can be committed with machetes, science was indispensable for the Holocaust.[94] Science entwined with military aims and agendas, which often are also bereft of any universal moral framework, selectively seeks to save those deemed "one of us" or, broadly, those considered saveable and valuable. Others are terrorists, enemies, or collateral damage.

---

90. Wagner and Briggs, *Penultimate Curiosity*, 440.

91. Firestein, *Failure*, 221.

92. See Mahon, *Posthumanism*; Cargill, *Sea of Rust*; and Jeff Lemire and Dustin Nguyen's comic series *Descender*.

93. Harari, *Sapiens*, 337.

94. See Sherratt, *Hitler's Philosophers*. On genocide's origins, see Sands, *East West Street*; and Bloxham and Moses, *Handbook of Genocide Studies*.

Today, science is increasingly dependent upon market forces, stock prices, and other capitalist agendas and aims, also bereft from sustained moral, let alone theological, inquiry and engagement. The question is often not whether this can be done, but the more difficult and slippery, should this be done? Such involves faith in our actions, means, and hopes, in the worldview in which we enact such tests, and the meaning and value of what is studied. What is more important than the dialogue of religion and science?

Faith can be a plastic enough principle or position to incorporate everyone, whether the radical skeptic (who exhibits a certain faith in his perspicacity of doubt), the nihilist (having faith in no professed faith); or the scientist who depends upon his calculations, statistics, and experiments, trusting that meaning and value are not possible outside of what can be calibrated, quantified, verified, and categorized. What doesn't fit is an anomaly that science will eventually configure and name. Does not such hope resemble faith, closer to what atheist Michael Ruse rebukes as "scientism," which falsely claims to have every solution?[95]

Easy, no-doubt answers today are not warranted. Theists have plenty of reasons to doubt their positions; but so should atheists and nontheists.[96] Such doubt provides greater space for learning and partnership within scientific and religious worldviews. As Jonathan Sacks writes: "[Science] tell us what and how but not why."[97] The why question is aided by the what and how conditions; this is why religions and moral philosophies need to study, reflect, and incorporate scientific truths and challenges. Science, though, should not dismiss or forego the all-important why question, and so benefits from religious and ethical voices and inputs, too.[98]

A good barometer here, as in many things, is Einstein, who ascribes to the "genuine" scientist a "faith in the possibility that the regulations valid for the world of existence are rational, that is, comprehensible to reason."[99]

---

95. Ruse, *Atheism*, 118.
96. Bowker, *Why Religions Matter*, 103–4.
97. Sacks, *Dignity of Difference*, 40.
98. Harari, *Sapiens*, 304–5.
99. Einstein, *Ideas*, 46.

The Journey

This is an ambitious work, with a "mighty theme,"[100] unabashedly interdisciplinary, and (gasp!) eclectic. But before I explain its architecture and literary structure, a comment on attempts at artistic flourishing—think of gargoyles with the faces of a building's architects, engineers, and owners (Woolworth Building). In *Humbling Faith*, readers may notice the acrostic in the table of contents spells "humility." It was like Ariadne's thread helping me through the maze in my vision of what is before you. I also imagined humility would blush at blatant exposure (and likely for good reason).

Readers may also notice a quotation in each chapter from a nineteenth-century French novel, fitting here for its narrative of a human "ascent secular in rhetoric but with a Dantesque ambition and even a glow of transcendence."[101] This was also my version of "Where's Waldo?"—though obvious with footnotes and the index. Also of marginalia-relevance is the reference to Silenus near the book's middle, which has a rich literary and philosophical history. It was also a nod to a literary magazine, *The Silenus*, which Michael Colaresi (now a Professor at the University of Pittsburgh) and I edited while in Oxford during our junior year of study abroad at the Centre for Medieval and Renaissance Studies in 1997. The journal proudly sits in my office, and I always liked the idea, as Rabelais noted, that the hidden treasure in the middle would be found in a rather ordinary box. Silenus may seem drunken and slurring, bald and fat, but was really "a noble and inspired Prophet," as Michael wrote in the introduction to our journal. Once again, a work of humility seems anything but!

Here is a brief outline of each chapter:

The first two chapters are foundational on humility (and its partner-in-crime, pride). Chapter 1 examines humility in the Jewish tradition (Tanach and Talmud); presents Islamic views of humility in the Qur'an and hadiths, and analyzes humility's role in the Gospels and in four Christian thinkers.

Chapter 2 evaluates humility in major faith traditions from South and East Asia: Hinduism, Buddhism, Taoism, and Confucianism. It also

---

100. Melville, *Moby-Dick*, 376.

101. Schmidt, *Novel*, 349. For the record, I don't think it's the greatest novel of the nineteenth century (contra Bellos, *Novel of the Century*) as *The Brothers Karamazov, Moby-Dick,* and *War and Peace* edge it out.

aims to highlight the importance of primal/indigenous traditions for humility studies.

Chapter 3 turns to the first area to humble faith: the reality of religious pluralism. It addresses the variety of religious plurality and examines the limitations or misconceptions of pluralism. It also explores pluralism in Hinduism, Buddhism, Islam, and Judaism. It closes with a presentation of pluralism in nature through the writings of anthropologist (and atheist) Loren Eiseley.

Chapter 4 incorporates the second area of humbling faith: interfaith dialogue. It provides an overview of the aims, types, and hopes of interfaith dialogue and briefly examines the way hope within interfaith dialogue has changed and developed in the Catholic Church and presents some contemporary Jewish critiques of Christianity as test cases for how dialogue humbles (and enriches).

Chapter 5 evaluates the third area of humbling faith: the secular/religious dialogue. It builds on the growing literature in the area of religious/secular dialogue and seeks bridges with and towards the New Atheist debates. As a humbling exercise, I argue for the importance of secular ethics, meaning, and humility as a Catholic theologian.

Chapter 6 presents the fourth area of humbling faith: history. I argue for the need to read history from multiple perspectives, linked with memory studies. Ethical and just reading of history necessarily should have deep repercussions, defining and humbling our identities. As a representative example, I will examine the ongoing problems of racism against black Americans in the United States.

Chapter 7 presents a fifth area of humbling faith: witness testimonies of mass atrocity and genocide. As argued in my previous books, contact with such witnesses humble all our worldviews and are enough on their own to shatter and disinvest us of any claimed superiority or comforting truths. This road will be similarly daunting and humbling.

Chapter 8 presents a sixth area for humbling: the need to accept and seek forgiveness, without losing sight of justice. It will evaluate the limits and questions surrounding forgiveness, the links of humility and forgiveness, the reality of the unforgivable, and evaluate the strengths of secular forgiveness. It also includes a trip to Dublin Zoo (to study forgiveness among elephants).

In the Conclusion, I assess the paths taken in the book and reiterate why we need to recognize our universal brokenness and dependence, moral failures, and human limitations. I argue that from this recognition, we can reach greater solidarity and hope in one another, removing the hubris that clouds our judgments and dismisses the needs and moral dreams of others—our faith humbled, but our horizons, hopes, and vision expanded. So, at least is the hope and the dream, but it is now time for the dread.

The Dread

Can one dread in a riad in Fes, sitting on a rooftop, sipping mint tea, as the melodious call for prayer (*adhan*) echoes along the rooftops, in the distance, nearby, intermingling, blending: religion in stereo sound? Or moving down in the courtyard, lounging on a settee, admiring the intricately, hand-painted cedar doors, the ornate patterns of mosaic tiles (*zellij*), the floral stucco designs wrapped around windows and along walls, the painted wooden ceilings, the silver lamps emitting shades of green, red, yellow, and blue? Colors, serenely, exploding?

For my 40th birthday, my wife let me travel for a few days in Morocco with my friend Boubker who is originally from Casablanca. I have just finished a warm conversation with an Irish Catholic priest now living in Birmingham and a Moroccan student from Fes working in the riad. My mind and soul are peaceful, and any dread is far, far removed from my thoughts. I had sat in the riad's courtyard to finish this introduction: a way to minimize the dread, surrounded by beauty. I had not planned on the conversation, the late hour.

The priest had returned from a retreat at Notre Dame de l'Atlas, home to Trappist monks, one of whom survived the massacre of seven in Tibhirine, Algeria, in 1996. Still living as Catholics amidst a dominant Muslim population, they had not sought aggressively to evangelize and convert, but to learn and to live with those around them. The three of us spoke about the need to encounter other faiths and people, even as we were also reminded that such does not always end well.

I began this introduction a few years ago, when the book was merely an idea, and there was so much, too much, to dread, not only of its value, but whether ideas sketched could be formed and structured. Had I been another hapless Reverend Edward Casaubon, filing cryptic notes in books for some supposed future use?[102] As Don Quixote warns Sancho: "for there are some who exhaust themselves learning and investigating

---

102. Elliot, *Middlemarch*, 166–67.

things that, once learned and investigated, do not matter in the slightest to the understanding or the memory."[103] Here the dread can be linked to apprehension, maybe awe, even reverence. But reverence for what? Those who persevere, amidst the futility, amidst the hopelessness?[104]

There are, of course, other dreads, endless dreads, diurnal dreads: similar dreads many of us have, about our children, spouse, parents, job, bills, health. Some dreads I remain oblivious to, shielded and protected by luck, obstinacy, God, or a jinn. Others, meanwhile, languish, mourn, and succumb. Some dreads manifest and destroy any in its path. Then there are dreads of a personal nature, of various failings and rejections: do I even fear a loss of faith amidst another work so deeply pummelling and stripping away? For how long can a believer flirt with such ideas, encouraging and dreaming of them?

Even after beginning this introduction, the dread loomed. I told myself I'd wait to work on it in Fes, and if not Fes, Marrakesh or Casablanca, and there I could face, and name, and maybe release the dread, like a flock of birds taking off for flight. Sitting here amidst the architectural beauty, the dread seems absorbed, if not quelled, by the multi-colored light and patterns, and the call to prayer that had unnerved me the first time I heard it in Istanbul, and is now no longer strange or unfamiliar; but anticipated, even missed.

Yes, some dread is vain or useless, but this elephantine book is dominated by dreams of a humbled faith serving to unite peoples of all faiths, and no faith. It humbly dreams elephantine dreams. Perhaps we need both the dread and the dream just as one needs humility and pride. But how to achieve the balance, how to achieve a humbling that elevates, not crushes or suffocates? Hopefully this work serves such a humble, but pivotal task.

---

103. Cervantes, *Don Quixote*, 601.
104. See Ammaniti, *Anna*, 14.

1

Hubris and Its Modest Foe
Jewish, Muslim, and Christian Views

There is something slimy, slippery, and self-serving when endorsing humility. In reflecting upon it, we should shudder and stutter like Moses before the burning bush: sibilance par excellence. For such hissing and rasping should be a warning: humility, sadly, can embody the sinister and serpentine, sloughing and shedding what is good, noble, and true.[1] Failures in humility come at great cost: an excess of humility primarily injures oneself; a lack of humility primarily injures others. Either way, suffering and pain increase.[2] Too many of us think writing the word "humility" (like despots quote "democracy") garners a modest mien and estimation. Instead, apertures open for revealed hypocrisy and duplicity.

Ultimately, learning from one another is the tinder for any lasting humility to remain alight within and for others. Think of humility like a controlled fire removing the detritus, dead wood (of excessive pride), and other dross. It can seem destructive but the result can be moral growth, verdure, and regeneration. Of course, controlled fires are rarely controlled;[3] and humility, like fire misused and left rampant, can be

---

1. While no herpetologist, I note the wise role snakes play in many ancient texts and folktales. The feathered serpent Quetzalcoatl in the Aztec tradition, "was the teacher of the arts, originator of the calendar, and the giver of maize" (Campbell, *Hero with a Thousand Faces*, 358). For James Kugel, the serpent in Genesis is just a talking snake with no explicit links to later Christian interpretations about the Devil (*How to Read the Bible*, 51). For the positive role snakes may have played in human evolution, see Isbell, *Fruit*, 2.

2. Pascal, *Pensées*, 240. See also Austen, *Pride and Prejudice*, 47.

3. Anthony with Spence, *Elephant Whisperer*, 179; on controlled fires by Native Americans before Columbus, see Mann, *1491*, 279–84.

dangerous.[4] But without humility, a different means of self-destruction is almost guaranteed. Think of such lack as a type of moral spontaneous human combustion, if not metaphorical then literal as depicted of the alcoholic Mr. Krook in Dickens's *Bleak House*.[5] Humility is life-sustaining and life-giving, but comes with a warning to use with care.

This chapter assesses some key resources and texts on humility, principally in the Christian tradition, but also drawing upon Jewish sources, notably in the Tanach and the Talmud, and from the third Abrahamic faith, Islam.[6] But first: opening thoughts on humility without God.

Godless Humility, Part I

In the introduction I espoused a spunky humility (or humbled pride).[7] Shakespeare, for example, couldn't credibly claim he was a middling playwright. The humble should be immersed in reality as Jon Sobrino notes, especially in solidarity with the poor and oppressed.[8] Here, theists and nontheists both suffer, are immersed in the causes, or work for healing.

Can only God truly humble us? Perhaps, but don't I feel humbled in the presence of the Grand Canyon, wild elephants, an exploding supernova, or a sugar cube's intricacies? I do, but this awe stems more from the wild and fruitful diversity of creation by a Creator. Cynically, humans destroy such things with indifference, even glee. While some boast (others lament) of God's death, I cling to the idea that God as a mystery, source, question, and (ultimate) quest mirrors our search for meaning and purpose. To alter such an attribute would seem to alter humanity's fiber and essence. God doesn't vanish by claiming God's demise. Does not a haunting and spectral afterglow remain?

Of God in Auschwitz, Elie Wiesel questions: "Why do you go on troubling these poor people's wounded minds, their ailing bodies?"[9] Here God seems mere echo and nuisance, an enervating remnant of guilt preying on the weak and defenseless; a type of phantom faith-itch. Or maybe

---

4. See Wohlleben, *Hidden Life*, 205–9.

5. Dickens, *Bleak House*, 463–64.

6. For a critique of the term Abrahamic, see Levenson, *Inheriting Abraham*, 207.

7. Henry James writes of a "noble humility or an enlightened pride" (*Portrait of a Lady*, 248).

8. See Sobrino, *No Salvation Outside the Poor*.

9. Wiesel, *Night*, 66. See also Morris, *Tattooist*, 169.

God's presence can still be glimpsed amidst our moral decrepitude? Remember that for Wiesel, belief in God (which amounts to wrestling with God) restores and maintains some sense of hope and meaning in this world.[10] Even great human beings are still flawed, yearning, frail, and seeking. The saint and the heroic and, sadly, the murderer and degenerate, are still like us in many ways (think Shylock's "hath not a Jew eyes" speech,[11] or Buddhist interdependence).

The tinges of awe and humbling before creation, then, are not as pervasive and magnanimous as the existence of a Creator God, for whom one may rail and curse, deny and "kill," but who still seems to remain, ever remain, as long as we, and the intricacies and convulsions of life, remain.

And yet, perhaps needing God for authentic humility is a sign of my own weakness and pride. If there is no God so now anything (supposedly) goes, then the genuinely humble still respect and dignify others in their words, gestures, and actions. Is true humility only possible for atheists? Should humility be easier for theists—another reason theists should be humble? Or is humility too tainted by patriarchal, anti-womanist, and anti-marginalized voices to be retrieved for any lasting or foundational role today? I'll return to secular humility in chapter 5.

Humility, Judaism, and the Tanach

Humility has been fiercely claimed (with a dearth of humility) by many Christians. But as a virtue or moral quality, it is neither contained nor solely represented in any one tradition. Christians may highlight Jesus as the highest embodiment of that term. Non-Christians would humbly offer their own exemplars. The Hasidic Rebe, Menahem-Mendl of Kotzk, for example, said of [Zusia of Lizensk]: "Just as there are scientific geniuses, there is one in matters of humility, and I mean Rebbe Zusia."[12] Zusia was a renowned figure of Galician Hasidism, along with his brother Elimelekh. Many other examples could be cited. Any Christian conception must begin with the Tanach and Jewish tradition.

---

10. Wiesel, *And the Sea is Never Full*, 70.
11. Shakespeare, *Merchant of Venice*, III.i.53–69.
12. Wiesel, *Souls on Fire*, 96.

"The virtue of humility," Daniel M. Nelson writes, "was central to the moral-religious understanding of traditional Judaism."[13] Nelson cites seminal biblical passages (with subsequent rabbinic discussion) like Micah 6:8: "to walk modestly with your God." Stanislaw Krajewski adds that the principle lesson in the Bible of humility is in the story of Moses, who is called humble, *anav*, while a great man and foundational leader of the Jewish people.[14]

Moses is not just called humble, but "a very humble man, more so than any other man on earth" (Num 12:3). Such a claim was more problematic when Moses was thought to be the author of those words. As James Kugel writes: "Surly, interpreters reasoned, a very humble man would not have said such a thing about himself."[15] More excessive claims have been made against Moses by the likes of Freud in *Moses and Monotheism*, or in Zora Neale Hurston's *Moses, Man of the Mountain*.[16] Regardless, everyone is humbled in the Tanach. Think of Adam and Eve, the satan, Moses, and David, whether forced to flee Eden; to slither on the ground among the dust and detritus; be barred from the Holy Land; or to endure chastising at the words of one's prophet (Nathan) and later through the vanity of one's son (Absalom).

Of the great rabbinic sage Hillel, Rabbi Telushkin writes: "Hillel is most famous as a teacher, but the Talmud makes it clear that his ability to teach anyone was connected to his ability to learn from anyone."[17] Nelson, furthermore, contends humility, according to the Sages, would be rewarded by God (*Erubin*: 13b; *Shabbath*: 104a); was an "essential virtue" for a rabbi (*Sotah*: 21b); counters a pride deemed equal to idolatry (*Sotah*: 45, 5a); worth all the offerings in the temple (*Sanhedrin*: 43b); and "is identified as a central feature of God's nature."[18]

This rabbinic interpretation is further buttressed in the twentieth century by Emmanuel Levinas. Humility is particularly present where the mightiness of God is humbly caring for the poor and the widow.[19] As Levinas emphasizes, to speak of the holy is to acknowledge what is

---

13. Nelson, "Virtue of Humility," 298.

14. Krajewski, "Meditation on Intellectual Humility," 242–43.

15. Kugel, *How to Read the Bible*, 31.

16. See Caruth, *Unclaimed Experience*, 66–72; Leys, *Trauma*, 275–92; and Schweizer, *Hating God*, 113–14.

17. Telushkin, *Hillel*, 76.

18. Nelson, "Virtue of Humility," 300–301.

19. Levinas, "Judaism and Kenosis," 105.

separate, which he links to terms such as yielding and kenosis (especially as they pertain to our responsibility to the face of the Other). Humility "means mainly the proximity of God to human suffering."[20] God's greatness is made manifest through solidarity with the lowly and oppressed. For Jewish feminist Melissa Raphael, writing in a post-Auschwitz context: "it should be asked how we could and can protect God's presence as it is this which makes it possible to know God in the other and for God to know God-self in creation."[21] For Raphael, God's presence as Shekhinah was manifest in the camps through acts of individual kindness among female inmates.

Elie Wiesel, in the context of discussing Rabbi Tarfon, remarks: "True humility is judging oneself with severity and judging others with understanding."[22] Wiesel also wondered why the call to be humble was not a commandment. Continuing his discussion of Rabbi Tarfon, he notes that individuals may try to outdo one another in various moral virtues and religious commitments—but not in humility. "True humility lies in the subconscious,"[23] and for Wiesel, Rabbi Tarfon exemplifies humility for his "readiness to admit ignorance." As Reuven Kimelman highlights, for Wiesel, Talmudic areas that hone humility most importantly present a range of opinions known as *Eileh ve'eileh divrei e-lohim hayim*. "The point is that you don't have to be wrong for me to be right."[24] Such humbling engagement also resonates in many Qur'anic passages and in the faith-expression of Muslims.

Humility and Islam

In *Islam in the West*, a study of Iraqi Shi'i communities in exile and transition in the UK and Ireland, Kieran Flynn transcribes important sermons from imams from 2004 to 2010. Many of them express sincere respect for democracy, Christianity, and humility. One memorable sermon (Flynn chose not to identify each speaker) depicts Muhammad debating with Christians to stress there must be freedom in choosing one's faith, as the Qur'an proclaims (2:256). "The Prophet with all his knowledge,"

20. Ibid., 102. The context is Psalm 68.
21. Raphael, *Female Face of God*, 156.
22. Wiesel, *Wise Men*, 209.
23. Ibid., 209.
24. Kimelman, "Wiesel and the Stories of the Rabbis," 46.

the imam said, "was not successful in convincing the Christians."[25] Part of humility is transparency and honesty: while admitting such a truth can also negatively color those Christians from a Muslim perspective (as Christians viewed "obstinate" Jews who would not profess Christ as Divine), it also can humble any Muslim claim to clear superiority. Perhaps, in other words, religious truths lucid to me are understandably not so for others?

In discussing the golden rule in Islam, Th. Emil Homerin states how "humility is the key to any understanding of it."[26] Madhuri M. Yadlapati, moreover, helpfully highlights how the five pillars of Islam foster religious humility in Muslim believers, constantly reinforcing the greatness of Allah and the need for ethical living. Such practices recall Allah's promise but also our individual longing and frailty and so the need to maintain trust in God.[27] Whether through fasting during Ramadan or showing obeisance to God by prostrating during *salat*, there is a continual reminder of the call for humility.

"For Muslims," as Afra Jalabi remarks, "humility is a model for practice."[28] Fethullah Gülen, moreover, notes that *Tawadu* (modesty and humility) "can also be interpreted as one's awareness of one's real position before God, and as letting that realization guide one's conduct toward God and with people."[29] Tarif Khalidi narrates this interesting conversation in Islamic literature involving Jesus: "'Why do I not observe in you the best of worship?' he asked. They said, 'What is the best of worship, Spirit of God?' He said, 'Humility before God.'" Khalidi comments: "Humility before God is the most central aspect of worship, as opposed to *kibr*, or pride, a prominent Qur'anic sin."[30] As the Qur'an notes: "The Servants of the Lord of Mercy are those who walk humbly on the Earth, and who, when aggressive people address them, reply with words of peace" (25:63).

The Prophet Muhammad is an exemplar of such humility for Muslims.[31] Among many applicable hadiths, we read: "Allah revealed to me

---

25. Flynn, *Islam in the West*, 182. All Qur'anic translations, unless otherwise stated are from *The Qur'an*, translated by M. A. S. Abdel Haleem.

26. Homerin, "Golden Rule in Islam," 104.

27. Yadlapati, *Against Dogmatism*, 20.

28. See Jalabi, "Walking on Divine Edge," 183–84.

29. Gülen, "Tawadu (Humility)."

30. Khalidi, *Muslim Jesus*, 71.

31. Ramadan, *In the Footsteps of the Prophet*, 167; and 30–32.

that we should be humble amongst ourselves and none should show pride upon the others."[32]

Of humility and pride, there is much agreement among Jews, Christians, and Muslims, anchored in the belief and reality of a God of creation who demands faith and devoted, ethical action seeking justice for all. Humility abounds in such beliefs and actions: no orthodox strand calls for arrogance or independence bereft of God. Christianity reveres humility, perhaps its principle virtue, elevated to divine embodiment in the incarnation.

Humility and the Gospels

Turning to the Christian Gospels, Kenneth Bailey examines the relevant verses in the Sermon on the Mount: "Blessed are you who are poor" (Luke 6:20) and "Blessed are the meek" (Matt 5:5). He remarks: "The Hebrew word, *ānî*, (poor/humble) has to do with obedience in accepting God's guidance. The Greek term, *praÿs* ("meek"), refers not to a person in the presence of God but rather describes relations between people."[33] He also looks at the role of righteous anger and so turns to the Prophet Habakkuk who is horrified at the Chaldeans who concoct their own versions of justice and so must be rebuked for not discerning injustice by the justice of God. Bailey thus concludes that in the Lukan and Matthean sermons: "The meek are those who humbly seek God. They are neither too bold nor too timid"; and "Being meek is in harmony with being angry over injustice inflicted on others."[34]

Mary, the mother of Jesus, is humility personified. The most fitting scene is the celebrated Annunciation, here as interpreted by Tomas in *The Gospel of Solentiname*. In discussing Mary's words to the angel: "Here am I, the servant of the Lord; let it be with me according to your word" (Luke 1:38), Tomas comments: "That shows she's very humble. She feels like a poor humble thing, instead of feeling proud for what they told her."[35] Tomas's insight is a startling one: often Mary is praised for her obedience, but was she not also susceptible to inordinate pride? How could such a notion not swell up (like the deity in her womb)—for she among

---

32. Ṣaḥīḥ Muslim 6856. Online: https://muflihun.com/muslim/40/6856.
33. Bailey, *Jesus Through Middle Eastern Eyes*, 73.
34. Ibid., 75.
35. Cardenal, *Gospel in Solentiname*, 11.

all people was chosen to bear the son of God? How often do we take pride in our children's accomplishments, some of us, unhealthily so?[36] We burden them with our own unfulfilled desires or with unrealistic expectations. We use them as means to energize our own egos and power. Yet, Mary offers a model who maintains a humble outlook in the midst of the greatest Divine favor. The humility of Mary has often been misused by patriarchal overtones that emphasize a virginal, chaste, slavish, and mostly silent woman. But Mary is the one who first believed in Jesus as savior and hastened his ministry at the wedding of Cana, a fitting first miracle that celebrates joy and love. Unlike the male disciples, neither Jesus's detractors nor the Roman guards and their spears could temper her public fidelity to him. In this regard, she resonates with so many mothers in the world who strive for justice but who also must witness and endure the torture and humiliation of their offspring.[37] Central to these ideas is the wonderful Magnificat in Luke's gospel (1:46–55), which echoes other Jewish women like Hannah in the Tanach (1 Sam 2:2–10) seeking justice for the poor and forsaken.

Guided by Scripture, humility is deeply enmeshed and developed in the theology of church fathers like Clement of Alexandria, Origen, Hilary of Poiters, Athanasius, Basil of Caesarea, Gregory of Nyssa, Ambrose, John Cassian,[38] and Benedict of Nursia, the "Founder of Claustral Holiness . . . the Basil of the West."[39]). Cassian, moreover, remarks that: "none can attain the end of perfection and purity, except through true humility."[40]

We turn now from biblical accounts of humility to a Catholic saint who was less than impressed with the Bible (at least initially).

Augustine: Conquering the Self through Tireless Humility

Born in present-day Algeria to indigenous African parents and raised to be a member of the Roman nobility,[41] Augustine read pride and virility as

36. Confer Mrs. Morrell in D. H. Lawrence's *Sons and Lovers*.

37. See Gebara and Bingemer, *Mary: Mother of God*; and Lederach and Lederach, *When Blood and Bones Cry Out*, 147–69.

38. See Groppe, "After Augustine," 192; and Pardue, *Mind of Christ*, 66–110.

39. Hugo, *Les Misérables*, 445; see also Benedict, *Rule*.

40. Cassian, *Institutes*, 12.23. See also Taliaferro, *Golden Chord*, 176–77.

41. See Wilhite, "Augustine the African," 1–34; Chvala-Smith, "Augustine of Hippo," 90; Augustine, *City of God*, 45–46 (I.35); Bushlack, *Politics for a Pilgrim Church*, 3; and Ryan, *On Politics*, 169–73.

the baneful sins of humanity, sins that consigned us to eternal damnation if not for the mercy and sacrifice of Jesus. With Jesus's atonement, some could be saved through the gift of grace. Augustine initially spurned the gospels because they seemed to lack the rhetorical elegance and dignity of many pagan texts, especially of Cicero.[42] He eventually reversed course, later esteeming the Bible as the book par excellence. It was vanity that had degraded his initial conception. "Puffed up with pride," he wrote in *Confessions*, "I considered myself a mature adult."[43] Augustine's life overflowed with questioning and searching for truth until his restlessness found peace in Christ.

Augustine read his entire pre-conversion life through the optics of pride, seeing specious vainglory leading him down false and disordered paths. A man of immense talent, sagacity, ambition, and drive, he also excelled most others in seeing his own sinfulness and depravity. Deeply and systematically, Augustine reflected on his moral failures—perhaps most traditionally emblematic in the stealing pears episode[44]—though modern readers would focus more on his treatment of his concubine.

While Augustine claims he was faithful to her,[45] he seems to have viewed the relationship as one of sexual utility.[46] Perhaps this is why she is not named or given her point of view (perhaps to protect her?). Regardless, Augustine is susceptible to his mother's constant harassing to marry a "proper" girl, though he has to wait for her to be of marriageable age, which would have been twelve.[47] In consequence, he writes: "The woman with whom I habitually slept was torn away from my side because she was a hindrance to my marriage."[48] Her own intentions and desires are not depicted, but she returns to Africa, vowing never to be with another man (out of love for him or commitment to becoming a nun, as some allege?). She leaves Augustine their son, Adeodatus (who tragically dies at 17). In reflecting on his concubine's departure, Augustine's pride seems wounded as he writes: "But I was unhappy, incapable of following a woman's example, and impatient of delay."[49] Augustine, unable to wait until the

42. Augustine, *Confessions*, 40 (III.9). See also Armstrong, *Bible*, 121–25.
43. Augustine, *Confessions*, 40 (III.9).
44. Ibid., 29 (II.9).
45. Ibid., 53 (IV.2).
46. See Farley, *Just Love*, 40–43.
47. Augustine, *Confessions*, 108 (VI.23).
48. Ibid., 109 (VI.25).
49. Ibid., 108 (VI.25).

girl he could marry comes of age, takes another woman.[50] Meanwhile, the mother of his child is estranged from her son.

As Augustine often repeated in various ways: "Because man fell through pride, [God] applied humility as a cure."[51] In *The City of God*, written in part as an apologia for Christianity and a response to the traumatic experiences caused from the Visigoths' sack of Rome in 410, we read: "Against this arrogance of the demons, to which mankind was enslaved as a deserved punishment, is set the humility of God, revealed in Christ."[52] This *Deus humilis* elevates that virtue as empowering and redemptive in Christian ethics. For Jesus's passion and his consummate modesty should enflame humility among Jesus's followers.[53] Augustine also wants to uphold the example of Jesus against false deities and other failed leaders.

Augustine has plenty of detractors. Even books in his defense stand out more because of the greater moral failures of other Christians (I have in mind his statements and views about the Jewish people[54]), but care should be taken to distinguish Augustine's great zeal, especially the zeal (and blind spots) of the convert, with vanity. Augustine was driven to overcome pride (often encumbered by unhealthy sexual longing). While such attempts are inevitably tainted, or at least tempted, by ambitious aims and tendencies, many great moral and spiritual reformers engage in similar battles. Their spiritual acumen, despite or perhaps partly contributed by their ongoing battles with pride and vanity, is sharper, bolder. As Augustine wonderfully pens: "Nothing is superior to God; and that is why humility exalts the mind by making it subject to God."[55]

Despite legitimate critiques in many feminist, liberation, and postcolonial interpretations,[56] Augustine crafted a foundational core for a Christian theology of humility.

50. Ibid., 109 (VI.25).

51. Augustine, *On Christian Doctrine*, 15 (I.14).

52. Augustine, *City of God*, 366 (IX.20). See also Augustine, *Confessions*, 219 (X.68).

53. Pardue, *Mind of Christ*, 156. See also Groppe, "After Augustine," 206fn33.

54. See Augustine, *City of God*, 753 (XVII.19); Fredriksen, *Augustine and the Jews*; and Chazan, *From Anti-Judaism to Anti-Semitism*, 76–106.

55. Augustine, *City of God*, 572 (XIV.13). See also ibid., 657 (XVI.4); and Augustine, *Confessions*, 121 (VII.13).

56. See Wilhite, "Augustine the African"; and Chelius, *Feminist Interpretations of Saint Augustine*.

My next highlighted thinker's bio includes family members locking him in the family castle in Roccasecca and sending in a naked prostitute to entice him away from monastic life,[57] but you probably know him for other reasons.

Thomas Aquinas: Humility Balanced by Magnanimity

As all roads supposedly lead to Rome, all Christian theological routes eventually pass through, from, or to Thomas Aquinas. Given the least applicable nickname in theological history (the dumb ox for his silence and perceived dullness along with his evident girth), there are few intellectual equals to that great Dominican systematizer of thirteenth-century theological and philosophical thought.[58] Aquinas's influence on Catholic Christianity in particular has been as pervasive as Paul and Augustine, though elements of his thoughts have been rightly critiqued since Vatican II, especially among feminist, postcolonial, and liberationist thinkers.[59] Care should also be given to distinguish "Thomas as far as possible before imperial Thomism,"[60] as Mark D. Jordan instructs.

Beyond Aquinas's obviously enormous intellect, exemplary is his genuine learning from wide sources, whether Jewish (Maimonides), Muslim (Avicenna), or what was considered "new" and untrustworthy (Aristotle).[61] Such praise does not diminish his thirteenth-century orthodox position that divided the world into Christians and non-Christians but shows creative space and innovation despite those restrictions and blind spots.

For our purposes, Aquinas examines humility in some particular depth in question 161 (*Secunda, Secundae partis*) of his magnum opus, *Summa Theologiae*. The question is posed with six articles. First, whether he deems humility a virtue (he does[62]). Second, where it resides ("it moderates the movement of the appetites"). Third, whether one should be humble towards all people (we should, praising God for the good in

---

57. Turner, *Thomas Aquinas*, 12.

58. See Kerr, "Thomas Aquinas," 211–20; Crosthwaite, "Thomas Aquinas on Servitude," 33–40; and McGinn, *Thomas Aquinas's "Summa theologiae."*

59. Hill, "Thomas Aquinas," 56; but see also Boff, "Thomas Aquinas and the Theology of Liberation," 458–71.

60. Jordan, "Thomas Aquinas," 153.

61. See Burrell, "Aquinas and Islamic and Jewish Thinkers," 60–61.

62. See Keys, "Monkish Virtue," 4.

man and recognizing everyone has some greater good or less evil in some area than oneself, thus requiring humility). Fourth, whether humility is part of modesty or temperance (it is of both). Fifth, whether it is the greatest of virtues (no, that would be charity).

While Augustine claims humility is foundational, Aquinas clarifies: "after the theological virtues [faith, hope, love]; after the intellectual virtues which regard the reason itself, and after justice, especially legal justice, humility stands before all others."[63] Somewhat of a veiled compliment, humility gets a good lesson in humility from Aquinas. Though Aquinas quotes Augustine on a number of occasions in his praise of humility, he "decisively reduced humility to a form of modesty," as Jane Foulcher notes.[64]

In the final question, he studies whether Benedict's twelve degrees of humility[65] are "fittingly distinguished." Aquinas cities Anselm's seven steps[66] as a possible challenge but ultimately argues that Benedict's degrees are fittingly distinguished, though he reverses Benedict's order, purposefully according to Mary M. Keys.[67]

Of most value is Aquinas's linking humility with magnanimity, which he had analyzed in an earlier question (129). In his discussion, Aquinas particularly has in mind Aristotle, who in the *Nichomachean Ethics* saw the virtuous man as someone who is concerned with great things, seeks for great things, and is aware that he deserves great things. Aquinas's critique of pride as the "most grievous"[68] and the "beginning"[69] of all sins, rendering the proud man sinful, seems to contrast with Aristotle's more positive account of pride, or what is better translated as greatness of soul (great-souled)—*megalopsychia*.[70] Augustine, as Michael P. Krom writes, would consider Aristotle's magnanimous man as "a failure to achieve self-knowledge, a denial of the human condition."[71]

For Aristotle, one is vain who erroneously believes he is worthy of great things or mistakenly believes he deserves more than he actually

---

63. Aquinas, *Summa Theologiae*, 2.161.5.
64. Foulcher, *Reclaiming Humility*, 8.
65. See Bernard, "Twelve Steps."
66. See Sadler, "Anselm and the Seven Levels of Humility."
67. Keys, "Monkish Virtue," 6–7.
68. Aquinas, *Summa Theologiae*, 2.152.6.
69. Ibid., 2.152.7.
70. See Williams, *Tragedy*, 58fn17. See also ibid., 123–24.
71. Krom, "Modern Liberalism and Pride," 459.

does. One is temperate who believes he is not worthy or believes himself not worthy of great things (he may also consciously aim lower than what he can achieve). One is unduly humble if he does not recognize his just deserts, and most unduly humble if he is a great man deserving of great things but feels otherwise. Aristotle thus concludes: "The proud man [*megalopsychos*—the great-souled man, possessing *megalopsychia*], then, is an extreme in respect of the greatness of his claims, but a mean in respect of the rightness of them; for he claims what is in accordance with his merits, while the others go to excess or fall short."[72] Aristotle, moreover, is clear that being unduly humble is a mistake by those who are great.[73] Such a man "robs himself of what he deserves, and seems to have something bad about him from the fact that he does not think himself worthy of good things, and also not to have known himself; else he would have desired the things he was worthy of since these were good."[74] Pride, then, is a mean between the extremes of one unduly humble or vain, though neither of these extremes are "malicious"—only "mistaken."[75]

Christian thinkers are unanimous that all good comes from God. In this sense, there is no robbery (of deserved deserts) for Christians cannot claim what isn't due to them ultimately.[76] Those who reach a high level of humility accept praise with graciousness and love knowing it is God that is really praised. Such language would make little sense to Aristotle.

Much of what Aristotle says about pride, however, seems balanced and practical.[77] In our contemporary human rights era, theists and nontheists highlight any misuse of power by the powerful against the marginalized. Any emphasis on self-contempt and constant focusing on one's sinfulness seems inordinate.[78]

Aquinas's inclusion of magnanimity may clarify the issue, though as R. E. Houser contends, "Magnanimity is arguably the most difficult virtue for Aquinas to explain."[79]

---

72. Aristotle, *Nichomachean Ethics*, 383 (IV.3).
73. Ibid., 387 (IV.3).
74. Ibid., 387 (IV.3).
75. Ibid., 387 (IV.3). For a critique, see Curzor, *Aristotle and the Virtues*, 129–42.
76. Merton, *Seeds of Contemplation*, 112.
77. See Sarch, "What's Wrong with Megalopsychia?," 231–53; and Kristjánsson, "Liberating Moral Traditions," 397–422.
78. Merton, *Seeds of Contemplation*, 113.
79. Houser, "Virtue of Courage," 310.

Thinking especially of Aristotle, Aquinas notes that "Magnanimity by its very name denotes stretching forth of the mind to great things."[80] According to Craig A. Boyd, while Aristotle's notion of magnanimity is "highly intellectualistic," Aquinas in contrast "sees magnanimity in terms of appropriate desire not accurate self-knowledge."[81]

For Aquinas, pride (*superbia*) instead is deemed an "inordinate desire for great things."[82] What Aquinas contends is that human beings are not only created in the image and likeness of God but are called to seek God, the greatest good and highest end by striving, with the gift of grace, to live as God ordains.[83] This is the essence of stretching forth and aiming to accomplish great things, with any successes as signs of God working through us. Such is by no means any Pelagian sense of our own right or desert, though we certainly play a role through exercising free will[84] in acts of charity[85] and thus earn some merit.[86]

Taken together, "Humility restrains the appetite from aiming at great things against right reason: while magnanimity urges the mind to great things in accord with right reason."[87] However, there still remained some tension as magnanimity was often deemed a pagan virtue and had traits praised by Aristotle (and in the Homeric epics) that, according to Houser, would seem unworthy of a Christian: "ignoring benefactors, overplaying *gravitas*, irony, unwillingness to associate with others, and preferring useless to productive possessions."[88] Aquinas carefully works around these objections by stating how magnanimity is a special virtue, which according to Houser, "recognize[s] that gifts natural and acquired, for which one is due some measure of honor, are ultimately owed to God."[89] Aquinas also distinguishes four vices opposed to magnanimity which all exhibit undue or excessive characteristics of a vice: pusillanimity—showing little or insufficient courage (or even awareness) in seeking goods

---

80. Aquinas, *Summa Theologiae*, 2.129.1.
81. Boyd, "Pride and Humility," 247.
82. See Aquinas, *Summa Theologiae*, 2.161.1; and Sweeney, "Vice and Sin," 163.
83. Aquinas, *Summa Theologiae*, 2.1.8, 2.2.8; on grace, see 2.5.6 and 2.109.
84. Ibid., 1.83.1.
85. Ibid., 2.114.4.
86. Ibid., 2.114.1.
87. Ibid., 2.161.1.
88. Houser, "Virtue of Courage," 310. The relevant section in Aquinas' *Summa Theologiae* is 2.129.3 (obj. 5).
89. Houser, "Virtue of Courage," 311.

that are commensurate with one's potential;[90] presumption (especially of honor), ambition, and vainglory. The truly humble are both aware of human beings' dependence on God and on others, even, or especially if they are considered great. Contra Aristotle's *megalopsychosos*, such people are more attuned to the reality that they are not self-made, self-sufficient, and fully independent, but live within, aware of, and grateful towards community.

Such fellowship was highlighted, for example, by Pope Francis during a mass celebrating the Feast of Saint Mark in April 2013. There he urged the Church to proclaim the gospel with magnanimity and humility. In his sermon, he drew in particular upon Aquinas's reflections above, although as P. Bracy Bersnak competently argues, Francis most likely also had another source for his reflections in the "back of his mind."[91] Humility has been one of Mario Bergoglio's dominant themes throughout his life and he is deemed by many as someone in a powerful position who still exudes humility. As Paul Vallery writes: "In him humility and power come together."[92] Such a union of seeming opposites is present in many of Bergoglio's fellow Jesuits, and certainly in its founder: the "someone else" Bersnak alludes to above who will be my next highlighted example.

Ignatian Humility: Ruined for Life

I am continually humbled (if not haunted) by my service in the Jesuit Volunteer Corps after college. Modelled after Ignatian spirituality and the Jesuit calling and obligation to serve others, the JVC entails one or two years of service to live among and with the poor and marginalized. Its slogan—"Ruined for life"—expresses the hard-earned truth that once embarked upon this path, FJVs (former Jesuit volunteers) will see the world differently: from glimpses of the perspectives of the many impoverished and vulnerable in our midst. Such perspectives, usually clashing with contemporary capitalist and materialist aims and goals, ruin—but in a liberating way. Seeing the world more transparently, a world of much goodness but also much underserved pain and suffering, can free us from

---

90. Aquinas, *Summa Theologiae*, 2.133.1.

91. Bersnak, "Magnanimity and Humility."

92. Vallely, *Pope Francis*, xi, 142, and 165. Vallery refers to Bergoglio's "audacious humility" and rightly critiques his refusal to testify at an Argentinean "crimes against humanity" trial in 2010; ibid., 196. See also Admirand, "Pope Francis," 163–78.

false attachments and spiritually vacuous career choices and lifestyles. For Ignatius (like Augustine, but with greater hope in the world), overcoming inordinate attachments is a crucial step towards spiritual maturity.

The JVC, like the Jesuit order, is rooted in the life and teachings of Iñigo López de Loyola, who according to historian Diarmaid MacCulloch, we know "as Ignatius after a scribal error over his Christian name when he matriculated in the University of Paris."[93] He sought worldly success through diplomatic and then military means, until injured from a cannonball. His subsequent recovery time involved deep reflection and readings of religious texts (no other options were available where he was convalescing). A cathartic transformation involving pilgrimages and visions ensued. At Manressa, he vowed to become a soldier for Christ, striving to bring the Word of God to non-believers. In seeking devoted followers to his cause, he developed and honed what became the *Spiritual Exercises*. That Pope Francis from the Jesuit order chose to be named Francis is not surprising—not only to his own temperament but also to Ignatius who in many ways sought to emulate Francis of Assisi, another wellspring of Christian humility.[94]

Through the foundational guidance of the *Spiritual Exercises* as taught and lived among Jesuits today, the JVC has transformed the lives of many volunteers, and hopefully the people those volunteers have served and learned among. As Ignacio Ellacuría notes, in the "case of St. Ignatius in his deliberations on poverty—explicit reference is made not only to the personal, but also to the institutional."[95] Thus, such service and compassion need to be reflective and informed about larger socioeconomic and political realities.[96]

After college I served in the JVC in California (Casa Santa Rosa, 1998 to 1999), working with Catholic Charities as a pastoral care advocate (delivering food to the needy, visiting the elderly and infirm) and teaching about life goals, ethics, and healthy relationships to students from the ages of twelve to eighteen throughout Northern California. I lived with other volunteers, who each earned eighty dollars a month, with half of those pooled for food (we did not pay rent and utilities). We

---

93. MacCulloch, *Reformation*, 220; on Pope Francis and the Latin American context, see Aguilar, *Pope Francis*.

94. See Ignatius, *Ignatius' Own Story*, 9–10. For humility and Frances and Clare, see *Francis and Clare*, 58.

95. Ellacuría, "Utopia and Prophecy," 316.

96. See Rubio, *Hope for Common Ground*, 10.

lived amidst and almost as the poor—almost, because unlike the genuine poor,[97] this was chosen poverty. An escape option was always viable. Outside my window I could see homeless children sleeping in their parents' cars as they waited for an open bed in the crowded Family Shelter next door. They had nowhere else to go. We did.

Much has been written about the *Spiritual Exercises*. Here I only want to focus on the role of humility within them. They are ideally undertaken in a guided thirty-day retreat and demand deep, but practical, introspection and examination of conscience to assess and evaluate how one has lived spiritually and ethically. For Ignatius this means praising and serving God through serving one another.[98] The *Spiritual Exercises* challenge and inspire participants to lead a more balanced and Christ-infused life of love to reach that end.[99] Such sentiments are summarized in an often heard phrase in Jesuit circles: "seeking and finding God in all things."[100]

"The purpose of these Exercises," the manual begins, "is to help the exercitant to conquer himself, and to regulate his life so that he will not be influenced in his decisions by any inordinate attachment."[101] Especially resonant is Jesus's instructions to the rich man to deny himself and take up his cross—in addition to giving everything to the poor, as Ignatius himself did.[102]

In the five points of the General Examination of conscience, exercitants begin with gratitude to God and prayer for the grace to discern and evaluate their sins and be freed from them, followed by a careful, daily accounting of their thoughts, words, and deeds. After each accounting, exercitants ask for forgiveness and resolve to change. Uttering an Our Father closes the examination. Throughout the four weeks, meditations are guided on various themes like the powers of the soul, sin, hell, the incarnation, the nativity, and to employing imagination, visualization, and other senses to penetrate various biblical scenes and our own fragilities and sinfulness. Guided questions and thoughts are intentionally structured for the exercitant to see himself abased, such as: "1. What am

---

97. See, Edin and Shaefer, *$2.00 a Day*, 60.
98. Ignatius, *Spiritual Exercises*, 48.
99. Martin, *Jesuit Guide*, 1.
100. See Himes and Pope, *Finding God*.
101. Ignatius, *Spiritual Exercises*, 47.
102. Ignatius, *Ignatius' Own Story*, 16.

I in comparison to all men? . . . 4. Let me consider all my own corruptness and foulness of body. . . . [and] 5. Let me see myself as a sore and an abscess from whence came forth so many sins, so many evils, and the most vile poison."[103]

The examples can seem stark and unhealthy, which is why such an exercise needs to be guided by a mature retreat leader and spiritual advisor. Some people's already low self-esteem will likely not benefit from such an approach. While initially typing Ignatius's words above, I wanted to denounce them as extreme, but then, just this morning, I lost all calm and patience at one of my kids when trying to get everyone to school. I screamed and cursed like a madman: sins, evil, vile poison, indeed.

And yet, I must admit, chills begin to tingle as I write: the temptation to delete and hide, pervasive. Ignatius insists that such sinfulness is not the final word: we are called to think of the great wisdom and mercy of God and all of creation in sustaining us. The exercise closes with expression of gratitude to God, praying an Our Father, and promising to make amends. Let's hope I do.

The *Spiritual Exercises* can be a rich repository for reflection and purification. They can also be painful and challenging, but for believers, there is always hope and the promise of God's love and mercy. Of humility, Ignatius writes that it (along with poverty and scorn from the world) can "lead men to all virtues."[104] While pervasive throughout the *Spiritual Exercises*, humility is explicitly highlighted under three modes (or degrees) in week two. As Brian Daley explains,[105] the reflections on humility for Ignatius and his early associates, "is really the concluding piece of a strategy developed throughout the Second Week, of preparing the exercitant to be involved in the work and lifestyle of Christ as fully as possible."[106] Principally the Exercises were linked with young people discerning vocation to religious life (especially men becoming Jesuits), but were also used in other contexts and for a range of people.[107] The first mode demands "I humble or abase myself as much as is possible for

---

103. Ignatius, *Spiritual Exercises*, 57; for parallels in Buddhism see Lopez, *Buddhist Scriptures*, 74.

104. Ignatius, *Spiritual Exercises*, 77; on perverted humility, see Ignatius, *Personal Writings*, 129.

105. Daley, "'To Be More Like Christ,'" 26.

106. Ibid., 31. See also Brackley, *Call to Discernment*.

107. Daley, "'To Be More Like Christ,'" 32.

me, in order that I may obey in all things the law of God our Lord."[108] Such a calling is an obligation for everyone to achieve salvation, but a higher state (the second mode) entails preferring poverty, dishonor, and a short life so long as the opportunity to serve God is possible. In such a state, one would never choose to commit a venial sin even if that means preserving one's life. Finally, the third mode of humility, deemed the most perfect, is an explicit link to serve with Christ who suffered and was poor and debased. It entails "willing to be considered as worthless and a fool for Christ."[109] Interestingly, this final mode is a type of honor: "he should implore our Lord to be pleased to choose him for this third type of humility."[110] And even here there is the caveat and reminder that such a state is perfect as long as it is to serve God selflessly and purely.[111]

Such love of God, entwined with love of the Other,[112] returns me to the Jesuit Volunteer Corps. Have I been sufficiently ruined enough and in the right way? The JVC experience helped orient my path as a theologian, but along with my work on liberation theology, I am reminded of those who do so much more concrete good. Here I inevitably mention that I have five young children, and there are so many needs and bills to pay. Yet even in my insular, provincial family context, I often hurt and disappoint. The ideals of the JVC constantly remind me (which is why I added haunting above) of my ongoing present moral breakdowns and negligence. The reality, if I am honest, is that I not only often fail my immediate family, but I generally forsake those most in need of aid and justice. In the context of liberation theology, words are never enough (here, many may also think of Irving Greenberg's working principle about words uttered in the presence of the burning children).[113] The *Spiritual Exercises* similarly haunt—but can also guide and heal, which is why they remain such an important resource for humility.

Another resource of spirituality and humility from the sixteenth century is my final exemplar in this chapter. She is also the only saint whose displayed finger I have seen.

---

108. Ignatius, *Spiritual Exercises*, 81.
109. Ibid., 82.
110. Ibid., 82.
111. Daley, "'To Be More Like Christ,'" 38.
112. Ibid., 36. See also Daley, "Pursuit of Excellence," 11–35. I thank Professor Daley for telling me of this work. Private email: 17 September 2014.
113. Greenberg, "Cloud of Smoke," 7–55.

Teresa of Ávila: Sincere but Calculated Humility?

Born in Ávila in 1515, the daughter and granddaughter of *conversos*,[114] Teresa of Ávila was the founder of the Discalced (or barefoot) Carmelites and of seventeen convents. Her remains (that finger mentioned above) can be viewed as a relic in the Convent of St. Teresa in Ávila today. More importantly, she is one of only four women doctors of the Catholic Church.

Teresa's deep contemplative prayer life is candidly depicted in a number of works including *The Interior Castle*, *The Way of Perfection*, and her autobiography, *The Life of Teresa*. As a woman, Teresa's experiences and expertise were constantly doubted or undermined by men. Humility needs a lot of explaining amidst such sexism that expects women to be submissive and humble. As a start, seeing gender as a fluid (but often fixed) societal construction encourages humility's worth and purpose towards all. It is a moral failure to posit that humility is not of value to the great-souled and successful (as we stressed above), is only a religious virtue (and so of little worth or role for the purely secular), or—and this is the point now—only an obstacle for the oppressed, particularly women. The presupposition is that such individuals are already "low" enough and so only need to be raised and not deflated. While noble, deciding some people don't need humility renders a disquieting evaluation of a range of people and perhaps undermines their dignity, too. Let me explain.

In the Talmud, the rabbis emphasized that everyone is expected to tithe (*tzedakah*, righteousness; often translated as charity) and to give some of their earnings to the needy—even the already poor should do so. Why? Because the rabbis recognized that enabling everyone to give to others is a means of providing and maintaining dignity. The thirteenth-century kabbalist text *The Zohar* says a person should exult when meeting someone poor who is a gift from God.[115] In Maimonides's *Treatise on Tzedakah*, he, too, stresses that the dignity of the poor should be protected, and this dignity is enhanced by their giving to others in need.

When first reading about the poor also needing to give charity (in part for their own dignity), tears moistened my eyes, I who generally seem stoic to most people. After getting my PhD (I had three young children then), I finished a one-year university contract as a head of a postgraduate program that only turned into a part-time one. The Celtic

---

114. On Teresa's Jewish heritage, see Williams, *Teresa of Ávila*, 26–38.
115. *Shemot* 2:3a, quoted in Unterman, *Kabbalistic Tradition*, 203–4.

Tiger had just crashed; the government froze new full-time university posts; and I was the only paid worker in the family. We had no savings, only loan and credit card debt. While also needing to be grateful for available government resources, my pride rankled as I had to attend various social welfare agencies for a year and a half (along with a later second stint before getting a permanent job). There were many painful and humiliating experiences (and I will forever be grateful for my parents for helping us especially during that time). Am I more empathetic towards others and humble towards my own failures and weakness (sinfulness)? Usually acknowledged as kind and patient, I was depressed, angry, and bitter during that period. Perhaps those were not my true colors (but then it is easy to be kind when all is basically fine). Such memories shame me. In a particular low point, my then four-year-old daughter drew a family picture. Everyone was smiling and happy except me. I don't want that to ever happen again. Hopefully such experiences help me to be more compassionate to others who usually deal with severe burdens.

During this difficult time, a social worker was evaluating our monthly budget to gauge what should be cut based on my then part-time salary and welfare benefits. There was little-to-no trim available but one thing stood out: a monthly meagre pittance to charity. We struggled to pay for basic necessities, so that charity, too, apparently had to go. I felt horrible, helpless, and low. I did not know of the Jewish wisdom then, which is why I cried years later when encountering those rabbinic words—even the poor should tithe, as giving reinforces one's dignity and sense of worth. The call to be humble should also not be restricted.

Fittingly, Teresa's approach encourages personal reflection, bare honesty, spontaneity, and humor. Humility for Teresa was both genuine and a needed strategy in a patriarchal culture that expected women to be mostly silent and passive. As Lisa Fullam writes: "Teresa's more substantive difficulty with humility [than Aquinas's] was political—specifically the politics of gender in which she lived and worked. Women in sixteenth-century Spain were systematically disempowered in Church and society."[116] Teresa's highlighting of her wickedness and lack of humility in her autobiography are both strategic and heart-felt. Heart-felt because she carefully distinguished between true and false humility[117] but also strategic because so-called humble men would pounce on any woman who had the audacity to want to be heard. As Fullam adds: "Her

---

116. Fullam, "Teresa of Ávila's Liberative Humility," 176.
117. See also Aquinas, *Summa Theologiae*, 2.161.1.

exaggerated claims of inadequacy are a rhetorical mask for a bold stance of self-assertion and resolve, the humility of the oppressed."[118] This resolve both liberated her to have the space she needed as a mystic in a world ruled by men while subsequently challenging them through her holy visions and acumen.[119]

If a conscious strategy, Teresa's is one that bore more fruit, for example, than the brilliant mystic Juana Inés de la Cruz. She was a Hieronymite nun who initially entered the Discalced Carmelite order. Her courageous and outspoken call for women's equality led to her being censured by the Archbishop of Mexico. Her publications then virtually ceased.[120] Teresa chose a different path, balanced by both calculated and genuine humility. Striving to live for God and believing God was working through her, she endured power-focused men but still maintained her integrity and a degree of independence.

One well-known story, a poem, and a line from her Constitution for the Discalced Nuns can flesh-out her flexible humility. In the story, Teresa, on her way to visit some nuns, had been knocked off a donkey and injured her leg. "Lord," she said, "Why would you let this happen?" The response in prayer that she heard was, "That is how I treat my friends." Teresa answered, "And that is why you have so few of them!" In addition to her sense of humor, it reveals "her playful way of addressing God" and "her assumption of God's playfulness with her."[121]

In her poem "Sea mi gozo en el llanto" (Let my rejoicing be in tears), notice the irony and paradox in the title, echoing the last shall be first and first shall be last refrains in the gospels. Here is a particularly relevant stanza:

> En olvido mi memoria,
> mi alteza en humillación,
> en bajeza mi opinión,
> en afrenta mi Victoria.[122]

---

118. Fullam, "Teresa of Ávila's Liberative Humility," 175.

119. Ibid., 197.

120. See Juana Inés de la Cruz, *Poems, Protest, and a Dream*; and for commentary, see Gonzalez, "Sor Juana Inés de la Cruz," 229–42; and Gebara, *Out of the Depths*, 29–45.

121. Martin, "Humor of St. Teresa of Ávila."

122. Teresa of Ávila, *Complete Works*, 305–6. Translation: "My memory in oblivion lives / I'm highest when I'm brought most low / Humbled, no greater fame I know / The mere affront a victory gives."

Here the self is not effaced into nothingness but becomes all the more raised, victorious, and remembered because it is a life rooted in Christ:

> En Cristo mi confianza,
> y de Él solo mi asimiento,
> en sus cansancios mi aliento,
> y en su imitación mi holganza.[123]

All ten stanzas celebrate the unexpected reversal of the meaning of the cross (life through shame and death). Though unconsciously ironic for a daughter of a *converso*, Teresa here echoes Paul's notion of Christ as foolishness and a stumbling block (1 Cor 1:23). She finds wealth in poverty, honor in being humbled, flourishing in vilification, new life from her eventual death.[124] It is a poem that beautifully reveals a healthy dependence in a world lavishing praise on autonomy and self-survival.

The third example is contained in the section of the Constitution for Discalced Carmelite Nuns, called "Of the Humble Offices," in which Teresa writes that the mother prioress is the first one on the rota for sweeping "to set a good example in everything." What then follows is a wonderful case of her practical wisdom. She stresses that no one should be raised above anyone else and adds that we must pay attention to unique needs, "for sometimes the oldest nuns require the least."[125] Here there is a deep sense of the uniqueness and irreplaceability of the individual. It also challenges hasty assumptions and generalizations about people: a so-called elder can be more sprightly than many a callow youth.

All three examples beautifully negate those accusations of an unhealthy, lacerating self. In the story, Teresa jocosely scolds God, while in the poem, God's existence is entangled with her own. She is not reduced to nothing because of God, but is instead elevated, finds joy and new life. These sentiments are far removed from any traditionally humble claim of passivity and self-denial. Her reply to God is something one would expect from Aristotle's *megalopsychos*, though one perhaps not surprising in her seeking Jesus who "combin[es] majesty with humility."[126] Also notice there is a rich bravery here, expected of the magnanimous person;

---

123. Ibid., 305–6. My translation: "In Christ is my self-assurance; and I am attached only to Him / in his weariness is my nourishment / it is a pleasure to imitate Him."

124. Ibid., 305–6.

125. Teresa of Ávila, *Complete Works*, 225.

126. Teresa of Ávila, *Life*, 280.

so, too, deep honesty. As she writes: "Humility is truth simply, and it is the imitation of Christ."[127] While Aquinas hedged a bit on the foundational role of humility, Teresa is clear on the issue: "The entire edifice of prayer is founded on humility."[128]

Within Teresa's works are copious lines about humility and claims of self-contempt (or is it a healthy sense of self?), from the *Life* to the *Interior Castle*, along with her Letters. "We must consider ourselves as nothing," she writes in her autobiography, "or less than nothing. In this way great humility is gained, and then the flowers begin to grow again."[129] Some contemporary scholars, however, have considered Teresa's asceticism under various unhealthy eating disorders. Such a blind spot (though differing from today's context) should be mentioned.[130]

Teresa often had to battle self-doubts and the doubts of others.[131] Like Anselm's guardians on the mountain of humility,[132] constant watchfulness and humility were required.[133] She was also watched, though. At one point she feared others' reactions to her contemplative and mystical union with God. She stopped praying, reasoning that the devil approached her "under the disguise of humility." She instead mimicked the majority in their ways of prayer[134] employing a "false cloak of humility."[135] She eventually overcame these temptations, realizing that true humility accepts gifts and blessings from God, which are not given because of any merit on our parts, so we must be grateful and appreciate their value and richness. We show our thankfulness by using these gifts for others and valuing them without forgetting "our poverty."[136] Teresa's sharing of her prayer experiences can be seen in this light. A soul in rapture will seek to teach others—though a woman doing so will be considered "lacking

---

127. Fullam, "Teresa of Ávila's Liberative Humility," 180.

128. Teresa of Ávila, *Life*, 158 and 85. See also Teresa of Ávila, *Interior Castle*, 131.

129. Teresa of Ávila, *Life*, 102.

130. Corrington, "Anorexia, Asceticism, and Autonomy," 59. See also Reda, "Anorexia and the Holiness of Saint Catherine," 38.

131. Teresa of Ávila, *Life*, 212.

132. Translation from Sadler, "Anselm and the Seven Levels of Humility."

133. Teresa of Ávila, *Interior Castle*, 9. See also Teresa of Ávila, *Life*, 314.

134. Teresa of Ávila, *Life*, 50.

135. Ibid., 132. Elsewhere: false, excitable, and "lacking in tranquillity," 179; 89, and 215

136. Ibid., 72.

in humility."[137] But "True humility," she notes, "does not bring darkness or aridity, but on the contrary gives the soul peace, sweetness, and light."[138] True humility entails feeling our limitations, sense of shame and knowledge of offence of God, but also God's mercy and love. This love is profoundly, and perhaps ironically present even, or especially as we see ourselves as nothing. Such a position intersects with other major figures.

For Simone Weil, humility is deeply tied to our nothingness before God. It is a supernatural virtue.[139] For Weil, what makes the Christian virtues special[140] is the kenotic, sacrificial love of Christ. Like Pascal, Weil's humility is rooted in self-denial. It also, unfortunately, borders on the unhealthy. Consider, for example, Weil's term "decreation," which she connected with God's loving act of creation. The more we renounce and decreate ourselves, the closer we are to truly loving God. She writes: "May God grant that I become nothing. In so far as I become nothing, God loves himself through me."[141] There is a hard, spiritual truth in this that parallels much Buddhist wisdom on overcoming craving and attachment, and which also resonates with Jesus's call to deny oneself and take up one's cross. The Dalai Lama's focus on emptiness linked with co-dependent arising may also be of help: we are nothing—empty—because we only are because others were: "'Empty' is shorthand for 'empty of intrinsic, inherent existence.' Or to put it another way, empty is another word for interdependent."[142] For Christians, this idea echoes humanity's dependence on God. Eckhardian spirituality also richly resonates[143]—but so long as human beings made in the image and likeness of God are also upheld.[144] Here again we have humility balanced by what Aquinas and Ignatius call the virtue of magnanimity—seeking excellence and greatness—neither below nor above one's status and dignity. For Pascal, moreover, the aim and intention is to remember he is nothing,[145] but that in

---

137. Ibid., 145.

138. Ibid., 215. See also Merton, *Seeds of Contemplation*, 109–10.

139. Weil, *Simone Weil Reader*, 329.

140. Ibid., 220.

141. Ibid., 329. For an optimistic view of Weil's de-creation, see Courtine-Denamy, *Three Women in Dark Times*, 213–16.

142. Dalai Lama and Chan, *Wisdom of Forgiveness*, 149.

143. See Meister Eckhart, *Selected Writings*, 42, 64, and 156.

144. For a discussion of imago Dei, evolution, and natural law, see Pope, "Theological Anthropology, Science, and Human Flourishing," 13–30.

145. Pascal, *Penseés*, 240.

such acceptance is the means of exaltation.[146] Of Teresa, Pascal writes that her "profound humility in her revelations" pleased God, while men are pleased by her enlightenment.[147] Pascal is noting that human beings miss the key point: they need to be humble as Teresa is, for only then, will such enlightenment be possible. Most human beings focus on the goal attained but not the way to reach that goal. Teresa exemplifies both.

Conclusion: Uneven Foundation

Lest there be any doubt, I still question how much of humility remains applicable as an essential moral foundation without clarifications. Humility is a flawed virtue, easily manipulated and often injuring those that it should protect. There is a lot of translation that has to occur, from the language of denigration to a healthy self-esteem. How much gets lost along the way—and is what I am advocating sufficiently present in its foundations and origin? The language of seeing ourselves as nothing seems as extreme as Hume's curt dismissal of monkish virtues. There has to be a healthy middle ground. It would also seem the hallmark of hubris to dismiss these great thinkers and rich traditions. Perhaps having such flaws renders humility appealing; like us, it is fragile and wounded, but promises hope and potential for good. Let's see what other religions claim.

---

146. Ibid., 62.
147. Ibid., 319.

2

Umble Pie

Eastern and Primal Views

Economist Thomas Piketty praises nineteenth-century novelists like Austen and Balzac (and I would add Dickens[1]) for their economic insights without our reliance on statistics and computer data. As he pens: "the distribution of wealth is too important an issue to be left to economists, sociologists, historians, and philosophers."[2] We can say similar things about humility, which by no means is the purview of only Christian theologians or Hasidic rebbes.[3]

To add more breadth to our discussion, I will present humility within some major faith traditions from South and East Asia, namely (what by convention we call) Hinduism, Buddhism, Taoism, and Confucianism,[4] followed by insights from primal/indigenous faiths.

Although nuance and distinctions will be evident among these traditions, it shouldn't be surprising that all these religious and philosophical traditions advocate forms of humility that often overlap and complement one another.

---

1. The chapter title alludes to Uriah Heep in Dickens's *David Copperfield*, 581.
2. Piketty, *Capital in the Twenty-First Century*, 2.
3. On architects and the need for humility, see Moore, *Why We Build*, 245.
4. For Jainism and humility, see Rankin, *Jain Path*, 193–222; for Zoroastrianism see Skjaervo, *Spirit of Zoroastrianism*; for Sikhism, see Singh, *Japji Sahib*. Emblematic is the interfaith gesture of the fifth guru, Guru Arjan Dev Ji, who asked Muslim Mir Mohammed Muayyinul Islam to lay the foundational stone of The Golden Temple in Amritsar. I thank Dr. Jasbir Singh Puri for insights regarding humility in the Sikh tradition.

Humility and Hinduism

Hinduism, at its finest, is the faith system of both/and, wonderfully encompassing and containing plurivocality, diversity, and delectable contradiction. As Wendy Doniger remarks: "Hindus nowadays are diverse in their attitude to their own diversity, which inspires pride in some, anxiety in others."[5] Partly a result of British colonial naming and trying to categorize and constrain what could not be tidily catalogued and contained,[6] Hinduism defies borders and marked lines. To be Hindu is more than being monotheist, polytheist, atheist, or agnostic. It's also more than promoting, denying, or overcoming the essence of existence and the soul. It's a way of life formed through the mores, customs, myths, beliefs, and thought of the ancient peoples within the Indian subcontinent and their dialogue, borrowing, and intermixing among surrounding and invading peoples and cultures. It is also more than that.

Humility in Hinduism is etched and formed through religious ritual, meditation, intellectual reflection, yogi, and ethical practice. In Sanskrit, humility (*vinaya*) is linked with education (*vidya*) so that students who finished their studies were "*vinit*—perfected in humility."[7]

Humility suffuses Hindu practice and belief. As Yadlapati remarks: "Hindu puja articulates one's small but sacred place in a larger world in which human beings are vulnerable to suffering."[8] The Hindu devotional practice to one or more deities accentuates dependence on and connections with Shiva or Vishnu, and/or another deity, perhaps as envisioned as the one Supreme reality or Brahmin. While reinforcing the need to be humble, such devotions instill hope of prayers answered and deeper spiritual connections. The plural reality within many strands of Hinduism are further testaments of humility. In the way of knowledge (*jnana yoga*), advocates seek to encounter one's true self (*atman*) beyond ego and deception or to accept the reality of no permanent self (*anatman*). Through *bhakti yoga* as pointed devotion to God, we hear Krishna advocate to Arjuna in the *Bhagavad-Gita*: "Let your understanding enter me; / then you will dwell / in me without doubt."[9] To achieve such dwell-

---

5. Doniger, *Hindus*, 14.

6. Lawrence, "Buddhist-Hindu Dialogue," 187.

7. See Rogers, "Hindu Influence on Christian Spiritual Practice," 205fn6. Another Sanskrit term for humility is: *namrata*.

8. Yadlapati, *Against Dogmatism*, 30.

9. *Bhagavad-Gita*, 112.

ing, devotees' actions should seek no reward, purely done for the love of Krishna.[10] Detached from any fruits, adherents fulfill obligation with purity and sincerity. In *karma yoga,* daily service to others endorses the interconnectedness of all within our karmic world. As *The Upanishads* state: "According as a man acts and walks in the path of life, so he becomes."[11] In *raja yoga,* the royal way to God, believers hone deep exercises of contemplation and meditation, holistically uniting mind and body to reach a state beyond the self.[12] All are ways of transcending the ego and self, inscribing and promoting humility.

More will be said in the next chapter of Hinduism's pre-eminence in the discussion of religious pluralism, but consider Hindu Anantanand Rambachan's remark that he finds inspiration and guidance in Jesus[13] for his "spontaneous and limitless compassion" and "unconditional love, tenderness, and humility."[14] As a Christian theologian, I am touched by Rambachan's openness and joy at his own humbling through contemplating the experience of Jesus. Thus glints the rich potential of interfaith encounter.

Amidst the depth and breadth of Hindu thought, some entry point is needed, and the life and writings of Mahatma Gandhi are accessible for his commitment to peace; his awareness but rejection of Christian theology (Gandhi was somewhat of a defensive dialogue partner with the West[15]); and his upholding of humility. As he writes in his *Autobiography*, "I feared humility would cease to be humility the moment it became a vow. The true connotation of humility is self-effacement. Self-effacement is *moksha* (salvation)."[16]

In achieving liberation or moksha, Gandhi elaborates that humility is a crucial component of overcoming the self, but he fears that ritualizing it could denude humility of its cathartic power.

Gandhi's rejection of Christianity should serve as a challenge to Christians who deeply respect if not revere his moral and political

10. Ibid., 144.

11. *Upanishads,* 140.

12. See the Dalai Lama's presentation of Hinduism in *True Kinship of Faiths,* 45–48.

13. Rambachan, "Christian Influence on Hindu Spiritual Practice," 213.

14. Ibid., 213.

15. Webster, "Gandhi and the Christians," 81 and 95. For a more positive view, see McDaniel, *Gandhi's Hope.*

16. Gandhi, *Autobiography,* 396.

commitment to the poor and can appreciate his wise and reflective writings.[17] Although he admitted much worth in parts of the gospel, especially the Sermon on the Mount, which he compared to the *Bhagavad-Gita*, he argued that the Gita is "the book *par excellence* for Truth."[18] He studied Christian doctrine, but was candid that "the arguments in proof of Jesus being the only incarnation of God and the Mediator between God and man left me unmoved."[19] He rejected Christian atonement theory, remarking: "I do not seek redemption from the consequences of my sin. I seek to be redeemed from sin itself, or rather from the very thought of sin."[20] He also saw the Buddha as more compassionate to all compared to Jesus in the Gospels,[21] who was a martyr and sacrifice, even a "divine teacher, but not as the most perfect man ever born." He thus contended there is nothing unique in Jesus and Christianity that is not found in other faiths philosophically, and that the moral goodness and deeds of Jesus and his followers are not superior to those of other faiths.[22] Buttressed by his holy and moral life, Gandhi's arguments against Christian uniqueness are powerful ones.

Claims of uniqueness often need humbling. If Jesus is a manifestation of God, and Christian orthodox belief does not claim Jesus of Nazareth as a human being could embody and contain all that is Divine, then why can't there be other incarnations? So many questions remain. And yet, there are false messiahs (Shabbetai Tzvi); anti-theistic gurus (Buddha); and pseudo-gods (Romans and Greeks).

"The seeker after truth," Gandhi notes, "should be humbler than the dust."[23] The world crushes such attempts to seek and know. Can we still persevere in such chosen humbling if only to glimpse the truth? Shouts from underground prisons, gulags, and unmarked graves elicit no easy answers. Those like Gandhi press ever onward.

He challenges us: "I must reduce myself to zero. So long as man does not of his own free will put himself last among his fellow creatures, there is no salvation for him. Ahimsa is the farthest limit of humility."[24] Ahimsa

17. Ibid., 68.
18. Ibid., 67.
19. Ibid., 123.
20. Ibid., 124.
21. Ibid., 160.
22. Ibid., 136–37.
23. Ibid., xiv.
24. Ibid., 505.

is non-violence, and so humility is demanded in placing the needs of others before our own.[25]

All traditions are also burdened by limitations and blind spots: presently we cannot ignore the rise of Hindu fundamentalism (Hindutuva) and its disparaging of what is deemed not Hindu and so not Indian; the pervasiveness of the caste system in many parts of rural India and in the slums; and the ongoing failures of integrating Dalits into wider society and acceptance.[26] Regardless, anticipating my argument in the next chapter on religious pluralism, exposure to dissenting views from respected and revered sources necessarily challenges and humbles any exclusivist or triumphalist position within our own faith. Hinduism is particularly situated to face and overcome such positions.

Buddhism and Humility

Whether as manifest in Mahayana, Theravada, or Vajrayana schools or traditions, Buddhism's tireless denial of any lasting self—and its highlighting of disordered desires or craving for what is ephemeral—are intensely humbling. Its challenging doctrine of Śūnyatā (emptiness or voidness) stresses, according to the Dalai Lama, that "any belief in an objective reality grounded in the assumption of intrinsic, independent existence is untenable."[27] Thus we should recognize our interdependence and compassion. Many of us cling to the I, to a permanent, continuous, unique self, for whom we often devalue all other concerns as secondary. Buddhism, especially Engaged Buddhism, promotes healing that overcomes false attachment without denigrating the life of all sentient beings.[28] Joy is also possible. Bill Porter tells the story of an old Buddhist nun living in a hut in China's Chungnan Mountains. He had asked her to write down the essence of Buddhist practice. She took the paper and said nothing, but then two months later gave it back to him with the words: "goodwill, compassion, joy, detachment."[29]

25. See also Weil, *Simone Weil Reader*, 389; and see Admirand, *Mass Atrocity*, 74.

26. See, for example, Brueck, *Writing Resistance*; Mallet, *River of Life*, 93–94; and Trawick, *Death, Beauty, Struggle*.

27. Dalai Lama, *Universe in a Single Atom*, 46; in Christian-Buddhist dialogue, see Tracy, "Kenosis, Sunyata, and Trinity," 135–54.

28. On Engaged Buddhism, see Senauke, *Bodhisattva's Embrace*; and Hanh, *Interbeing*.

29. Porter, *Encounters with Chinese Hermits*, 109.

Emblematic of humility (and the above virtues) in Buddhism are the Bodhisattvas, who vow to achieve buddhahood in order to "free all beings in the universe from suffering."[30] Such beings are the quintessence of courage, compassion, and humility: courageous for embarking on such an unknown path; compassionate for seeking to alleviate the pain and delusions of others; and humble for seeing a need and value in helping others despite any status already achieved. In the *Munimatālamkāra*, the Bodhisattva vow stresses that concern for others is one's only aim and drive.[31]

As with all major figures of faith traditions, the historical founder of Buddhism, Siddhartha Gautama, exudes humility and reaches the state of enlightenment (*moksha*) because of his deep awareness of the illusory nature of all life (*dukha*) and the interconnectedness of all life (*Pratī tyasamutpāda*, dependent origination or dependent arising). Through many lives and life cycles, as told in the *jātaka* stories, we read countless acts of compassion and self-abnegation in the previous lives of the Buddha, whether as a human male or (more rare) female, or other animal like a fish, deer, or rabbit. In some versions, the Buddha sacrifices body parts or life itself, as in his previous birth as a beautiful young woman Rūpyāvati.[32]

In the tale, Rūpyāvati encounters a starving woman on the verge of eating her child because of a severe famine. With no other immediate option and reflecting on the impermanence of life, Rūpyāvati cuts off her breasts and gives them to the woman to eat. Rūpyāvati then runs to her husband to get him to prepare more food for the woman. Two miraculous transformations then occur. First, her breasts regenerate after her husband performs a rite of truth on her. Then, after the god Indra questions her purity and motives, she asks to be transformed into a man. He grants her request, and she becomes the male Rūpyāvati who eventually is made a king.[33] The story is problematic when read with a feminist lens, not merely because of the sacrifice of her body (in another version, the Bodhisattva as a man gives away his head[34]) but because much of traditional Buddhist thought promotes men over women, as touched upon

---

30. Lopez, *Buddhist Scriptures*, 388.
31. Ibid., 390.
32. Ohnuma, "Story of Rupavati," 103–46.
33. See Lopez, *Buddhist Scriptures*, 159–71.
34. See ibid., 142–58.

further below. For our immediate purposes, the story highlights radical self-sacrifice to save lives and a deep, penetrating humility infused with compassion and guts.

Such humility is also a cornerstone of the Four Noble Truths, especially the first precept that all is *dukha*, impermanence/suffering. What pride can occur when foundations cannot be trusted and what we perceive or know is not trustworthy or real? Sustained contemplation on the fleeting states of everything further relinquishes claims of grandeur and superiority, or what John M. Thatamanil rebukes as "religious self-sufficiency."[35] Along with the diagnosis, the Buddha provides hope and a cure through the noble eight-fold path, formulated as right view, right thought, right speech, right action, right livelihood, right effort, right mindfulness, and right concentration. Of especial importance is mindfulness in all moments, "to know what is going on within and all around us."[36] Humility is intimately linked with mindfulness and an awareness of others beyond the needs of the self.

Chen Yu-Hsi situates humility in Buddhist thought as "a norm of personal conduct and a mark of supreme attainments that is consistent with the Buddhist 'middle way.'"[37] The Middle Way is one of the most appealing elements of Buddhism, avoiding the extremes to find a liveable, practical center from which to live and act. Anchored in the life of the Buddha, who had tried the extremes of a hedonistic and radically ascetic lifestyle, the latter eerily presented in many famous sculptures of the withered, emaciated monk, there was a need to balance the demands of the body and the strivings for liberation. Just as Aquinas employed elements of the Aristotelian mean (*mesotes*) to highlight how magnanimity and humility can balance one another, humility in Buddhist tradition is also fine-tuned to prevent excessive self-hatred or extreme asceticism. Yu-Hsi, for example, employs criteria for genuine humility in Buddhism, which includes acting free of ego and selfish tendencies or trying to impress others; taking a selfless concern and interest in the welfare and interests of others; candidly identifying our strengths and weaknesses; and accepting the reality of our imperfections and the need for learning and growth.[38]

---

35. Thatamanil, "Learning from," 290.
36. Hanh, *Living Buddha*, 14.
37. Yu-Hsi, "Buddhist Perception of Humility."
38. Ibid.

Returning to the fraught issue of gender in Buddhism, an issue still unresolved in all the major faiths, Kim Gutschow has highlighted how Buddhist nuns in the Himalayan Kashmir are "judged relentlessly on how generously they serve others and how sparingly they serve themselves."[39] According to Gutschow, many of the nuns also perpetuate the cycle of gender discrimination and gender injustice through their eagerness to be reborn as monks and in accepting humiliating treatment as a form of merit.[40]

The majority of Buddhist nuns she observed in the late nineties and early oughts were discriminated against on account of their gender, which had firm support not only in the wider cultural context but in a key foundational Pali text of Tibetan Buddhism, *Mūlasarvāstivādin Vinaya*, citing rules regarding women's ordination, including precepts that a nun cannot "reveal the corruptions of monks," and especially: "nuns must prostrate before all monks, even one who has been newly ordained a day."[41] While the Dalai Lama promotes equality for all, even stating in 2013 that his successor could be female,[42] the issue of foundational gender inequality remains insufficiently addressed at all levels of Buddhist thought.[43]

Humility in Classical Taoism

The famous Taoist story of Chuang-Tzu waking from sleep and wondering if he had been a man dreaming he was a butterfly or a butterfly dreaming he was now a man testifies not only to the interconnectedness of the Taoist world but a call for humility and circumspection about everything, as even self-knowledge could be contested.[44] So much is flux and appearance: as even morality has been entwined with societal convention and misappropriation of language, leading to pervasive emptiness and pretense.[45] As Qianfan Zhang writes: "what is branded as 'moral'

---

39. Gutschow, *Being a Buddhist Nun*, 149.

40. Ibid., 160.

41. Ibid., 171.

42. McGregor, "Next Dalai Lama."

43. See Swanepoel, "Blossoms of the Dharma," 569–99; and Goodwin, "Right View, Red Rust, and White Bones," 198–343.

44. Chuang Tzu, *Book of Chuang Tzu*, 20. See also Yao, "I Have Lost Me," 511–26; and the *I Ching*, 30–31 (15).

45. Such ambiguity has also been used against literature more generally. See Marx, *Hatred of Literature*, 103–54.

or 'good' often amounts to no more than the adulation of the powerful, which renders a large part of moral teachings to mere hypocrisy."[46] Perspective and place are mired in ego and striving.

In the proclamation of the paradoxical *wu-wei*, action less action,[47] resonant in many ways with the teaching of Krishna in the *Bhagavad Gita* above, we are called to detach ourselves from the fruit of outcomes, to divest ourselves of drives and plans for external awards and praise and so be content.[48] As Chuang-Tzu enlightens: "Empty, still, calm, plain, quiet, silent, actionless action is the foundation of all life."[49] We are called to seek internal cultivation[50] by following the Tao and stripping and simplifying ourselves, free from seeking praise, honor, and external attachments. Humility is suffused in the concept *wu-wei*: and ironically and paradoxically, both imply a weakness and passivity that nevertheless are deemed to be freeing and empowering—although both terms are also open for wide misunderstanding, for *wu-wei* entails action, but of a specific kind: not sloth, apathy, or laziness.

Linked to *wu-wei*, early Taoists portrayed the sage as an uncut piece of wood or the property of water.[51] As the *Tao Te Ching* instructs: "Have little thought of self and as few desires as possible."[52] Uncarved, they are beauty in themselves, not needing extraneous adornment. Of water, the *Tao Te Ching* comments: "In the world there is nothing more submissive and weak . . . yet for attacking that which is hard and strong nothing can surpass it."[53] Chuang-Tzu, moreover, contends to be still as water and similarly reflective: "Empty, still calm, plain, quiet, silent, non-active, this is the centeredness of Heaven and Earth and of the Tao and of Virtue."[54] Water is a metaphor of many possibilities; but applicable here is its durable potency to erode what seems more powerful: an insight crucial to

---

46. Zhang, "Human Dignity," 495.

47. Lao-Tzu, *Tao Te Ching*, xliii (50), xlviii (55), lxiii (70); and Chuang Tzu, *Book of Chuang Tzu*, 123; on *wu-wei*, see Slingerland, *Effortless Action*; and Loy, "Wei-Wu-Wei," 76.

48. Lao-Tzu, *Tao Te Ching*, xlvi (53).

49. Chuang Tzu, *Book of Chuang Tzu*, 107.

50. See Roth, *Original Tao*.

51. Lao-Tzu, *Tao Te Ching*, lvii (64).

52. Ibid., xix (23).

53. Ibid., lxxviii (85).

54. Chuang Tzu, *Book of Chuang Tzu*, 106.

geologists like Charles Lyell.[55] With enough time, raindrops could carve immense canyons. As Loren Eiseley wrote of Lyell's key forebear, Scottish geologist James Hutton: "He saw, with the marvellous, all-seeing eye of Shakespeare, that 'waterdrops have worn the stones of Troy and blind oblivion swallowed cities up.'"[56] Taoists had expressed similar notions over two millennia earlier.

Not confined to someone of supposed low stature, virtues like modesty, yielding, and humility became the hallmarks both of the Taoist sage and the ideal political ruler. The sage, for example: "does not consider himself right, and so is illustrious; / He does not brag, and has merit; / He does not boast, and so endures."[57] Just as the humility of Christ ironically renders him potent and divine for Christians, so too we read in the *Tao Te Ching*: "It is because it never attempts itself to be great that it succeeds in becoming great."[58] Such claims oppose every fiber of Western, capitalist culture: be aggressive, proactive, assertive, carved, unyielding, forcing the issues. "Weakness is the means the Tao employs," as Lao-Tse remarks.[59]

Humility is again prominent as we must recognize our finitude in the presence of infinity. Think of Chinese Buddhist or Taoist scrolls depicting cavernous mountain ranges and forests spilling over into vast stretches of empty space, and somewhere within that great immensity a tiny figure, a monk perhaps in meditation. Such images signal not only the great connections of Taoism and nature but humanity's tenuous place. Shen Zhou's (or Chou's) "Poet on a Mountaintop" depicts the painter himself, staff in hand, peering into the gorge beyond and below the receding cliffs and clouds.[60] The scroll includes these poetic lines: "I lean on my bramble staff / and gazing into space / make the note of my flute / an answer to the sounding torrent."[61]

In the ethereal poetry of Li Po or Tu Fu we encounter timeless Taoist images, reflections, and wisdom. In Li Po's "On Yellow-Crane Tower," we

---

55. Livio, *Brilliant Blunders*, 66–67.

56. Eiseley, *Firmament of Time*, 25. The Shakespeare quote is from *Troilus and Cressida*, III.ii.185.

57. Lao-Tzu, *Tao Te Ching*, xxii (27); and xxix (34); and see Chuang Tzu, *Book of Chuang Tzu*, 139–40.

58. Lao-Tzu, *Tao Te Ching*, xxxiv (39).

59. Lao-Tzu, *Tao Te Ching*, xl (47).

60. See Steuber, *China*, 10–11.

61. Sullivan, *Three Perfections*, 48–52. See also Clunas, *Art in China*, 101–3 and 137.

hear: "From Yellow-Crane Tower, my old friend leaves the west. / Downstream to Yang-chou, late spring a haze of blossoms, / distant glints of lone sail vanish into emerald-green air: / nothing left but a river flowing on the borders of heaven."[62] Yellow-Crane Tower, on Snake Hill in Wuchang, was initially built to commemorate a story about a Taoist monk, who in gratitude for free wine given to him in a wine shop in Wuchang, drew a magical crane with instructions to dance whenever it heard clapping. Throngs visited the site. Ten years later, the monk returned, played on his flute and rode the yellow crane to heaven.[63]

While powerful in visual and poetic terms, the application of these ideas can seem utopian. As Qianfan Zhang notes: "The Daoist rejection of reason, knowledge, and civilized society is, however, at best a simplistic solution; it is both unrealistic and self-defeating."[64] We have also seen the ripe possibilities for misunderstanding inherent in the term and application of *wu-wei* in Taoist thought. Yet, conceptions of humility without turning to Taoist resources would seem empty and insufficient: *wu-wei* of the worst kind.

Humility in Confucian Thought

A similar insufficiency would entail the omission here of the thought of Confucianism. Confucius appears in *The Book of Chuang Tzu* in ungraceful terms. A supposed sage in need of humbling or further enlightenment, Confucius in Chuang Tzu's stories marvels at the wisdom of the old fisherman.[65] In another story, Confucius is chastised by the Taoist teacher, Lao Lai Tzu: "Confucius! Rid yourself of your pride and your smug look on your face."[66] However, similar to the erroneous and slanderous portrait of the Pharisees in the gospels, Confucius's portrait by his Taoist rival and interpreter does not match the rich, nuanced, and moving sayings in *The Analects*. While notions of *wu-wei* and opposition from the world are not featured in that major work, Confucius also praises and promotes yielding and humility (*qian*)—deep moral virtue taught

---

62. Li Po, "On Yellow-Crane Tower," 83; see also Barnstone and Ping, *Anchor Book of Chinese Poetry*, 469.
63. On cranes, see Ziegler, *Black Dragon River*, 48–59.
64. Zhang, "Human Dignity," 493–510.
65. Chuang Tzu, *Book of Chuang Tzu*, 280–86.
66. Ibid., 239.

through education and as embedded in the golden (or silver) rule—and living by the Mean. These elements can be linked to Taoist thought but are also distinctive and bear some comment in relation to humility. As Catherine Hudak Klancer writes, for Zhu Xi, often compared to Thomas Aquinas for his masterful synthesis of Confucianism and subsequent impact on Confucian tradition,[67] humility entails responsibility for one's thoughts and actions and always striving for greater improvement and moral refinement.[68] "Striving" is a word that demarcates the Taoist and Confucian, but one can say that the end, harmony (*he*), is advocated by both through different means.

Much has been written about Confucius's promotion of *shu* when asked if there was a word that could guide one's conduct in life, followed by his comment: "Do not impose on others what you yourself do not desire."[69] Empathy is a mutually reinforcing virtue for humility: each needs the other which is why any attempt to establish a universal ethic is best sought in promoting the golden or silver rule in the world's faiths.[70]

In *Humbling Faith*, I repeatedly praise following the Mean in various religious and philosophical formulations, and so, too, we hear from Confucius: "Supreme indeed is the Mean as a moral virtue."[71] Though Confucius's thought and system are sometimes deemed to be overly deferential, many sayings rebuke such extreme positions. Thus, we read: "You will be looked upon as obsequious by others if you observe every detail of rites serving your lord."[72] The notion of yielding is often advised in the context of illustrating or advocating two fundamental Confucian virtues: *ren* (benevolence) and family reverence or filial piety (*xiào*).[73] Jing Lin and Yingji Wangwe write: "In the Chinese language, the word ren, is the symbol of two people standing together, implying that human beings are always engaged in the reciprocal relationship of sharing kindness and love."[74]

---

67. Berthrong, "Christian-Confucian Dialogue," 297.

68. Klancer, "How Opposites (Should) Attract," 672.

69. Confucius, *Analects*, XV.24 (135); and Xii.2 (112). See also Mencius, *Mencius*, VII.A.4 (182). See also Csikszentmihalyi, "Golden Rule in Confucianism," 157–69; and Allinson, "Hillel and Confucius," 29–41.

70. For an opposed view, see Bloom, *Against Empathy*.

71. Confucius, *Analects*, VI.29 (85).

72. Ibid., III.18. (70).

73. See Patt-Shamir and Zhang. "Confucian-Jewish Dialogue," 450–67.

74. Lin and Wang, "Confucius' Teaching of Virtues," 3–17.

When seeking to learn about the government in an unfamiliar area, Confucius instructs that this information is earned by being: "cordial, good, respectful, frugal, and deferential."[75] Elsewhere Confucius says regarding family reverence: "Never fail to comply."[76] In his famous account of his growth in various stages throughout his life, Confucius seems to embody the Taoist way by concluding: "at seventy I followed my heart's desire without overstepping the line."[77] Bolstered especially by Mencius's positive presentation of human nature (as Confucius was silent on this issue[78]), Confucianism can be another viable source for refining and developing humility.

Humility and Primal Faiths

For my World Religions module, I had asked Dr. Jude Lal Fernando to give two guest lectures. I gladly sat in on them. "Primal traditions," he remarked, "humble the world religions because they are reminders that they existed before them and would not have existed without them." It was a sobering thought—all the more sobering when contemplating how "grateful" such world religions have been for such gifts. That any primal, aboriginal, tribal, indigenous, or traditional religious faith remains is a testament to the perseverance and boldness of its peoples to endure persecution, violence, and genocide of various kinds. Regarding the devastation of small pox brought by the Europeans, Pretty-shield—medicine woman of the Crows—told Frank B. Linderman: "When a woman sees whole families wiped out, even whole clans, and cannot help, cannot even hope, her heart falls down and she wishes that she could die."[79] Similarly the nineteenth-century Native American writer William Apess wondered: "Now I ask if degradation has not been heaped long enough upon the Indians?"[80] Unfortunately, two centuries on, while the rights of Native peoples on paper have been strengthened by the adoption of "The

---

75. Confucius, *Analects*, I.10 (60).

76. Ibid., II.5 (63).

77. Ibid., II.4 (63).

78. See ibid., V.13 (78); Mencius, *Mencius*, 164–65. Hsün Tzu believed human nature needed education and ritual to curb its negative tendencies (*Hsü n Tzu*).

79. Linderman, *Pretty-shield*, 21. See also Linderman, *Plenty-Coups*; and Lear, *Radical Hope*.

80. Apess, "An Indian's Looking Glass," 1398.

Declaration on the Rights of Indigenous Peoples" by the UN General Assembly in 2007, maintaining indigenous ways remains precarious.[81]

First, what constitutes a primal or indigenous faith, or cosmic spirituality? While all faiths were once localized, some traditions have transcended and spread from their provincial contexts all the world over. Such globalized faiths (so-called world religions) are also contextual and localized in multiple spaces, while primal traditions remain more rooted to a specific territory, even if in theory a vast one or suffused by a cosmological perspective. The sacred is all around us as space, time, and place—think of the Dreamtime among Aboriginal peoples.

These traditions are also the most vulnerable.[82]

Once again I'm wading into worlds within worlds, encompassing vast stretches throughout the globe. I will restrict myself to a few indigenous voices, mostly from Native American studies, which as Lee Irwin notes, is also immensely diverse and complex, "grounded in very specific languages, places, lifeway rites, and communal relationships."[83] After centuries of oppression and cultural genocide, are European and American governments and religious institutions more open to promoting indigenous spiritualities for guidance and wisdom, especially in the areas of ecological sustainability and justice?[84] Hopefully, more of us can see how Native wisdom can also deeply enlighten core religious and philosophical beliefs.[85] As Lee Miena Skye notes, Australian Aboriginal women transformed the violent Christology of the colonizers into a gentle Christ;[86] a transformation that should also deeply humble European and American theologies and legacies. For too long in the Christian world, indigenous faiths and traditions were deemed inadequate, pagan, sinful, or perhaps at best, *preparatio evangelium*, preparation for the gospel.[87] Many indigenous people, if not hostile to Western (or Eastern) hegemonic faiths, are today urged by their leaders to promote and weave in their indigenous

---

81. See especially Suzman, *Affluence without Abundance*.

82. May, *Transcendence and Violence*, 123. See also Grann, *Killers of the Flower Moon*.

83. Irwin, "Native American Spirituality," 4. See also Byrd, "American Indian Transnationalisms," 179.

84. On the West's failure to face climate change, even after the facts, see Rich, "Losing Earth."

85. See Peelman, "Native American Spirituality and Christianity," 346–59.

86. Skye, "Australian Aboriginal Women's Christologies," 195.

87. See Graber, *Gods of Indian Country*.

traditions. As Tink Tinker argues: "Christian Indians need to think of our traditional Indian cultures—with their rich stories and powerful ceremonies—as part of an 'old testament' tradition that might become for Indian Christians the only appropriate foundation for affirming Jesus and expressing a christian commitment."[88]

To highlight the shameful facts of European and American conquest and genocide of Native peoples and beliefs is not to create some false dichotomy that primal ways and beliefs are good, while the religions of the colonizers are bad, dividing "those filled with light and those filled with darkness."[89] Such binary or Manichaean thinking is both unhelpful and misleading. Tinker, for example, calls on White Christians to "acknowledge the american history of violence" and "*resist judgment* of [Native American] religious and ceremonial tradition," but also challenges Native Americans to "take their cultures and traditions seriously," which includes exhibiting the cultural values of Native spiritualities in daily living.[90]

Humility is suffused within indigenous worldviews where all life is harmonious and intimate with nature. As Churchill notes, Native peoples' civilizations exist within nature seeking neither domination nor destruction.[91] The idea is beautifully expressed as "The Way" by Granpa, a full-blooded Cherokee in Forrest Carter's controversial (but still deeply moving) novel *The Education of Little Tree*: "Take only what ye need. When ye take the deer, do not take the best. Take the smaller and slower and then the deer will grow stronger and always give you meat."[92]

Perceiving the sacred throughout nature encourages respect and partnership. Vine Deloria Jr. describes interspecies communication dependent upon whether the human being's moral life is attuned with creation, showing respect to non-human life in particular. "If we are worthy in their eyes," he writes, "they adopt us."[93] Similarly, Guatemalan activist Rigoberta Menchú comments: "So we think of the earth as the mother

---

88. Tinker, "American Indian Liberation," 63.

89. Hugo, *Les Misérables*, 810.

90. Tinker, "American Indian Liberation," 65–66.

91. Churchill, "I Am Indigenist," 282.

92. Carter, *Education of Little Tree*, 9–10. For critique, see Admirand, "Should We Still Teach?"

93. Deloria, "Indigenous Peoples," 552–59.

of man, and ... This is why, before we sow our maize, we have to ask the earth's permission."[94]

As Black Elk, warrior and medicine man of the Oglala Sioux, told John Neihardt, the White Man, or Wasichus, instead slaughtered the bison without purpose. "They just killed and killed because they liked to do that."[95] These Native voices, as Dr. Lal reminded my students, are indictments of the hypocrisies and moral failures of the more forceful religions: offering means of humbling for all expansionist faith systems, from Christianity and Islam to commercial and economic advocates of capitalism, industrialization, communism, and globalization.

In the context of nineteenth-century America, the Native Americans were on the cusp of annihilation through death, disease, broken treaties, trails of tears, reservations, and forced removals. Recall Chief Seattle's famous words, warning the white man that he will never be alone, even "when the last Red Man shall have perished," because their spirit and soul will remain in the landscape and in memory, haunting the white man amidst and after his misdeeds and destruction.[96] Who can credibly refute Chief Seattle's warnings, and how can the First World not be chastened and humbled?

Humility Humbled by Pride

Humility personified may be bashful, but as seen above, it is fundamentally praised in many circles with a wide enough following for more than a little sense of justified pride. But humility is also susceptible to injustice and misuse and so ultimately must be balanced by healthy pride (or the virtue of magnanimity from chapter 1). While discussing the famous eighteenth-century Jewish Hasid and preacher Maggid of Mezeritch, Elie Wiesel contends that: "*Umilbashto anava*, God's cloak is humility, was interpreted in Mezeritch as meaning: humility should be like a cloak; one must know how to take it off sometimes."[97]

Pride, construed as arrogance or blindness to the needs and esteem of others, deserves all the rebuke heaped upon it in religious circles.

---

94. Menchú, *Rigoberta Menchú*, 56.

95. Neihardt, *Black Elk Speaks*, 181; see also Irwin, "Freedom, Law, and Prophecy," 295–316.

96. Chief Seattle, "Speech of Chief Seattle," 1421–22.

97. Wiesel, *Souls on Fire*, 61.

However, is pride balanced by humility still pride? We can't have healthy haughtiness but is it not possible to have a healthy pride? What do we mean, for example, when we take joy and feel justified pride in ourselves or someone tied to us?

When teachers tell my wife and I that our kids are kind and compassionate, we billow with joy, and well, pride. It is the kind of feeling where we want to tell others (like now). It is a joy balanced by awareness and guilt of our failures in other ways towards them but hoping we are not burdening themselves too much with our baggage and maybe even helping to make them good little people who mature into good big people. Is such a vicarious pride, as Nicholas Nixon calls it, wrong?[98] It can be, but as Nixon notes: "vicarious pride that is proportionate to a realistic appraisal of the help we have given our children is appropriate."[99] Such pride, I would add, should have an ethical thrust towards values like goodness, truth, and community, free from ownership, pressure, or ego. Ma Thanegi, imprisoned for her support of Daw Aung Suu Kyi in Burma, speaks of how pride helped many political prisoners endure their ordeals: "they lived with a pride that left no room for self-pity."[100]

As noted in the introduction, the humility I am elevating is necessarily scrappy, rugged, and obdurate, willing to be fierce in the midst of oppression and injustice. Theologically, it is a wounded or broken faith, as Elie Wiesel and Irving Greenberg have noted, or fractured, in my language[101] and "limping" for Kevin J. Vanhoozer.[102]

We are left with a humility seeking knowledge but also admitting ignorance; a humility humbled by clarification and explanation, and a need to build "an inter-dependent society."[103] Humility without editing, explanation, and refinement is likely to cause harm. Such admissions are again tied with the need for self-critique.[104] This sense of not knowing

---

98. Nixon, "Modesty, Snobbery, and Pride," 415.

99. Ibid., 416.

100. Thanegi, *Nor Iron Bars a Cage*, 10.

101. See Admirand, *Mass Atrocity*, 141.

102. Vanhoozer, "Scripture and Tradition," 168; see also Francis, *Adventures in Human Being*, 199–209.

103. Gebara, *Out of the Depths*, 132.

104. Greenberg, Feinstein, Schulweis, and Ellenson, "On the Role of Denominations," 114.

and openness to self-critique are fuelled by an interdisciplinary and especially interfaith context.[105]

According to Michael von Brück, interreligious endeavor requires humility.[106] In a similar vein, the Dalai Lama has highlighted the Tibetan word *soe pa*, often translated as patience, but also including "the virtues of tolerance, forbearance, and forgiveness."[107] While *soe pa* often means enduring suffering, he clarifies how such is not passive or impotent.[108] Recall Gandhian *satyagraha* (commitment to truth) and *ahimsa* (total non-violence), as peaceful, active means to combat violence and injustice.[109] It is courageous, committed, and capable of defeating empires or racist, institutional mind-sets. It also knows it's fragile and cannot be borne alone. As Martin Luther King Jr. proclaimed while condemning the Vietnam War: "We must speak with all the humility that is appropriate to our limited vision, but we must speak."[110] He knew his words would be unpopular.[111] Humility is a virtue that is often forged in agony but perseveres.

Such is a rugged, scrappy humility or humbleness. It is transparent, patient, steeped in hope, faith, and love; but not indifferent and inert in the face of injustice (nor rash, either). True humility does not denigrate me, another, or life in general; even in acknowledging or celebrating greatness, beauty, and uniqueness. We should recognize the interconnection of all life and know and understand that many of our successes and failures are intertwined with the actions or non-actions of others, which neither detracts from our sense of ultimate responsibility nor removes our need to take responsibility for what we say and do (or do not say or do not do). Theists at this point may accentuate the greatness of God, perhaps in a Jobian sense: "Where were you when I laid the earth's foundations?" (Job 38:4), though the enigma of God's words to Job remains impenetrable, and perhaps, deficient from a pastoral standpoint. And if they are wise, theists will often remain silent, saying nothing after

---

105. See Admirand, "Seeking Humility and Self-Critique."

106. von Brück, "What do I Expect Buddhists to Discover in Jesus?," 174–75. See also Hanh, *Going Home*, 22.

107. Dalai Lama, *Beyond Religion*, 138.

108. Ibid., 138.

109. See Scalmer, "Mohandas Gandhi," 337–52.

110. Carson and Shepard, *Call to Conscience*, 140.

111. Ibid., 140.

uttering such devout phrases, letting the silence humble them and their piety, feeling foolish and humiliated for their holy words.

In the epilogue to *Learned Ignorance*, Rabbi Reuven Firestone asks one of his Christian co-editors, James Heft: "Can one ever arrive at a true understanding and truly respectful view of the religious other if one insists that one's religious tradition is truer?"[112]

Such is one key question to investigate in our next chapter on religious pluralism and its potential to humble faith.

---

112. Heft, Firestone, and Safi, "Epilogue," 303; italics in original have been removed.

3

Many Ways or One Way?

Religious Pluralism and Sheltering Another's Hopes

Master Lao Yang, a blind Taoist monk, told Bill Porter (Red Pine): "Buddhists and Taoists walk the same path. They just dream different dreams."[1] It's a wonderful and hopeful image to lead us gently into the often dreamy (to some, wistful and vague) landscape of religious pluralism. Master Yang is not belittling or conflating difference but highlighting where congruence and overlap can exist. He envisions what can unite. Yet to say we all dream different dreams may not go far enough: for some people's dreams are others' nightmares. At their core, religious pluralists are helplessly optimistic and hopeful, trusting in what they do not fully know or understand but is apparently beloved by others. For theists, religious pluralism is anchored in a resounding trust in a compassionate Creator beyond full grasp and definition—fullness overflowing. For nontheists, there is trust in the goodness of life, the holiness of living reality.

Rabbi Harold Schulweis tells a story of a rabbi's disciple who became aware of a village atheist prepared and ready to challenge his master's theistic beliefs. One day, the atheist burst into the rabbi's study, glared at the rabbi, and prepared to deliver his arguments. "Their eyes met, and the rabbi spoke a single word: *Efshar*, 'Perhaps.' With that one word, the tension was broken, and the two fell into each other's arms."[2] The present work is a paean to perhaps, and the embrace of faith and doubt.

Religious pluralists say: "I may not know or understand why you believe what you do, but you must have valid reasons, and as they don't

---

1. Porter, *Road to Heaven*, 218.
2. Greenberg, Feinstein, and Schulweis, "On the Role of Denominations," 149–50. See also Lane, *Age of Doubt*.

cause harm, and even promote the good, that's enough for me." Religious pluralists may not want everyone to dream the same dreams—for such could be dreadful. Must we not discern and name (and where necessary, rebuke or prioritize) one dream (or nightmare) from the other? But they want to nurture as many dreams as they can.

I contend that religious or secular faiths develop into mature, authentic positions and contain qualities crucial for ongoing relevance through otherwise often self-defeating and compromising attributes. They would include the following:

1. roots in doubt and questioning;
2. deeply cognizant of foundational gaps and scriptural or doctrinal inconsistencies;
3. painfully apprised of its real-life, historical and present failures;
4. diurnally humbled in the presence of various holy and authentically good Others; and
5. allergic, if not hostile, to religious or secular language that claims "fullness of truth," "only," "universal singularity,"[3] exclusivity, and so on.

Otherwise, such triumphalist positions risk becoming shrivelled and predatory: a type of zombie faith munching on the fears and hopes of the seeking and needy. Such faiths pledge the unrealistic and the unverifiable, whether manufactured and sold as pure, scientific Truth, immediate financial prosperity (with stock options), or definitive salvation (no rebirth or purgatory for you). Arrogance masked as hope.

Instead, humility should foster pluralism just as pluralism should heighten humility. Raimundo Panikkar, for example, emphasizes how our lack of total knowledge and complete certitude are revealed the more we engage with other perspectives and views.[4]

Our focus here is beyond the mere fact of the diverse existence of theistic and nontheistic faiths and humanist and atheist options, or what Paula Fredrikson calls practical or pragmatic pluralism,[5] and which, from a Hindu perspective, Arvind Sharma labels cultural pluralism.[6]

---

3. López, "Divine Revelation," 231.
4. Yadlapati, *Against Dogmatism*, 160.
5. Fredrikson, "Paul, Practical Pluralism," 87–118.
6. Sharma, "One Kind of Pluralism?," 57.

Religious pluralism here means the possibility or real validity of other ways of knowing, being, believing, and seeking. Religious pluralism incorporates a realistic understanding of the frailty and fragility of all faith-paths, especially our own. While hoping and believing our unique path or way is true, holy, or salvific, it neither claims, nor even hopes, to be the only way. Perhaps against strands of tradition or doctrine and even the apparent rudiments of logic, such pluralism wants meaning and truth to be as sweeping as the galaxy, ethereal and sidereal, just as the orbs and planets of the sky guide the journeys of the living and the dead. For theists, such positions enfold a God of Love who is present to every individual in this world, often through inscrutable and impenetrable ways.[7] For nontheists, pluralism is a feast of diversity within our world, providing security to what is unknown or beyond.[8] Pluralism is a tendency to seek both/and solutions rather than either/or ones. It evaluates, judges, and critiques, though always through humility and expansiveness.

When guided by the option for the poor,[9] a pluralist framework should aim for transforming worldviews through a dialogue of openness and mutual learning. For liberationist Jon Sobrino, there is a "limit on pluralism" in our responsibility to aid the poor and oppressed, which takes precedence over any other type of communion so that such a partnership cannot conceal or minimize such suffering."[10] This too, is humbling. It is also freeing as it sets a ground for a pluralist attitude to be principled and discerning. If acknowledging that the pluralist attitude is guided and constrained by the option for the poor (embedded in a culture of life[11]) does this also admit a bias and subjectivity, even the potential for intolerance and exclusivism? Does it mean anything to insert the words "holy" or "ethical" before a term like pluralism?[12] Fundamentally and primarily, if secular or religious positions promote life, and especially the life of the vulnerable, defenseless, and poor, they are holy, authentic, and meaningful, which is to say, salvific in the sense of saving and redeeming.

My awareness (or begrudging acceptance) of the potential or real validity of other ways impacts how I envision and validate my own way.

7. See Romans 11:33.

8. Wohlgreen, *Hidden Life*, 53.

9. Knitter, "Toward a Liberation Theology of Religions," 196–97.

10. Sobrino, "Communion, Conflict, and Ecclesial Solidarity," 629. See also Dube, *Postcolonial Feminist Interpretation of the Bible*, 193–94.

11. See John Paul II, *Evangelium Vitae*, chapter 4.

12. See Knitter, "Toward a Liberation Theology of Religions," 181–82.

Such awareness, as Chester Gillis rightly notes, is particularly important for "traditions with long histories of felt superiority [who] must [now] approach the religiously other with a new humility and openness."[13] Such humility demands deep introspection and self-criticism coupled with appreciation of outside critique.[14]

Some would welcome the challenge of being proven "wrong." If Jesus is God, then a materialist conception of the universe could not be maintained and some may welcome the refutation and the lesson learned; the proof and evidence shown. If there is no God and no afterlife, atheists will not be around to get their deserved last laugh or console their theist friends; the same may not be the case if there is a God and afterlife—though it may be the moral atheist who is vindicated if compared to an immoral, hypocritical theist. Such is to say that as a Catholic, if the Catholic way is proven irrevocably right (so that all other faiths are wrong or only preparation for the gospel), then I am tempted, like Ivan Karamazov, to return my ticket. This is an undeniably frightening and problematic assertion (for me, anyway) so the next two chapters will work through this dilemma while arguing for why pluralism is a necessary humbler. Is it possible that the richer and deeper my love of Christ becomes, the more open to other ways I could be? That my religious identity may become all the more tightened and confirmed as I leave room for alternative ways for others? Or is this simply a further sign and step of the eventual desiccation or dissipation of my Catholic, then Christian, then theist, identity?

This chapter will proceed in five steps. It will first seek to address the plurality of types within religious pluralism. It will then examine the limitations or misconceptions of pluralism. Third, it will present various qualifiers to clarify why pluralism is not relativism and grapple with whether pluralism is really another form of exclusivism. Fourth, it will briefly look at pluralism in Hinduism, Judaism, and Islam, and then close with a short overview of pluralism in nature through the writings of anthropologist (and atheist) Loren Eiseley.

---

13. Gillis, *Pluralism*, 37. See also Bowden, "Religious Pluralism and the Heritage of the Enlightenment," 16.

14. Tillich, *Dynamics of Faith*, 33. See also ibid., 146.

Defining Religious Pluralism?
Types, Models, Overlaps, and Contradictions

While discussing the Glorious Revolution of 1688, Daron Acemoglu and James A. Robinson note how part of that revolution's success (in addition to contingency) was the granting of more rights to more individuals because a broad coalition had to be formed preventing one group gaining a "monopoly at the expense of the rest."[15] This broad coalition helped form a Parliamentary body bolstered by more checks and balances. Similarly, Rabbi Rudin believes religious pluralism is an antidote to religious terror and violence.[16] I am also contending that pluralism humbles rigid perspectives and unblinkered certitude—but in a vivifying and freeing way. Some religious violence is fuelled by uncertainty, with religious pluralism deemed to oppress and suffocate claims of singularity and unique meaning. Acts of rash desperation are sometimes chosen to thrust and restore religious identity and power. Religious pluralism becomes the enemy to resist and outlaw. Yet it need not be that way. Religious pluralism humbles certain aspects of faith, but may also refine and strengthen faith in the process: removing the dross of insecurity and narrowed thinking and allowing its core essence to glimmer: its golden gleam restored. No alchemy is at work as[17] humbling may also erode and tarnish faith; the need for smelting may be long overdue.

Perhaps because of these possibilities, there is much trepidation and resistance to religious pluralism in some religious circles. Gavin D'Costa, for example, is clear that "religious pluralism is inconsistent with orthodox Christianity and some of it is neo-Christian in its presuppositions."[18] Elsewhere he further confirms: "pluralism is not an orthodox option for a Roman Catholic theology of religions."[19] D'Costa identifies Christian pluralists as those who hold such positions as the following:

1. Other ways are salvific.

2. Other faiths' founders or books are sources of valid revelation.

3. Missionary attempts are unwarranted as other peoples are already touched by God.

---

15. Acemoglu and Robinson, *Why Nations Fail*, 211.
16. Rudin, *Christians & Jews*, 232. See also Sifton, *Violence All Around*.
17. For a discussion of these terms, see Admirand, "Why Liberation Theology."
18. D'Costa, *Christianity and World Religions*, 9.
19. D'Costa, "Reflections on Philosophical Presuppositions," 329.

4. Christianity can learn "new ontological truth" through interfaith dialogue.

5. Inclusive and exclusive claims regarding Christianity are no longer viable and operable.

6. Christians should instead seek to live and partner as equals with those of other faiths.[20]

Note that my current work here is not explicitly engaged in systematically refuting or supporting D'Costa's above claims, but I wonder whether adherence to the opposite views is more indicative, for example, of Christian spirituality and mercy and a God of universal love and grace. Perhaps one can maintain humility by claiming, for example, that:

1. Only Jesus (the source of one's faith) is salvific.

2. Any holy figures outside Christianity are invalid sources of revelation.

3. Christianity already exhausts all knowledge of ontological truth and so Christians have nothing substantial to learn from non-Christians in this regard.

4. Christians must tirelessly work to convert even the so-called holiest non-Christians until they accept uniquely viable Christian truths.

It would seem, however, that either such humility should be unwarranted and undesired (because of its impossibility to cogently maintain) or would have to be reconfigured as holy pride in one's faith. D'Costa's fears, however, of an eroding Christian identity and a failure to discern and evaluate clear differences and values remain pressing. Gillis, for example, asks: "Is God the one and indivisible Allah, the Father of the Lord Jesus Christ, the ultimate Dharmakaya of Mahayana Buddhism, the all-powerful creator of Judaism, whose name cannot be spoken, or that which is the true soul of each being, Brahman in Hinduism?"[21] Can an understanding of God encompass such diverse and often contradictory elements without becoming gibberish? Gillis supports focusing on God as transcendent while bearing in mind a God of revelation, presence, and mystery.[22] There are particular manifestations of God in particular

---

20. Ibid., 329–30.
21. Gillis, *Pluralism*, 178.
22. Ibid., 179–80.

histories and cultures—an idea we will see below in Jacques Dupuis (who still maintained the pre-eminence of the Christian revelation).

To provide a layered and nuanced portrait of religious pluralism, I will highlight five desired (or even required) attributes of the pluralism I am advocating as a humbler of faith. This pluralism should be:

1. Humble
2. Just
3. Compassionate
4. Pluralist
5. Dialogical

First Attribute: Humble

To support or be open to religious pluralism requires a humble stance of uncertainty at the exclusive claims of one's faith embodied by a deep love and hope for others' well-being and dignity. It should also acknowledge, if not be in awe of, the great mysteries, rituals, texts, and holy practices witnessed of those from other faiths and paths. It is humbling to see Muslim friends pray five times a day, Jains avoid killing insects, or Buddhists committed to mindfulness and meditative practices that instill love for others. It's humbling to try to learn and study from practitioners of other faiths whose language, terms, and perspectives can seem so foreign and jarring.

Pluralism without humility becomes hypocrisy and totalitarian. Humility thus permeates all the other attributes described below.

Second Attribute: Just

In the call for humility and in recognizing limits and doubts within all religious positions, it is crucial to apply those same qualifiers to all forms of pluralism, let alone to any exclusivist stance. As the post-Shoah Jewish theologian Irving Greenberg clarifies: "In principled pluralism, practitioners of absolute faiths do not give up their obligation to criticize that which is wrong (or what they believe to be wrong) or that which leads to less than full realization of truth, found in other faiths."[23] Here, undif-

---

23. Greenberg, *For the Sake of Heaven and Earth*, 208.

ferentiated pluralism or so-called relativism is a strawman (or woman!) in these types of arguments. As Greeberg adds: "the difference between relativism and pluralism is the fundamental difference we all have to learn."[24] The fear of relativism is always a threat to pluralism, but it should be balanced against its insular, self-referential extreme.

Two other points are essential for this attribute. The first entails an awareness of the potentially flawed criteria one uses to close (and then silence) disagreements. The second is an acknowledgment, no matter how painful, that the majority view today may become the minority view in the future, as the Talmud and other rabbinic writings beautifully illustrate (see *Tosefta Eduyyot* 1:40).

Notice that there is a strong element of an exclusivist faith, or what Greenberg refers to as "absolute" faith. Greenberg remains Jewish, though open to the paths and ways for others. God's covenantal partnership with the Jews "does not exhaust God's love."[25] For Greenberg, based on our religious or moral system (in his case, Judaism), we must rebuke injustice wherever we see it, whether within our traditions, or outside it. Pluralism is not an excuse for silence or indifference. In Greenberg's case, he is open to acknowledging that the Christian covenant may be valid for Christians—and not Jews—but when aspects of that covenant or how Christians perceive that covenant, are immoral, such as previously held supersessionist views, they must be challenged and rebuked.

For Greenberg, pluralism is also not enough. We must move beyond pluralism to partnership. We should even "take satisfaction in knowing that *harbay shluchim lamakom* (God has many agents/messengers)."[26] While still believing in the viability of our faith, the emphasis shifts. Our distinctive orthodoxies, while cherished, become displaced or recalibrated by the possibility that such beliefs may not, after all, be equivalent to God's all-encompassing and diverse aims. Or more likely, that every element of our traditions' orthodoxies are not universally proscribed; that there may be many chosen people and multiple covenants and paths which all reflect a love of God and one another. Can religious people prioritize living out that ethical message rather than obsessively trying to disprove and silence other truth claims which also spread mercy and compassion? Can they envision peace without attachment to such exclu-

24. Greenberg, Feinstein, and Schulweis, "On Orthodox and Non-Orthodox Judaism," 123.

25. Greenberg, Feinstein, and Schulweis, "On the Meaning of Pluralism," 151.

26. Greenberg, *For the Sake of Heaven and Earth*, 212.

sivist hopes or claims? Exclusivists and pluralists have a lot to learn in this regard.

In employing the term "just," I want to emphasize ethical justice with the principled stance identified above: some lines need to be drawn. There is also the question of justice towards whom. Is it towards the self, tradition, the Other, the Other's Tradition, or as entwined within all these relations, God? Such entwining can also seem restrictive and tense. Rebuking another's views or actions may be required but should be performed delicately, mercifully, and ideally, in dialogue with that person and worldview. It requires sustained purging and judgment of our own faults, failures, and hypocrisies—and a willingness to hear another's refutation and possible counter judgment.

This element of mutual critique resonates with Paul Knitter's ethical or soteriological pluralism.[27] Such "solidarity with the suffering"[28] demands listening to such voices and empowering them, whether articulated or merely embodied, to guide and lead our discernments. Such marginalized voices are prioritized, but are not the only voices in the discussion.

Knitter advocates a liberation-theology approach with its emphasis on the option for the poor, condemnation of structural injustice, call for praxis, and support of bottom-up base communities. This also coheres with my approach. Praxis and healing are yearned for everywhere, and all faith systems from secular humanism and Islam to Tibetan Buddhism clamor for such healing and praxis. Faith systems, theistic and nontheistic, secular and religious, need to cooperate to work towards best overcoming such oppression, for there is where salvation, Jesus, Krishna, nirvana, or moksha—and other ultimate names and hopes—are met and encountered. Knitter is right to promote "the mutuality of religions"[29] and "socially-engaged inter-religious dialogue."[30] All systems and faiths need one another for full development and maturing. The ethical takes priority. Not surprisingly, Knitter is also influenced by Emmanuel Levinas's

---

27. Perry Schmidt-Leukel describes Knitter's pluralism as monocentric and Cobb's as polycentric. See his "Christianity and the Religious Other," 144. See also his *Religious Pluralism and Interreligious Dialogue*.

28. Knitter, "Responsibilities for the Future," 85. See also Knitter, "Inter-religious Dialogue and Social Actions," 138 and 143.

29. Knitter, "Transformation of Mission in the Pluralist Paradigm," 94.

30. Knitter, "Inter-religious Dialogue and Social Actions," 138.

ethics before ontology and the pull of the face of the Other towards inhibiting violence.

In advocating the option for the poor and seeking justice for the most vulnerable, we are confronted with clear choices, priorities, and judgments. Perhaps we can believe almost anything (or not) about the Transcendent, but not the diminution of the sacred dignity of life. A God who tramples the oppressed and downtrodden is not worthy of veneration. The ethical and theological are inter-related (love of God and care of life are inseparable) even as I also contend that dignity of life is better translated in secular terms to be open to everyone (which does not hide or ignore thick religious conceptions for some believers). Pluralism is not syncretism.[31] Ultimately I agree with David Patterson's contention that ethics is intertwined within the pluralist view and seems the least likely to cause harm. He also reminds us that how we view the fate of outsiders to our tradition in the afterlife can influence how we treat such people in this life, especially on the question of God's care and love for all.[32] This seems reasonable, which is also to say I am humbled by those who maintain an exclusivist position but still treat others with dignity, respect, and care.

Third Attribute: Compassion

Compassionate is the third core attribute of pluralism, and so it is useful to examine how the Dalai Lama in particular links compassion with his examination of religious pluralism. Being compassionate is a guiding principle in identifying, responding to, and interacting with another's life, dreams, and meanings. In the name of compassion, we may refute or argue with another's truth claims and beliefs, but the means, ends, and results are filtered in both of our perceived best interests. A humbled pluralism, seeking what is just, open to other ways, dialogical in nature, and suffused by compassion will tread delicately amidst another's spiritual or doctrinal dreams, beliefs, and rituals.

The Dalai Lama asks: "Does acknowledging the truth of the Buddhist's taking refuge in Buddha, Dharma, and Sangha compromise [Christian] belief in the nature of Christian faith as call to discipleship of Jesus? Is faith in Christ one way to find Truth, while belief in the

31. Moffic, "Progressive Reform Judaism," 60.
32. Patterson, "Life and Afterlife," 38.

Buddha represents another path?"[33] As J. Abraham Vélez de Cea points out, the Dalai Lama works through this conundrum by holding onto a one-way-and-many-ways approach. While maintaining the Geluk school of Tibetan Buddhism is superior for him, he acknowledges other ways for other people. According to de Cea, His Holiness seems to equate private individualized religious practice (which is guided by distinctive and differing doctrinal beliefs) with a more public openness to the ways of other faiths in the realm of ethics.[34] Interestingly, both de Cea and D'Costa argue that the Dalai Lama speaks more liberally among Western audiences, while maintaining at the individual level the supremacy of achieving the ultimate end, Buddhahood, "only through the Geluk Presentation of emptiness."[35] While only hinted at by de Cea, in the Dalai Lama's more recent publications, he is moving in a more genuinely open and encompassing religious pluralism, emphasizing innate, universal, secular ethics as a greater resource for peace than religions.[36]

Although the Dalai Lama is open to the possibility of others' conversion, he prefers they experience their spiritual maturity and growth within their own traditions.[37] Such a position could not ethically and cogently maintain ultimate ends are only viable in the Geluk tradition but then discourage people from entering that path to remain within their own religious upbringing. Instead, the Dalai Lama discusses a transformation in meditation and practice so that "in following your own spiritual tradition, you will discover that a natural humility will arise in you, allowing you to communicate better with people from other religious and cultural backgrounds."[38] You see the "full worth" of others' faith traditions as you also appreciate the good of your own faith.[39]

The crucial piece for the Dalai Lama is compassion—which is not only transformative in general, but is promulgated and praised in all the world's faiths.[40] For the Dalai Lama, compassion "constitutes a basic

---

33. Dalai Lama, *Good Heart*, 19.
34. de Cea, "Buddha and the Dalai Lama," 62.
35. Ibid., 60–61.
36. See Dalai Lama, *Appeal to the World*.
37. Dalai Lama, *Good Heart*, 45.
38. Ibid., 41.
39. Dalai Lama, *Toward a True Kinship of Faiths*, ix.
40. Dalai Lama, *Good Heart*, xiii.

aspect of our nature shared by all human beings."[41] Such compassion, particularly present in (and sometimes exceeding) various configurations of the golden or silver rule, can help unite religious efforts to create and sustain a peaceful, just world for all.[42] The Dalai Lama distinguishes two levels of compassion. The first is at a biological level: and he often gives the example of a mother's love for her child. The second level has to be cultivated, and here religions can play an irreplaceable role.[43] He also carefully shows how compassion can inform justice and peacefully confront injustice.[44]

His notion of compassion is similar to recent work in relational justice that sees peace-making and reconciliation working with conceptions of justice as right relationships. Ethical mindfulness,[45] meditation, and mental cultivation[46] are especially valuable for training and meditating upon and radiating love and joy for others.[47]

While *Humbling Faith* highlights humility (or a humble pride), compassion is also essential. Can one be compassionate without humility? Unlikely. Can one be humble without compassion? Again, unlikely. They are mutually reinforcing. As Jane Foulcher writes: "Humility gives birth to compassion."[48]

The Dalai Lama sees the move to a pluralist position based on experience and exposure to other faiths while also fostering and developing commitment to personal faith. This exposure sharpens our appreciation and deeper awareness of our own faith and the spiritual riches of others.[49] For the Dalai Lama, openness to religious plurality need not seek to establish or prove "the ultimate oneness of all religions."[50] Instead, religious diversity should be celebrated.[51] Nor does he support the diminishing

---

41. Dalai Lama, *Toward a True Kinship of Faiths*, 109.
42. Ibid., 118.
43. Dalai Lama, *Beyond Religion*, 50.
44. Ibid., 70.
45. Ibid., 103.
46. Ibid., 164.
47. Ibid., 171.
48. Foulcher, *Reclaiming Humility*, 312. See also ibid., 195–96; and Metz, "Facing the World," 30.
49. Dalai Lama, *Good Heart*, 17–18 and 45–46; and Dalai Lama, *Toward a True Kinship of Faiths*, 146. See also MacFarquhar, *Strangers Drowning*, 186.
50. Dalai Lama, *Good Heart*, 148.
51. Ibid., 156.

of our own truth claims. He is clear: Buddhism is best for him—just not for many others, as religious truths are core elements forming religious identity.[52]

Also essential and useful is the Dalai Lama's highlighting of secular ethics, particularly in *Beyond Religion*. By secular, he does not mean an antipathy for, or rejection of, religion, but is strictly referring to how secularity is employed in the Indian constitution. In such an understanding, secular "implies a profound respect for and tolerance towards all religions. It also implies an inclusive and impartial attitude which includes nonbelievers."[53] Crucially, the Dalai Lama argues that ethics does not need a Divine source or ground, noting: "ethics can also emerge simply as a natural and rational response to our very humanity and our common human condition."[54] Compassion is practical because it promotes health and happiness.[55] While I remain tempted to posit God as the source to this core humanity, the Dalai Lama's approach is a way to call everyone to this ethical life.

Fourth Attribute: Pluralist

As emphasized above, one of the key attributes of pluralism should be its openness and celebration of difference. In this light, my fourth attribute of pluralism is what Anselm K. Min rightly calls pluralist.[56] There are no shortages of types and varieties of pluralism to choose from, like ritual pluralism,[57] committed and agnostic pluralisms,[58] complementary

---

52. Dalai Lama, *Toward a True Kinship of Faiths*, 157–58. For an opposing view, see D'Costa, *Meeting of Religions and the Trinity*, 90.

53. Dalai Lama, *Beyond Religion*, 6. For accounts of Indian secularism, see Bhargava, "How Should States Deal with Deep Religious Diversity?," 73–84; and Bhargava, "Multiple Secularisms and Multiple Secular States," 17–41.

54. Dalai Lama, *Beyond Religion*, 13; in the context of attrition and war, see Yarov, *Leningrad*; and in imaginary moral dilemmas, see Edmonds, *Would You Kill the Fat Man?*

55. Dalai Lama, *Beyond Religion*, 28.

56. Min, "Loving without Understanding," 59. See also Sharma, "One Kind of Pluralism?," 60–61; and von Brück, "Theology of Multiple Religious Identity," 181–206.

57. Telushkin, *Hillel*, 119. See also Boyarin, "Hellenism in Jewish Babylonia," 347.

58. See Newbigin, *A Word in Season*, 168.

pluralism,[59] or covenantal pluralism.[60] That there is a plurality of types of pluralisms should be celebrated.

My listed attributes of pluralism, moreover, should accept revision, change, correction, and addition. It is also reasonable that there is no one way of understanding and defining pluralism as examined here. This attribute clarifies that a truly pluralist view is hospitable to exclusivist claims and exclusivist dialogue partners—a critique often levelled against pluralists. John Cobb Jr. calls this "fuller pluralism," which also avoids relativizing unique beliefs.[61]

Muhammad Legenhausen, on the other hand, promotes degree pluralism in which "each religion has some particular positive status, [but] they do not have that status equally."[62] He prioritizes Islam as the highest embodiment of such pluralism, arguing that though Islam is the superior religion, it does not deny "divine light and truth" in other faiths and calls for believers to respect one another.[63]

In Universal Pluralism, advocates seek places of congruence and shared interests and aims in order to show deep overlap, consensus, and ultimate synergy between faiths. Min believes such a pluralism best describes the work of Hans Küng and Leonard Swidler.[64] Through the Global Ethic Foundation, Küng's vision and works have relentlessly brought together religious voices for dialogue around ethical aims. While Küng and Swidler seek to maintain distinctiveness among religions, they want to highlight their potential for partnership and deeper dialogue and relations.[65]

Contra the Dalai Lama, Raimundo Panikkar argues that "Pluralism affirms neither that the truth is one nor that it is many."[66] Min calls Panikkar's approach an ontological pluralism[67] (Gavin D' Costa labels it

59. See Phan, "Peacebuilding and Reconciliation"; and McDaniel, *Gandhi's Hope*, 9.

60. For covenantal pluralism, see Soulen, "Israel and the Church," 169.

61. Cobb, "Rethinking Christian Faith," 22. See also McEvoy, *Leaving Christendom for Good*, 115.

62. Legenhausen, "A Muslim's Non-Reductive Religious Pluralism," 52.

63. Ibid., 70.

64. Swidler, "History of Inter-religious Dialogue," 16.

65. See Küng, "Global Ethic," 186; and Swidler, "Interreligious and Interideological Dialogue."

66. Panikkar, "Jordan, Tiber, Ganges," 109.

67. Min, "Loving Without Understanding," 60.

"pluriform plurality":[68] a further nuancing of the plurality of types of plurality!). For Min, Panikkar's ontological pluralism "means passing beyond absolutism without falling into relativism with its agnostic tendencies."[69] This delicate balance seeks to embrace the unique differences of various paths that have their own criteria, beliefs, and systems but which all reflect, though imperfectly, some higher sense of reality and "the totality of human experience."[70] For Min, moreover, such ideas do not resemble the limitations of what is called a super-system.

Such super-systems can be located in John Hick's contention that all faith systems are ultimately meaningful as emblematic in some way of the Real. Though to be fair to Hick, he also challenged what he called ultra-pluralism or polyabsolutism (all faith systems are real) and so preferred a "single ineffable Ultimate Reality whose universal presence is being differently conceived and experienced and responded to within the different human religious traditions."[71] Returning to Panikkar, the focus on being insures that no system gobbles up unique identities and lives, the lifeblood of belief systems.

Finally, in Jacques Dupuis's inclusive pluralism (or pluralist inclusivism) there are attempts to maintain the ultimate supremacy of the Catholic position of Jesus's theological and soteriological uniqueness, while arguing that other traditions can serve "as 'meditations' of the mystery of salvation in Jesus Christ for their followers within God's design for humankind."[72] This position entails arguing that religious pluralism (or as he writes, "pluralism in principle" (or de jure[73]) is "based on the immensity of a God who is Love and communication."[74] Such communication is especially viable in the model of a Spirit or Trinitarian Christology[75] that cannot be fully contained in the historical, contextual finite life of Jesus of Nazareth. Building on *Ad Gentes* §9, Dupuis writes that "elements of divine '"truth and grace"'—which he also calls "additional and autonomous"—are at work "outside the Christian tradition springing

---

68. D'Costa, "Reflections on Pluralist Theology of Religions," 329–44.

69. Min, "Loving Without Understanding," 66.

70. Ibid., 68.

71. John Hick, "Next Step beyond Dialogue," 12.

72. Dupuis, *Christianity and the Religions*, 253.

73. Dupuis, *Toward a Christian Theology of Religious Pluralism*, 386.

74. Dupuis, *Christianity and the Religions*, 255.

75. Dupuis, *Toward a Christian Theology of Religious Pluralism*, 385. See also Lane, *Stepping Stones*.

from Jesus Christ, though not unrelated to his person and his work."[76] We have seen how much of this shared focus, or what Dupuis calls asymmetrical "mutual complementarity,"[77] is located in various understandings of the golden rule or in compassion as illustrated by the Dalai Lama above. It is a generous development and heightening of *Nostra Aetate* §2 (other faiths reflecting a ray of truth) or *Ad Gentes*' language of "seeds of the Word" (§11, 15) while still maintaining the language of fullness only in the Christ event. Dupuis had hoped to maintain the centrality and necessity of a salvific Christ while still leaving space and means for other faiths. Such space not only would enlighten Christianity but could also be means of salvation and signs of a covenantal relationship with God. Hence, Christ is central "in a qualitative and not quantitative way."[78] As is well known, Dupuis's works were brought under investigation by the Congregation of the Doctrine of the Faith.[79]

An intriguing question is how Dupuis's work would have been received if initially published in the papacy of Francis. Despite its flaws, it provides rich resources for change and development within a fairly conservative Catholic understanding of salvation and non-Christian religions.

While I am most supportive of Knitter's ethical model of pluralism that focuses on praxis, peace, dialogue, and liberation,[80] it is important to study and engage with diverse models to insure that the pluralism advocated is as rich and nuanced as possible—in a word, pluralist. Such diversity encourages dialogue, conversation, interaction, and partnership.

Fifth Attribute: Dialogical[81]

The fifth attribute is dialogical, and here we are referring to all modes and ways of dialogue (examined further in the next chapter), from highly academic to interfaith social-justice partnership, to the dialogue of life.

---

76. Dupuis, *Christianity and the Religions*, 256.

77. Ibid., 257.

78. Schmidt-Leukel, "Christianity and the Religious Other," 143.

79. For Dupuis's response, see Burrows, *Jacques Dupuis Faces the Inquisition*. For additional critique, see Schmidt-Leukel, "Christianity and the Religious Other," 143.

80. See especially Knitter, *Without Buddha*.

81. For dialogical pluralism, see Dietrich, "Globalization, Human Rights, and the Catholic Response," 143; and Tennent, *Invitation to World Missions*, 221.

As a simple example: I was in the car with four of the kids while my wife took our older daughter with her into a store. It was a cold day and the car windows began to steam up. One of the kids sketched away with his finger. A veiled Muslim woman, getting out of her car, noticed what he was doing, smiled, and traced a few squiggles back. She then saw me in the car, glanced apologetically, and walked towards the store. Beyond a simple human-to-human encounter, what occurred between my child and the unknown woman was also an interfaith or intercultural one. Her playfulness and smile may register in his memory—and hopefully was reinforced by his pedantic dad commenting on the happy exchange after my wife and daughter returned.

In this vein, I want to extend this dialogical approach by turning to discussions of the relationships between exclusivist, inclusivist, and pluralist approaches—for they are almost always intertwined in some way. As part of dialogue is hearing critiques, I will first present some of the salient ones against pluralist approaches.

The Limitations of Pluralism

Of the merry-go-round explanations of exclusivism, inclusivism, and pluralism, think of it this way: exclusivists already have the answers—and you don't. Inclusivists have the answers, too, but you may, partially so. You just don't know the real reason.[82] Inclusivism has an initial appeal, and almost seems palatable, but is really exclusivism light or incognito.

Pluralists also have the answers, and you do, too, as long as your answers are also theirs in the end. Does any sound position not claim to have all the answers? Pluralism is no panacea to belief, but it is a crucial piece of humbling. It does have risks and drawbacks, though.

Equality as Silencing the Marginalized

Uniqueness, trauma, marginalized, the other—these are ubiquitous words claimed by a wide-range of people, especially in many postmodern contexts. When all are rendered other and different, as theologian Joerg Rieger reminds us, true distinctions seem to flounder and a failure to

---

82. Eck, "Is Our God Listening?," 36.

clarify needs and wants renders the desperation of survival of some to be equal (or less equal) than the wants of the privileged.[83]

Thus Rieger advocates an option for the poor from the margins in which our postmodern discourse is expanded to the themes, calls, and actions espoused within postcolonial studies. Such a discourse, like the option for the poor in liberation theology, demands action and changes to structural inequalities in society. The mere reality of pluralism is not enough.[84]

In a celebration of the many and the multiple, we must be weary of token or cheap pluralism, symbolized by a celebration of a people or culture for one day or month but neglecting (and exploiting them) the rest of the year. Such exploitation is particularly rife when past and present failures and discriminations are downplayed, distorted, or silenced. Such exploitation—rendered as moral indifference—can also conceal itself under a religiously pluralist banner.

Pluralism as Moral Indifference

Any undifferentiated or radical pluralism can be narcissistic, prone to moral apathy. Recall traditional missionaries who renounced their material connections and embarked to foreign and treacherous places to save souls. Differences of belief were deemed a matter of life and death. With the erosion of such fervid religious convictions, coupled with awareness of historical wrongs and a greater appreciation of other traditions, the need to convert another seems inappropriate, if not distasteful. There is a call to not interfere but to respect other traditions. How do we distinguish between an apparent respect for difference and moral indifference? Do pluralist worldviews contribute to such indifference because there is little urgency to confront, let alone, save others? If we believe that salvation, liberation, or scientific truth is fully present in our own tradition (and that such beliefs are contradicted, minimized, or non-existent in other traditions), how can we not seek to evangelize and convert out of love for others? If our life is a journey to uncover truth and such discoveries are integral to our fulfillment and happiness as human beings, how can we squirrel away this revelation and not seek to share it with others?

---

83. Rieger, "Introduction," 14 and 4.
84. Sobrino, "Communion, Conflict, and Ecclesial Solidarity," 629.

If my fellow Catholics in particular believe this is even remotely true (and at what cost to their Catholic identity if they do not so believe?), the deeper question becomes how can they not witness their faith to non-Christians?[85] The CDF's "Doctrinal Note on Some Aspects of Evangelization" and *Dominus Iesus* highlight the lacuna within those who do not know Jesus and disavow salvation outside the Church founded by Christ.[86] Both implicitly, if not explicitly, proclaim other faiths limited, incomplete, or imperfect.

Such witnessing is often deemed a return or purification of faith, especially against the fear of a faith breakdown. We move not only into how we witness our faith and the impact such witnessing (or the dearth of such witnessing) has on our identity, but how to evaluate the questions of urgency and responsibility to witness our faith to another.

Eroding Identity and Tradition

In discussing *Dominus Iesus*, Daniel Madigan rightly contends that "Pluralists can easily become exclusive and intolerant," especially when they minimize distinctive qualities of various faith positions to claim that all paths ultimately lead to the same God. This is especially common in regards to concepts of salvation.[87] David Tracy notes "how pluralism can collapse into a repressive tolerance,"[88] and calls for suspicion if this plurality leads to a complacence that fails to critique injustice (an "ethical-political criteria"[89]) and is bereft of "a particular vision of resistance and hope."[90] Tracy rightly argues that such openness is the beginning but not the goal of a pluralistic attitude.[91] While pluralists must be willing to learn from everyone, they should take definitive stands where needed.[92]

---

85. Benedict XVI, *Porta Fidei*, §4.

86. Congregation for the Doctrine of the Faith, *Aspects of Evangelization*, §7; Congregation for the Doctrine of the Faith, *Dominus Iesus*, §6.

87. Madigan, "Saving *Dominus Iesus*," 268.

88. Tracy, *Plurality and Ambiguity*, 31. See also Legenhausen, "A Muslim's Non-Reductive Religious Pluralism," 59.

89. Tracy, *Plurality and Ambiguity*, 92. See also Tracy, *Dialogue with the Other*, 54–55 and 95–96.

90. Tracy, *Plurality and Ambiguity*, 91.

91. Ibid., 92.

92. Ibid., 92–93.

Tolerance can be another byword for marginalization, silence, and exclusivism by other means.

Is Gillis correct, then, to argue that pluralism does not seem to meet the important David Tracy/Schubert Ogden criterion of remaining faithful to the original witness of tradition? Does pluralism seem to call for too radical an alignment?[93] Gillis notes how "Pluralism as parity has devastating theological effects."[94] But could these devastating effects be purifying ones—a type of honor for faith lived and embodied well? Does pluralism accept the distinctive uniqueness of the other person and that person's faith and belief systems?[95] Can genuine openness and hope in the salvific or meaning-generated system of other faiths co-exist with individual, specific religious commitment?[96]

Evidence is murky. The sociologist of religion Steve Bruce contends that believers with a pluralist sympathy or outlook (privatized, compartmentalized, individualized) are less successful in passing on a sense of commitment for their core religious identity and beliefs to the next generation.[97] In all my pluralist comments to my children—about, for example, good and holy Muslims who only see Jesus as a prophet—am I undermining any possibility of their strong Christian identity? As a Christian, does not my eager openness to the Jewish covenant, which refutes any divine or salvific role to Jesus, inevitably begin to deny or erode my own faith? Is such pluralism doubly weak because it erodes an individual's faith-identity while in reality (as we saw above) sharing many traits with exclusivist tendencies—a pluralism that is really exclusivism with a smile?

Exclusivism in Disguise as Pluralism

Douglas Pratt contends that all forms of pluralism and inclusivism "collapse into some form of exclusivism."[98] Pratt instead approaches the issue in terms of a faith's uniqueness, or what makes it exclusive rather

93. Gillis, *Pluralism*, 27.
94. Gilkey, "Plurality and its Theological Implications," 40.
95. Amaladoss, "Pluralism of Religions and the Significance of Christ," 86.
96. Cornille, "Multiple Religious Belonging," 335.
97. Bruce, *Secularization*, 48.
98. Pratt, "Fundamentalism, Exclusivism, and Extremism," 241. See also Gillis, *Pluralism*, 21.

than in arguing for why only its way is correct.[99] For Pratt, exclusivity, unlike exclusivism, is not antithetical towards religious diversity, and so he identifies further distinctions or "variants" of the "paradigm of exclusivism": namely, open, closed, and extreme/rejectionist.[100] According to Pratt, too often the pluralist camp lumps exclusivists together, and Pratt's classification is helpful to show the diversity and complexity of exclusivist views.[101]

Similarly, Gavin D'Costa remarks: "it is not clear to me why 'pluralists' who also believe that theirs is the only true tradition should not equally be described as exclusivists."[102] So-called openness can be very restrictive and close-minded, indeed. D'Costa importantly raises the question of a pluralism in name only that seeks to avoid confrontation or the appearance of an exclusivist position and so speaks of a type of unity among faiths (or a lack of urgency or even danger in converting to another faith) but in reality still privileges their position. For D'Costa other traditions are actually stages or lesser vehicles because pluralism (if it involves holding any one faith position) is inevitably exclusivism disguised. Inclusivism and pluralism, therefore, mask as tolerance. While tolerance is a far cry from any dynamic religious pluralism, both are susceptible to an apparent openness to the Other that is really an encoded moral indifference.

Pluralists and Exclusivists Mutually Indebted

There is no lack of opportunities for my Catholic faith to be humbled. The sex-abuse scandal could silence any Catholic claim about the truth subsisting in the Catholic Church.[103] Most missionary, medieval, or Holocaust histories contain so many tragedies, embarrassments, and sins committed by Christian individuals or institutions that no corner seems dark enough to hide. Consider this prosaic but still potent humbler: Islam and its traditional view of Christianity and Christ.

While a college junior studying abroad in 1998, I visited the Great Cathedral-Mosque of Córdoba. I walked through the interior and

99. Pratt, "Fundamentalism, Exclusivism, and Extremism," 246.
100. Ibid., 247.
101. See also de Cea, "The Buddha and the Dalai Lama on Religious Pluralism," 58.
102. D'Costa, *Meeting of Religions and the Trinity*, 46.
103. See Admirand, "Pedophile Scandal."

examined the changes Christians made to the mosque to transform it "back" into a church. As a Christian (and an American one at that), the geographical and architectural space of the restored cathedral seemed to reinforce my (then admittedly limited) notion of so-called progress and history. Without explicitly saying it, I believed that the space reverting back to a church was right and just. Pride bubbled in my limbs and my eyes.

Fast forward twelve years later to Istanbul where I was a guest of advocates of the Fetullah Gülen movement, which contra Erdoğan, are committed as Muslims to interreligious dialogue, social justice, and democracy.[104] While on a tour of Hagia Sophia, I couldn't overcome pangs of melancholy, especially when thinking how the Christian altar was removed. I was struck by the immense medallions hung on columns under the dome with the names of Allah, the Prophet Muhammad, the first four caliphs, and the two grandchildren of Mohammed. I had to repel the words: "They don't belong here." I later discovered those medallions were part of a remodelling of Hagia Sophia in the mid-nineteenth century under two Swiss-Italian architects, Gaspare and Giuseppe Fossati. Such a fact may or may not have enhanced my melancholy. I was also reading Philip Jenkins's *The Lost History of Christianity* and William Dalyrimple's *From the Holy Mountain*, both narrating Christianity's decline in the Middle East and Western Asia.[105]

Standing on the balcony of Hagia Sophia, I thought back to Córdoba. I perceived my choice on the losing or conquered side. It did not feel fair. Almost everywhere else I travelled in Turkey gave me a similar sense of being conquered. But slowly, gradually, I began to empathize, and see the crossing of victor and vanquished, and moved away from reflecting on what only concerned me.

Exclusivist claims or those that boast of superior or triumphalist beliefs are not generally embraced by those promoting a religiously plural agenda. Pluralists tend to look upon exclusivists as remnants of some bygone, antediluvian age or as dangerous ideologues preaching their myopic views and creeds against the dignity of others who are not on their side. Exclusivists often portray pluralists as wishy-washy liberals with no sense of loyalty, identity, or coherence. Incapable of judgment or critique, these pluralists surrender to the siren-song of relativism and so

---

104. See McMaster, *A Word Between Us*.

105. On contemporary Christian responses to persecution, see Philpott and Shah, *Under Caesar's Sword*.

seem paralysed to decree anything as universally or intrinsically wrong or good.

In reality, both groups need each other. Pluralists need the sense of urgency, identity, and the importance of discernment and critique traditionally espoused by those who adhere to an exclusivist agenda. Exclusivists need to embrace the necessity of humility in any genuinely pluralist approach that promotes deep trust in the goodness and common sense of others. Much conversation and dialogue are needed.

Pluralism in Hinduism, Judaism, and Islam

It is helpful to be reminded of the rich pluralist possibilities in the world religions. Hinduism, for example, is the pluralist religion par excellence. "For ordinary people in ancient South India," Doniger remarks, "religious pluralism was more of a supermarket than a battlefield. Laypeople often gave alms to Buddhist monks or, later, prayed to Sufi saints, and still visited Hindu temples."[106] Such pluralist practices remain salient features of the Hindu faith—though being challenged by Hindutva ideology and a tendency in some circles to assimilate, in other words, undermine other faiths. For Doniger, the roots of Hinduism are pluralist in how "the Vedas regards the world, or the deity, or truth itself as plural."

While Jeffrey D. Long warns that Hinduism's ability to absorb other faiths can be a mixed blessing if the uniqueness of the other tradition is lost,[107] positively, it also reveals the broad reach and depth of the spiritual. In Hindu temples, devotees see statues of the Buddha or Jesus, inviting reverence.

Although Hinduism may be the religion that most extensively practices such assimilation, all religions have been influenced or even partly founded within other religious faiths. No religion, let alone human being, is an island. Just as early post-70 CE Judaism was influenced by Christian (and later Islamic) encounters, Christianity is founded upon the Jewish faith (not to mention its Greek and Roman influences). Islam unabashedly sees itself as linked with, and a fulfillment and final word of, Judaism and Christianity. The Sikh tradition, while maintaining its uniqueness, is heavily indebted to its Hindu and Muslim predecessors and sixteenth-century dialogue partners.

---

106. Doniger, *Hindus*, 368.
107. Long, "Hinduism and the Religious Other," 59.

Peter Phan has highlighted Christianity's missionary attempts to seek greater connection and contact with Asian peoples through using a language of Christ that reflects the historical Buddha, calling him "The Enlightened One," or the "Buddha."[108] Jesus's portrayal and interpretation in Arabic Literature (especially as depicted in Tarif Khalidi's *The Muslim Jesus*) or via Buddhism through Thich Nhat Hanh's *Living Buddha, Living Christ*, or via Hinduism in the work of nineteenth-century Hindu thinkers like Keshab Chunder Sen[109] also testify to similar attempts at assimilation by other faiths.

In Judaism, while there has been a tension between seeing the faith as a light unto the nations or employing a narrowed, isolationist stand, there are rich possibilities for accepting other traditions, provided there is a basic respect for God and human beings. Jonathan Sacks locates diversity and pluralism as part of God's plan and being. As God created diversity, so we must honor and protect it, even as covenantal Judaism endures.[110]

The key rabbinic notion of pluralism is in the Noahide laws,[111] in biblical passages like Isaiah 19:25 ("Blessed be My people, Egypt") that highlight other nations coming before God, or in the Talmud when God weeps as Egyptians perish in the Red Sea (Sanhedrin 39b). While there are some exceptions in the Talmud, Rabbi Joshua ben Hananiah's contention that the *tzadikkim*, the righteous of all nations, share in the world to come "was accepted as the normative one."[112] Such a tradition was developed in the Middle Ages by the likes of Menahem Meiri of Perpignon.

Contemporary Rabbi Or N. Rose raises crucially difficult questions regarding choseness and being Jewish today (similar for Christians examining Jesus's uniqueness).[113] Irving Greenberg (as noted above) links the growth and recognition of a principled pluralism to engaging with the presence of God in a world during and after mass atrocities, especially

---

108. Phan, *Being Religious Interreligiously*, 136; See also Sugirtharajah, *Jesus in Asia*.

109. See Neufeldt, "Hindu Views of Christ," 162–75.

110. Sacks, *Dignity of Difference*, 200; and Sacks, *Future Tense*, 74 and 80. See also Boteach, *Kosher Jesus*, 197; Kogan, *Opening the Covenant*; Patterson, "'Where is Your Brother?,'" 43; and Rose, "Spiritual Mappings," 65.

111. Maimonides, *Mishneh Torah*, Shoftim, ch. 9.

112. Rosenthal, "Salvation Jewish Style," 28.

113. Rose, "Spiritual Mappings," 69.

the Shoah.[114] He goes further to argue that Christianity and Judaism are linked to God's plan of love and justice.[115] This gracious attitude to another faith tradition is also characterized by a certain leniency even where some of its doctrines may be in need of greater reformulation or engagement.[116]

Similar openness to other faiths is also fairly pervasive in Islamic thought. For Islam, like Judaism, recognizes the spiritual riches of other ways (while also containing strong polar tendencies).[117] This initial broad-mindedness resonates in Qur'anic passages like 2:112: "In fact, any who direct themselves wholly to God and do good will have their reward with their Lord: no fear for them, nor will they grieve"; and especially 2:148: "Each community has its own direction to which it turns: race to do good deeds and wherever you are, God will bring you together."[118]

Roger Boase helpfully extracts seven interfaith principles from the Qur'an:[119] no compulsion in religion (2:256); no mocking other faiths (6:108); no association with those who ridicule one's faith (5:57-58); speak politely to those of other faiths (29:46); invite the use of reason in all interfaith conversation or dealings (2:111); eschew idle speculative talk about God or the truth of revelation (40:4); and each faith should compete in piety (5:48).[120]

Muslim theologian Mahmut Aydin bravely asserts "we suggest Muslims do not consider God's revelation to the Prophet Muhammad as *full, definitive and unsurpassable*, but as *universal, decisive, indispensable* messages of God."[121] Asma Afsaruddin agrees, citing how religious

---

114. Greenberg, "Judaism and Christianity," 154.

115. Ibid., 155.

116. Ibid., 157.

117. See Michel, "Religious Pluralism in Islam," 170–85.

118. For commentary see Sirry, "'Compete with One Another in Good Works,'" 423–38; Afsaruddin, "Finding Common Ground," 67–86; Homerin, "Golden Rule in Islam," 99–115; Thomas, "Islam and the Religious Other," 148–71; and Admirand, "Ethics of Displacement and Migration," 671–87.

119. Boase, "Ecumenical Islam," 252.

120. Ibid., 254. On his claim of Islam's superiority, see ibid., 260.

121. Aydin, "Islam in a World of Diverse Faiths," 50. See also Afsaruddin, "Finding Common Ground," 70; and Jalabi, "Walking on Divine Edge," 181.

pluralism is "divinely mandated"[122] in the Qur'an, and present within the early constitution of Medina.[123] The Middle Way is again essential.

The Middle Way

Muslims see Islam as the middle way, based on Qur'an 2:143: "We have made you into a middle community." Numerous meanings are invoked here: Muslims are the middle way between extreme positions (traditionally, the asceticism of Christianity and the legalism of Judaism); they are the mediators between the words of Muhammad and the other nations; while other scholars link justness with middleness or moderation, following the examples of the thirteenth-century Andalusian exegete Muhammad b. Ahmad al-Qurtubi and the fourth caliph and first imam of Shi'a Islam, Ali b. Abi Talib.[124] There is much interfaith and intercultural potential here. Consider the Aristotelian mean as formulated in *The Nichomachean Ethics*, where, for example, courage is praised as the mean to aspire (and teach one to aspire) between the extremes of recklessness and cowardice. In Buddhism, the middle way (Sanskrit: *madhyamā-pratipad*) is embodied in the life and teachings of the Buddha. After a life of extremes, Siddhartha Gautama saw moderation while recognizing all life as *dukha*, becoming enlightened and so finding and teaching the Middle Way. In Judaism much Talmudic and post-Talmudic discussion on ethics also praises moderation.[125]

Maimonides writes how "the Sages instructed that a person measure (lit., estimate) his character traits, directing them in the middle path so he will be whole."[126] We can hear the influence of Aristotle; so too, with Aquinas, who also draws on Maimonides at various points in the *Summa Theologiae* (1.2.64, a.1 and a.3).

From the mean to the golden rule, most of the world's faiths and major philosophical and ethical systems show tendencies, if not qualified (sometimes divinely-sanctioned) support, for some pluralist positions. They recognize mutual goodness and value, even if with the caveat

---

122. Afsaruddin, "Finding Common Ground," 70.

123. Ibid., 75.

124. Ibid., 78–79.

125. Buxbaum, *Life and Teachings of Hillel*, 143–44.

126. Maimonides, *Mishneh Torah*, Law 3–4; See also Rosenfeld, "Maimonides on Life."

that such ways remain imperfect or are somehow founded on their own system. Diversity is similarly abundant in the natural world around us and also provides challenges and depth to the discussion of religious pluralism. The more we study non-human life, the more we marvel, and if honest, are humbled.

Pluralism in Nature

Nature is a wonderful repository and testament to the flourishing of plurality, a truth acclaimed by theists, atheists, and nontheists.[127] The fertile, abundant notion of plurality in nature is wonderfully reflected upon in the writings of Loren Eiseley, the American anthropologist, poet, and naturalist.[128] What is most striking about Eiseley's essays is his penetrating awareness of encroaching upon worlds within worlds, spaces where the human is a foreigner and stranger.[129] Such worlds, while devoid of meaningful glimpses of any Supreme Being, still reflect a sense of wonder. Eiseley, an atheist, has much to teach about the sacredness of life and human responsibility for life on this planet. In his stories and encounters with non-human life, he reminds us that our ways are not the only ways, our thoughts not the only thoughts.

Such privileged moments often involve being solitary; so, too, "the time has to be right; one has to be, by chance or intention, upon the border of two worlds." Eiseley does not limit these encounters solely to the human being. In "The Judgment of the Birds," he imagines the sensations of a crow, who while lost in a dense countryside fog, suddenly finds itself at a strange level, where he encounters Eiseley, "a harbinger of the most profound evil a crow could conceive of—air-walking men."[130] While playful, Eiseley's sensitivity and openness to non-human worlds and perspectives are authentic and humbling. Once he tussled and played with

---

127. Sacks, *Dignity of Difference*, 53; and Shanor and Kanwal, *Bats Sing, Mice Giggle*, 12. See also Gyger, "Religions and Birth of New Humanity," 92.

128. This section is adapted from my "Dirt, Collapse, and Eco-responsibility," 1–24. See also Lynch and Maher, *Artifacts and Illuminations*.

129. Eiseley, *Star Thrower*, 114. See also his *Immense Journey*; *Firmament of Time*; and *Night Country*. For contemporary naturalists who also encounter such worlds, see Cowen, *Common Ground*, 161; and Foster, *Being a Beast*.

130. Eiseley, *Star Thrower*, 30; and ibid., 281.

a baby fox and picked up a bone with his teeth. He described it as "the gravest, most meaningful act [he] shall ever accomplish."[131]

In one memorable journey, Eiseley was trekking in a wilderness of mountain and ridge. He soon "observed that something ropelike which glittered in the sun appeared to be dangling from the ball-shaped object."[132] It was a rattlesnake coiled about a pheasant too large to eat who was pounding the snake against the earth. Both were in a desperate dance-clasp of mutual death over "whether a clutch of eggs was to turn into a thing with wings or scales—this problem, I say, of the onrushing nonexistent future, had capitulated bird against serpent."[133] Understanding that "Man could contain more than himself,"[134] and wanting this senseless struggle to end, Eiseley uncoiled the serpent from the bird, wrapped it around his arm, and released it away from any further hazard to all involved.

Reflecting on this incident, Eiseley recognizes how he had embodied the role of a reconciler, uncoiling this dilemma that was also a part of him. "I had transcended feather and scale and gone beyond them into another sphere of reality. I was trying to give birth to a different self."[135] This different self, guided by compassion and moral responsibility, could transcend mere survival. For Eiseley, the scientist-poet, Darwin's "tangled bank of unceasing struggle, selfishness and death"[136] seemed etched into his scientific formation. Yet, he continued to see beacons of compassion and a love of live. In "The Star Thrower," Eiseley joined a man who picked up nearly lifeless starfish and threw them back into the sea: "The task was not to be assumed lightly, for it was men as well as starfish that we sought to save."[137]

While we can study and even immerse ourselves in the worlds of other species, there is also a responsibility and cost to that unique ability to see outside ourselves. This envisioning of others is at the heart of why human beings, even in Eiseley's godless world, have a responsibility for all of life; and in our terms, a call to celebrate pluralism.

131. Ibid., 64.
132. Ibid., 293.
133. Ibid., 292.
134. Ibid., 293.
135. Ibid., 295.
136. Ibid., 185.
137. Ibid., 184.

"Here I no longer cared about survival," Eiseley writes in "The Inner Galaxy," "I merely loved."[138] Tying together the themes of creation, meaning, responsibility, and compassion, he continues: "I felt, sitting in that desolate spot upon my whiskey crate, a love without issue, tenuous, almost disembodied. It was a love for an old gull, for wild dogs playing in the surf, for a hermit crab in an abandoned shell."[139]

Conclusion

While advocating that religious pluralism is a key humbler of faith positions, I have argued that it should be mixed with a modicum of an exclusivist stance, resulting in a principled religious pluralism, deeply linked with the option for the poor and marginalized. I also highlighted five key attributes for a viable pluralism, namely that it should be humble, just, compassionate, pluralist, and dialogical.

Questions, nevertheless, proliferate, stretching and challenging foundational identities. No answers are easy—but that is the beauty and potency of engaging and embracing pluralism. Immersed in another's emotionally and spiritually rich ideas, practices, and rituals, we are confronted by mystery and boundlessness. Other ways, other systems of language and hopes parallel, collide, and sometimes coincide or co-exist. Sometimes, such systems seem untouched by one another, even at their deepest core. Yet all these faiths seek to save, liberate, heal, or guide the human person—always in tandem with deep respect and moral demands towards life. Pluralism encourages such openness and searching.

In the final episode[140] of the reimagined *Battlestar Galactica*, Lee Adama (call sign "Apollo") and Kara Thrace (call sign: "Starbuck") are standing amidst a vast prairie, having just discovered Earth after their war with the Cylons is "over."

"Well," Apollo says to the mercurial Starbuck, whom he has deeply, and painfully, loved: "I always thought when this was all done I would kick back. Relax. Spend the rest of my days doing the absolute minimum humanly possible."

"And now that you're here?" Starbuck asks.

---

138. Ibid., 309.
139. Ibid., 310.
140. *Battlestar Galactica*, "Daybreak Part 2."

"I want to explore," Apollo utters, his eyes widening, "I wanna climb the mountains. I wanna cross the oceans. I wanna—gods, I can't believe I'm saying this." He glances away into the expanse and then turns back to look at her.

Starbuck, though, is gone. Had Apollo simply dreamed she was there all along?

Pluralism can also be a misty enterprise. It collapses too many boundaries and foundations. Yet, it still seems to be a dream worth believing in: seeking to shelter the spiritual yearnings and hopes of others. It can play a crucial role in humbling, in reminding ourselves that other ways may also be true and meaningful. This is a simple idea, but one that could do much to bring interfaith healing, and perhaps, at a crucial moment, to delay or hinder any urge for oppression or violence.

Extending Master Lao Yang's thoughts, are we all on the same path but dreaming different dreams?

In Eiseley's autobiography, he recalls finding a satchel left to him by his mother after she had committed suicide. Inside the bag was a prehistoric bone discovered from one of his early digs. He recalls a similar bone, now buried, with a shepherd dog named Wolf "who wandered much with me and upon my head once rested by a fire."

"I think," Eiseley continues, "we dreamed the same dreams, that dog and I."[141]

A crucial way to interpret such dreams is through interfaith dialogue, our next main feature of humbling faith. As Diana Eck remarks: "Pluralism is based on interreligious dialogue."[142]

---

141. Eiseley, *All the Strange Hours*, 272. See also Heuer, *Lost Notebooks*, 160 and 255; and Eiseley, *Unexpected Universe*, 93–119, and ibid., dedication page: "To Wolf, / who sleeps forever / with an ice age bone, / across his heart, / the last gift / of one / who loved him."

142. Eck, "Is Our God Listening?," 44.

4

Interfaith Dialogue as Challenge and Catharsis

Apparently, elves and dwarves didn't always get along. Although Tolkien scholars and bloggers still debate the cause, the celebrated friendship in *The Lord of the Rings* of the dwarf, Gimli, and the elf, Legolas, has become legendary—if not "downright ecumenical."[1] While cracking orc skulls may have been a major contributor to their friendship (and cracking any literal skulls is not advocated here) their bond does illustrate how personal encounters can weed-out barriers and bloom relations in the most unlikely of places. In other words, it deeply humbles. We are immersed in such stories in all kinds of mediums: from children's picture books, film, and poetry to religious texts that highlight unlikely connections and relationships.

In children's stories, think of Marianne Dubuc's *The Lion and the Bird* or Mac Barnet and Adam Rex's *Billy Twitters and His Blue Whale Problem*. Emblematic in film is the friendship of "Nerf-herder" Han Solo and Chewbacca, the Wookie, in the *Star Wars* universe. In Brian K. Vaughan and Fiona Staples's comic *Saga*, Alana and Marko try to raise their child, Hazel, while the warring planets they come from don't want their love to exist. In video games, there's the cathartic moment of Ellie (and Joel) encountering a herd of giraffes amidst the apocalyptic landscape of *The Last of Us*, or the exploits of Asaris, Krogans, Salarians, Turians—and other galactic species—in the *Mass Effect* universe.

---

1. Goldman, "Christianity and Myth." For a funny intercultural (actually intrahobbit) dialogue, see Tolkien, *Lord of the Rings: Two Towers*, 854; and between Gimli and Legolas, ibid., 713–14. For other interspecies dialogues, see Chambers, *Record of a Spaceborn Few*; and Herbert, *Dune*, 250.

Examples are endless. What holds a lot of these relationships is their ongoing communication and face-to-face encounters. As David Tracy writes: "Dialogue demands the intellectual, moral, and, at the limit, religious ability to struggle to hear another and to respond."[2] Such a struggle also, of course, comprises humility.

As employed throughout this work, I use interfaith as opposed to interreligious to encompass non-religious systems and beliefs.[3] In chapter 5, I focus on the so-called religious-secular dialogue as a further test and means of humbling and partnership.

Recall Hans Küng's famous dictum: "No peace among the nations without peace among the religions. No peace among the religions without dialogue between the religions. No dialogue between the religions without investigation of the foundation of the religions." It is that foundational call that has been at the heart of this project.

Theologically, interfaith dialogue still has its naysayers and skeptics.[4] Most critiques want to express limitations to dialogue and stress they are a means and not an end. Dialogue with another person can also lead to greater separation and enmity. We may meet individuals who exceed every negative stereotype launched upon their affiliated group.[5] Most meetings and dialogue, thankfully, can forge a humility birthed from exposure to what is unknown and new.

In this chapter, I will first provide an overview of the aims and models of interfaith dialogue and then examine the way hope within interfaith dialogue has changed and developed in the Catholic Church. I will close with a brief overview of the current state of Jewish-Christian dialogue, and in particular of some contemporary Jewish critiques of Christianity.

Dialogue cannot be sheltered from some pain, or even danger; anything that humbles bears both risk and responsibility.[6]

---

2. Tracy, *Dialogue with the Other*, 4.

3. For distinctions, see Valkenberg, *Sharing Lights on the Way to God*, 113–16.

4. See Becker and Morali, "Conclusion," 509; and Millbank, "End of Dialogue," 190. In terms of "multiple religious identity," see Tang, "Identity and Marginality," 95.

5. On interfaith dialogue and mass atrocities, see Admirand: "Dialogue in the Face of a Gun?," 267–90.

6. Williams, *Dostoevsky*, 10.

Interfaith Dialogue amidst Bounce Passes

Interfaith dialogues are built on stories.[7] I grew up in a lovely seaside town, Port Washington, in New York. Like other towns dotted across America, it was named after a nearby visit of the eponymous first US President. My parents had moved there in the 1960s from predominantly Christian enclaves in Astoria and Bay Ridge. To their surprise, few Christmas lights blinked on their block during their first Christmas in their new home. Their neighbors were predominantly Jewish. It took some getting used to, but by the time I was born in the mid-seventies, it was just the way it was. Not having Jewish neighbors would probably have been strange to me.

One day when I was about ten years of age (in 1986), I was playing various games with my neighbor and friend, Yuri. At some point between dribbling and passing a basketball, Yuri mentioned Jesus as a prophet. I don't remember why and if it seems unlikely to you, it still does to me as well. But that is why I remember it. Yuri was Jewish, originally from Israel, and though I did not know it at the time, he would soon be returning there.

After Yuri mentioned Jesus, I momentarily paused, confused. I knew I was Catholic and I knew he was Jewish and knew that Jesus was someone I believed in whom he did not. Having the familiarity of being friends and the bluntness of youth, I immediately said, "But you don't believe in Jesus."

"We don't believe in him the way you do," he said, "but we think he was a great teacher and holy person." He passed me the ball.

"Oh," I said, passing the ball back to him. "Really? I thought you didn't even think he existed."

"No, we do. We just don't believe he was the Messiah like Christians do."

The conversation soon changed to the Mets or movies, but I felt happy, though couldn't explain why. As I thought all Jewish people denied Jesus's mere existence, it felt comforting to know that wasn't true. While only the beginnings of an interfaith dialogue, there is perhaps more in that little story than even I comprehend. Perhaps it even played a role in why I later chose to study theology and especially Jewish-Christian relations and interfaith dialogue.

Such face-to-face moments of contact, no matter where they are, can form the lifeblood of interfaith learning and dialogue. Think also of

---

7. See Peace, Rose, and Mobley, *My Neighbor's Faith*.

the movie and book examples given above. These encounters shape and expand our own world and dreams. Interfaith dialogue is not something extra that we do in our spare time. If we are truly attuned to the history, spirit, and hopes of our faith or philosophical tradition and texts—and the current state of our world today—interfaith dialogue and learning are obligations for everyone.[8]

One key, as Leonard Swidler argues in his fourth commandment of the "Dialogue Decalogue," is to "not compare our ideals with our partner's practice, but rather our ideals with our partner's ideals, our practice with our partner's practice."[9] Sincerity and honesty matter.

Dialogue as Gift and Presence: Six Types of Interfaith Dialogue[10]

The meeting, clashing, and blending of faiths have been transpiring for millennia. In *A History of the World in 100 Objects,* Neil MacGregor discusses the Vale of York hoard, Viking objects found near Harrogate, England. In the hoard was a coin, MacGregor informs us, minted at York around 920, in which "we find the sword and name of the Christian Saint Peter but, intriguingly, the 'I' of Petri—Peter—is in the shape of a hammer, the emblem of the Norse god, Thor. The new faith uses the weapons of the old."[11]

While history bears the record of one faith conquering and subsuming another, dialogue presupposes mutual respect and dignity. Interfaith dialogue and learning thus involve presence and gift. Ideally, it should be a sacred, trusting environment where individuals of different faiths and cultural backgrounds allow themselves and their creeds to be as exposed and transparent as possible. Participants offer their values, hopes, and beliefs to one another while also sharing and being present to each person's related, but distinct stories and language. The benefits and aims can be rich and multi-dimensional. For our purposes here, it humbles as much as it inspires: forcing us to admit that the world (let alone, God) is

---

8. For a helpful overview, see Merrigan and Friday, *Theologies of Interreligious Dialogue.*

9. Swidler, "Dialogue Decalogue."

10. An expanded version of this section analyzing "A Common Word" can be found in Admirand, "Seeking Humility."

11. MacGregor, *History of the World,* 364–65.

greater than our communal, individual, and religious outlooks—a blessing as much as a burden.

The forms of interfaith dialogue can vary but can be grouped into at least six models. First, Raimundo Panikkar highlights intrapersonal dialogue, "an inner dialogue within myself, an encounter in the depths of my personal religiousness."[12] In this crucial and ongoing dialogue, we work through many of our own insecurities, doubt, and strengths, perhaps waiting to test and try some of these ideas in the presence of another, only to return to that inner-space for greater reflection and evaluation. For Catherine Cornille, such returning requires "an act of intellectual and spiritual humility."[13] All the other dialogues below are in some way in on-going dialogue with this one.[14]

At a more general level, there is the dialogue of life (think of the example given in the previous chapter of the Muslim woman joking around with one of my kids by scribbling on the fogged-up car window). The dialogue of life can be the most pervasive and elemental through such slim, even transient encounters.[15] In the presence of another person, abstract labels (like Christian, atheist, or Hindu) are shed or bracketed. Particular eyes interlock, and the distinctive voice that communicates inevitably connects and joins two human beings sharing interrelated hopes, concerns, and dreams. Or perhaps you both simply confirm the right bus to take ("number 16"), or have kids play on the same soccer team ("Go Flyers!").[16] It has to start somewhere.

Third, interfaith dialogue can be social-justice oriented. Those of various religious and non-religious faiths support a certain cause or work together to help the destitute and oppressed. They seek mutual partnership and solidarity; to heal the world, *tikkun olam*, in the Jewish context; the reign of God in a Christian one. Such justice is rooted in basic humanity, warts and all: "Err, stumble, commit sin, but be one of the just."[17]

Interfaith dialogue can also occur formally at a theological or philosophical level where knowledgeable experts or deep practitioners of faith

---

12. Panikkar, *Intrareligious Dialogue*, 40.

13. Cornille, *Im-Possibility of Interreligious Dialogue*, 80.

14. See also Kujawa-Holbrook, *God Beyond Borders*, 37–40.

15. Francisco, "Migration and New Cosmopolitanism," 586. For an example, see Kassabova, *Border*, 156.

16. For fifteenth-century examples in Jerusalem, see Boehm and Holcomb, *Jerusalem*, 68.

17. Hugo, *Les Misérables*, 13.

meet to discuss possible connections, clarifications, comparisons, rapprochement, or differences.[18]

Such dialogue also occurs at the leadership level, as major, acknowledged faith representatives or leaders convene in formal, often institutional settings.[19] Lastly, consider recent intermonastic meetings and encounters in which those of one faith tradition study, meditate, and reflect in the sacred settings and methods of another.[20]

Gender and Interfaith Dialogue

While gains of women in many so-called first-world societies should be celebrated, there is increasing concern that young boys and men are being left behind.[21] In 2015, *The New York Times* published a wide-ranging discussion with reader responses on the "crisis" of boys in education.[22] Most of the world, however, still discriminates against girls and women as full, equal contributors in fields like science, business, law, medicine, and religion; and still maintains rigid gender roles.[23] Interfaith dialogue can show similar biases.

As I am alleging that interfaith dialogue is another vehicle to humble our philosophical, theological, and scientific positions, this shared weakness must be addressed.[24] The so-called masculine and feminine are abstract general means to classify but also label and limit. Of God and gender, most monotheists insist that God transcends gender (or employ a gender neutral term, as in Arabic) but often explicitly or implicitly name God as masculine. Goddess language thus seems to smack of the pagan as if interchangeably referring to God as "she" or with feminine language is not appropriate. Like parenting roles (with the sidelining of many fathers

---

18. See the apt anecdote in Andrić, *Bridge*, 129.

19. Dalai Lama, *True Kinship of Faiths*, 139.

20. Mitchell and Wiseman, *Gethsemane Encounter*; Foulcher, *Reclaiming Humility*, 294–97; and Bucko and McEntee, *New Monasticism*.

21. Rosin, "End of Men"; Bolick, "All the Single Ladies."

22. Online: https://www.nytimes.com/2015/03/01/opinion/how-to-educate-boys.html. On men and the rise of women in religion, see Allen, *Future Church*, 204; Meszler, "Where Are the Jewish Men?," 165–74; and Plaskow, *Coming of Lilith*.

23. See Fonrobert, "Regulating the Human Body," 270–94.

24. Gebara, *Out of the Depths*, 10–12; see also King and Beattie, *Gender, Religion and Diversity*.

or the overburdening role of mothers), most societies could use a healthy dose of a gender restart.

In the context of interfaith encounters, broadly concerned, especially in the dialogue of life, women are usually widely present but at the official leadership levels remain underrepresented. In a 1998 article, Ursula King wrote that interreligious dialogue "is strongly marked by the absence of women."[25] King felt the status of women in religions remained undermined and excluded. She even asked if interreligious dialogue was "relevant" for women.[26] Writing fifteen years later, Jeannine Hill Fletcher paints a similarly limited role for women.[27] Despite many gains from the feminist movements, patriarchal structures of religions still weave through their traditions, rituals, applicable scriptures, dogmas, and roles. It is reasonable to argue that greater inclusion among women in such dialogues could alter unjust structures opposed to women's equality.[28] Perhaps as a sign of the times, Pope Francis echoed these ideas in a speech at a plenary assembly of the Pontifical Council for Interreligious Dialogue in June 2017.[29]

Humility and Interfaith Dialogue

Even in moments of frustration or missed opportunities for connection, interfaith dialogue and face-to-face encounters can humble. For theists, such humility is anchored in acknowledging no ownership of God.[30] Along with respect towards viable atheist and nontheist views, there should be an expansiveness expected in any viable conception of God or the transcendent. This openness ties in with a healthy view of the value and gifts participants bring to any dialogue or interactions.[31] Such a stance is aware of our need for one another and so will require appreciation and

---

25. King, "Feminism," 42.

26. Ibid., 47.

27. Fletcher, "Women in Inter-Religious Dialogue," 168–83; see also Cornille and Maxey, *Women and Interreligious Dialogue*.

28. King, "Feminism," 52; see also Weissman, *Memoirs*; among scientists, see Pappas, "5 Reasons."

29. See: http://en.radiovaticana.va/news/2017/06/09/pope_francis_central_role_of_women_interfaith_dialogue/1317917.

30. Eck, "Is Our God Listening?," 37.

31. Boyd, "Pride and Humility," 259.

reception for learning, growth, and development.[32] Faith systems closed to the gifts of others not only lack gratitude but humility.

We all strive for some sense of meaning and hope, but always with varying levels of inadequacy, stumbling, and doubt. As Marianne Moyaert pens, humility is "an important requirement for the success of inter-religious dialogue."[33] Similarly, Mary C. Boys contends, "If dialogue does not grow out of true humility, it certainly contributes to it."[34]

In *The Im-possibility of Interreligious Dialogue*, Catherine Cornille structures her work around the argument that conditions of humility, commitment, interconnection, empathy, and hospitality are interrelated and necessary for genuine interreligious dialogue. She writes: "the first condition for inter-religious dialogue is recognition of the very possibility of change or growth within one's own tradition."[35] In particular, she highlights epistemological humility; that is a recognition and acceptance that one may still learn and grow in understanding through study and encounters of other faiths and traditions. For Cornille, the virtue of humility in Christian circles needs to be sharpened to promote the "development of a less absolute attitude towards its own conception of the truth and a more open attitude towards the possible truth of other religious traditions."[36] Crucially, this practice of humility demands both faith commitment and knowledge for interreligious dialogue to flourish. Nor are such participants blind or closed to how other paths could rejuvenate or enlighten certain neglected or underdeveloped aspects of their traditions.

Cornille also rightly emphasizes the requirement of empathy as we try to understand another's position and beliefs.[37] Such empathy is sustained by striving for interconnectedness nurtured upon moments of enlightenment and solidarity. Lastly, she focuses on hospitality, especially towards strangers with differing views to our own.[38]

Citing Cornille, Moyaert helpfully highlights how renouncing possession of truth is both a practical and ethical act. It is practical because

32. Ibid., 260.
33. Moyaert, "Interreligious Dialogue," 212.
34. Boys, "This I Believe," 127.
35. Cornille, "Conditions for Inter-Religious Dialogue," 21.
36. Cornille, *Im-possibility of Interreligious Dialogue*, 56.
37. Ibid., 176.
38. Ibid., 210.

no human being can claim to possess the full truth. As all belief systems depend on the words, actions, and rituals of fallible humans, to claim otherwise, is not just hubris but impractical.[39] The move is also ethical (here I am building on my own concerns) because for others, their belief system has sustained and sheltered them, provided guidance and purpose through perhaps dark and difficult times, illuminated the joys of community and meaning, and reinforced their identity and connection to the outside world. To hope that this joy, especially as translated into acts of kindness and goodness, can remain meaningful and viable for others is to seek their full well-being and integrity. Who wants anyone's ethical worldview destroyed? Such a stance is not because it is better to be happy and ignorant despite clinging to alleged false beliefs, but leaving a space so that such beliefs can be affirmed and valued, even as clear differences arise. Again, is this cogent and desirable? Can I still have "my" Christ—and others "their" Buddha, Qur'an, Torah, bhakti, or Vedas? Can my conception of God create such a possibility or does such a possibility disservice God or the Truth?

To reach such a point requires great trust and hope in both another and oneself. Sadly, such hope was traditionally lacking, especially (though by no means solely) in Christian circles in the context of interfaith dialogue. Are recent signs of growth and hope evident?

Inconstant Hope in Interfaith Dialogue[40]

For St. Paul, humility was not the pre-eminent virtue. As he famously penned: "And now faith, hope, and love abide, these three; and the greatest of these is love" (1 Cor 13:13). Hope, while not greater than love, can be as complicated. It need not be static, though. Hope, like faith and love, can mature and grow. And we can hope in the transformation and growth of hope. We may even live to see this transformation. As true hope is essentially bonded to love, its growth will depend more on that premier virtue's development. These next few sections will trace one such development and transformation: hope within Catholic views of interfaith dialogue, especially Jewish-Christian dialogue.

---

39. On hubris as a political vice, see Button, *Political Vices*, 33–59.
40. For an expanded version, see Admirand, "No Dialogue without Hope."

Prior to the twentieth century, genuine interfaith dialogue involving Christians and non-Christians was a rare and exotic occurrence.[41] Speaking broadly, in early dialogues between Catholics and other faiths (which were often closer to monologues or debates), if hope was present, it was a hope to prove the other wrong. For most of Christian history, encounters with the Other were often nasty, brutish, and short. Consider the 1263 Disputation of Barcelona in which Rabbi Moshe ben Naḥman (Naḥmanides) was summoned to defend against a recent Jewish convert in the presence of James I, King of Aragon. Despite the King's assurances of his safety, Naḥmanides had to flee the country when "he ran afoul of church authorities."[42]

More tragically, consider Christianity's role (intended or not) in the destruction or near-destruction of indigenous cultures and beliefs. While many well-meaning Christian missionaries hoped to save the souls of such so-called pagans, their hope, whether grounded in provincial, legalist, or doomsday frameworks, or even if touched with a certain kind of love, was nevertheless misguided.[43] Hope was often aligned with an aggressive, if subtle, means of defeating or silencing the Other.[44] This hope was conversion.

The most noteworthy contemporary event to accelerate interfaith dialogue is sadly rooted in genocide. Six million Jews were murdered during the Shoah in lands deemed to be Christian. The facts eventually forced deep soul-searching and moral reckoning. In the Roman Catholic Church, the modern interfaith movement essentially commences with *Nostra Aetate*. The 1965 document can seem flawed and outdated today. Nonetheless, it played a pivotal role in inspiring Catholics to learn and study other faiths and to grant, even if hesitantly and all-too-subtly, the transformation and maturity of a virtue (hope), and thus the transformation and maturity of a faith. The document was originally meant to focus solely on the Church's relationship with the Jewish people and the Jewish faith, but a more expansive vision, along with politics and some intransigent anti-Judaic tendencies, altered the document to include Catholic attitudes towards all faiths. The few paragraphs on Judaism, though, are

---

41. See Abelard, *Ethical Writings*, 59–148. For an overview of some pre-1960 interfaith developments, see Pratt, *The Church and other Faiths*, 31–47. From a Jewish perspective, see Cook, *Modern Jews Engage the New Testament*, 15.

42. Mittleman, *Short History of Jewish Ethics*, 127.

43. Las Casas, *Destruction of the Indies*, 6.

44. Ruston, *Human Rights and the Image of God*, 75.

the longest.⁴⁵ Much has been written about *Nostra Aetate*, especially the claim that "The Catholic Church rejects nothing that is true and holy in these religions" and decrees that their good actions and teachings "often reflect a ray of that Truth which enlightens all men."⁴⁶

While the compliment is understated, it was leap years ahead of earlier positions.⁴⁷ According to Dermot Lane, this shift involves "a burgeoning awareness and recognition of the active presence of God outside the Christian reality within other religions."⁴⁸ Interfaith dialogues and the Catholic study of other faiths blossomed in the decades following *Nostra Aetate*.

Developing from *Nostra Aetate*, the life and work of John Paul II is particularly noteworthy.⁴⁹ Recall his various apologies for Christian injustice, particularly against the Jewish people, and his tireless effort to partner with other faiths, especially in the 1986 World Day of Prayer for Peace in Assisi. He provided flawed, but still crucial leadership on the contemporary Catholic relation and attitude towards those of other faiths. His prayer at the Wailing Wall in Jerusalem nicely summarizes his recognition of the Catholic need for atonement and repentance vis-à-vis the Other. Important as well was John Paul calling the Jews people of the covenant, denying any notion of supersessionism or replacement theology that erroneously sees the Church or Christianity replacing the Jewish faith and people as beloved of God.⁵⁰

For John Paul II, Judaism is a living faith whose example had much to teach Christians. Most importantly, in 1980 in Mainz, he echoed the Pauline notion of the Jewish covenant, "never revoked by God."⁵¹

To stress that the particular Jewish covenant is not revoked is to open up a range of exciting but complicated areas for theological reflection, especially in Christology and soteriology. In other words, what is

---

45. See Cunningham, Hofmann, and Sievers, *Catholic Church and the Jewish People*; Poorthuis, "The Diplomat and the Pioneer," 471–88; Berger, *Post-Holocaust Jewish-Christian Dialogue*; and Burrell, *Toward a Jewish-Christian-Muslim Theology*.

46. *Nostra Aetate*, 2. In the context of the Soviet Bloc, see Kosicki, *Vatican II Behind the Iron Curtain*.

47. Lane, *Stepping Stones*, 70.

48. Ibid., 70.

49. See Admirand, "Rifts, Trust, and Openness," 555–75.

50. See Pollefeyt, "Christology After Auschwitz," 229–48; and Cunningham et al., *Christ Jesus and the Jewish People Today*.

51. John Paul II, "Address to Representatives of the Jewish Community in Mainz."

the salvific role of Christ for Jews living within the still viable Jewish Covenant? Does this not imply more than one path and way that respects both faiths, what Jewish theologian Michael Kogan calls a Jewish path and a Christian path to God?[52] Theologians (and not the Magisterium) are the Catholic trailblazers here, expanding these notions in Catholic dialogues with all the world's faiths.[53] Unfortunately, certain signals or statements from the Vatican have also seemed intended to halt or hinder such insights, most pronounced in *Dominus Iesus* (2000) and in some further Notes and Clarifications issued by the Congregation of the Doctrine of the Faith. During Benedict XVI's pontificate, he stressed evangelization and mission and repeatedly challenged secular and so-called relativist outlooks. The employment of hope within interfaith dialogue seemed again to be changing (or reverting).

Interreligious Hope as Interreligious Love

Despite some setbacks, interreligious hope shifted into a more ethical and dialogical framework: Catholics could hope for opportunities to present their views and listen to another's views; they hoped to gain insights and truths from their dialogical partner. While not minimizing difference, Catholics guided by this new understanding hoped to find shared spaces of communion, partnership, and solidarity. Such has been especially evident in contemporary Jewish-Christian dialogues. With the election of Pope Francis and encouraging accounts of his support and role in interfaith dialogue, hope may again be transforming.[54] Throughout his papacy, Francis has stressed the value and contribution of interfaith dialogue, testified in his longstanding friendship with Rabbi Abraham Skorka.[55] He also teaches that such dialogue involves participants remaining knowledgeable and firm in their faith commitments and convictions.[56] Like his predecessors, Francis sees evangelizing as inseparable from witnessing our faith.

---

52. Kogan, *Opening the Covenant*, 34–35.
53. See Boys, *Has God Only One Blessing?*
54. See Povoledo, "Pope Appeals for More Interreligious Dialogue."
55. See Bergoglio and Skorka, *On Heaven and Earth*; Rubin and Ambrogetti, *Pope Francis*; and Vallely, *Pope Francis*.
56. Wooden, "Pope, Rabbi Skorka."

While I maintain that dialogue is not a tool for converting another, evangelizing is always present in interfaith dialogue. Evangelization occurs in listening to and learning from one another. It is witnessed in how participants act, show respect, and dialogue. Such testifies to humility and those three cardinal virtues—hope, faith, and love. Hope that yearns for partnership, learning, and respect within dialogue is built with a faith sustained by a humble, mature, expanding love. For Christians, such love is founded on the Sermon on the Mount (Matt 5:1–12) and that important phrase: "Whoever is not against us is for us" (Mark 9:40). This compassionate love knows the power and meaning of faith for others and treads carefully where the possibility of conversion could become a tangible reality.[57]

Ultimately, Christians should be sustained and guided by a vision of God that is Love (1 John 4:8). Such a conception is what steers and empowers hope in interfaith relations and dialogue. It is a hope that believes in universal dignity and God's care for all. It is hope deeply dependent on faith formulated by love. It does not claim all answers and truth—and out of respect and love for God and the Other, may, to repeat, not even hope for such a possibility. In Benedict's encyclical "*Spe Salvi*," he opens with the Latin translation of Romans 8:24—"*Spe Salvi facti sumus*"—in hope we were saved. Linked with Paul's higher ranking of love (1 Cor 13:13) and viewed interreligiously as mutual learning and growth, such a hope may not only abide, but indeed, save.

But what if such a hope comes in the form of critique and humbling? Can such a faith still endure?

Christianity's Maturing Appreciation for Judaism

While often overlooked, the most lucid example of a Copernican revolution in terms of evangelization of non-Christians is in Christianity's post-Shoah relationship with Judaism.[58] Many Christian groups have publicly professed that systematic and organizational attempts to convert Jews to Christianity are no longer supported. Any statement advocating a conversion agenda also emphasizes the right of religious freedom of

---

57. Ueda, "Jesus in Contemporary Zen," 56. See also Admirand, "Mission in Remission," 95–104; and Admirand, "Overcoming 'Mere Oblivion,'" 30–38.

58. See Rosenthal, *Jubilee for All Times*.

choice and the importance of never denying one's own faith.[59] Consider the Catholic religious order of the Sisters of Our Lady of Sion. Formed specifically in 1852 to convert Jews, their members are now committed to partnership and dialogue with Jews and to educate Christians on the value and beauty of Judaism. The Sisters' ground-breaking approach has been tacitly confirmed, for example, in December 2015 by the Vatican's Commission for Religious Relations with the Jews. The Commission formally decreed that Catholics should not participate in any "institutional mission work" to convert the Jews and should instead promote dialogue and works of social justice.[60]

Also important is the earlier document, "A Sacred Obligation," signed by a wide-range of Christian academics and pastors, and which also contended "Christians should not target Jews for conversion."[61] It was a response to the Jewish Document *Dabru Emet*, which acknowledged and praised Christians for instituting key changes in their approach towards—and views of—Judaism. Also significant is the December 2015 "Orthodox Rabbinic Statement on Christianity," where we read: "Now that the Catholic Church has acknowledged the eternal Covenant between G-d and Israel, we Jews can acknowledge the ongoing constructive validity of Christianity as our partner in world redemption."[62] Christians endorse Jewish life and faith as salvific by affirming the eternal validity of the Jewish covenant and renouncing any systemic conversion attempts.

In a 2016 article, "Landmines and Vegetables: The Hope and Perils of Recent Jewish Critiques of Christianity,"[63] I praised the current healthy status and gains of Jewish-Christian dialogue but contended that the real test is when more Jewish participants present their critiques of Christianity and how Christians on the whole respond. My title was based on the idea that these critiques in most cases were like vegetables to a child: needed for growth but maybe difficult to swallow. Sadly, Christians had a record of violence—the landmines aspect of Christians towards Jews. Could Jewish critiques renew Christian violence against Jews or reveal

---

59. See Committee on Doctrine and Committee on Ecumenical and Interreligious Affairs, "A Note on Ambiguities," §7–9.

60. Commission for Religious Relations with the Jews, "'The Gifts and the Calling of God Are Irrevocable.'"

61. "A Sacred Obligation."

62. "Orthodox Rabbinic Statement on Christianity." On the problems of evangelical Christian support of the State of Israel, see Goldman, *God's Country*.

63. See Admirand, "Landmines and Vegetables," 81–96.

true dialogue maturity? I examined some Jewish challenges and critiques towards all facets of Christian belief: such as Christology, the Trinity, and the historical validity of gospel passages. These challenges deeply humble.

Ultimately, I contended that within Jewish-Christian dialogue, Christians must both cleanse the messes they have created and continue repenting and re-educating themselves; in short, planting vegetables and not landmines. What is presented can serve as a model in other contexts; and those with the landmines or vegetables may find themselves with roles reversed.[64]

It is thus heartening for many Christians to hear how Jewish study of the Gospels and of Jesus has been productive for them as Jews. In *The Jewish Annotated New Testament*, Amy-Jill Levine and Marc Zvi Brettler write: "Indeed, for many Jews, including the editors of this volume, study of the New Testament has also made us better, more informed Jews."[65] Crucially, many Jewish scholars and groups have recognized how an increasing number of Christian churches and individuals have irrevocably separated from many of its insensate and nullifying beliefs and traditions, minesweeping and de-mining anti-Judaic passages and assertions within Christianity. Consider the following developments among many Christians:

1. Jews are again proclaimed by Christians as a people of God.
2. The Jewish covenant is deemed irrevocable by Christians.
3. Jewish tradition, beliefs, and practices are praised and studied by Christians.
4. The ongoing existence of the Jewish people is cited as a sign of their fidelity and perseverance in faith.
5. Supersessionist ideology is deemed wrong and sinful.
6. The deicide charge is annulled.
7. The Jewish faith is deemed living and valuable in itself.
8. Any systemic conversion attempt of the Jewish people by Christians is rebuked.
9. The Jewishness of Jesus is promoted.

---

64. Novak, "Introduction," 5–6.
65. Levine and Brettler, "Editors' Preface," xi–xiii. See also Kessler, *Jesus*.

10. Deeper awareness of Jewish readings of the Tanach and the wisdom of the Talmud (and other Rabbinic writings) are considered viable and valuable.[66]

This is all deeply promising. Jewish critiques also raise further challenges for many Christians. Let's take the critiques of Jesus as the Messiah as an emblematic example.

No to Jesus as Messiah

There is no scarcity of Jewish arguments for why Jesus should not be deemed the Messiah.[67] In his reading of Matthew's gospel, Jacob Neusner pragmatically asks: "To follow him, do I have to violate one of the ten commandments?"[68] Neusner is referring to Jesus's invitation to leave one's family and follow him. For Neusner, the answer is clear: Jews are called to faithfully practice the Torah which sanctifies family life. Moreover, for many Jewish people, the most telling reason to reject Jesus is our still unredeemed world where sin, injustice, and war dominate. As Cook asserts, Israel remained under Roman oppression. There was no liberation at the time of Christ.[69]

For others, it is the incarnational and Trinitarian belief of Christians. Patterson and Berger contend: "The primary concepts that define the creeds—incarnation, virgin birth, Son of God, the Trinity, and so on—are not contrary to Jewish teaching; they are unintelligible to Jewish teaching."[70] Here dialogue seems impossible: how do you speak coherently of what is unintelligible? Rudin, furthermore, critiques the standard notions of the Christian atonement—often the main reason given for the incarnation. He remarks: "The Covenant requires no intermediary or

---

66. See also Cunningham, *Seeking Shalom*, 146–52.

67. Rudin, *Christians & Jews*, 41. See also Boteach, *Kosher Jesus*, 148–98.

68. Neusner, *Rabbi Talks*, 58 and 103. See also Patterson, "The Ashen Earth," 117–26. In the Qur'an, see 56:28–33 and 80:25–32. See also the blog, *Green Muslims*. Online: http://www.greenmuslims.org/.

69. Cook, *Modern Jews Engage the New Testament*, 57.

70. Berger and Patterson, *Jewish-Christian Dialogue*, 92. See also Boteach, *Kosher Jesus*, 149; and Levine, *Misunderstood Jew*, 56–62. For an opposite view, see Boyarin, *Jewish Gospels*, 6 and 22–23.

vicarious savior."⁷¹ Patterson and Berger also claim: "certainly nowhere do the prophets conceive of the Messiah as the Son of God."⁷²

Commenting almost twenty years after his 1986 essay that introduced the notion of Jesus as a failed rather than a false Messiah,⁷³ Irving Greenberg further clarifies his terminology: "As a Jew I look at the case of Jesus and I say, 'I'm sorry—he didn't make it. He tried to be the Messiah, but the world is still unredeemed. I should be such a failure!'" Greenberg acknowledges the arguments were misinterpreted by Jews and Christians, but remarks: "The truth is, [Christians] shouldn't have rejected it when I said 'failed.' That's how Jesus presents himself in the New Testament."⁷⁴

Byron Sherwin acknowledges that Jesus was a failed Messiah, but still calls Jesus a "Messiah Son of Joseph" who prepares the way for the Messiah Son of David.⁷⁵ The claim is appealing, but still unsatisfying. Criticizing Greenberg and going further than Sherwin, Steven Leonard Jacobs has suggested to consider Jesus as a "potentially redemptive messiah." Of Christ's death, Jacobs writes that it "has not, either at that moment, or up to this moment, redeemed our world, but only opened the door to that possibility. But it was not then, nor is it now, the only possibility."⁷⁶ Jacobs offers an enticing and generous claim that can resonate with the language of liberation theology, for example. Such theologians speak of the Reign of God as both inaugurated (by Christ) but not yet completed in this world.⁷⁷

Like Jacobs, Michael Kogan also critiques Greenberg's terminology, referring to our limited knowledge of the diversity and development of Jewish messianic expectations during Jesus's time.⁷⁸ Because of this ambiguity, "There is no question of 'failure' here."⁷⁹ As a Jew, Kogan prefers to speak of Jesus "as the one sent by Israel's God to bring gentiles into the covenant."⁸⁰ Does such a positive position undermine the Jewishness of

---

71. Rudin, *Christians & Jews*, 40.

72. Berger and Patterson, *Jewish-Christian Dialogue*, 87. See also Rudin, *Christians & Jews*, 40.

73. Greenberg, *For the Sake of Heaven and Earth*, 145–61.

74. Greenberg, et al., "On the Meaning of Pluralism," 152.

75. Sherwin, "'Who Do You Say That I Am?,'" 40–41.

76. Jacobs, "'Can We Talk?,'" 146.

77. See Admirand, *Mass Atrocity*, 133–66.

78. Kogan, *Opening the Covenant*, 149.

79. Ibid.

80. Ibid.

INTERFAITH DIALOGUE AS CHALLENGE AND CATHARSIS   113

Jesus and ignore his predominant focus on the Jewish people throughout his ministry—with notable exceptions like his interaction with the Roman centurion (Matt 8:5–13), the Samaritan woman (John 4:1–42), or the Syrophoenician woman (Mark 7:24–30)?

Neusner's often-cited comment—"I will not praise with excessive, irrelevant compliments someone else's God: it is demeaning and dishonest"—may strike the right tone by accepting that most Christians will not compromise on the Divine status of Jesus and so Jews should not try to appease Christians by calling him a rabbi or teacher.[81] Furthermore, as such interpretations are even debated among Jews, their subjective, academic, and hypothetical tendencies can seem less offensive than Jewish claims about Jesus's thoughts or beliefs that are contrary to basic Christian positions. For example, Boteach states: "But [Jesus] absolutely did *not* consider himself divine . . . Nearly all the expressions Christians use to prove that Jesus declared himself God are textual misunderstandings."[82] Cook similarly claims: "Jesus did not imagine himself divine or as Daniel's supra-human 'Son of man.'"[83] Patterson and Berger also ask: "Just as a proselytizing Christian might approach a Jew and ask, 'Do you know Jesus?' so might the Jew reply, 'Do *you* know Jesus?'"[84] Like Qur'anic words attributed to Jesus in which he denies being Divine or the Son of God (5:120), such Jewish assertions are offensive and insulting to Christians.

Does this mean silence is the preferred option? Contra Neusner above, portraying Jesus as a rabbi, or a Jew like us, is not irrelevant. Such an approach has garnered important insights into the gospels and Jesus's words and actions. In orthodox Christology, Jesus is fully God and fully human and his Jewishness is certainly relevant for his humanity, and in fully unexplored ways, his Divinity, too.[85]

Christological belief, intrinsic for Christians, is also moored in faith (Heb 11:1). The Catholic faith likes to speak of the certitude of one's faith.[86] Belief in Jesus, however, need not be without tinctures of doubt, or the possibility for such doubt. Faith must tread where reason falters and doubt and questioning thrive. It is endemic in Jesus's praise for those who

---

81. Neusner, *Rabbi Talks*, 58.
82. Boteach, *Kosher Jesus*, 47; 52, xvii, and 154.
83. Cook, *Modern Jews*, 57.
84. Berger and Patterson, *Jewish-Christian Dialogue*, 75.
85. John Paul II, "Old Testament Essential to Know Jesus."
86. Benedict XVI, "Porta Fidei."

could not touch and see him (John 20:29). Where we believe and another doubts may cause little anxiety for our own position. However, when Scripture—the bedrock of either all or the bulk of a Christian's faith—is shown to be faulty, erroneous, or immoral, what then?

Shared Judeo-Christian Beliefs?

In trying to bring together Jews and Christians after hundreds of years of struggles, differing beliefs cannot be minimized. Thus, for the majority of Jews:

1. Jesus can never be considered the Messiah.
2. Christological and Trinitarian theology have little to no connection to their Jewish understanding.
3. Many parts of the Gospels are circumspect and historically flawed, riveted by anti-Judaic bias and Roman flattery.
4. Little of what Jesus says or does is unique, except claims (that cannot be believed) about his divinity.
5. Christian reading of the Tanach, particularly in using typology and prophetic passages like the Suffering Servant sections in Isaiah, are misreadings, often out of context and sometimes dependent upon poor translation of the original.[87]
6. Christian atonement theology in almost any guise is morally repellent (especially if God demands such a violent sacrifice and human free will and responsibility are minimized).[88]
7. Any apparent unresolved issues of God, justice, and repentance are dealt with in the Tanach, Talmud, and other rabbinic writings.

How Christians examine and accept such differing beliefs and critiques within interfaith dialogue will demand a healthy dose of humility.

---

87. See Pardue, *Mind of Christ*, 30–65; Kugel, *How to Read the Bible*, 555–58; Batnitzky, "On the Suffering of God's Chosen," 203–29; and Kogan, *Opening the Covenant*, 50–53.

88. See Admirand, "Healing the Distorted Face," 302–17.

Conclusion: Holy Work[89]

Interfaith dialogue can be a demanding, exhausting, and mind-rattling exercise as our seemingly firm grasp of the world and its truths suddenly feel exposed and delicate. Through uncertainty, humility, and frailty, faith can also grow and mature. Amidst uncertainty and fear, there can be hope that two strangers from different faith traditions may reach the point, where as adults they can be present to one another—whether passing basketballs or standing together against injustice—with the familiarity of friends and the bluntness of youth.

In short, a world where wookies and nerf-herders, lions and birds, and elves and dwarves are humbled and supported by one another.

Such hope is also sought in our next area of dialogue and humbling.

---

89. Boys, "This I Believe," 121.

5

Linking Theist-Atheist Dialogue
Bridges and Platforms[1]

Meet the Mets: Ya Gotta Believe—in This (Post) Secular Age

During baseball season, I always check the New York Mets score and read daily analysis about them. So many memories—good, but mostly painful (these are the Mets, after all) involve the team from Shea Stadium (now Citi Field). Especially memorable was the cathartic Mike Piazza home run in the first sporting event in New York after 9/11 in 2001. My wife and I went to the game without tickets—and a fan in the stadium called down to us as we approached the gate to buy some. "You want free tickets? Here you go." He dropped them down to us. Manna from heaven: field level, second row, right behind first base.

Through mostly down years (like 2018) and a few good years (especially 1969 and 1986), Mets fans love to echo pitcher Tug McGraw's words in 1973: "Ya Gotta Believe." In *The New Yorker,* Roger Angell listed the lessons young kids would have learned from a huge series between the Mets and the Nationals in September 2015, even if it meant staying up too late, exhausted for school the next morning. Of the seventh lesson, he wrote, "Joy. Nothing else comes close." While tempted to put things in perspective, my guttural, ecstatic cheers while watching those games didn't exactly prove him wrong, either.[2]

While Mets readers will grimace and nod if I mention our shared pain, other readers will be less impressed with this fanaticism: the

---

1. I thank my colleague, Dr. Joseph Rivera, for his comments on an earlier draft of this chapter.

2. Angell, "Back to School."

devotion, the rituals, the worship, the memorials, the chanting—didn't you say you were a theologian?

This chapter is about the relationship of the secular and the sacred, secular ethics, and atheist–religious dialogue. I contend that religious beliefs are humbled by encounters and dialogues with strictly secular or atheist positions, but that the deeply atheistic or rigidly secular are also humbled by religious convictions. Thus, this chapter aims to build on the growing literature in the area of religious/secular dialogue, it seeks bridges with and towards the post-New Atheist debates, and contends how and why the secular and the sacred are deeply interrelated, interdependent, mutually humbling, and reinforcing of each other's strengths. Lastly, although a Catholic theologian, I advocate (with a nod to the Dalai Lama), the promotion and importance of secular ethics, secular meaning, and secular humility.

But why the Mets introduction above? I want to show a blurring of the line in the case of Mets fans who should be Christian—even in the presence of Yankee fans (sorry, Dad). This is not ground-breaking, fresh, or provocative. It is commonplace, which is the point. I'll return to this blurring of lines further below—as the blending of the secular and the religious (without negating clear differences) is a crucial step in the recognition of mutual humbling.

The Secular and Secularities: Definitions and History

Secular, secularization, secularity, secularism, desecularization, sacralization, the sacred, public sphere or square, overlapping consensus, secularization thesis or paradigm, the post-secular, unsecularity, comprehensive faith—there is no shortage of overused or highly technical words and phrases that seem to mean different things in different contexts.[3] Misconceptions are rife on many sides.

Much has been written distinguishing secularity from secularism.[4] Often the latter is deemed an ideological position expecting and working towards the removal of religion from the public sphere, while the former seeks a more neutral position, neither privileging nor undermining any ethical, religious, or secular system. This chapter will not religiously

---

3. Bowker, *Why Religions Matter*, 1. See also Zuckerman and Shook, *Oxford Handbook of Secularism*, 1–122.

4. See Durham and Clark, "Place of Religious Freedom," 289.

separate the terms and will often interweave them, especially as many key authors don't maintain a strict distinction. No one, apparently, likes isms—but there are some still important ones to keep around, like altruism, feminism, and many religious and philosophical systems that can be softened with a simple adjective—think liberal or liberation Catholicism, and so on. As Scott Hibbard opines, moreover, we can speak of an "ecumenical secularism"[5] (or secularity)—or a humble secularity in our context. Here the non-religious arms of the secular also preach and practice this open form of secularism. Such secularity praises the hopes and strengths of the religious, or eventually concedes the need or reality of acknowledging religion's value. Think John Rawls's greater acceptance of comprehensive doctrine in the public square, or Jürgen Habermas's growing support for the role of religions in the public sphere after 9/11.[6]

Any history of the secular, as Charles Taylor notes, is "complex and ambiguous."[7] William E. Connolly, for example, highlights the religiously combative definition of the secular in the OED: "According to it, *Seculere*, in Christian Latin, means 'the world' as opposed to the One Church or heaven."[8]

In the Middle Ages, as William T. Cavanaugh notes, the distinction was minimal and tangential, at best, "to distinguish between two different types of clergy, those who belonged to orders such as the Dominicans, Franciscans, and Benedictines, and those who belonged to a diocese."[9] In *The Unintended Reformation*, Brad Gregory clarifies that "secular" in his work refers to the "institutional and jurisdictional meaning of non-ecclesiastical, not the intellectual or ideological meaning of non- or anti-religious. Thus, 'secular authorities' throughout most of European history have been nonecclesiastical, lay Christian authorities who exercised power in the public sphere, not atheistic or unbelieving authorities."[10] Ul-

5. Hibbard, "Religions, Nationalism, and the Politics of Secularism," 101.

6. See Rawls, "The Idea of Public Reason Revisited," 766 and 805; Habermas, "Religion in the Public Sphere," 1–25; for commentary, Swindal, "Habermas,"; Biggar and Hogan, *Religious Voices*; and on Catholicism and democracy, see Schuck and Crowley-Buck, *Democracy, Culture, Catholicism*.

7. Taylor, "Western Secularity," 34. On definitions, see Casanova, "The Secular, Secularizations, Secularisms," 55–74.

8. Connolly, *Why I Am Not a Secularist*, 21.

9. Cavanaugh, "Invention of the Religious-Secular Distinction," 112. See also Zimmerman, *Humanism and Religion*, 16–29; and MacCulloch, *Reformation*, 28–34.

10. Gregory, *Unintended Reformation*, 439fn2. See also Rubin, *Soul, Self, and Society*, 58.

timately, Gregory contends that the sixteenth-century Reformation unintentionally contributed to our hyperpluralist, obsessively consumer-oriented, and morally and politically fractured, secularized society. Such a society, Gregory laments, has removed any substantial public God-talk and marginalized or devalued the essential investigation of Life Questions (Why are we here? What is our purpose? Is there a higher, unifying Good or principle? Is there a God?).

The promotion of the (private) individual conscience and the priesthood of all believers (flattening the monastic life and the non-monastic life) played important parts in loosening the hold of the sacred from its institutional footing for millions of Christian believers. The so-called discovery of the New World also raised issues of salvation and responsibility previously unimagined. Were these discovered beings human, or fully human like (apparently) civilized Europeans, and how did the story of salvation history account for such discoveries?

As importantly, the sway and power given to reason, logic, science, and experiment through the Enlightenment further eroded the aura and glow of the sacred. Human beings were no longer the undisputed center of the universe. Political revolutions, especially in France and America, sought to overthrow the King, previously thought aligned with God. The great thinkers of the French Enlightenment, especially August Comte and Nicolas de Condorcet, played foundational roles in establishing the "increasingly mature secularization theories of Marx, Weber, and Veblen."[11] In America, a vociferously religious land, deep structures were laid to avoid any theocratic rule.[12]

Nature red in tooth and claw also reared its head, and the disenchantment of the world rolled on. Species that once existed were now only bone fragments or imprints in rocks. Time stretched beyond the finite mind of humankind. There was no going back, despite the desperation of creationists then or intelligent design enthusiasts today. Such critical thinking filtered into biblical criticism—and so much was suddenly questioned. Truths once normative had a diminished sheen. Economic liberalization, hastened by technological advances, the earlier invention of the printing press (but more importantly its spread and fine-tuning, especially of paper production[13]), the movement toward universal educa-

11. Shah, "Secular Militancy," 385; and Wilson, "Secularization," 9–20.

12. For the unholy alliance of religion and corporate capitalism in the US, see Kruse, *One Nation Under God*.

13. Puchner, *Written World*, 137–42.

tion—all these played their parts in foreshortening the reach, sway, and depth of the transcendently sacred. With the horrific, dehumanizing world wars and the Shoah, moral progress joined the death heap of previously cherished ideas and hopes. The spread of pluralism, urbanization, technocratic societies, growth of bureaucracies and job differentiation, family changes—no list can be exhaustive here—and what was sacred and what was secular were no longer ambiguous as the former seemed to be absorbed or purified by the latter. Yet, this process was far from straight-forward or necessarily as one-sided as portrayed. The religious and the sacred were also clarifying, accounting for, interpreting, justifying, purging, correcting, and adapting to this secular understanding and development. For Catholics today after the Second Vatican Council, such a narrative need be neither negative nor one of loss, but enlightenment and growth: greater understanding of the world we live in. Much can be said of other religious systems as well—which had less struggles with these realities, or had already embraced them as normative and valued.

What remains important in any such narrative for theists is to highlight the historical embeddedness of the secular within an overarching religious worldview.[14] Such is similar, for example, to the Jesuit notion of seeing God in all things (panentheisim), as opposed to pantheism (all things are God).[15] Aquinas writes that God is present throughout creation, especially in all human beings who strive to live and unite with God and whose soul is eternal.[16] Creation is a work of God and is inherently good as God is good. Going further, the presence of God is wherever there is faith, hope, and love. Contra Tertullian, there is no strict separation of Athens and Jerusalem.[17]

Against such a unity, however, much has been written of the supposedly far-reaching and persistent religious divide between a Europe often deemed secular and a religiously-infused United States.[18] Secularists of the eighteenth and nineteenth centuries had initially viewed America as a bastion of hope from the European religious climate and interpreted a society's level of secularization (and anti-clericalism) as a key indicator of its progress and modernity. Consider that many of the so-called

14. Eagleton, *Culture and the Death of God*, 119 and 203–4.
15. See Schaab, *Creative Suffering of the Triune God*.
16. Aquinas, *Summa Theologiae*, 1.8.1 and 1.8.3.
17. Tertullian, *Prescription against Heretics*, 7.15–22; see also Hazony, *Philosophy of Hebrew Scripture*, 219–64.
18. See Howard, *God and the Atlantic*.

1848ers who sought sanctuary in America grew bitterly disappointed by what they saw as a helplessly religious people without a sense of authority and history. For the traditionalists, America was often a degenerate land, lacking culture and sophistication, experimenting and changing with little sense of tradition and its core principles. In short, European dissatisfaction with the religious climate in America was generally agreed upon across the right/left divide.

Interestingly, historian Thomas Albert Howard exposes the provincial, zealous, and close-minded tendencies within many early secular advocates. For example, some foundational voices who argued for public school in America exhibited a ravaging anti-religious position, seeking not mere tolerance, but "the necessity of unbelief," as publicist Christian Esselen claimed in regards to the Wisconsin school system.[19] Sociologist Jean-Paul Willaime's argument—that France needs a "secularization of secularism" more open to religious views—could be particularly apt in establishing a way to bridge these ideological divides within and between America and Europe.[20]

As Austin Dacey notes, however, "etymology is not destiny . . . in modern usage, *secularism* has no more connection to Jesuits and Dominicans than *lunacy* has to the moon."[21] Austin instead promotes a different historical origin for the secular in George Jacob Holyoake's popularization of secularism in the nineteenth century. For Holyoake, "Secularism means the moral duty of man in this life deduced from considerations which pertain to this life alone."[22] Such a system's principles include living according to the insights of science, seeking to improve our world by material means (based on utilitarianism and ethically guided by Positivism) and acknowledging the duty to be good towards others.[23]

While Holyoake was not promoting atheism (nor strictly against religion[24]), the secularism promoted is still usually seen as opposed to the sacred or the religious, eliding over historical contexts and ending up replacing the hegemony of religious faith. Instead, I broaden William

---

19. Ibid., 121.

20. Ibid., 204.

21. Dacey, *Secular Conscience*, 31; on the value of religious conscience in the public square, see ibid., 52.

22. Holyoake, *Principles of Secularism*, chapter 9.i.

23. Ibid., chapter 3.i–viii.

24. Zuckerman, *Living the Secular Life*, 13.

Connelly's claim that "Secularism needs refashioning, not elimination,"[25] to include religious positions as well. Connolly's focus on refashioning is to remind us how the secular was embedded in the religious to show that stated oppositions are forced, while also challenging anti-religious rhetoric in secular conceptions that only denude the potency and vigor of the term. I contend the secular and the religious empower and strengthen themselves in how they protect, nurture, and support the possibility of flourishing for the other. Christianity did not invigorate itself through crusades, inquisitions and militant evangelizing. Secularization's spread also failed through violent or militant tactics. In terms of humbling, secular studies and supporters need to go beyond the secularization thesis and learn from its weaknesses. Theists must also show restraint in religion's apparent growth or reinvigoration as much of the secularization thesis still remains challenging and valid.

The Secularization Thesis

In *On Politics*, philosopher Alan Ryan notes: "In most of the world, secularization has not happened."[26] In the West, or what Taylor calls the North-Atlantic world,[27] the secularization thesis once seemed a near established truth and was widely heralded among many sociologists of religion and other academics as the death knell of religious faith. The blueprint was pretty straightforward: the more a country was secularized by the forces of greater economic opportunities, material benefits (especially a life free of poverty and characterized by healthy living), modern ideas and notions, non-partisan education and formation (especially through Enlightenment principles), coupled with the reality of religious and ideational pluralism, then religious belief and hegemony would inevitably decline.

Religious institutions once controlled and directed public entities and spheres like schools (education, research, publishing, and experiments); work (economics), government (politics), marriage, the family—even time and space (nearly all aspects of social, imaginative, and cultural life). With modernization, the exclusively religious had ceded or was coerced to cede power and influence to non-religious but (supposedly)

---

25. Connolly, *Why I Am Not a Secularist*, 19.
26. Ryan, *On Politics*, 985.
27. Taylor, *Secular Age*, 1.

religiously-neutral, secular powers and authorities. Such public spaces once dominated by religion were "allegedly emptied of God or of any reference to ultimate reality," as Taylor writes.[28]

Religion was supposed to be relegated to the private sphere, or at best, translated into a language all could debate and argue. But, as Cavanaugh contends, the distinction of the religious and secular is forced and "invented." The State gets sacralized while the sacred is secularized.[29] His aim is to correct the idea of religion as irrational, prone to violence, and needing to be controlled—while the secular is more prone to peace and neutrality.[30] History bears out neither claim fully—as discussed further in chapter 6.

Opposing such a narrative, some theories have tried to account for this limbo space between traditional belief and standard unbelief. Linda Woodhead, for example, has argued that religious belonging has fallen, but belief is still present—though in some new or unexpected ways.[31] She has called this "belief without belonging." Abby Day evaluates those who want to maintain a religious label even if knowing and living out little of that faith. In this sense, "belief is performative and relational."[32] It is also what Day calls "anthropocentric," as opposed to theocentric. Such terms describe people who identify themselves as a certain faith (like Christianity on a survey in the UK) because it is linked with cultural, national, or familial identity or augments other types of belongings.[33] They believe in belonging. Part of the problem is not only trying to quantify religious belief, but also unbelief. Atheist philosopher Ronald Aronson shows how surveys are often vague or imprecise on the nuances of unbelieving with questions like "I don't believe in anything beyond the physical world" seemingly ruling out justice, love, and hope. He contends the number of atheists or agnostics would be even higher if greater care in the questions were taken.[34] Thus, there are still a few prominent believers in the

---

28. Ibid., 2.

29. Cavanaugh, "The Invention of the Religious-Secular Distinction," 105 and 114.

30. See Cavanaugh, *Myth of Religious Violence*.

31. Woodhead, "Neither Religious Nor Secular," 137–61.

32. Day, *Believing in Belonging*, 99.

33. For an analysis of British identity after Brexit, see Scruton, *Where We Are*.

34. Aronson, *Living without God*, 29; see also Zuckerman, *Living the Secular Life*, 5.

secularization theory, or those who insist, like Peter Watson, that "it was right all along."[35]

Living in Ireland, I find it difficult to avoid seeing the secularization thesis on fast-forward, especially during the years of the Celtic Tiger and amidst the child abuse scandals in the Catholic Church. Ireland, like Poland, was an exception to the European secularization model, but the Catholic Church's sway over Ireland has greatly diminished, emblematic in the successful 2015 referendum legalizing gay marriage and in the abortion referendum in 2018.

Typical accounts of secularization paint a picture (and overarching narrative) of the subtraction theory of secularization, linked with what Taylor, in *A Secular Age*, calls secularity 1 (secularized public spaces) and secularity 2 (the decline of belief and practice).[36] Taylor, however, focuses on what he calls secularity 3, explicating how unbelief and belief are now two real, if not equal possibilities of choice and worldview.[37] This reality, I aver, is one to neither mourn nor obsessively battle. Aggressive forms of secularization, however, whether embodied in New Atheist invectives toward religious belief in the works of PZ Myers or as propaganda of communist governments sullying genuine religious belief, should not be met with silence or acquiescence.[38]

Remember, it is a rugged, scrappy humility celebrated here—or better a humble pride. Such humble pride is important in navigating and bridging the secular-religious divide.

Helping to overcome this divide is one of the original supporters of the secularization thesis who then joined the unconvinced. Sociologist of religion Peter Berger deserves credit for admitting he was wrong[39] and acknowledging the reality of ever-thriving religious belief in our world,

---

35. Watson, *Age of Atheists*, 13 and 14. See also Bruce, *Secularization*, 199; Norenzayan, *Big Gods*, 210fn1; and Aronson, *Living without God*, 34.

36. See Admirand, "Embodying an 'Age of Doubt,'" 439–54. See also McEvoy, *Leaving Christendom for Good*; Barbieri, *At the Limits of the Secular*; Smith, *How (Not) to Be Secular*; Warner, VanAntwerpen, and Calhoun, *Varieties of Secularism*; Leask et al., *The Taylor Effect*; and Bilgrami, *Beyond the Secular West*.

37. Taylor, *Secular Age*, 20. On secularity 4, see Barbieri, "Post-Secular Problematic," 132–33.

38. For atheist critiques of radical atheists, see Ruse, *Atheism*, 52; Stedman, *Faitheist*, 14; and Crane, *Meaning of Belief*, xi and 22. From a Christian perspective, see Davies, "New Atheism," 1834. For attempts to go beyond the divide of religion and atheism, see Carroll and Norman, *Religion and Atheism*.

39. Berger, *Many Altars*, 53.

even and especially in places where material prosperity and a good dose of Enlightenment thinking flourish. In *The Many Altars of Modernity*, Berger aims further to readjust and reformulate his views on religious belief and the secularization thesis, predominantly through the lens of pluralism. For Berger, modernity need not lead to secularization, but it will "necessarily lead to pluralism."[40] He notes two kinds of pluralisms: the first includes the reality and interactions of various religions in society while the second pluralism describes the range of those differing religious beliefs co-existing with secular discourse and ways of living.[41] Although I employ the term interfaith dialogue to combine these pluralist realities, Berger's separation also has its strengths.

Sacred/Secular Blending

One of the strengths of such separation is to then stress, as Nancy Ammerman opines, that "the sacred and the secular are intertwined."[42] Instead of the secular discourse replacing the religious one, Berger notes that "the secular discourse inserts itself into the turbulent world of religious pluralism."[43] Sometimes there is an overlapping of the secular and the sacred, sometimes the secular becomes just one more competing voice and option in the marketplace of religious and non-religious ideas. Either way, there is co-existence, if not mutually reinforced flourishing.

For Berger, the exclusively secular requires the expansive and creative imagination and hope of the religious with its passion to render this world holy and sacred; while the exclusively religious needs the secular's pragmatic, efficient, and flexible tendencies, cognizant of realities "on the ground" and the practical need for partnership, dialogue, and pluralism. Such co-existence or overlapping, as Berger contends, promotes doubt and questioning, further eroding any sense of religious or ideational triumphalism.[44] Such pluralism is humble, not concealing its brokenness. It is rooted in shared failures and participatory triumphs.

Jewish theologian Irving Greenberg contends "the religious-secular distinction is no longer adequate." Particularly after the Shoah, religions

40. Ibid., 20.
41. Ibid, 53; for a helpful localized study, see Hanson, *City of Gods*.
42. Ammerman, "Response," 106.
43. Berger, *Many Altars*, 53.
44. Ibid., 64.

are broken. Religious voices were silent or perpetrated heinous crimes. Likewise, secular voices were also wanting or guilty. No ideological system, religious, philosophical, corporate, scientific, or secular can claim any moral high ground. All failed and were complicit. All are morally fractured, especially if they try to distance themselves from moral questions. For Greenberg, the profound secular person should recognize how the idea of God can be a bulwark against human attempts to deify themselves at the expense of others, and so should support this notion in the lives of holy believers. Spiritual blindness of theists and failure to acknowledge their God was a driving force in the Shoah. Even if atheists believe theistic faith is delusional, what about those few whose faith lead them to oppose injustice?

In my most recent trip to Germany (2017), I visited sites commemorating the Four Lübeck Martyrs and of Karl Leisner and Cardinal von Galen in Münster. Maybe even God can't heal the black holes of Auschwitz, but we ignore any light at our peril.

For Greenberg, we all need to acknowledge our brokenness and limitations, which are keys to ensure that "religion and secular cultures both function as forces for good and healing—rather than for destruction."[45] For Aronson, acknowledging such limits is a "statement of humility."[46] Such positions can help us view the Other as beneficial and complementary. In seeing mutual wounds and brokenness—and most importantly recognizing such failures within our traditions, leaders, and goals—can strengthen religious–non-religious partnerships. Such ideas are the fulcrum of this chapter, and—embedded in humility—throughout this work.

Solidarity with the Religious: A Secularity of Openness, Dialogue, and Humility

Fortunately, discussion of religions and the secular are becoming more nuanced through sharper awareness of the plurality of secularities.[47] We also need nuanced (and theological) readings of the variety, contradictions, and minimal overlap of the secular within inter- and intra-

---

45. Greenberg, "Dialectic Living and Thinking," 184–85.

46. Aronson, *Living without God*, 145; on brokenness, see ibid., 40.

47. See Baker and Smith, *American Secularism*, 6, 14, and 24; and Froese and Bader, *America's Four Gods*.

religious contexts. While religious fundamentalism is an important piece of the discussion, thankfully it is not (or should not be) the only one. This chapter on the secular-religious dialogue is complimentary with the chapter on interfaith dialogue among religions. While dialogue between religions is highly valued as a crucial component of mutual humbling, the atheist-theist dialogue cannot be overlooked, especially in the context of a supposedly neutral public sphere. Such is the fifth (but no less crucial) tier in an all-encompassing dialogue with the Other, as developed in chapter 4; here, the religious-atheist one.

It is important to recognize (and celebrate) the differing positions and complexities within each tier and aspect of such dialogues. Thus, the idea of multiple secularisms, a phrase from Rajeev Bhargava,[48] is useful to highlight the variety and nuance of the secular. Such discussions are often disappointingly myopic and Eurocentric or ones that merely gesture at Asia (perhaps with a nod to Turkey and India). Works on the secular and sacred need to become ever more globalized and far reaching to begin to do those terms justice if seeking to move through and beyond the provincial and local.[49] Three examples here can suffice.

In *Beyond Religion: Ethics for a Whole World*, the Dalai Lama cogently argues for the embrace of secular ethics. By the secular, he does not mean an antipathy for, or rejection of, religion, but is strictly referring to how the secular is employed in the Indian constitution. In such an understanding, secular "implies a profound respect for and tolerance towards all religions. It also implies an inclusive and impartial attitude which includes nonbelievers."[50]

Located within Indian conceptions of the secular, the Dalai Lama's approach highlights the foundational and universal reach of ethics and compassion. The secular is "a position equidistant from all faith traditions, including nonbelievers."[51] As J. Rosario Narchison further elaborates: "All [India's] religious indigenous traditions are secular in the

48. Bhargava, "Multiple Secularisms," 18–41; for a critique of multiple secularisms, see Mahmood, *Religious Difference*, 10.

49. See Juergensmeyer, Griego, and Soboslai, *God in the Tumult of the Global Square*; and Rectenwald, Almeida, and Levine, *Global Secularisms*. On Black secularism (in dialogue with Black theology), see Lloyd, *Religion of the Field Negro*; for secularism in Nigeria, see Vaughan, *Making of Nigeria*, 163–65.

50. Dalai Lama, *Beyond Religion*, 6. On Indian secularism, see Bhargava, "How Should States Deal with Deep Religious Diversity?," 73–84.

51. Dalai Lama, *True Kinship of Faiths*, 37.

twin sense of accepting of many ways (to God) and many cultures, and concern for this world (*saeculum*) in all aspects of its life."[52] Such a conception of the secular is deeply rooted in pluralism.[53] Narchison deems this "*open secularism*, open to the influences of social ethics inspired by religious beliefs. Secularism is needed to make religion more tolerant and politics more moral."[54]

As promoted by seminal figures like Amartya Sen and Raimundo Panikkar,[55] Indian secularity has many strengths and could even serve as a model for others to emulate, though critiques are not wanting. T. N. Madan and Partha Chatterjee contend that secularism cannot be foundational in a state where most people are religious, leading to failures to address forms of violent religious fundamentalism, if not inadvertently aiding them.[56] Thus, in the Dalai Lama's Indian context, there is also reason for humbling.

This openness and tolerance towards all faiths and none is also advocated in *Secularism and Freedom of Conscience*, co-written by Charles Taylor and Jocelyn Maclure. The book stems from their work on a government commission in Quebec examining questions of citizenship in the context of pluralism, religions, and the secular. They sought to "reconceptualize the meaning and ends of secularism,"[57] and succinctly present how secularism is not only intrinsic to any flourishing, pluralist democracy but to religious and philosophical freedom as well. They successfully provide a reasonable and balanced approach for how to disentangle the inevitable secular and religious knots, while envisioning why and how a state and its citizens can benefit from deeper engagement with those of differing views and persuasions. Essentially, Maclure and Taylor advocate a "liberal, pluralist model of secularism" sustained by an ethics of dialogue.[58] They oppose a republican model that promotes the secular

---

52. Narchison, "Theological Education for Pluralism in India," 67.

53. Ibid., 67.

54. Ibid., 69.

55. Sen, "Threats to Secular India."

56. See Jakelić, "Secular-Religious Encounters as Peacebuilding," 127; Balagangadhara and De Roover, "The Dark Hour of Secularism," 111–30; and Doniger, *Hindus*, 14.

57. Maclure and Taylor, *Secularism*, 105.

58. Ibid., 110.

at the expense of the religious in the name of sustaining a cohesive civic identity that supports moral equality and freedom of conscience.[59]

This linking above is significant as Taylor and Maclure stress that such principles demand that the secular does not replace the religious sphere in "an all-encompassing secular philosophical conception,"[60] but respects, and sometimes protects, its citizens' religious preferences and views.[61] Comprehensive doctrines, as Rawls eventually conceded, should not be marginalized in the context of a vibrant and plural democracy. Too many thoughtful people are inspired by deeply held religious (and secular) beliefs. Silencing or marginalizing such voices weakens and dishonors the civic integrity and potential partnership of all parties. Maclure and Taylor are also cognizant of this error in some circles, which is why their conception of secularism entails protecting "core beliefs and commitments" by both religious and secular adherents.[62]

In another nod to Rawls, they promote an "overlapping consensus."[63] While there are shared convergences, such a perspective also protects each group's internal reasoning and ways of operating. Reaching such a consensus depends on what Maclure and Taylor call an ethics of dialogue.

In his contribution to *At the Limits of the Secular: Reflections on Faith and Public Life*, a collection of essays examining key phrases through readings of *A Secular Age*, David Tracy examines what he calls the "three forms of publicness," ideally for Tracy representative in any viable Catholic vision.[64] Tracy is writing about the public realm in which freedom of expression and inquiry are prerequisites. Thus, publicness one is highlighted as "rational inquiry" calling for dialectic and argument. The aim is to provide reasoned arguments for positions that are comprehensively presented, debated, justified, challenged, re-examined, and perhaps, reformulated, or maintained. The second form of publicness returns to an area that has been one of the cornerstones of Tracy's intellectual life: the dialogue with classics. In his reading of the classics, Tracy advocates the methods of hermeneutical suspicion, testing, and retrieval, to recognize how past works and ideas have helped to form and sustain us, giving

59. Ibid., 34.
60. Ibid., 15.
61. Ibid., 20.
62. Ibid., 13.
63. Ibid., 15. For a critique, see Mahmood, *Religious Difference*, 177–78.
64. Tracy, "Religion in the Public Realm," 29.

us language of proper ends and identity while remaining fruitful for development and new readings.[65] Thus, Tracy rightfully calls for religious classics to be part of the public dialogue and discussion seeking the best means and values for flourishing.[66]

In publicness three, he highlights resources beyond reason's limits, arguing that religions need to be more than just "another consumer item," entailing not only their rational thrust and focus, but their obligation and responsibility for the Other, especially as embedded in the option for the poor.[67] Elsewhere Tracy has written that Levinas's turn to the face of the Other "can open us to ethical responsibility and even to the call of the prophets to political and historical agency and action."[68] As a Catholic he also highlights Jesus's second coming, in the call to prepare and be present to the hiddenness of God in the world, that spurs the need and foundation for an option for the poor and justice for all.[69] Such again is to return us to the quest for a source of secular ethics, of a godless ethic, or an ethic without metaphysical foundations. As Terry Eagleton writes: "Of the artificial respirators on which God has been kept alive, one of the most effective is morality."[70] Yet, can such a respirator be "turned off" without severe consequences, as Nietzsche, for example, was so acutely aware?[71]

Godless Humility, Part II

I support ethical flourishing without God—which for me ultimately, and more importantly, hints at the existence of God. But I see little need to wield God as a hoop one has to jump through to make viable ethical claims. Plenty of God believers have made and make egregious moral claims. Moreover, I see little, if any, direct, unvarnished, unambiguous link from the Divine to the human. Such is not to deny the possibility of grace, or as a Catholic, any role, for example, to the Magisterium of

---

65. See Tracy, *Analogical Imagination*; and Tracy, *Plurality and Ambiguity*, 14–15.
66. Tracy, "Religion in the Public Realm," 39.
67. Ibid., 44–45. See also Tracy, "Christian Option for the Poor," 119–31.
68. Tracy, *Naming the Present*, 17.
69. Tracy, "Christian Option for the Poor," 131.
70. Eagleton, *Culture and the Death of God*, 156; see also 164–65.
71. Nietzsche, *Thus Spoke Zarathustra*, 272–78; and Nietzsche, *Gay Science*, 181. See also Walsh, *Luminosity of Existence*, 178–321.

the Catholic Church, but theirs is a responsibility that must be weighed and performed humbly, delicately, and inclusively. Too many failures and sins have been left in its wake to do otherwise. A Church leading by humble example (entailing interfaith partnership and learning) is more profound, holy, and "infallible" than mere proclamations. Think of Pope Francis not only urging all Catholics to help and aid the mass migrants of Syria and the Middle East, but taking in refugee families in the Vatican.[72] Citing revelation may give a clout and history to moral norms, and offer reassurance and guidance for many, but revelation is often muddled and ambiguous and no argument for the nonbeliever.

Contra Hume, and as noted in chapter 1, spiritual nourishment, prayer, and monastic life can provide testimony and models to the moral and spiritual flourishing of individual and communal life. But of paramount importance remains how best to help the poor and defenseless (materially, emotionally, spiritually) and to avoid war and exploitation of people and the land. Atheists, agnostics, nontheists, and misotheists all contribute to such a reality, even without embracing theistic impulses or ends. We all can agree that "if we must tip the balance, let it be on the side of the people, for they have been suffering longer."[73]

Theologian James Swindal suggests that "the secular is not only consistent with the religious, but might actually, under certain conditions, perfect it."[74] He cites biblical examples like the last-judgment discourse of Matthew 25 in which the king rewards people for good deeds with eternal life. The King (typically interpreted as Christ/God) links the people's good deeds to others as good deeds performed for the King. The individuals seem confused by this connection. Swindal wonders if this is because their motives were purely secular, done with no connection to God.[75] It is a wonderfully liberating thought—one I would add even to those who do good deeds while candidly rejecting God. Swindal asks: "More radically, would a religious motive for these selfless acts of charity in any way undermine their salvific power?"[76]

Opening up the language of ethics and the good for all, without demanding exclusive recourse to Scripture, natural law, revelation, or

72. On the war in Syria, see Glass, *Syria Burning*; and Solomon, "Syria"; on the refugee crisis, see McDonald-Gibson, *Cast Away*.
73. Hugo, *Les Misérables*, 36.
74. Swindal, "Habermas, Religion, and a Postsecular Society," 234.
75. Ibid., 234.
76. Ibid., 234.

visions, could be the most profound religious act a theist can offer as hope and testament of God. There is little value in scriptural references as proof-texts—far too much in Scripture, especially the Tanach, is ethically ambiguous, if not unethical: the biblical God, especially so. Scripture, at best, points to a people moving toward God, but stumbling often along the way, with their interpretation, discussion, and representation of God. Is such still revelation? For believers, I maintain a positive response but understand the hesitation, if not scorn and distrust heaped on religious texts by non-believers. If Christians proudly hail Christ as a supreme ethical guide, I say "Amen"—but also contend little in Christ's ethical call is radically new, though of the highest caliber (especially his commitment to nonviolence and a growing sense of universal love).

Aptly titling his book *After the New Atheist Debate*, Phil Ryan, like the Dalai Lama, supports the need to articulate and defend a post-religious ethics.[77] Ryan is also concerned with arguments and claims of the New Atheists and their equally zealous opponents to stake out a balanced and judicious space for dialogue. Such an ethics does not gainsay the living, ongoing contribution of religious faith and doctrine in establishing and formulating moral rules and ways of life, but practices and affirms those views in a pluralist environment. As David Hollenbach notes in the context of human dignity's development in Catholic Social Teaching, faith traditions and beliefs are evaluated in light of practical, lived experience. So long as faith systems maintain this sense of development and innovation, they are crucial voices and pieces in striving for greater ethical norms.[78]

Thus, Ryan is right to rebuke Richard Rorty's claim that religion is a conversation stopper.[79] Likewise, atheism should not be a conversation stopper for theists discussing ethics and morality. Ryan is also correct in supporting ongoing ethical dialogue in which religious and secular voices are encouraged to partake and contribute, though his exclusion of comprehensive doctrine would not be beneficial.[80]

Contrary to many exclusivist Christian claims, the Dalai Lama, as noted, argues that ethics need not be founded upon any notion of a Divine Guarantor to avoid a claim of baselessness in advocating right from wrong or in calling for "restraining selfish and destructive impulses and

---

77. Ryan, *After the New Atheist Debate*, 85.
78. Hollenbach, "Human Dignity in Catholic Thought," 250–59.
79. Ryan, *After the New Atheist Debate*, 135.
80. Ibid., 148 and 150.

cultivating inner values." Untethered to any divine source, ethics springs from within our daily living through our humanity. Instead "ethics can also emerge simply as a natural and rational response to our very humanity and our common human condition."[81] Compassion is practical because it leads to a healthier, happier life.[82] It can also be self-evident as we reflect on something like the golden or silver rule.[83]

The Dalai Lama employs an argument for secular ethics via the language of karma (action) and not God. He states he is not minimizing religion's great potential and actual role for good, but advocating that religion is not essential for understanding and implementing ethics; nor that religion is "indispensable to the spiritual life."[84] He separates spiritual well-being, which he deems as an inner resource—"innate human nature"—available to everyone and inclining all of us to "compassion, kindness, and caring for others"—and a "religion-based spirituality that is acquired from our upbringing and culture."[85] I respect such a turn even if I remain a bit befuddled by it, struggling to speak of essence or what is intrinsic without recourse to purpose, teleology, or God. Yet, clearly speaking the language of universal compassion and the golden rule unites more easily and widely than the loaded words like Jesus, the Qur'an, Krishna, Talmud, or dharma.

Human Dignity and Human Nature: Atheist Values

German Catholic theologian Karl Rahner has famously argued that such a tendency towards the good and our seeking for answers and ultimate truths are existential signs of our calling and search for the Transcendent within us.[86] If we are geared toward kindness, any such evidence supports our being created for love by a God of love. Scientific literature[87] adds to the discussion with an evolutionary understanding of religion, showing

81. Dalai Lama, *Beyond Religion*, 13.
82. Ibid., 28. On core tenets of secular ethics, see Dalai Lama, *Appeal to the World*, 37.
83. See Zuckerman, *Living the Secular Life*, 13–14.
84. Dalai Lama, *Beyond Religion*, 16.
85. Ibid., 17.
86. See Rahner, *Foundations of Christian Faith*; for commentary, see Kerr, *Twentieth-Century Catholic Theologians*, 87–104; Kärkkäinen, *Christology*, 140–46; Lane, *Stepping Stones*, 133–68; and Regan, *Theology and the Boundary Discourse*, 71–89.
87. See Norenzayan, *Big Gods*.

how religion benefitted societies' development and so was "naturally" cultivated and advantageous through natural selection. Consider as well neurobiological and philosophical arguments for the origin of altruism, though deeply debated. The benefit of promoting secular ethics is to recognize various routes in achieving and understanding peace and in developing greater interfaith communion.

Contra the bleak, or at best clean-slate, picture of humanity in Golding's *The Lord of the Flies* (or the negative anthropology of Hsün Tzu),[88] I cling to the notion of humankind made in God's image and likeness. Can there be a secular ethic and human rights discourse where metaphysical foundations can be bypassed and still maintain permanence and objectivity?[89] I am doubtful theoretically, but plenty of secular humanists and other moral atheists testify otherwise.[90] Can I accept human life as merely chance and contingency, and how would that alter any metaphysical conception of dignity in human beings? Are not secular theorists more prone to contend rights do not exist in biology, for example, and are just myths human beings decide to enforce (or not)?[91] "Human dignity" is a phrase that the present and future of humanity is built upon. Where it flourishes, so does humanity and the future of this planet; and where it falters or is attacked, nothing less than the meaning and value of our lives and endeavors are exposed and threatened.

What matters is a world imbued and charged with a divine beauty and grandeur (Hopkins) even if such is an atheist world, a so-called secular one. But whether we need God for such ideas to mean something, to be believed and followed, still remains divisive. Again, can such ideals be maintained or humbly enforced without God? As promised in chapter 1, let's now look at secular—or atheist—humility.

Atheist Humility

Holocaust scholar Eliezer Berkovits deemed "holy" both the positions of those who could no longer endure their faith after the Shoah and those

---

88. Golding, *Lord of the Flies*; for analysis, see Paulson, *Sin and Evil*, 313–15. On Hsün Tzu, see *Hsün Tzu: Basic Writings*.

89. On the tension between universal human rights and the ordinary virtues, see Ignatieff, *Ordinary Virtues*, 214; for an interdisciplinary account of key philosophical questions regarding human rights, see Etinson, *Human Rights*.

90. See, Pinker, *Enlightenment Now*; and Epstein, *Good without God*.

91. Harari, *Sapiens*, 123.

who could.⁹² He acknowledged the pull and legitimacy of each position, though he contended ultimately that he remained on the side of the believers. Ever since admiring Dr. Rieux in Camus's *The Plague* or reading essays in college from Kai Nielsen,⁹³ I have been intrigued, and to be honest, in awe, of secular humanists. While I would not concur with Yuval Noah Harari's description of humanism as those worshipping homosapiens, he reminds me of the need to clarify what kind of humanism: liberal, socialist, or evolutionary, for example, the last one containing the pernicious ideology of National Socialists.⁹⁴

My respect for liberal humanists falls under those who, unable or refusing to believe in any Higher Power, often because of the extent of useless evils in our world, nevertheless commit themselves to mercy and justice, striving to make the world safer, happier, and healthier for everyone.⁹⁵ My sense of everyone, moreover, would entail, as much as possible, respect for non-human species as well (a point not always evident in much humanist discourse).⁹⁶ Too often so-called religious people seem mired in petty doctrinal issues, intrafaith battles, interfaith triumphalism, saying much and doing little—or perhaps acting morally to gain a postmortem reward or avoid postmortem or karmic punishment. Who could not be humbled by Dr. Rieux who devoted his life to healing others without belief in God or any hope for a redeeming afterlife?⁹⁷ As he tells the journalist Tarrou: "For the moment I know this: there are sick people and they need curing."⁹⁸ As a Christian theologian, I praise (and almost cheer) secular humanism, and in this context, atheist or humanist humility. The more we minimize or remove claims of religious uniqueness and distinctiveness rooted in superiority and triumphalism, the closer we approach the essence and source of authentic faith, deeper communion, and partnership. If being good depends upon solely being a Christian or humanist, for example, what a sorrier state our world would be. The call to be good as fundamentally universal, regardless of language about, or absence of, deities, is a great hope of our times. This is not only because

---

92. See Berkovits, *Essential Essays*.
93. Nielsen, "Ethics without Religion," 361–69.
94. Harari, *Sapiens*, 254–63.
95. See Hammer, "Imperilled Bloggers of Bangladesh."
96. See Singer, "Taking Humanism Beyond Speciesism," 19–21.
97. See Thiemann, *Humble Sublime*, 147–88.
98. Camus, *Plague*, 127.

theists can claim such truths as proof for some divine purpose of creation, but more importantly, because it includes all of us without exception in the endeavor to strive in love, mercy, hope, and justice.

We should aim to locate and promote the notion that individuals can be good and define the good in terms of respect and dignity for life without full dependence on strictly religious education, contexts, and language. Theists should not only build bridges towards nontheists but know that a similar building is occurring from the side of nontheists: dual travelling and complementarity; ultimately, building-with. For theists, such striving and maintaining of the dignity and justice of the least and marginalized should lead to joy in partnership for justice, not the language of anonymous Christians or Buddhists. Paraphrasing the ending of the *Communist Manifesto*, I would call all the humble to unite. It is not that secular and religious views of humility overlap, though they may, nor that they are interchangeable and equal (which they are not), but proponents of humility are best served in seeking solidarity among the humble instead of merely elevating their own religious version. Thus, when atheist philosopher Louise M. Antony writes that "Humility is a premier religious virtue," and then praises her fellow atheist philosophers for their humility, we know we are moving into mutually sacred ground of some sort.[99]

Foundations of ethics in all the faiths are deeply murky, convoluted, and insufficient without some element of faith. As atheist Phil Zuckerman contends: "I get my morals from the people who raised me, the culture within which I live, the kind of brain that I have, and the lessons I have learned from things I experience as I navigate life."[100] There are a lot of unknowns here, reasons to doubt, the threat of limited knowledge, vision, and experience. But religious believers' descriptions would be fairly similar. What matters more, Zuckerman continues, is "how those morals are enacted in daily life."[101] Knowledge remains finite and partial.

Secular humility, whether deemed Kantian, epistemic, ontological, or intellectual is often better placed to uphold such an acknowledgment. All these terms in some way call us to recognize our limitations and ignorance about our ability to know things fully in themselves and the cause and reasons for existence; it is also linked to our inability to know

---

99. Antony, "Introduction," xiii.
100. Zuckerman, *Living the Secular Life*, 36. See also Smith, *Secular Faith*, 214.
101. Zuckerman, *Living the Secular Life*, 36.

who we are with certainty—let alone truly knowing other manifestations of life. Apophatic theology shares some similarity with its focus on the transcendence and ultimate mystery and unknowability of God's essence, but is still reinforced by faith and trust in a God of ultimate Love.[102] God as your argument remains tempting for too many theists not to employ—even as atheists shrug.

Thus, in examining ethics or virtues from religious and non-religious viewpoints, there is the need to acknowledge difference and points of strength or weakness, but to be careful about—or to avoid—extremes in self-promotion or self-critique. For too long, the former was the claim of theists, arguing that atheists could not lead meaningful lives or avoid moral relativism.[103] With a certain decline in full theistic commitments in some parts of the world coupled by a rise in atheist or God-indifferent voices, it is understandable that atheists feel emboldened to emphasize why their positions are superior to theistic ones. Humility in this context would be effective and instructive, though.

Exemplary in this regard is the approach of Jeffrey Stout in his 2007 Presidential Address at the American Academy of Religion annual meeting in San Diego. As an atheist, he argued that democracy in America is strengthened by the voice and commitment of moderate religious believers who need to be supported and heard.[104] While I would quibble with his qualifier, moderate (for what or who defines the label?), an atheist's humble acknowledgment of seeking and needing theistic voices is inspiring for theists.

Contra the narrative that argues denying or bracketing God corresponds with replacing God with human beings, Julie Cooper, for example, highlights strands in select Enlightenment thinkers (Spinoza, Rousseau, Hobbes) who instead redefine humility by opposing any self-deification while still endorsing human freedom, the empowering of human beings, and a secular critique of pride.[105] Cooper narrates a type of secular humility that accepts and celebrates human finitude, even as it denies any higher power. This denial, Cooper contends, does not attempt to replace God or theistic religion. Rather, secular humility, as developed

---

102. See Caputo and Scanlon, *God, the Gift and Postmodernism*; Caputo and Scanlon, *Questioning God*; and Shah, "Secular Militancy," 381.

103. See Blessing, "Atheism and the Meaningfulness of Life," 107.

104. Stout, "2007 Presidential Address," 533–44; and Stout, *Democracy and Tradition*.

105. Cooper, *Secular Powers*, 141.

by the core foundational thinkers she focuses on, empowers humanity through acknowledging limitations in our means, aims, and goals.[106] By acknowledging we are only mortal, space forms for greater freedom and empowering within limits.[107]

In Cooper's account, Spinoza reinterprets modesty as a means for human empowering,[108] Rousseau develops a healthy love of self that still admits (though inconsistently) failures and sins,[109] and for Hobbes, modesty (and recognizing human limits) is needed if civil society can flourish while promoting human self-sufficiency and agency without the pessimism perceived in Augustinian or seventeenth-century Protestant accounts.[110]

While Cooper downplays the potential for her book to serve as a bridge between Christian and secular conceptions of humility,[111] it remains useful for our context.

Atheist-Theist Dialogue: Shared Platforms

Theists, nontheists, and atheists have their differences, but what is surprising (if not distressful) can be the distaste or disrespect levied among the groups. Historically, theists (especially Christians and Muslims) claimed that disbelievers would be punished and languish in some form of fire and flame. When such theists also inhabited or oversaw seats of political power, such pronouncements had serious, sometimes deadly consequences.

For all the bickering and fighting between atheists and theists (at least in the West[112]), it can also be argued, as Ronald Thiemann does, that "The Christian tradition has a long history of seeing deep connections between belief and unbelief, between believer and unbeliever, in large part because the tradition at its best has always recognized the unbeliever

---

106. See Aronson, *Living without God*, 117.

107. Cooper, *Secular Powers*, 105.

108. See also Clayton, "Religious Spinoza," 66–86; on his reading of Scripture, see Spinoza, *A Theologico-Political Treatise*, 165; and Spinoza, *Ethics*, 145.

109. Rousseau, *Confessions*, 344. On his hypocrisy, see Mendham, "Rousseau's Discarded Children," 131–52.

110. See Hobbes, *Leviathan*, 89; Cooper, *Secular Powers*, 56–57; and 45.

111. Cooper, *Secular Powers*, 152.

112. See Frazier, "Hinduism," 367.

in all of us."[113] The same can be said of all world religions—and many atheist positions, too. As Louis Dupré notes: "Atheism has from the beginning been a steady companion of religious belief."[114] Religious belief, at its best, has been a steady companion of atheism, too.

It is when the one veers too far from the other that problems arise; when theists shout infidel to the unbeliever, secure in their righteousness, while the atheist scoffs at the childish neediness of the believer. Further degradation: they each then seek to purify and enlighten. Finally, they try to save another, regardless of that person's desires and lived ethical life. Humility can be a guard both to deter that false sense of superiority and obsessive, almost narcissistic need to save someone else. An unavoidable question: who are you really trying to save?

For atheist participants, six features for viable and humbling atheist-theist dialogue should include the following:

1. Aiming to be fair to all sides of the atheist-theist debates while arguing for and maintaining one's atheist position.[115]

2. Trying to be open to new or challenging truth claims. Atheist philosopher Michael Ruse writes of the "deep existential seriousness of religious commitment."[116] Without seeking and feeling respect for the other, such openness remains blocked or veiled. Humanist Chris Stedman was shocked when fellow atheists called him a "faitheist" because of his respect for theists. He noticed the same "sure-handed certainty and dismissal" of the other in the atheist as he heard from many religious fundamentalists.[117] He soon embraced the term "faitheist" if such meant "exploring godless ethics and identifying and engaging shared values with the religious—in putting 'faith' in my fellow human beings and our shared potential to overcome the false dichotomies that keep us apart."[118] Presumably the term works both ways, and so is a label I could embrace as well. The ultimate bridge would be a term that encompasses both theists and atheists and which does not obviously distinguish one from the other. If

---

113. Thiemann, *Humble Sublime*, 117.

114. Dupré, "Dialectic of Faith," 39.

115. See Ruse, *Atheism*, 4 and 210; Kitcher, *Life after Faith*, 38 and 67; and from a theist's view, Bullivant, *Faith and Unbelief*, 105

116. Ruse, *Atheism*, 99.

117. Stedman, *Faitheist*, 4; as an example, see Sparks, *Devil You Know*.

118. Stedman, *Faitheist*, 15.

Stedman and I are both faitheists (he for his interest in religious themes and concerns and I for my deep sympathy for and pull towards atheist tendencies), the divide becomes less obvious; the potential for partnership renewed.

3. Through words and deeds, showing deep respect for genuine religious arguments and religious lives. Philosopher Todd May opines: "I am atheist as the day is long, but I am fascinated by Trappist monks or Trappistine nuns, who speak only when necessary and in some cases not at all."[119] He cannot help but admire their commitment. Fellow atheist philosopher Ronald Dworkin called himself a "religious atheist."[120] Ruse deems himself an atheist who is religious.[121] Kitcher aims to depict religious views "as sympathetically and precisely" as he can.[122]

4. Embracing in name, if not spirit, an intellectual and spiritual humility: a humble pride. In a similar vein, I have highlighted how theists armed with doubt and humility, wrestling with the same issues as atheists, are often best positioned to live much of their theistic faith. A Doubting Thomas can be commendable.

5. Acknowledging there is much still to learn—and that resources in our own traditions or worldviews are not enough.[123] Stedman, for example, admits: "there is a storied history of religious social justice, and we would do well to learn from it."[124] No one likes a know-it-all theist or atheist.

6. Advocating and striving for ethical living and in making the world a more just, meaningful, and peaceful place.[125] Some of the particulars and specifics may be debatable, but core agreement through human rights law cement atheist-theist ethical ties. Various humanist manifestos, like The Amsterdam Declaration of 2002, can be very similar to theistically-infused ones.

---

119. May, *Significant Life*, 79.
120. Dworkin, *Religion without God*, 4.
121. Ruse, *Atheism*, 5.
122. Kitcher, *Life after Faith*, 61.
123. Ruse, *Atheism*, 245.
124. Stedman, *Faitheist*, 169. See also Bissell, *Apostle*, 102.
125. Kitcher, *Life after Faith*, 117 and 122; and Stedman, *Faitheist*, 11.

7. A willingness to show a sense of humor—and be laughed at—doesn't hurt either.[126] Such humor entails the humility to laugh at ourselves and our beliefs—their ludicrousness and stubborn paradoxes and odd slants. It is also to jest at what we cannot, should not, dare not, or can no longer believe. Such is not the "unthinking laughter of the secure"[127] but the thoughtful smirk of the searcher and wanderer. It may also be the easy giggle of children. For here, youth has much to teach and remind the jaded and severe. Dworkin writes of fellow atheist Woody Allen that when "told he would live on in his work, he replied that he would rather live on in his apartment."[128] Or perhaps better, take Calvin from the *Calvin and Hobbes* strip. Procrastinating about his math homework, Calvin argues that math is really a religion as you have to believe all this stuff that requires faith, like adding two numbers that miraculously become a new one. He tells Hobbes: "As a Math atheist, I should be excused from this."[129]

Atheist Reflections: Seeking Bridges

While Math atheists may raise an eyebrow, Ronald Dworkin calling himself a religious atheist no longer seems out of place (especially in the West, while in much of Asia it has been historically normative). For Dworkin, religious atheists share in the beauty, mystery, and sublimity of the created world,[130] strive and seek for purpose, success, fullness, and meaning, and are committed to healing, justice, and love. Taking a nod from Einstein, Dworkin writes that "Religion is deeper than God."[131] Of special importance is the call for moral and ethical living sustained by a deep awareness of the complexity and aesthetic richness of our world. For Dworkin and Einstein, such a basis is universally shared.[132] For Einstein, "teachers of religion" who move beyond a personal god filtered through

---

126. An openness to laugh at oneself and our convictions, imbibed in the jester, Shakespearean fool, or Silenus is also apt here. Note also how Erasmus refers to Christ "as the most extraordinary Silenus of them all."

127. Bowels, *Travels*, 402.

128. Dworkin, *Religion without God*, 149.

129. Watterson, *Calvin and Hobbes*, March 6, 1991.

130. Dworkin, *Religion without God*, 10.

131. Ibid., 1.

132. Einstein, *Ideas*, 37.

controlling priests could then "avail themselves of those forces which are capable of cultivating the Good, the True, and the Beautiful in humanity itself." Einstein calls this true religion, which can see science as a partner and ennobler.[133]

Dworkin is more conciliatory to traditional religious views as partners, believing that all share in this prior commitment and responsibility of core values.[134] Such can be a "shared faith" enabling greater communication and partnership among theists, atheists, and nontheists.[135] Dworkin claims that all people have "a fundamental religious impulse" expressed and manifested in different ways—most often through belief in a supernatural force or being—a god—or "a set of profound ethical and moral convictions."[136] His atheist prayer is that atheists and theists can recognize and embrace the shared moral, religious space they inhabit.[137]

Also relevant is *The Oxford Handbook of Atheism* (hereafter *OHA*) jointly edited by a Christian theologian (Stephen Bullivant) and an atheist philosopher (Michael Ruse). *OHA* is no sounding board to harangue believers against the existence of God or gods, nor one to conflate the obvious differences, but recognizes the range of types and practices of atheist positions coupled with sincere and trenchant analysis and critiques of atheist and theistic arguments.[138] Its purpose is balance, not to convert or reconvert but to enlighten and inform.

Such balance is also the aim of Philip Kitcher's *Life After Faith: The Case for Secular Humanism*. Kitcher's arguments are centered around key themes or areas of loss "religious people foresee in the transition to a secular perspective."[139] Relevant questions, resonating with some points above, include:

1. What grounds are there for ethical living for humanists?

2. Can life have meaning without belief in the Transcendent?[140]

---

133. Ibid., 48.
134. Dworkin, *Religion without God*, 24.
135. Ibid., 2.
136. Ibid., 146.
137. Ibid., 146.
138. Bullivant and Ruse, "Introduction," 5.
139. Kitcher, *Life after Faith*, 125.
140. See Lightman, *Searching for Stars*; and Lewis, *Finding Purpose in a Godless World*.

3. Does not denial of any afterlife expunge meaning, value, and happiness in this world and deter the possibility of coping with suffering and death?
4. Does not a denial of the Transcendent entail a loss of depth and breadth to the world, flattening it, in the language of Charles Taylor's *A Secular Age*?

These are all important questions and Kitcher provides honest assessments and generally tries to maintain a balanced focus, even acknowledging where religious systems deserve praise (especially in their ability to fuse community, provide heightened contexts for ethical living, and give comfort and meaning to billions of people).[141]

Kitcher considers his position "soft atheism," meaning that he does not unequivocally deny the possibility one day of scientific evidence proving the existence of a theistic framework, though based on the extant evidence, he deems this increasingly unlikely.[142] Raised in the Anglican tradition, and acknowledging much beauty within it (especially religious music), he aims to be fair and sympathetic to religious views in presenting his arguments. Like Stout, he further classifies religious beliefs under the rubric of refined religion against those of a more literal or fundamentalist bent.[143] This move thankfully distinguishes him from the likes of a Dawkins who often lumps all theistic believers together or unduly focuses on the most literal-minded ones.

Kitcher also movingly addresses why not believing in an afterlife need not diminish value in this life nor inhibit coping with death. Freud-like, he supports a need to face reality and avoid infantilizing myths for false comfort. Freud, for example, chides: "Men cannot remain children forever, they must in the end go out into 'hostile life.'"[144] Kitcher wants us to accept the reality of death to make this world more meaningful. In facing our mortality we can also recognize and help those who suffer in the process.[145] Such "musings on mortality," as Victor Brombert notes,

---

141. Kitcher, *Life after Faith*, 2.
142. Ibid., 23–25.
143. Ibid., 90.
144. Freud, *Future of an Illusion*, 62–63.
145. Kitcher, *Life after Faith*, 118. See also Phillips, *Problem of God*, 184. For my analysis of Phillips's purifying atheism, see Admirand, *Mass Atrocity*, 69–77. For other thoughtful atheist critiques on death, see Aronson, *Living without God*, 151–86; and Dworkin, *Religion without God*, 149–59.

"implies being alive, questioning how to live, raising moral issues."[146] Atheists like Brombert and Kitcher can provide deep insight and perspective on how to face, or even celebrate, the reality of death. They can remind believers on how sacred and special this life can be—and how tragic when it is not.[147]

Conclusion: Secular-Religious Fusions

Does the religious inevitably oppose the secular and does the secular oppose the religious—or is there another term to express the reality of religious/non-religious partnership and the space and description the Dalai Lama refers to above as the Indian form of the secular? Such a space is plural, dialogical, and seeking social justice, whether guided by John Rawls's difference principle, Gustavo Gutiérrez's option for the poor, or the economic arguments for a global wealth tax on the wealthy to help the struggling and poor as in Thomas Piketty's *Capital in the Twenty-First Century*. It is more than tolerance and transcends the secular—even as it also transcends the religious because it incorporates and is guided by multiple strands within those overarching ones. Is there a tidy name for a beautifully messy idea—beyond the sterile terms "civil society" or "the public square" or "sphere"? Raimundo Panikkar writes that "Only worship can prevent secularization from becoming inhuman, and only secularization can save worship from being meaningless."[148] A world without those like Camus, Orwell, or Eiseley is a god-diminished one, its radiance weakened, its aching despair augmented.

The so-called secular and religious divide is usually a misnomer. We do not live in a secular or post-secular age, but in a world where the majority of people can barely survive—marginalized, forgotten, and obscure. Whether the victims, perpetrators, or bystanders profess belief in Allah, Christ, Zeus, Nature, humanity, or nothing is often irrelevant. Whether one imbibes the religious and embraces the secular, shuns the secular and clings to the religious, scorns the religious and upholds the secular, (somehow) rejects both the secular and the religious or does not

---

146. Brombert, *Musings on Mortality*, 165.

147. See Chuang Tzu, *Book of Chuang Tzu*, 151. On death and atrocity, see Pinnock, *Facing Death*.

148. Panikkar, *Worship and Secular Man*, 1–2; for commentary, see Dallmayr, *Being in the World*, 126–34.

differentiate them, wars proliferate, children perish, and religious and secular hypocrites thrive.

But that is not all: hope and kindness endure, too. Sometimes, a (so-called) religious voice subverts and liberates; other times, a (so-called) secular voice prophesies and saves. In short, we are many-sided selves, solitary and social, of various yearnings, constitutions, failures, and joys. We conflict within ourselves, where doubt and faith—and despair and hope—mix, mingle, and uncomfortably reside, like the Canaanites and the Israelites of the Bible. Am I secular and/or religious, and regardless of the answer(s), is such a state consistent throughout the day, throughout my life? Am I only religious when I am good and so not religious when I falter? If so, then is the secular somehow shorn of the good, a neutral playing field of pluralist, borderline-relativist activities and paths, viable so long as not inflicting unjust harm? Is the secular enmeshed in a lowest-common denominator of interpersonal (non)action? Am I truly secular (and so not religious) when I:

1. espouse interfaith learning and dialogue;
2. am intrigued by multiple religious belonging;
3. appreciate postmodern, pluralist frameworks of multiple truths, fragments, and unanswerable questions;
4. view atheism as a potentially meaningful choice;
5. encourage the separation of religion and the State (but expect religious voices of integrity at the negotiating table arguing their claims in the public sphere); and
6. send my children to a non-denominational public school?

If the ground and labels of the secular and the religious are so contested and seemingly meaningless for one individual, then what about for a culture, nation, geopolitical region, time period—the world?

Let me close with an almost forgotten personal memory—and then a return to the Mets. During a homily years ago, a priest recommended to talk to Jesus every morning when we rise and every evening before bed, even with a simple "Good morning, Lord," or "Good evening, Lord."

"Just talk to him," the priest spoke, "tell him about your day, your troubles. And be sure to thank him every day. Remember, he's your friend."

This advice has comforted me tremendously, and to this day, I try to say "good morning, Lord," also addressing various saints and my grandparents. On one level, it seems so childish and simple, and yet as I'm more likely to complicate matters, holding unto this seemingly "childish" act is wonderfully spiritual and peaceful.[149]

When I was a parish-outreach coordinator in Northern California through the Jesuit Volunteer Corps, I was blessed with one client, Grace. Her name alone was fitting. She was a particularly eccentric and needy (which is to say, too-often forgotten) elderly woman. Grace lived alone in the second floor of an apartment complex, making it difficult for her to leave and communicate with others. Repeated attempts to find her a roommate failed, as she would never tell them (or me) how much money she wanted or how the apartment was to be shared. She called every day—sometimes two or more times. Her mood often varied. The problem was usually one we had talked about previously. Sadly, her children lived nearby, but refused to visit her. One previous Christmas, a son slipped a card under her door. How she cherished that (now tattered) card! She would proudly read it to me during almost every visit. "Look what my son gave me the other day."

I stopped by her apartment every week for an hour or so and talked to her and helped her with bills. Usually, what I did was never enough and the hour or so would pass too quickly (for Grace!). My leaving her apartment was always a calculated, slowly planned maneuver. Since she often asked me questions about prayer (and since we would pray together), I mentioned in passing how Christ was always with her. Incredulous, she asked me again: "Really? You mean all the time, even when I am alone?" I nodded. Her face lit up. "Oh, Peter, that makes me so happy. All the time?" Every visit or phone call subsequently, Grace would always remark: "It makes me so happy to know Christ is even here with me now."

I'm glad those words comforted Grace, but it also absolved me of some guilt and no doubt bequeathed me more free time (certainly fewer phone calls). Reflecting almost twenty years later, I can only think how an atheist would have it so much more difficult—be called to go so much further—to be that presence or find a community that could try to fill that gap. There would be no supernatural crutch, or exit. The believer in me says the grace of God led me to those words, but false pride says that would be the only salve to soften, if not heal her heavy loneliness. Instead, faith in my atheist friend would cohere in the desire, the intention, in the presence to heal. And going further, perhaps even without God's grace.

---

149. Teresa of Ávila, *Life*, 84.

Postscript

While the Mets' 2017 and 2018 seasons were hopeless, the successes of 2015 and 2016 helped unite atheist, agnostic, theist, nontheist, polytheist, multifaith, and secular Mets fans. As for the future, as Mets blogger Jason Fry commented: "in the face of considerable evidence to the contrary—ya gotta believe."[150]

---

150. Fry, "Welcome Home."

6

Illuminating Past Sins
History and Memory in Dialogue

Three Maltese Snapshots

1

I awake peering out a hotel window in Sliema. Colorful fishing boats (*luzzu*) slowly sway on the serene Marsamxett Harbour. Painted on both sides of their prows are the eyes of Osiris, said to ward off evil, a remnant of pagan testimony on a very Catholic island. In the distance stretch the walls and fortifications of the old city and newer capitol, Valletta. The ramparts, bastions, curtains and ravelins remain as testaments to the obsessive building-frenzy of the Knights Hospitaller of St. John of Jerusalem. They called it "Humilissima Civitas Valletta"—The Most Humble City of Valletta. Church spires and domes soar above the walls and the dominant chalky-cream patina of its limestone houses and buildings. Shades and tones of azure, cobalt, sapphire, and cerulean, shimmer in sea and sky. From Neolithic people to the Phoenicians, Carthaginians, Greeks, Romans, and onto various medieval city states and fiefdoms through the Ottoman Empire, Napoleon, and Great Britain, the tiny island is a witness to the rise and fall of the once potent and mighty: world conquerors joining the conquered.

The Knights were bequeathed Valletta by Charles V in 1530 and spent the next two centuries obsessively constructing ways to thwart Muslim advances and parries. Such precautions had precedents. Sometimes entire populations of islands were enslaved by raiding pirates or corsairs. Gozo lost almost 6,000 people in a raid in 1551. Of the fortifications, slaves tirelessly dug and entrenched. Their testimony is buried with their anonymity. The walls are thick and immense, sending a message of insularity and defensiveness.

Dividing lines of us/them seem riddled all over these islands—even among Christians themselves with the Inquisitor's Palace. There are glimpses of integration, inter-mixing, and immersion. To Allah, the Maltese Muslims pray; and to Allah (sometimes spelled Alia) the Christian Maltese pray: the pronunciation indistinguishable to the outside observer. Here, too history presents a complicated picture, where identities are hybrid and mobile.[1] While Catholic statues guard most street corner niches, and house plaques enshrine Catholic saints, there's no denying the remains of Muslim influence from their rule of nearly three hundred years, from the eighth to the eleventh century. While Catholic lore boasts of unremitting belief once St. Paul had converted the inhabitants of Malta after his supposed shipwreck here in 60 CE, alternative historical accounts depict later wholesale conversions to Islam. These conflicts, repressed desires, and truths still linger and subsist, if not in the bedrock of Malta's physical structures than in subterranean and unconscious realms.

Shipwreck images are harrowing now, becoming almost a daily occurrence around the shores and shoals of Europe. I had arrived in Malta after one of the worst incidents of reported refugee deaths, the sinking of a ship with North African immigrants seeking a better life in Europe. The ship sunk off the coast of Libya on April 19th, 2015, with deaths of perhaps 900 people.[2] An editorial cartoon in the *Sunday Times of Malta* (26 April 2015) depicted portly tourists diving into a Mediterranean sea of skulls.

2

I'm watching children play soccer on an astro pitch. I reflect on my childhood, a video of me as a six-year old, looking at the camera each time I scored, beaming with pride. Now I watch the Maltese kids dart, stumble, pass, cheer, sulk, and shout. It all seems so familiar, yet I'm less than one hundred yards from the ruins of Ġgantija, a Neolithic megalithic temple

---

1. I thank Professor Adrian-Mario Gellel of the University of Malta for his hospitality and knowledge; see also Abela, *Malta*. On the duality of cities, see Carr, *Rule of the Land*, 284.

2. Yardley, "Rising Toll on Migrants."

complex. I just finished my tour, and am about to exit through the gift shop for a bus to the station and then onto the ferry back to Sliema. The temples may be the oldest, freestanding structure in the world (3600–3000 BCE). The kids just want to score goals.

I'm in Gozo now but residing in some mixed dimension, hearing the children play soccer and trying still to envision what the Temple was like thousands of years ago. When Neolithic man and woman looked upon it, what did they feel or say? What happened there, not just in how it was built (there are theories) but why and for what purpose? Why those random holes in the boulders or in the ground by the portal doors? What, if any, is the significance of the spirals embedded in immense stones; of the dotted patterns in the rocks, of the androgynous figures and statues unearthed? If constructed for some deities, how were they portrayed? Was it predominantly from hope or loving awe?

Even with archaeological insights, so much is mystery and unknown. Illusive. We call it pre-history as if we can draw a line and claim other times are known. But sites like Avesbury or Stonehenge in England, or New Grange in Ireland or Ħaġar Qim (in Qrendi, Malta) only belie our own uncertainty about foundations and murky origins, whether of big bang or some primordial ooze, a reptilian and ape past as Eiseley would pen. We have theories, diverse readings, some no different than divination in the past despite our sophisticated technology and scientific terminology. Neolithic man is as much a mystery as we are. Contemplating the past we see a reflection of ourselves and both remain blurry, as much rubble as beauty.[3] Probing origins, we confront present mists, adrift in perpetual seeking.

Still lost in a haze, I watch the kids play for another minute, wondering if they even notice the temples. Perhaps not: I wouldn't have. There's so much I still don't see and don't know.

3

Further echoing the repressed, but extant reminders of Islam in Malta are place names like Mdina. I'm now in that walled city after having visited St. Paul's Grotto in nearby Rabat. Once this was the center of power for the ruling Aghlabids in Mdina, but little visible presence of that time remains

---

3. Hennessy, *Dorothy Day*, ix.

to casual visitors—only fragments in museum displays or in place names or words—and yet there is a presence, an influence in the air.

There are Muslims living, working, and studying in Malta today. Many female students wearing hijabs passed me in the campus of Malta University as I walked to the bookstore before teaching my class. I think of the refugees, most are Muslim—though Christians fleeing the Middle East are increasing.

Almost everywhere we venture there are signs of obliteration, of buildings rising on and over one's enemies, erasing their foothold and imprint. But even in stories of triumphs, there remain tragedies, loss, violence.[4] History traditionally echoes the bombast of victors, but as Clive Finlayson notes in the context of *Homo sapiens*, "prehistory is no different."[5] Yet, cracks and fissures remain, peek out in shards, place names, and DNA. The losers, the victims, the humble, the silenced, the exterminated: their bones, perhaps even their spirits, linger, and demand re-telling.[6]

History, Memory, Humility

Narratives are enfleshed in our thinking. We dream stories as much as we live them. They lurk in our biological origins, in our myths—historical, religious, and familial. Even the silent and taciturn tell stories. Most of us gravitate towards history, "exhausting" as it can be.[7] This chapter investigates the effect of history and memory as humblers of identities, egos, presentiments, revelations, institutions, nations, faiths, and gods. It is a humbler of history as well. A history that doesn't humble is merely hagiography, if not much worse; not just dead history, but deadly history, leaving cadavers in its wake. All histories are messy, smeared in greyish hues and tones. Some souls are even barred from it, a white-washing of sorts.[8]

Memory, suffused with dialogue and discernment, can evaluate and purge positions of hubris, close-mindedness, and superiority. Such are

---

4. See Roth, *Failures of Ethics*, 101; Saunders, *Lincoln*; Admirand, *Mass Atrocity*, 275–305; and Fallada, *Nightmare in Berlin*, 259.
5. Finlayson, *Humans Who Went Extinct*, 105.
6. See Redbanks, *Shepherd's Life*, 6.
7. Tillinghast, *Finding Ireland*, 273.
8. Baldwin, *Evidence of Things Not Seen*, 80.

the realms of ethical memory and the obligation to remember truthfully and transparently.[9] Ethical memory employs the past neither as a weapon for revenge nor as a tarp to hide discomforting and vulnerable truths. Seeking justice, it both judges and expects to be judged. It assigns where failure occurred and improvement or purification is needed. How we face, analyze, or ignore what occurred in the past creates and informs that history. James Baldwin interpreted this confluence of past, present, and future through our ethical relation to memory and history. If there is no love for the Other, he sung, then the history we create will sully our present and future, imprisoning us and the Other as well.[10] Sadly, few escape from censure and blame.[11]

What follows in this chapter is an examination of an ethics of memory and the sometimes fraught relationship between history and memory. I will present five key lenses needed for reading history, the 5 Ps as I call them: poverty, pluralism, postmodernism, postcolonialism, and pardon. These five lenses in reading history can humble and challenge our sacrosanct identities while also strengthening our potential and past success. As an example of such reading and seeking, I will turn to the still fraught and unresolved history of racism in the Unites States, examining some prominent, recent texts in the area of black studies and black-white relations. Reading my native country's history through these lenses contests, if not shatters, any still remaining idealistic claims ("with hard work, the great American (con) Dream is yours";[12] "there is no classism in America"; "we are now a color-blind society"[13]). My overall point here should be a ho-hum, no-brainer: history humbles. More demandingly, this reality is applicable to whatever identity and -ism you identify with. Our identities, let us remember, are welded to the images we paint of others, our slurs and silencing—or hospitality, care, and praise. Those whose histories have no sin can cast the first stone, but be forewarned: such stones are more like boomerangs.

While we are shaped by our histories, they are more mysterious, convoluted, intertwined, and blemished than most of us want to admit.

---

9. Blustein, *Moral Demands of Memory*, 180.

10. Baldwin, *Evidence of Things Not Seen*, xvi.

11. Gandhi, *Autobiography*, xii; in the political sphere, see Phan and Tan, "Majority-Minority Dynamics," 220.

12. Williams and Milton, *Con Men*, 5 and 155.

13. See Formisano, *Plutocracy in America*, 30–51; and Anderson, *White Rage*.

They're replete with dangerous memories as Johann Baptist Metz writes,[14] breaking present triumphalism. They remind us of our weakness and negligence in combating injustice and suffering: "a memoria passionis: a memory of suffering."[15] Not addressing past historical failures leads to loss of one's own sense of freedom and moral vision.[16] Any attempt to seek foundations or development in various identities—religious, ethnic, national, family—must respond to those buried voices, must seek to uncover, locate, and hear them.

Especially through testimonies, and the act and responsibility of bearing witness (see chapter 7), history deeply, agonizingly humbles. We may claim purity, certitude, and victory, but honest evaluations seeking multiple voices will reveal failures and fragility. Reading history humbles in at least three ways and so is a crucial component of humbling faith and identity:

1. It reveals mystery and nebulous origins and possibilities (we do not have all the answers or the entire narrative).

2. It highlights our interdependence, despite or through previous attempts to overcome some Other.

3. It divulges blunders, frailties, and sins, even as it couches them as endurance, perseverance, and triumphs.

Memory and History in Dialogue

Memory and history are both paralleled and opposed. French-Jewish historian and Holocaust survivor Pierre Nora has highlighted his concern about the growing separation of history and memory.[17] For Nora, "History is perpetually suspicious of memory, and its true mission is to suppress and destroy it."[18]

Yet even as their means or aims may vary, memory and history are too enmeshed in one another to be diametrically opposed.[19] How can

14. Metz, *Faith in History and Society*, 107, and Metz, "Future in the Memory of Suffering," 3–16.

15. Metz, *Faith in History and Society*, 106.

16. Ibid., 91.

17. Nora, "Les Lieux de Mémoire," 8. See also Yerushalmi, *Zakhor*, 94.

18. Nora, "Les Lieux de Mémoire," 9.

19. Stone, "History, Memory, Testimony," 25. See also Leydesdorff, *Surviving the Bosnian Genocide*, 141.

there be a full flowering of history without testimonies, and the sometimes fluttering, but body-felt synaesthesia of memory: the smell of a blue sky on a lazy summer day; the glowing brightness of a favorite song drifting from headphones? Or—the depthless, deadening silence of horrid loss, imprinted on the body, and sadly, the soul?[20]

Without history as an academic discipline, how can the gaps and depth of testimonies and memory be addressed, appreciated, articulated, and understood?[21] Timothy Snyder sees historians as objective interpreters, perhaps possible if they recall the humble attributes listed above. Objectivity though is another phrase needing humility. "The ultimate affront of history," Christopher Coker writes, "is that it rarely takes sides."[22]

Forgetting: Moral Indifference or Life-Necessity?

So much of our conscious, and even unconscious, memory is about whether we are willing to recall, listen, and learn. Forgetting and remembering are facets of ethics; circumstances, too. They inform and usually guide how we live. They can dictate how we aid or afflict others in our midst, especially those anonymous souls teetering on the brink of poverty or the maw of war and tragedy.

Wendy Doniger contends: "Often the future is shaped not by what we remember but by what we forget."[23] So, too, Margaret MacMillan reminds us: "History is about remembering the past, but it is also about choosing to forget."[24] In choosing the problem lies. Is forgetting a privilege of the powerful or a crux for stagnancy?

There can be valid reasons to forget. We can be buried by a surfeit of memory.[25] Some memories cripple with regret or grief, paralyzing healing and growth. How tempting to dip in the river Lethe, dripping with clarity and lightness. Some form of forgetting can be conducive for humility. Consider the extreme example of Borges's Funes the Memorious. He couldn't forget any detail, no matter how trivial. Memories over-

---

20. Baldwin, *Evidence of Things Not Seen*, 153. See also Baldwin, *Notes of a Native Son*, 30–31.
21. Snyder, *Bloodlands*, 402.
22. Coker, *Men at War*, 26.
23. Doniger, *Hindus*, 689.
24. MacMillan, *Dangerous Games*, 113.
25. See Maier, "Surfeit of Memory?," 136–152.

whelmed him.[26] There was no escape or respite but death. Contemporary philosopher W. James Booth thus talks of a qualified "duty to forget, to heal ourselves, and to allow a rebirth or a strengthening of our civic ties."[27]

For Nietzsche, "active forgetfulness" could unburden the mind for deeper contemplation, if not basic living: "there could be no happiness, no cheerfulness, no hope, no pride, no *present* without forgetfulness."[28] We have seen that Nietzsche is no advocate of humility, so it's interesting that forgetting is needed for pride. The issue is how, why, and what we forget, especially if such merely sustains a false pride. It's convenient not to remember our wrongdoing, what Geoffrey H. Hartman calls anti-memory, a wilful planned position of denying historical truths and devising alternative and authoritative versions in their place.[29]

Totalitarian regimes tend to be proficient in anti-memory propaganda. Louisa Lim reports how the Chinese government concealed a June 4th-related uprising and government crackdown in Chengdu, a city in South-western China.[30] Lim writes: "what happened in Chengdu was very nearly the perfect case study in first rewriting history, then excising it altogether."[31] The powerful have a monopoly on authoritative memory, which also includes how and why people died.[32]

The need to forget is sustained by both the authorities and the masses: "There is no benefit to remembering, so why bother?"[33] some lament to Lim.

Remembering—especially via history—fuels humility. For some, to achieve what I call a humble pride may demand a type of forgetting (perhaps as minimizing) various accomplishments, praise, and accolades. Again, for those beaten down already, this step is unnecessary. Humility instead becomes another blunt weapon of the powerful, grinding the downtrodden.

---

26. Borges, "Funes the Memorious," 66. See also Blustein, *Moral Demands of Memory*, 15–19.

27. Booth, *Communities of Memory*, 145. See also Blustein, *Moral Demands of Memory*, 293.

28. Nietzsche, *Genealogy of Morals*, 58.

29. See Hartman, "Introduction," 10.

30. Lim, *People's Republic of Amnesia*, 1.

31. Ibid., 205.

32. Ibid., 205.

33. Ibid., 211.

But those individuals—or our institutional, national, and religious affiliations—smothered in claims of superiority or fame, should try to "forget" their apparent renown, uniqueness, and greatness. Why? Because such forgetting can avoid a conceit that crushes others and obstructs our need to reform, repent, and renew.[34] People believing their faith, nation, or scientific method is superior do not suddenly disbelieve their sense of grandeur. They retain it in the peripheral vestiges of their thoughts. But they can try to imagine a context (no matter how trying) in which this status would be questionable or (blasphemy) not true. Some people or institutions need inordinate help to even consider they could be wrong. Sadly the rub is how to entice the self-intoxicated to engage, not the already humble, the salt of the earth.

Failure to take responsibility for our past reveals more than a dearth of humility. Self-delusion and bloated self-importance linger and contaminate self and others.

Death No Longer the Equalizer

How we formulate or silence a memory's meaning, urgency, or value, and how we prioritize our monuments, media coverage, and media consumption, translate into life or death for millions. Memory thus effects who gets consumed, who thrives, who merely endures. It can be the difference between eternal oblivion and the hope of ongoing presence through a memorial mass or ancestor shrine. Tombs of the anonymous soldier deserve hushed silence, while for some: "Their name, their years, spelt by the unlettered muse"[35] can reveal a love more lasting than marble and diamonds. Even our pets garner such lavishing words.

For other human beings, there are only unmarked graves, or worse—lives pass and no one notices or cares. Perhaps the worst death: unmourned because unseen or forgotten while breathing and waking.

Death does not equalize all. Some deaths fuel copious tears of grief; others of exaltation. Some bodies are preserved, frozen in hope of one day resurrecting—a Lazarus of the future—others are said miraculously to fight decay, incorruptible. Some bodies are desecrated after death: Achilles dragging the body of Hector; the torture of those hung, drawn, and quartered.

---

34. See Volf, *End of Memory*, 145.
35. Grey, "Elegy."

The world remembers victims unequally. A terrorist attack from ISIS[36] in Europe garners world-wide coverage, but victims of war and atrocities in places like Syria, Afghanistan, Iraq, South Sudan, and Nigeria have almost become expected, our response blasé. The diurnal deaths of the poor even more so.

Avishai Margalit, in *The Ethics of Memory*, evaluated whether it was possible and commendable to support a thick ethic of memory in which deep concern and an expectation to remember would extend beyond our family members or tribal, national, or religious identities.[37] Viet Thanh Nguyen calls for an "ethic of recognition" and a call to remember our shared humanity and inhumanity, not simply "to remember one's own."[38] Such a hope collides with the ever-growing cases of atrocities, the impossibility of remembering them all.[39]

Memory Shards

Different theories of memory, what I'll call shards of memory, are not lacking. As historian Dan Stone writes of Holocaust Studies: "it is easy to find oneself 'at the edge of memory' (James Young), 'preserving memory' (Edward Linenthal), or 'committed to memory' (Oren Baruch Stier), examining the 'vectors of memory' (Nancy Wood), or 'remembering to forget' (Barbie Zelizer)."[40] Consider also terms like postmemory (Marianne Hirsch), collective memory (Maurice Halbwachs), prosthetic memory (Alison Landsberg), dangerous memory (Metz), intergenerational memory (Arlene Stein and Eva Hoffman), and deep memory (Lawrence Langer). In Michael Rothberg's multidirectional memory, there is solidarity both among the oppressed and among their memories, which while distinct can reinforce and not cancel the other in mutual regard or study.[41] Thus, examining postcolonial atrocities in Africa does not denude the horrors of the Shoah.

---

36. See Gerges, *ISIS*.
37. Margalit, *Ethics of Memory*.
38. Nguyen, *Nothing Ever Dies*, 79 and 9.
39. Crownshaw, Kilby, and Rowland, "Preface," x.
40. Stone, "Beyond the Mnemosyne Institute," 19.
41. Rothberg, *Multidirectional Memory*, 3.

This pluralism of memory should not be surprising, especially as I also highlight the pluralism of history,[42] another reason for humbling. Too many of us think we own history, standing on its right side. How to read history becomes a crucial task in the aim of a humbled pride, a realistic self-assessment to proper self-love and self-respect. In addition, note that "memory work is often highly gendered."[43] Gender influences how victims are treated, and how they survive or suffer.[44] Being a woman also entails additional, almost omnipresent dangers and worries in many contexts, especially from rape and other sexual violations.[45] While men commit most bodily violence, works like Wendy Lower's *Hitler's Furies* also highlights women as accomplices, if not architects, of great evils and suffering.[46] Who is exempt?

The Meaning and Ethics of History: Reading, Identifying, and Interpreting

In the West, history was suffused with progress and linearity. Whether linear or cyclical (as in China), history was rarely written (let alone endorsed) by the vanquished and subdued. History, really histories, are the stories and accounts of past and present realities and embodiedness, of peoples, tribes, nations, religions, places, objects,[47] and ideas, coded and spoken through laws, thoughts, and hopes, of records and archives, testimonies and memories, visual, auditory, olfactory, tactile, and gustatory (think Francis Bacon's "Of Studies" or Ezekiel 2:9—3:3 and Jeremiah 15:16[48]). History is this and more, buried in layers of eyewitnesses silenced, the powerless shunted, ghettoized,[49] and the potent bellowing on towering stelae, war-ravaged scrolls, grandiose or fading monuments, dusty law books and decrees, and weighty academic tomes. As Yehuda Bauer writes: "a historian's tools include the analysis of written documents of the period, of diaries, of letters, and of testimonies of

---

42. Pilario, "Revisiting Historiographies," 541.
43. Stein, *Reluctant Witnesses*, 138.
44. See Cubilié, *Women Witnessing Terror*.
45. See Bennhold, "Women Travel Migrant Trail Rife with Risk," A1.
46. Lower, *Hitler's Furies*.
47. Holzer, *Civil War in 50 Objects*.
48. For commentary, see Cook, *Hear, O Heavens*, 194.
49. On ghettoes, see Duneier, *Ghetto*.

survivors, not to mention remnants of sites."⁵⁰ Norman Davies adds: "The historian needs to use counterparts of the telescope, the microscope, the brain-scanner, and the geological probe,"⁵¹ while Jürgen Osterhammel promotes, "A feel for proportions, contradictions, and connections as well as a sense of what may be typical and representative; and second, to maintain a humble attitude of deference toward professional research."⁵²

History entails listening, an eagerness to visualize and depict multiple sides. It demands humility to acknowledge we may be wrong, unenlightened, blind, and entangled in a righteousness that seems so infallible and pure. Can only the humble perform legitimate history, really see and identify the patterns and carcasses, the slaughterbench,⁵³ as it were, and can history truly humble despite the intentions of victors who generally craft it?⁵⁴

History can and should build-up where needed; it can inspire with stories of achievement; of deep dreams reached; an evil vanquished; an overflowing of peace and healing. It can uncover what the guilty wanted to inter. It can humble through both tales of triumph and accounts of failure and despondency. History, at its best, presents the face of the other (again, not limited to human beings), and brings that face and that life to as full a flourishing as possible—the historian as novelist, detective, and artist. Historians must be attuned to varying voices, angles, and perspectives. "True history involving everything, the true historian gets involved with everything."⁵⁵

For history as a humbler, consider these five key attributes (five Ps).

History and Poverty: The Option for the Poor as Normative?

If an economic system should be judged by how it serves the most marginalized, how the destitute live and how they die, can similar assessments be made of history?⁵⁶ In Catholic Latin American liberation theology, the

---

50. Bauer, *Rethinking the Holocaust*, 24–25

51. Davies, *Europe*, 2.

52. Osterhammel, *Transformation of the World*, xvii.

53. See Hegel, *Reason in History*, 27; for commentary see Ryan, *On Politics*, 664.

54. MacMillan, *Dangerous Games*, 169.

55. Hugo, *Les Misérables*, 809.

56. National Conference of US Catholic Bishops, *Economic Justice For All*. For examples, see Dunbar-Ortiz, *Indigenous People's History*, 1; and Zinn, *People's History*, 1.

preferential option for the poor is a starting and endpoint for theological language, decrees, dogma, tomes, and study. As poor women of color are often triply oppressed, the option for the poor also demands a gendered focus.[57]

It is rooted in an active praxis committed to encountering, assessing, and changing societal injustice, whether personal, institutional, structural, religious, political, or militaristic. It has its biblical roots in the Exodus story, but is especially immersed in the life of Jesus who lived as and among the poor and marginalized, who had no money when pressed to decide whether it was lawful to pay Caesar (Mark 12:17); and who was humbled by the Syrophoenician woman (Matt 15:21–28).[58] Jesus wore humility as both an inner and outer garment, in solidarity with the stunted and condemned, the dead, the so-called dregs and scum of the world. Challenging political, economic, religious, and military injustice, speaking truth to power, he was betrayed by the leaders of his people, arrested, tortured, and murdered by the State. A typical story, but the embers of hope and a resurrection of good news—the reign of God—spread to every corner of the globe, enflamed and enveloped like meadow flowers at dawn.

All the major religions and most societies share some interest in, and require, aid for the needy.[59] The option for the poor deeply humbles the non-poor, demands humility as a foundational lens for reading and writing history. When greatness is unequivocally attached to Alexander, Emperor Wu of Han, Caesar, Augustus, Genghis Khan, Napoleon, Mao, Hitler, and Stalin because of their military hubris and political potency, at the cost of millions of lives, history fails. Representative instead is the story of Emperor Ashoka, truly great once he renounced the violence in his name after the Kalinga War.[60] He then sought to rule through peace and interfaith dialogue. History constructed of the option for the poor can liberate, indeed, transform the world.

---

57. See, Beattie, "Maternal Well-Being in Sub-Saharan Africa," 175–88.

58. Sugirtharajah, "Syrophoenician Woman," 14; see also Admirand, "'Traversing Towards the Other,'" 157–70.

59. Ryan, *On Politics*, 712.

60. See Frankopan, *Silk Roads*, 27

History and Postmodernities: The Humbling of Grand Narratives?

Situated in the context of post-Holocaust discourse, Elie Wiesel asks: "After? Did you say: after? Meaning what?"[61] Wiesel rightfully challenges the prefix placed before the Shoah as if we have moved beyond it. Instead, we remain disturbed by unanswerable questions or are too timid to trace their damning conclusions.[62] As anti-Judaism remains prolific and as genocides continue to plague our world, the prefix 'post' seems highly problematic beyond the chronological sense.

The use of postmodernism, or post-postmodernism, or postsecularism is also problematic. Where the so-called modern ends (or begins) and the postmodern commences, whether in literature, art, music, or theology is usually a matter of generalizing, and then effacing any exceptions.[63] As David Tracy notes: "There are only postmodernisms."[64]

With both hubris and a touch of humility, Western theorists like Jean-François Lyotard declared the death of grand narratives, or metanarratives. The failure of such Western narratives culminated in the Shoah. Beyond any so-called modern/postmodern divide is the ethical failure within the events and ideas constrained under both periods or notions. For Berel Lang, we should speak of a moral history ("that is ethics within history"[65]) that blends any supposed distinction between the modern and the postmodern because both deal with vast injustices.[66]

Postmodernity, inspired or in dialogue with God-talk, can liberate and attune ourselves to the needs of the peripheral. It humbles by its upstart challenges and questioning of power, identity, and continuity. It can support theologies or histories on the margins, especially for women.[67] A postmodern approach can help us see we are fragmented souls with fragmented thoughts and dreams, living fragmented history. Such fragments, as David Tracy opines, are "our spiritual situation."[68]

---

61. Wiesel, *One Generation After*, 57. See also Patterson and Roth, *After-Words*.

62. Boschki, "Teaching through Words," 248.

63. Anderson, *Origins of Postmodernity*, 3–4.

64. Tracy, "Fragments," 170.

65. Lang, "Evil Inside and Outside History," 23.

66. Ibid., 17. See also Glover, *Humanity*; and Brombert, *Musings on Mortality*, 101.

67. Fulkerson, "Feminist Theology," 125.

68. Tracy, "Fragments," 173; on literature, the postmodern, and belief, see Samway, *Flannery O'Connor*, 250.

Without fragments any semi-coherent notion of postmodernism would be impossible. Fragments provide evidence of what was once possibly whole. It may elide a God of fragments amidst an evolutionary whirling. The unknown can lead to humility (panic, too).

We are immersed in ruptures, vacuities, the trace. If there is a time of day, it is the gloaming or the aurora. Humility shares a similar opaqueness: it is both hope for illumination and renewal; or the dying of light, submission to darkness. Relevant faiths are broken, wounded, fractured, alienated,[69] momentary. While radical and extreme, we also encroach upon Mark Taylor's A/Theology.[70] We question permanent, ongoing religious identities, awash in the plethora of religious and atheist choice and conversions, what Charles Taylor refers to as "fragilization."[71]

Postmodernism's strengths are in its hesitations and traces, as evidence remains murky and conflicting. Acknowledging ignorance can obligate us to go beyond treating one another with mere deferential respect. Such self-doubt can propel us to uphold another's way of life. It is this shred of doubt that I want to uphold.

Historians, too, need to incorporate such doubts even while combatting falsity and promoting truth. They should also be leery of promoting what is definitive or unchallengeable. Postmodern critiques help to avoid this error. They expect doubt and welcome evidence that challenges final claims. Doubt propels the historian for more viewpoints, fact-checks, and transparency.

With grand narratives questioned, more competing local and contextual versions flourish. Although truth-claims are not neutralized, seeds of doubt demand ongoing study. Hearing all sides becomes standard.[72]

History and Pluralism: Truth and Objectivity Dethroned?

Historian Norman Davies writes: "History can be written at any magnification. One can write the history of the universe on a single page, or

---

69. Fasching, *Ethical Challenge of Auschwitz and Hiroshima*, 5.
70. See M. C. Taylor, "Erring," 514–33.
71. C. Taylor, *Secular Age*, 834–35 n. 19.
72. Beard, *Confronting the Classics*, 171–72. For critiques of postmodernism, see Rieger, "Theology, Power of Margins," 189; Field, "On (Re)Centering the Margins," 46–47; Gonzalez, "Who is Americana/o?," 60fn6; and Loomba, *Colonialism/Postcolonialism*, xii.

the life cycle of a mayfly in forty volumes."[73] Either way, choices must be made.[74]

Multiple perspectives hint at our need to acknowledge limitations.[75] Such limits challenge patriarchal, monopolistic, or totalitarian tendencies. Pluralism, aligned with postmodernity, allows the possibility that another history, path, or tradition may be more or equally true. As David Tracy states: "All our religious traditions are pluralistic, fragmentary, and ambiguous in their histories."[76] Such ambiguity is a further acknowledgment of our limits and need for humility in order to understand, write, and interpret history.[77]

Pluralism is most useful as a background philosophy of how we approach, analyze, and judge the truth-claims of one another and the history we are trying to construct, revise, or evaluate.

Postcolonial History: Past Events as Power-Plays?

Postcolonial studies brutally paints a picture of the powerful dominating the subaltern with moments of liberation often followed by ongoing or hidden neo-colonialist laws, agendas, or practices. As an academic movement, it developed in the 1970s, especially through the work of pioneer figures like Frantz Fanon and Edward W. Said, and after the liberation movements in Africa and Latin and South America[78]—along with the realization that many of the people in these countries were still subjugated and not truly free. In theology, it builds upon the tenets of liberation theology and the option for the poor addressed above.[79]

Salient truths include:

1. A postcolonial perspective highlights past and present tendencies to dismiss the Other and her views, hopes, and needs as misguided and unenlightened. Such dismissal corresponds with acts of injustice through economic, political, social, religious, and military

---

73. Davies, *Europe*, 1.
74. Cunliffe, *Europe Between the Oceans*, viii. See also Meier, *Culture of Freedom*.
75. Gebara, *Out of the Depths*, 76.
76. Tracy, "Western Hermeneutics and Interreligious Dialogue," 17. See also Cornille, "Conditions for Inter-Religious Dialogue," 22.
77. Tracy, *Plurality and Ambiguity*, 70.
78. See Coronil, "Latin American Postcolonial Studies," 221–40.
79. Keller, Nausner, and Rivera, "Introduction," 5.

institutions. Such histories render the Other absent, powerless, expendable, and exotic.

2. Postcolonial studies unmasks imperialist or colonial agendas. Like postmodernity, postcolonialism challenges injustice within foundational religious, literary, and legal texts and traditions.[80]

3. When all is contestable, dialogue becomes crucial as we are called to question, challenge, and listen to one another explain, enact, and illustrate these changing, flexible, and still-to-be discerned meanings.

4. Postcolonial studies demands action and structural change.

History as Pardon: A Surfeit of Apologies—Or Not Enough?

History demands awareness and need for apology, for seeking pardon, and where feasible, making amends and restitution. History as the study of the past, reveals conditions and hopes in the present; and where those conditions and hopes are stunted, history can provide analysis and explanations of causes, culpability, and negligence. In the concluding chapter, I will speak more on forgiveness, so only a few words here need suffice, drawing together what has been seen through the other lenses above. History viewed through the optics of the impoverished exposes how individual, societal, governmental, and structural choices, laws, and practices create, sustain, and augment the gap between the wealthy and the abysmally poor.

With such awareness and solidarity come deeper questions of how this state of affairs has arisen, and the sheer number of desperate and struggling people, demanding investigation, responsibility—and more than likely—forgiveness. Usually, forgetting, blame, and excuses are the arsenal of replies.[81]

Together these five lenses of history not only help us craft the most authentic and liberating accounts; they humble. In such humility, perhaps, is the hope for rectifying past failures, the facing of present calamities, and the avoidance of future ones.

---

80. See Sugirtharajah, *The Postcolonial Biblical Reader*; Pui-lan, Compier, and Rieger, *Empire*; Dube, *Postcolonial Feminist Interpretation of the Bible*; Donaldson and Pui-lan, *Postcolonialism, Feminism, & Religious Discourse*; Treble and Russell, *Hagar, Sarah, and Their Children*; and Pui-lan, *Hope Abundant*.

81. See Isenberg, *White Trash*, 1–14.

To illustrate these ideas, I will turn to the fraught history (and ongoing moral failure and responsibility) of the present repercussions of black slavery, racism, and historical and political silence in the United States. As Michael Eric Dyson writes, while reflecting on the inauguration of Trump in 2017: "America is in trouble, and a lot of trouble—perhaps most of it—has to do with race."[82]

"I Feel Good, Coach, Real Good": Ethics, History and the Forsaken: Autobiographical Sketches

I don't know how to begin, which is to say, we must begin before the beginning, before the once upon a time cliché. I already mentioned I grew up in a neighborhood with a rich Jewish presence that likely contributed to my interest in Jewish-Christian dialogue. There were no black people on my street, nor in my grammar school. Little changed in the high school and universities I attended. This contrasts deeply to my wife who was a minority as a white girl in Poughkeepsie High School. She laughs at the idea of my writing this section—reflecting on race relations in America. What I still don't get, my wife reminds me, is that in addition to the race divide, where she grew up class and money further separated people. Both the poor black and white kids may not have had dinner the night before.[83] I had at least two separations with those kids I want to talk about now: race and class. As usual, my wife is right and I am humbled, but I persevere.

Growing up, fuelled by what I now see as a mixed bag of pity as condescension and a genuine need and privilege to give back, to volunteer, I left my safe, sheltered privileged world and entered the worlds of them, the (whisper) black people. It started as volunteer work, serving as a type of big brother in the predominantly black and poor neighborhood of Spinney Hill, hidden away, but also surrounded, by the excessively wealthy homes of Manhasset, Plandome, and Great Neck, New York. Spinney Hill, named after a white rich export merchant named Joseph Spinney, is an area originally inhabited by the servants of the rich estates that then became a predominantly black area. I came to volunteer in an

---

82. Dyson, *Tears We Cannot Stop*, 3. See also Whitehead, *Underground Railroad*, 285.

83. See, Vance, *Hillbilly Elegy*; and Gest, *White Working Class*.

after-school program called Adventures in Learning, which remains a safe place for kids to go, do homework, and receive guidance and support.

When volunteering, I would sit down with various kids at one of the homework tables, and help with reading or math. The families they came from were often troubled, but I knew so little back then. As a Big Brother to two of the kids, I would sometimes take them for pizza or to play basketball at the park.

It pained me, nearly broke me, to hear the stories, either from the children, or from my mother who taught at their school and also volunteered: kids smelling when they came to school, wearing the same clothes, while wealthy classmates wore designer outfits. Many Spinny Hill fathers were in jail or gone; young single mothers struggled with poverty; drug abuse; stories too common now, but drowning ones nonetheless.

In college in Washington DC, my education on America and race really began. 1994: the city was perhaps starting to recover, but signs of blight and a racial apocalypse seemed evident almost everywhere, outside the enclaves of Georgetown and Military Avenue—areas I wouldn't know until I returned to DC after my year in the Jesuit Volunteer Corps. There was a hostility I sensed, or fear from the propaganda or reality. In a car with friends, on North Capitol Street, where broken homes and broken families looked out in the distance to the morally-broken US Capitol, a black man angrily punched the hood of my friend's car while crossing the street: "You don't belong here." He glared menacingly.

I could feel the racism—conscious or unconscious—creeping into my thoughts and rationalizations, succumbing to the us/them language. At a crossroads, I wanted to do something positive, even if under the false mantle of "savior."

Throughout college, I was privileged to volunteer as a basketball (and soccer) coach at St. Gabriel's Grammar School in the Petworth area of Northwest DC. Then it was predominantly African American: a no-go area to the white college kids of CUA. To the kids, I was "Coach," but also Larry Bird, both a joke and a compliment as they respected my jump shot. Bird was also the only decent white player they could name. If white people were spoken about in a true but cutting way, I'd get, "Not you, of course, Coach." I'd like to think skin color has a way of blending and blinding in a good way, too. But a few years of tender smiles and care are not enough. My wife rightly corrected me: skin color never went away. I only imagined otherwise, another betrayal of my race and class privilege.

Memories spill over, but just a few to reveal my own limited awareness of the gaps and holes, the hypocrisies and injustice in the racial landscape of America. When I first started coaching, I usually took the bus back to CUA at night from Petworth. Standing in the darkness by the mostly deserted street, I knew this was risky, but what other choice did I have? One night, the grandma of our point guard Charles (nicknamed Smurf because of his size), called me over. "That you, Peter?"

She asked what I was doing out here alone, and said it was too dangerous at this time of night. She needn't add for someone like me. She insisted I go to her home and wait until her older son could give me a lift. I walked back to her house. It soon became clear that her son would be delayed. I suggested a cab, but the reality was: "Not too many cabs will come out here." Too dangerous. It became too late for any bus and walking was not an option. After another hour, still no cab came. Eventually the son arrived and I was glad to get a ride. From that point on, the devoted CYO coordinator of the program, Darren Foster, would pick me up from CUA and drive me home in the school van, the same red van I would use to take all the kids to their games. I never had to take another bus from Petworth again. There were always options and resources, escape plans—for me, anyway.

Most of the teams the kids played in CYO were from wealthy, white suburban areas in Maryland. I always had my players dress in shirt and tie or the nicest clothes they had—mostly because that was what I had to do on the university soccer team—but also to teach them some life lessons beyond the court. None of these kids were going to make the NBA (it was the local B team, after all). For one outing, I took them to see the movie "Hoop Dreams" in Dupont Circle, a trendy area in the District that none of them had been to before. I wanted them to enjoy the outing but also think about life choices.[84]

Taking them to the games, I can still see others stare at me and 11 or 12 inner-city African American kids strutting into suburban gyms. In stores, the workers got nervous. At a 7-11, an anouncement sounds over the loudspeaker reminding us that we are being watched by security cameras. I never heard that voice when I entered the store on my own. For some of these kids, the practices and games were their safety net from the streets, where gangs, drugs, and violence were threats and companions. One year we had too many interested boys and I had to tell some

---

84. For an account of street basketball as a transcendent experience for black American men, see Woodbine, *Black Gods*.

kids they didn't make the team. I tried to plead with Darren to expand a few names but some were still left behind; there just wasn't enough room. I was crushed with guilt as I apologized to each boy individually. What happened to them after?

Our "gym" for practice was in the basement of a church. It had four cement pillars in the middle of the "court," like impenetrable, or slow-footed, opponents. You had to look up when you dribbled and be aware of where you were passing, or the ball would ricochet off a pillar, or you'd bang your knee or head. I incorporated drills where the kids had to dribble around the pillars or bounce pass between them. The ceiling was also ridiculously low, so most jump shots had to be angled just right, more like a line drive if you were tall.

What must the kids have thought of the spacious gyms of those other teams, with fiberglass backboards, airy, high ceilings? It reinforced the false notion that all white people were rich.

In one capacious gym, my players gaped at a closet-full of new basketballs. Their eyes widened, calculating. After the game, as my team climbed into the back of the red van, it appeared they had become pregnant, their bellies bulging.

"Let's go. Get the balls and bring them back," I said. "Now."

"Aww, Coach, come on, you see how many they have?"

We were lucky to have one or two among all of us for practice.

We were a good team, played in the championship game, won easily. One player, James, from a particularly troubled home, had missed the majority of practices. The rule was clear: you had to go to practices to play in the game. Wanting to make him feel a part of the team, I let him wear the uniform but told him he may not get in the game. He smiled broadly, glad to be accepted back. Easy going kid; I liked him. We won by 30 points, never close. I let James in the game for a few minutes. He was a big kid who could grab rebounds on both sides of the glass. When the game was over, I shook hands with the coach and that was that. Or so I thought. Weeks later I got a call from a very disappointed Darren. The coach of the other team had protested the game saying I didn't play one player on the team the required amount of minutes. Without CYO contacting me, his team was awarded the first place trophies. Devastating. What would the kids think?

I tried contacting the coach over a period of three weeks, like a detective tracking a crime scene. I was nineteen then, maybe he was in his early 40s, like I am now. He was used to success and getting his way, so why return my call? I was persistent. Eventually, I reached him at home, explained the situation: about the kids and their struggles and how hard they had worked amidst so many temptations and disadvantages. I explained why James was given limited minutes, that he could have been kept off the team, but I wanted to give him some hope for next year. Sometimes coaches don't play kids who aren't very skilled; that was obviously not the reason with James. I spoke to the coach as someone who was like him, using my race and class card, having played in a wealthy area, too, and argued for how this was not fair. What kind of message were we teaching the kids on both teams? He was unmoved.

I said why don't we play again to determine who should be in first? He hid in excuses. His players were busy with other sports. He said he appreciated my dedication and slinked off the phone. I had to tell my team the news.

They took it better than me, as if expected. Were they already schooled and jaded that things were stacked against them? That the rich white kids win even when they lose?

Fortunately, my parents volunteered to buy the kids first place trophies, which were presented to them at a pizza party I gave at CUA and paid for by my uncle, Mike Ryan.

One more story, which I have been delaying, avoiding, trying to decide whether to use another name, a false name. Eddie Ward. He was, as far as I knew, just another kid on the team trying to find his way. I see him now in a team photo, eyes a bit glassy, his skin almond, his black hair curly. He had gone missing for a bit, like some of the kids did: the streets or family problems or school problems. I only heard vague reasons why, but when he came back one practice, he was in good form, smiling. "I feel good, Coach. Real good." He said he was ready to be committed to the team. Then he disappeared again. Weeks later, Darren brought me the news. Eddie had been found dead in a house in Southeast DC. Initial reports in *The Washington Post* said Eddie's body was disfigured from roach and rat bite marks or from a fight. The report was unclear, as was potential drug use and signs of tracking on his arm.[85] 8th grade. He had been in and out of foster care and changed schools. "I feel good, Coach, real good." At various times I think of Eddie, especially if seeing him in that team photo I still have. While writing this chapter I reached out to Debbi Wilgoren, one of the journalists who wrote *The Washington Post*

---

85. Wilgoren and Thomas-Lester, "Boy Found Dead."

piece about his death. She sent me links to two subsequent reports that included autopsy details that Eddie died from an enlarged heart and showed no signs of drug use.[86] Why he ended up in that abandoned closest in a dilapidated home on Yuma Street in Southeast DC still remains unknown, though.

Back then I didn't know what questions to ask or how to interpret what I saw and felt, so different from my own upbringing. It was mostly "Unwritten history" to me, as W. E. B. Du Bois could contend.[87] But there remained something wrong, something not shared or told in the history and way of life in my head and textbooks and what these kids had to endure and live through. I needed to know more because there were links, bridges from my world and their world and the reasons for the separation that divides us. These are memories we want to bury and hide.[88] Conceal. Rationalize. Deny. As Toni Morrison remarks: "The United States is a culture where the past is always erased and America is the innocent future." It is a "national amnesia."[89] The deeper I read in past and present histories, the more I learned and the more humbled I became of my own identity and upbringing.

That's the beginning, anyway.

History in Color: White Trying to Read Black

America needs another civil rights movement. In Morrison's *Sula*[90] she writes how poor blacks were forced to live in "the Bottom" until even this land was purchased by wealthy whites.[91] False starts, false promises. Redlining occurred in various cities as black people bought homes on paper but were swindled by white lawyers and bankers who charged exorbitant rates and took back the property on the slightest of infrac-

---

86. Lewis, "Extensive Forensic Testing"; and Wartofsky, "A Lesson in the Language of Grief."

87. Du Bois, *Souls of Black Folk*, 23.

88. Buell, *Dream of the Great American Novel*, 66. The quotation in Buell's text is from Taylor-Guthrie, *Conversations with Toni Morrison*, 257; see also Morrison, *Beloved*.

89. Buell, *Dream of the Great American Novel*, 330. See also Baldwin, *Notes of a Native Son*, 35.

90. Morrison, *Sula*, 163.

91. Ibid., 166. For a forgotten history of such "bottoms" among emancipated blacks and poor immigrants in America, see Goff, *Shantytown*, 180.

tions, real or imagined.[92] More recently, the rollback of affirmative action and other civil rights achievements have picked up pace. Jim Ruttenberg reports how the successes of the 1965 Voting Rights Act and other civil rights milestones are being successfully challenged, watered down, and in some cases, overturned.[93] Perhaps Biggar Thomas was right to think: "Never again did he want to feel anything like hope."[94]

Tragically, what should have begun the healing and process of justice was instead denied through flagrant acts of racism and anti-black violence and discrimination or subtle forms of racism through segregation policies. The struggle still endures amidst Black Lives Matter and a US President who failed to immediately denounce white supremacists at a rally in Charlottesville, Virginia, in August 2017.[95]

Racism remains a latent, unaddressed sickness of false superiority, a malicious pride seeking to subdue and conquer. Racism has endured—just a little more slyly, covertly, and legally, evident from the failed relief effort towards poor, mostly African Americans after Hurricane Katrina[96] to racial rhetoric in Trump's 2016 successful presidential campaign. Consider also America's Third-World ghettoes, glaring reminders and evidence of the value, or lack of value, attributed to poor black and brown bodies and minds. Numerous studies also showed blacks and other minorities suffered disproportionately in the recessions from 2008.[97] Financial situations are so precarious that "even a small financial setback can be devastating."[98]

This denial is wilful and culpable. "I am invisible, understand," we read in Ralph Ellison's *Invisible Man*, "simply because people refuse to see me."[99] There are so many we do not see. "In our Baptist church," bell hooks reflects, "we had learned women were not supposed to preach, were not worthy enough to even cross the threshold of god's anointed space—the pulpit."[100] Layers of sightlessness, a hierarchy within hierarchy of the unseen.

92. Desmond, *Evicted*, 251–52. See also Moore, *Southside*, 31–33.
93. Rutenberg, "Dream Ondone."
94. Wright, *Native Son*, 340.
95. For theological responses, see Lloyd and Prevo, *Anti-Blackness*.
96. Crownshaw, "Natural History of Testimony?," 164.
97. Formisano, *Plutocracy in America*, 24.
98. Kiel, "Debt and the Racial Wealth Gap," 7.
99. Ellison, *Invisible Man*, 3.
100. hooks, *Memories of Girlhood*, 74. hooks's lesbian identity is a further mark of marginalization and oppression; ibid., 22.

How much of our identities are forged by false, concealed histories? Baldwin touches consistently on this linking and bond of the oppressed and the oppressor. In *Notes of a Native Son*, he writes: "Our dehumanization of the Negro then is indivisible from our dehumanization of ourselves: the loss of our own identity is the price we pay for the annulment of his."[101] Similarly, in *The Fire Next Time* he proclaims: "Therefore, whatever white people do not know about Negroes reveals, precisely and inexorably, what they do not know about themselves."[102] This awareness of the Other through history does more than humble. It restores and repairs identity and the potential for relationship. But only if we see, admit, and rectify.

Let me close this chapter with a few recent books that are required reading on the above issues.

Slavery by Another Name

In *The New Jim Crow*, Michelle Alexander convincingly shows how in a post-civil-rights age, where law in America is supposedly colorblind, slavery among poor African Americans goes by different means: prison, probation, and poverty. As Alexander writes: "Today it is perfectly legal to discriminate against criminals in nearly all the ways that it was once legal to discriminate against African Americans."[103] While there has been a black president[104] and praised black culture and sports stars—"black exceptionalism"[105]—the majority of black youth grow up in blighted neighborhoods with poor education and limited future opportunities. Prison time, or, more importantly a prison record or "label,"[106] further limits opportunities or even the use of government aid or housing. Much of the wave of black male imprisonment was unleashed during the age of the bloated and failed War on Drugs,[107] which grossly affected poor,

---

101. Baldwin, *Notes of a Native Son*, 30.
102. Baldwin, *Fire Next Time*, 44.
103. Alexander, *New Jim Crow*, 2; see also ibid., 94.
104. With Trump's election, the role and legacy of Barack Obama and the question of race in America remains widely debated. See Phillips, "Farewell to the Chief," 16–27; and Smith, *Invisible Man*, 195–215; on the Catholic vote and Trump, see Millies, *Good Intentions*.
105. Alexander, *Jim Crow*, 14.
106. Ibid., 14.
107. Ibid., 74–81. See also Hinton, *From the War on Poverty*.

black males more than any other group, especially compared to white Americans who were as frequent drug users and in many cases, the prime buyers and sellers.[108] Alexander notes: "In Washington D.C., our nation's capital, it is estimated that three out of four young black men (and nearly all those in the poorest neighborhoods) can expect to serve time in prison."[109] I think again of my St. Gabriel kids.

For Alexander, these policies have resulted in a "racial caste system."[110] The poor, young black male is a Dalit in America. Once born and raised within such a caste, odds were stacked against rising out of it.

Echoing Baldwin in the title of her final chapter, "The Fire This Time," Alexander reinforces the predominance of denial in this caste system—as the majority of us refuse to recognize the links between historical and present injustice.[111] She closes with a quotation from Baldwin, including these important lines: "But it is not permissible that the authors of devastation should also be innocent. It is the innocence which constitutes the crime."[112]

There is danger in such presumed innocence.[113] So, too, humility, which is why a humble pride or scrappy humility has been advocated; a humility brought down to earth by awareness of false and failed flight. It rises because it is earthbound. Humility indeed can reach the sidereal through its groundedness. Can the same be said for overcoming racism?

Running

This innocence is hard to maintain in light of the glaring evidence. Sociology Professor Alice Goffman spent six years living in a destitute inner-city neighborhood of Philadelphia (deemed Sixth Street). She narrates the lives of poor, black inner-city individuals caught up in the War on

---

108. On the dilemmas of African American leaders in the 1970s and their initial support of the war on crime, see Forman, *Locking Up Our Own;* on liberal Democrats supporting prison growth, see Ambar, *American Cicero,* 92; on the moral and civic responsibilities of urban African Americans despite unjust social and judicial structures, see Shelby, *Dark Ghettoes.*

109. Alexander, *Jim Crow,* 7.

110. Ibid., 12.

111. Ibid., 223. See also Dyson, *Tears We Cannot Stop,* 96–103.

112. Baldwin, *Fire Next Time,* 5–6.

113. In terms of innocence and violence, see Toumani, *There Was and There Was Not,* 6.

Drugs and the racial caste system, outlined by Alexander. Goffman is Caucasian. In her methodological note at the end of her book Goffman discusses how she "negotiated [her] privilege" as she came from "an educated and well-off family."[114]

Overcoming initial resistance, Goffman embedded herself with a group of young African-American men and their girlfriends and mothers. Moving, enlightening, frustrating, and absorbing, the work gives an outsider's inside/outside views of inner-city perils of a group of African Americans and their incessant and debilitating run-ins with the police and the law, affecting and dominating all aspects of their lives: jobs, love, family, and health. Depending on your background and upbringing (class and race, especially), this will seem possibly creepy and voyeuristic. While reviews gushed about the work, *Slate's* Dwayne Betts, who was convicted of carjacking and spent eight years in prison, argues: "The book suffers because it panders. Unwittingly, Goffman gives ammunition to tough-on-crime politicians who want to believe that urban areas are breeding grounds for crime and lawlessness."[115] I am partial to Betts's insights, but can also see how the work could be didactic and life-changing, as an educated white American tried to get a deeper perspective of the ongoing failures in many parts of American cities (and increasingly, the outer burbs where many of the city's poor are exiled).[116] Through this journey, Goffman can share these insights and struggles of the people she studied and came to call friends.

Goffman endangers her life and body in doing her research,[117] witnessing and experiencing acts of police violence and interrogation.[118] She testifies that "Fourteen times during my first eighteen months of near daily observation, I watched the police punch, choke, kick, stomp on, or beat young men with their nightsticks."[119] She immersed herself in the heartbreak and tragedy of the lives she observed. Controversially, she even crosses a legal line[120] between observing and abetting criminal

---

114. Goffman, *On the Run*, 228–29. See also Contreras, *Stickup Kids*, 17–18.

115. Betts, "Stoop Isn't the Jungle."

116. See Moskowitz, *How to Kill a City*.

117. Goffman hides Mike in her house for four days while he was "hot"—wanted by the police (*On the Run*, 46).

118. Ibid., 60–61 and 70–71.

119. Ibid., 4.

120. See Lubet, "Ethics on the Run"; Goffman, "Reply to Professor Lubet's Critique"; Lubet, "Alice Goffman's Denial of Murder Conspiracy"; and Lewis-Krauss, "The Trials of Alice Goffman."

actions when she drives with one of her confidantes, Mike, seeking the murderer of another, Chuck. Mike had a gun. As Goffman admits: "I got into the car because, like Mike and Reggie, I wanted Chuck's killer to die."[121] It is a touch dramatic and naive but hints at how visceral and sharp such feelings can be, illuminating a glimpse of daily, inescapable reality for many.

Goffman's text is very critical of the police.[122] Attending funerals or the birth of one's children, letting an uncle or brother stay at one's house—any of these actions, according to Goffman, could result in some indictment if the family member is wanted for a crime or, in the first two cases, you have broken parole.

Embedded in the perspective of those running from the law, Goffman's text does not include anyone like homicide detective John Skaggs, for example, who worked tirelessly to find the killers of those murdered in South Central Los Angeles when those deaths are often deemed unimportant through racist and classicist attitudes.[123] Nevertheless, police brutality remains a dark undercurrent in our history and present-day reality. Goffman's text, despite its flaws, testifies to America's racist reality and the failure of law to address and heal it.

Poverty, Drug-Dealing, Community

Like Goffman, Waverly Duck is a sociologist who embedded himself in a poor, predominantly African American city to study the lives of its marginalized members. As an African American who grew up in a similarly rough neighborhood, Duck has a different kind of insider/outsider status. In *No Way Out: Precarious Living in the Shadow of Poverty and Drug Dealing*, he achieves more balance than Goffman by consulting the views of local police working those beats. But he in no way conceals the harm and struggles the poorest residents must endure. He asks: "What options do families have when unemployment is unusually high, when schools are not performing, when neighborhoods are overrun with crime, when law enforcement does not consistently respond, and when a third of children live in poverty?"[124] Duck wants readers to see life through

121. Goffman, *On the Run*, 260.
122. Ibid., 197.
123. Levoy, *Ghettoside*, 128. See also Knafo, "A Black Police Officer's Fight Against the N.Y.P.D."
124. Duck, *No Way Out*, 134.

the eyes of the residents living under these difficult conditions.[125] How constricted is the freedom and potential of youth in such contexts? As he writes: "Practices such as zero-tolerance policies in the schools and the near-universal criminalization of young black men compromise their future prospects."[126] His work is based on "seven years of ethnographic observation and interviews" on a street he calls Lyford, in a town he calls Bristol Hill, based on a "small city in the northeastern United States."[127] Ultimately Duck contends that contrary to outside judgments looking at inner-city ghettos, there is often a moral and logical order, "a highly developed social organization,"[128] against the perceived anarchy and moral vacuum of areas burdened by drug dealers and crime. In the case of Bristol Hill, drug dealers were local, often kids who grew up on the block and were part of the community, even as they were also outsiders because of their role.

"The problems that plague Lyford Street originated in a history of racial discrimination in both employment and housing," Duck argues.[129]

Redemption and Hope

Bigger Thomas, broken, had cursed hope, but dreamers and the ever hopeful are desperately needed, especially in dark, wintry times of isolation, desolation, and rampant injustice. Martin Luther King Jr.'s dream may be somewhat tarnished by ongoing failures, setbacks, hypocrisy, and corruption, but it remains one of the most important dreams worth striving for. Bryan Stevenson has spent over thirty years seeking to defend those on death row, especially poor, black men, and incarcerated children.[130] Reflecting the best of humanity, let alone American ideals, he writes in *Just Mercy*: "The true measure of our character is how we treat the poor, the disfavored, the accused, the incarcerated, and the condemned."[131] Unfortunately, the facts bear a negative judgment. Bryant notes: "Today we have the highest incarceration rate in the world.

---

125. Ibid., 5. See also Rios, *Punished*.
126. Duck, *No Way Out*, 112.
127. Ibid., 2.
128. Ibid., 3.
129. Ibid., 57.
130. Stevenson, *Just Mercy*, 125.
131. Ibid., 18.

The prison population has increased from 300,000 people in the early 1970s to 2.3 million people today. There are nearly 6 million people on probation or on parole ... One in every three black male babies born in this century is expected to be incarcerated."[132] The so-called War on Drugs has accomplished little, not drastically lowering crime, but succeeding in normalizing incarceration for many black youth. This incarceration is also coupled by the daily assault and murder of black lives coupled with a societal acceptance of such loss. No media coverage, no justice. "We all share in the condition of brokenness," Stevenson writes, "even if our brokenness is not equivalent."[133] He continues: "We have a choice. We can embrace our humanness, which means embracing our broken natures and the compassion that remains our best hope for healing."[134] Seeing our brokenness is at the core of a robust humility coupled with a calling to mend and heal. Stevenson embodies such a balance.

Reckoning

The denial and blindness have endured too long, though. James Baldwin pricked white conscience with a razor-sharp honesty that was as rooted in love as it was in judgment.[135] A similar balancing act is found in the work of Ta-Nehisi Coates. Like Alexander's final chapter in *The New Jim Crow*, the influence of James Baldwin is stamped all over Ta-Nehisi Coates's memoir *Between the World and Me*. It's structured as a letter to his then fifteen-year-old son, Samori, like James Baldwin's letter to his nephew James in "My Dungeon Shook." The title of the memoir also comes from Baldwin's *The Fire Next Time*. In his memoirs, extended essays in *The Atlantic*, and his comic-book writing for the *Black Panther* series, Coates has helped raise the profile of extant racism in America.

Crucially, Coates calls for a "national reckoning that would lead to spiritual renewal."[136] Such a reckoning demands transparency and a

---

132. Ibid., 15. Jill Levoy adds that 40% of those murdered in America are black males (*Ghettoside*, 6).
133. Stevenson, *Just Mercy*, 289.
134. Ibid., 289.
135. Baldwin, *Fire Next Time*, 95.
136. Coates, "Case for Reparations," section IX. *The Atlantic* essays cited here have been collected in Coates, *We Were Eight Years in Power*. For an excellent review essay, see Pinckney, "Afro-Pessimist Temptation." On reparations, see Robinson, *Debt*; and Baptist, *Half Has Never Been Told*.

desire for repentance. "From America's very founding," he writes in a Baldwinian tone, "the pursuit of the right to labor, and the right to live free of whipping and of the sale of one's children, were verboten for blacks."[137] Like Duck, Alexander, and Goffman, Coates points to the devastating incarceration blight upon inner-city black Americans and other marginalized groups: "Our carceral state banished American citizens to a grey wasteland far beyond the promises and protections the government grants its other citizens."[138] The consequences for black families has been catastrophic, economically, politically, and spiritually. Unemployment or pay at minimum wage almost forces ex-offenders into illicit economic activity for survival.

Coates is haunted by the number of young black people killed in police custody in the last few years: Eric Garner,[139] Michael Brown,[140] Freddie Gray,[141] Tamir Rice,[142] and Prince Carmen Jones.[143] Looming over all of this is Coates's worry about his son. Such killings have a legacy and a history.[144] This chapter, and the work as a whole, is a small step in that return and reckoning.

Closing: History, Humility, and the Hood

Candid as always, Coates writes of humility: "'The meek shall inherit the earth' meant nothing to me. The meek were battered in West Baltimore, stomped out at Walbrook Junction, bashed up on Park Heights, and raped in the showers of the city jail."[145]

Such a reality has been looming over this work from its inception. The battered, bashed-up, and raped need a certain kind of humility, but it is not a priority. In a work extolling dialogue, what about dialoguing with the dead, or the dead-in-life as Holocaust survivor Charlotte Delbo

---

137. Coates, "Black Family in the Age of Mass Incarceration," section IV.

138. Ibid., section I.

139. Greenberg, "We're Not Going to Stand for This Anymore."

140. See Pinckney, "In Ferguson"; Flores, "When Discourse Breaks Down," 101–10; and Hill, *Nobody*, 1–29.

141. Stolberg and Oppel, "Suspects in Gray Case," A25; and Coates, "Nonviolence as Compliance."

142. Coates, *Between the World and Me*, 9.

143. Ibid., 77. See also King, "Our Demand."

144. Coates, *Between the World and Me*, 111; see also ibid., 6.

145. Ibid., 28.

writes?[146] What then? What truths remain? Do not all faiths get swallowed in the fires of Auschwitz, the killing fields of Cambodia, and the "machete season" of Rwanda?[147] In the next chapter, we turn to witnesses of such evils, in what I call testimonies of mass atrocities. On their own, they do more than enough to humble, if not annul, any kind of faith or sense of progress.

---

146. Delbo, *Auschwitz and After*, 224.
147. Hatzfeld, *Machete Season*.

7

Testimonies, Witnessing, and Moral Failure

Testimony: A Reflection

Some are wizened, others jaded, their eyes seeing through it all. Of the glories, achievements, celestial phrases and rituals of various religions, philosophies, and sciences, they know. Of national myths that lionize glory and freedom, their bruised bodies and souls shiver and stammer. Of petitions and prayers, covenants of protection and lands, of deities healing and resurrecting, they linger, bemused or forlorn, sometimes accusatory; sometimes foreboding. Of bright claims of superiority, purity, and near-perfection, they darken as reminder, as blight, as accusation, as witness, as testimony.[1] Histories blanket them in lies and anonymity; their mass gravesites eviscerated; legal rights and dignity crushed with impunity; identity and language ghettoized; memories disputed and denied counsel. Despite death, they still speak. We can sometimes even hear them, if we strain to listen.

But they smell. They reek of decay and god-killing loss. Their faces and stories repulse children. They yearn and mock justice. Nothing can fully heal, compensate, or punish. The unforgivable and the

---

1. See Felman and Laub, *Testimony*; Young, *Writing and Rewriting the Holocaust*; Langer, *Holocaust Testimonies*; Caruth, *Unclaimed Experience*; Cubilié, *Women Witnessing Terror*; Waxman, *Writing the Holocaust*; Wieviorka, *Era of the Witness*; Goldenberg and Millen, *Testimony, Tensions, and Tikkun*; Stover, *Witnesses*; Matthäus, *Approaching an Auschwitz Survivor*; Crownshaw, Kilby, and Rowland, *Future of Memory*; Glowacka, *Disappearing Traces*; Trezise, *Witnessing Witnessing*; Rowland and Kilby, *Future of Testimony*; Shenker, *Reframing Holocaust Testimony*; and Finkel, *Ordinary Jews*.

unredeemable shadow them. They sicken, painting dystopic pictures of our world and of our fellow human beings. They slay gods in their prayers and groans. They are part Medusa, part sun. They hold up mirrors and we desperately, cravenly, turn away. Because we have to: both for our sanity and to avoid shaming them. If we stare too long and too intently, without respite, without distracting joy, we, too, can become frozen and blinded. And those of us shielded and cocooned from such depravity can never really understand. No matter how much we read, watch, or even listen. We shame them with our facile use of facts and contextual references. We shame them when all they wanted was simple joys, unimaginable joys, whatever basic life consists of, and we mope and groan and curse—without real reason or substance. They want us to remember, seek justice, and prevent such ills from happening again. They do not want more martyrs. They want to know somewhere, some child is laughing, is happy; that innocent mirth is still possible.

Unlike them, the rest of us know nothing of that abyss of starvation, abandonment, or violation, of senseless violence and useless knowledge; of death and decay everywhere, pervading the living and the unborn. We still hope—or so we should. We speak of love and—and—humility as if these are meaningful, possible, and trustworthy. Humility is mocked and trampled in such worlds; an abettor and abattoir. The humble child sex victim; the meek, fleeing Tutsi or Auschwitz prisoner—easy prey. Humility is almost an accomplice to the crime. If such a virtue has any meaning, it's a new and possibly terrifying one.

Such testimonies can shatter all preconceived or elegant ideas. They humble in ways that can also destroy. To repeat: no religion, nation, philosophy, or science can avoid their gaze for too long. Once such witnesses are glimpsed or heard, faiths seek reassurance, closure, or relief. Such will never come, can never come; but how faiths understand and respond to such truths determine how and whether they perish, merely endure, or somehow still thrive.

When listening to and examining testimonies, there are no purely happy endings. To say they humble faiths is really to say they testify to their deep irrelevance and failures. Yet some can hint at hope, even if it rarely comes, for them. The rest of us can close the book, pause the film, go on worrying about bills and our kids at school. We can feel annoyed that someone left an empty box of cereal in the cupboard as hunger gnaws—and is immediately, indifferently quenched.

Structure: Testimony

The previous and current chapters are entwined within testimony, history, and memory.[2] Here I expand and build upon what I call "testimonies of mass atrocity"[3] to examine and highlight the reality and the process of humbling and brokenness further. "Can human nature," the question goes, "turn itself inside out like that, so completely?"[4] Sadly, yes. Accounts of victims of horrific suffering humble all of our religious, national, or institutional beliefs and affiliations. While needing proper assessment,[5] testimonies also provide closer contact with reality, what Pope Francis calls the "smell of the sheep."[6]

In an edited collection of essays paying tribute to Elie Wiesel, Holocaust scholar Alvin Rosenfeld provocatively titled his contribution "Améry, Levi, Wiesel: the Futility of Holocaust Testimony." The striking word is "futility." Rosenfeld's argument is that because Wiesel turned to prose fiction, he could express his darker thoughts of doubt and theological despair, thus leaving room for faith and a richer "spiritual vocabulary unknown to Améry and Levi."[7] For my purposes, the point is the need for a risky and expansive vocabulary to push one's spiritual (and/or theological) doubts and ideas to the limits, but also a deep engagement with that damning word "futility."

I first examine Liao Yiwu's *For a Song and a Hundred Songs: A Poet's Journey through a Chinese Prison* and Mohamedou Ould Slahi's *Guantánamo Diary*. I then analyze the role of witnesses for the witnesses through Matthew Desmond's *Evicted: Poverty and Profit in the American City*, Rohini Mohan's *The Season of Trouble: Life Amid the Ruins of Sri Lanka's Civil War*, and Laura Apol's 2015 collection of poems, *Requiem, Rwanda*.

Before doing so, though, let's head to Argentina.

---

2. See also Stone, "History, Memory, Testimony," 27–28; Browning, *Remembering Survival*, 9; Browning, *Ordinary Men*; Greenspan, "Survivors' Accounts," 441–27; and O' Neill, "Anthropology and Genocide," 189–92.

3. Admirand, *Mass Atrocity*, 280–81; and Admirand, *Loss and Hope*.

4. Hugo, *Les Misérables*, 77.

5. See Langer, *Using and Abusing the Holocaust*, 55; Ozick, "Rights of History and Imagination," 3–18; and Suleiman, "Do Facts Matter in Holocaust Memoirs?," 21–42.

6. See Francis, "Homily." See also Whitmore, "Peacebuilding and its Catholic Partners," 155–89.

7. Rosenfeld, "Améry, Levi, Wiesel," 228.

Buenos Aires

1

I'm sitting on a bench by el Río de la Plata. The weather is tenderly warm but the wind furls and spins. I'm staring out into the waters at a life-size sculpture by Claudia Fonts, commemorating a fourteen-year old boy (Pabló Míguez) who was murdered on May 12, 1972, at 3 a.m. The site was chosen because many bodies were dumped here by the paramilitary forces during the genocide in Argentina in the 1970s and early 1980s, erroneously called a "Dirty War."[8]

More specifically, I'm at la Parque de la Memoria: Monumento a Las Victimas del Terrorismo de Estado in the northern outskirts of Buenos Aires, a short walk from the University of Buenos Aires. Sculptures dot the park that is overwhelmed by zigzag, high walls of concrete inscribed with the names of the murdered. Thirty thousand people were estimated to be disappeared during the dictatorship with less than 1 percent of those targeted surviving.[9]

On each wall, divided by year, on individual porphyry plaques, are the names and ages of the disappeared. Most were very young. I pause at various points and years, reading out some names and writing them down in my notebook.

1983
Obreque, Sauro Antonio
    15 años
1980
Cabilla, Veronica Maria
    16 años
1978
Larrubia, Susana Alicia
    25 años
1977
Noroña, Hector Pablo
    46 años

---

8. See Partnoy, *Little School*; Feirstein, "National Security Doctrine in Latin America," 489–508; and Gandsman, "Ex-Disappeared," 31–55.

9. Gandsman, "Ex-Disappeared," 32.

1976
Torrano, Graciela Beatriz
    19 años
1976
Fote, Fortunato Leandro
    38 años

The need to remember is often overshadowed by politics, by inconvenience, cost, guilt. So many reasons to forget and move on. It can be so depressing to think about all these lives enveloped in merely three facts: year of murder, name, and age of death—and yet there is an obligation to honor such losses. It's the least we can do. To speak of honor, obligation, or duty may not satisfy philosophical purists who deny any intrinsic, eternal ought because there can be no proof, no certitude. All the same, we are obligated. We cannot know and remember the full extent of such victims. They seem endless—they are endless. But we must try to know and remember what we can. Collectively, such stories and witnesses not only humble, but can cleanse beliefs and institutions to hinder or prevent similar occurrences in one's name or ideology or -ism.[10]

At the memorial site, I also visit the Sala Pays, where there are exhibitions and computers to search the database for victims. How many people have sat here, searching, hoping? I view an exhibition called "Cosas del Rio" (Things from the River) by photographer Fernando Gutiérrez. There are photographs of one eyeglass and part of a frame; a sandal; a weathered small green pencil; a passport: what people had with them when they were dumped. Sometimes, no bodies, but only their belongings were retrieved.

At the front desk, I ask for more information or a tour and am given a book describing the monument site.[11] I feel blessed to be here and pay the victims small homage. This may sound like platitudes, empty phrases, an egotistical thrust, another genocide tourist, but the call to remember and witness is a potent one: and we need witnesses for the witnesses. It can seem useless and overwhelming. There has been too much loss. Names melt into names, into numbers. But as Timothy Snyder reminds us, we cannot stop here, but "must turn the numbers back into people."[12]

---

10. Patterson, "Jewish Reflections," 118.
11. Hochbaum and Battiti, *Monumento a Las Victimas*.
12. Snyder, *Bloodlands*, 408.

As I wander outside the memorial site, lovers have a picnic or lean into or on one another. Others walk arm in arm along the river. Some are lost staring at the river or in each other's eyes. One drops a cigarette into the water. It disappears. No trace.

It's the incongruity of it all—the mix of beauty and serenity with the murmurs and stains of past horrors. On the river, boats drift in the distance. There is a slight breeze. The sun kindly beams down, as it is "winter" here. The waves splish and splosh. Away from the bustle and grime of Buenos Aires's center, out here I find myself at peace, relaxed, even hopeful. And yet, the memorial wall, the reminders everywhere of the bodies dumped, washed ashore—or only their few belongings.

We are humbled. The witnesses and their testimony, the lives of so many lost, reveal failures of Church, State, and people. They demand a witness that spreads or retells their stories and does not hide painful truths. Theologically, we speak of "solidarity with the suffering."[13] In the face of the victim, in the presence of injustice and evil, religious and ideological difference can seem meaningless, petty.[14]

2

In Buenos Aires little plaques on the sidewalk memorialize who was kidnapped at a certain spot at a certain time or where the *desaparecido* had lived. Jogging one morning near my hostel in el Barrio Norte, I stop abruptly, having noticed one such plaque on the sidewalk. Pedestrians quickly file past me as I translate the phrases. In the afternoon, I get the address of a former site (Comisaría 23 at Santa Fe 4000 in Palermo) where the disappeared were taken, and walk there. It is now a police station, with no evidence or acknowledgment of its previous incarnation.

3

I also visit The Navy Petty-Officers School of Mechanics (in Spanish, Escuela de Mecánica de la Armada, commonly referred to by the acronym ESMA). The ESMA was supposed to be only an educational facility of the Argentine Navy. If only it had been so.

---

13. Knitter, "Responsibilities for the Future," 85.
14. Ibid., 85.

The base is divided by an area where access was restricted by ugly forest-green guard towers, resembling a top hat, propped up by four legs. The towers are made of concrete with two thin slits at eye level for guards standing. They access their post via a short ladder. Views of the school and the Avenida de Libertad.

I had joined a Spanish-speaking tour and the conversation among the guide and the visitors frequently became animated. Argentina is still working through this turmoil in its history and disagreements could be rife. I can only catch pieces of a conversation—*demasiado rápido para mí*. I wander off and another tour guide, a college student in her early twenties, kindly shows me around privately. We converse in part-Spanish, part English. The cells where prisoners had been tortured and beaten were refurbished by the military to hide their previous existence. She takes me through the spaces where kids were held, tortured; the room where the pregnant *mujeres* were kept. Their babies, once born, were given to families loyal to the military. Their identities changed. Emotions are high. She speaks in Spanish revealing her anger at such injustices. And I keep telling her: *más despacio, por favor*. She shows me the remains of some prisoner graffiti, a heart scratched into a wall. Evidence of what, of whom, was not supposed to be there.[15]

Despite the cover up and the concealment, it remains a ghastly place. Only 200 people out of the 5,000 brought here survived. Silent now, but it's not difficult to imagine the piteous cries. The hallways meander and zag: it is a chaotic place.

Liao Yiwu's Song

Twenty-nine years after the June 4th Massacre in Beijing, the protests, detentions, and silence continue.[16] As Rishi Iyengar wrote of the commemoration in 2015: "They want to make sure mainland China, and the rest of the world, do not forget. Some of the people also came so they themselves would not forget."[17] Of a typical day in Tiananmen Square in 2014, journalist Louisa Lim similarly remarked: "Over the course of the past quarter-century, in an extraordinary sleight of hand, China's rulers have managed to transform this site of national shame into one

---

15. See Actis, Aldini, Gardella, Lewin, and Tokar, *That Inferno*.
16. Deneyer, "On Tiananmen Square Anniversary."
17. Iyengar, "Tens of Thousands."

of national pride." Most Chinese tourists arrive there for the flag-raising exercise, not protests.[18]

Liao Yiwu, imprisoned for four years as an 89er, a political dissident from the June 4th killings, writes to limit such loss and forgetting. His memoir, *For a Song and a Hundred Songs: A Poet's Journey through a Chinese Prison*, had to be written three times because the Chinese security police had confiscated two previous versions.[19] I cannot fathom how Yiwu could begin, let alone finish, a third version. That he did so with such poetic grace and narrative verve is a further testament to his work and mission. Beyond his own testimony are his fascinating works of interviews and portraits of other victims in Chinese society, most notably, *The Corpse Walker: Real-Life Stories from the Bottom Up* and *God is Red: The Secret Story of How Christianity Survived and Flourished in Communist China*. The latter is a fascinating account of witnessing for the Other, as Yiwu professes no theistic faith but is drawn to the heroic beliefs and perseverance of many persecuted Chinese Christians. He believes their story and witness also need to be heard.

While the title of Yiwu's memoir might seem lyrically beautiful, its meaning is sullied in the vacuous pain and misery of the prisons. Officer Yu, as a punishment to Yiwu, ordered him to sing a hundred different songs. Whenever Yiwu lagged in pain, or his voice became hoarse, Yu threatened him with an electric baton. Yiwu plodded on, but grew weak and strained to remember any songs he could. After reaching the thirty-eighth song, Yiwu pleaded for water. All entreaties were refused. The temperature was also freezing. "My throat was dry," Yiwu writes, "as if a large ball of cotton were stuck in it. I squeezed out one song after another. Soon my mouth was moving but there was no sound coming out of it."[20]

Officer Yu zapped him with the electric baton on his head. Yiwu's skin burned. Yu ordered another baton when the juice died. Then Yiwu "was wrestled to the ground and [his] trousers were stripped off. 'Are you going to sing or not?' Officer Yu asked."

The sexual threat was evident but Yiwu was helpless, voiceless, a poet without any more words; with no more songs to sing. Yu wasted little time.

---

18. Lim, *People's Republic of Amnesia*, 1. See also Osnos, "Tiananmen Square," 156.

19. Yiwu, *For a Song*, xix.

20. Ibid., 301–2.

Yiwu testifies: "I could feel the baton on my butthole, but I refused to surrender. The tip of the baton entered me. I screamed and whimpered in pain like a dog. The electric current coursed through my flesh and burst out from my neck. I felt like a duck whose feathers were being stripped."[21] With unimaginable resolve, he managed to sing a famous Red Guard song, contending that "the American imperialists are afraid of the Chinese people."[22]

Shocked that Yiwu could still sing, Officer Yu laughed and joked, "Okay, now I'm afraid of you." The torture of singing those one hundred songs finally, mercilessly, ended.[23]

Witness

Referring to one prisoner, a former journalist called Old Yang, Yiwu comments: "As his memory dims and fades with time, I hope that my writing will serve as a record of this anonymous soul who once sparked a small flame of justice in a totalitarian prison."[24] Here Yiwu refers to an incident in which Old Yang, through his testimony in the prison, convinced the party secretary to change his faulty decision that a prison riot was caused by the '89ers.

After finally being released from the Chinese prison system for his performative poem, "Massacre," about the June 4th killings, Yiwu recalls the conversation he had with Liu Shahe, a poet condemned by Mao Zedong in 1958 but a seventy-five-old historian at the time of his conversation with Yiwu. "Why don't you abandon poetry and be a witness to history?" Shahe asks Yiwu. "So many people have suffered injustices, but only a few have crawled out of jail still clearheaded enough to remember and record what they have seen . . . But remember to tell the truth. False testimony will be condemned by the future generation."[25] We can see the fruit of this advice throughout Yiwu's oeuvre.

Hauntingly, Yiwu gives sparse details about his own life before the imprisonment, and much of it is critical. He was born in the throes of

21. Ibid., 302.
22. On the Red Guards, see Yang, *Red Guard Generation*; and Huang, *Little Red Guard*.
23. Yiwu, *For a Song*, 302.
24. Ibid., 22.
25. Ibid., 384.

a famine "which claimed the lives of thirty million people nationwide between 1959 and 1962."[26] He would have joined that unimaginable number of those murdered, dying of malnutrition if not for an herbal doctor.[27] Hunger and malnutrition, however, remained constant threats during those years. Still, from a young age his father taught him Chinese poetry, and it was a love that grew with Yiwu as he became a restless and wild teenager, reading banned Western books and writing poetry as if in a delirium: "Words poured out of me in buckets."[28]

He married A Xia, who was a secretary with the local municipal government and who had yearnings to be a poet and artist. They had exchanged correspondence about their poetry and soon began dating in 1984. Despite parental disapproval, they eloped that winter. But as a restless and morally desultory soul, Yiwu did what he wanted, when he wanted. After his wife broke a leg and he retrieved her from the hospital, he impetuously bought a boat ticket to get away, lying to her that it was bought before the accident, and ignoring her pleas and cries. He checked the time, wiped her tears, and left.[29] He had no planned destination and wandered for nearly two months in search of "literary and sexual targets."[30] The couple was pulling apart before his arrest, especially when Yiwu one day caught a man she had been seeing discretely. He could not accept the possibility of her infidelity, too.

Like an albatross he refers to one escapade years before his marriage but linked with the death of his sister Fei in a car accident. Having been away, Yiwu received a telegram about the funeral too late. While grief-stricken, he sought escape in a random woman at a bar. She was a newlywed whose husband was away. The images are stark: "My mourning outfit lay strewn on the floor."[31] The rustling of trees outside bespoke his sister's disappointment and anger. He felt he had "stained her memory by his carelessness." The guilt stayed with him but would not deter his lusts and needs when with his poet friends, or years later as his recuperating wife was confined at home. "I had turned into a ghost," he writes in closing the first chapter, "As we are well aware in Chinese culture, ghosts possess no heart and never need to repent."[32]

26. Ibid., 10. For more on the famine, see Jisheng, *Tombstone*.
27. Yiwu, *For a Song*, 10.
28. Ibid., 12.
29. Ibid., 13.
30. Ibid., 13.
31. Ibid., 8.
32. Ibid., 9.

A few months before the June 4th massacre, as his wife was now recovered, he again left her to enter a writing program at Wuhan University, and had a "scandalous" affair with an engaged graduate student. Her fiancée stabbed Yiwu repeatedly, sending him to a hospital. Expelled from the program, Yiwu briefly returned to A Xia, but again left soon after with a poet friend. Around this time the protests of Tiananmen Square were building in intensity. Annoyed that he had not won a literary prize, Yiwu headed away from Beijing and returned to Fuling a week later, "bitter and cynical."[33]

Near the height of the massacre, Yiwu describes himself as naked in his house, turning off the news, thinking that whether it succeeded or not would be of little benefit to him.[34] His explanation for what drove him to compose that poem of protest was almost a primal urge: "For once in my life, I decided to head down a heroic path, one on which I advanced with great fear, scampering at times like a rat with no place to hide."[35] Even while describing this cathartic moment, Yiwu does not conceal his own fragility and weakness.

The road he eventually took was more like a howl and a roar: the poem "Massacre" culminates in zealous, ironic shouts to "open fire" on the elderly, children, women, students; to "blast away." Yiwu made an audio copy of the poem and performance along with three copies. He later worked on spreading the poem with some of his poet friends.

It was not that Yiwu suddenly wrote political poems. In the spring of 1989 two of his longer poems were published in journals later deemed to be anti-communist. His house was searched and he was placed on a government watchlist. The massacre poem, the distributed copies, and some public readings of it garnered further unwanted government attention. After he and his wife momentarily reconciled and she became pregnant, he still went ahead with plans to do a "risky" film project that would be a sequel to the massacre poem, called "Requiem."[36] Yiwu (along with his pregnant wife and poet friends) were arrested in February of 1990. Yiwu received a four-year sentence that resulted in horrific abuse and torture perpetrated by many of his fellow prisoners with the consent of the guards and the authorities. Almost surreally, while in prison, Yiwu

33. Ibid., 14.
34. Ibid., 22.
35. Ibid., 30.
36. Ibid., 51.

TESTIMONIES, WITNESSING, AND MORAL FAILURE 191

was able to read Orwell's *1984* in the prison library at the No. 3 Provincial Penitentiary "at the foot of Daba Mountain."[37] Yiwu writes that reading it "was like walking through a gallery where there was no difference between art and life. On the page was an imaginary prison, while all around me there was the real thing."[38]

Yiwu is blessed or burdened with the prodigious—or "pathologically precise"—memories of Primo Levi and the "pathological keenness" of Nabokov's memory.[39] He thus writes voluminously both of his own experiences and of the conversations and interviews he has had with other prisoners or the marginalized in Chinese society. When Yiwu interviews fellow victims, he listens and records their travails, rarely accentuating or adding his own ordeals.

"The damn mute called God"[40]

Yiwu is an atheist. He tells Mao, a prisoner awaiting execution and seeking some kind of farewell prayer from him, "Nobody in China believes in God."[41] Yet, spirituality, faith, and God are often recurrent themes in Yiwu's work. For example, Yiwu's lawyer told him to admit his guilt and gave him letters from his wife telling him to confess, reminding him that he still hadn't seen his daughter. Yiwu writes how "Sitting in a small courtyard outside the lawyer's office . . . [t]he sun had broken through the clouds, and narrow shafts of sunlight hit the ground in a pattern that resembled hordes of heavenly sparrows flitting across the ground. 'What do I want?' I asked myself." Yiwu remembered the earlier "powerful words" on the back of Old Xie's Bible that stressed we are sojourners in this world and that "the soul is God's and that mistreatment of our body will not liberate our souls."[42] While the passage is unhelpfully cryptic and almost Manichaean (why are "our bodies the graves of our souls"?), the words struck a chord with Yiwu. He wept, acknowledging he had no idea where the passage or God came from.

37. Ibid., 341.
38. Ibid., 297.
39. Levi, *Periodic Table*, 213; and Nabokov, *Speak, Memory*, 55 and 248. See also Zim, *Consolations of Writing*, 267.
40. Yiwu, *For a Song*, 205: from a poem Yiwu recited to other inmates.
41. Ibid., 280; see, however, Johnson, *Souls of China*, 31.
42. Yiwu, *For a Song*, 306.

After his show trial, Yiwu had thoughts of a heavenly court of judgment.[43] Was that where God was? In another example noting how his poet accomplices were arrested, Yiwu explains that Xiao Min, the wife of his friend Big Glasses, was spared. Yiwu writes: "Fortunately, in one fleeting moment, God's invisible hand had shielded her and the unborn baby from danger."[44] At the time Xiao Min was three-months pregnant. But Yiwu seems to have Luck or Providence more in mind, than a benevolent deity. Either way, the moment is random, fleeting.

One day in the prison, Wang Er (the cell's main henchman) reported that the cook had said dinner was going to be special that night. He jokes that God is a "fat chef." Old Xie immediately asks God for forgiveness for their "ignorance and blasphemy." Another prisoner, Foreign Minister, then jokes he would believe in God if meat was added to the dinner. The only "treats" that night were two rotten, steamed sweet potatoes. Yiwu writes: "Our disappointment was indescribable. Curses and anger followed. God is later mock-addressed by Wang Er."[45]

God also arises in discussion with guards. Officer Cao was described by Yiwu as a guard who wrote poetry and had sympathy for political prisoners. He even expressed regret that he became a jailer and admitted reading Yiwu's poems. Remarkably, Yiwu showed compassion to him, seeing his sense of shame, and telling him he was lucky to have a job. Yiwu asked Cao if there was a biblical verse that could describe Yiwu's situation. "'If someone slaps you, turn the other cheek,' Officer Cao answered without hesitation. 'Too bad God is not Chinese.'"[46]

State Sanctioned, Prisoner-on-Prisoner Violence

In every cell was a big boss who had life or death power over his fellow inmates. Tyrants like Wang Er divvied up duties like washing the latrines to deciding how close to the latrine people would sleep, insuring he had the most space. Surrounded by his henchmen, he also ensured his sexual needs were met. Those prisoners, deemed "Slave boys," were raped and abused at whim. Yiwu describes how the slave boys were forced to perform fellatio and other sexual acts on the leaders, so that "Their loud

---

43. Ibid., 307.
44. Ibid., 78.
45. Ibid., 252–53.
46. Ibid., 321–22.

slurping conjured up the image of starving peasants gulping down a bowl of hot congee." Newer initiates cried "when their masters forced them to swallow semen."[47] In *The Corpse Walker*, Yiwu interviews Que Yao, a pop singer put in a detention center and blamed for an unruly crowd who had come to hear him perform and would not disperse in an orderly fashion. The police started breaking instruments, the crowd resisted, and mayhem ensued. Once imprisoned, the head of the prison gang in Que Yao's cell forced him to drink urine and later had him dress up and sing like a girl and "perform oral sex on him several times."[48] This lasted two weeks until Yao was sentenced to serve two years in "a youth re-education camp on the outskirts of Chongqing."[49]

In addition to such rapes, other horrific and elaborate tortures were devised and implemented in various cells. Yiwu recounts what he calls "Song Mountain's One Hundred and Eight Rare Delicacies," basically a "menu" of prisoner-on-prisoner torture, depredation, and humiliation. Yiwu comments: "I hope that someday, when the history of the prison system is written, other people will add to this testimony."[50] Two heinous examples will suffice, even as they make for difficult reading. "An Estranged couple: Two inmates are roped together back to back. At the enforcer's order, they are forced to grab each other's penis with their hands and pull it without seeing it." And "Noodles in a Clear Broth: Strings of toilet papers are soaked in a bowl of urine, and the inmate is forced to eat the toilet paper and drink the urine."[51] Reading through the whole list is nauseating.

In one instance, Yiwu, refusing to eat, gave his food to a migrant worker imprisoned for not having the right permit. Since his arrival, the migrant worker had been beaten mercilessly by the inmates. Ironically for a Communist country (and one whose ideology once lambasted the educated and Westernized), there were unsaid hierarchies in the jail against the lower class. Political prisoners or those deemed educated were often treated deferentially. To teach Yiwu a lesson that "in prison, sympathy is a crime" and also to remind him who was in charge, the jail chief had the migrant mentioned above served the torture dish of stewed pig nose. In

47. Ibid., 123.
48. Yiwu, *Corpse Walker*, 295.
49. Ibid., 295.
50. Yiwu, *For a Song*, 85.
51. Ibid., 85–89.

this act of torture, inmates pinch the migrant's lips together with a chopstick as he groaned pitifully.[52] As a second torture "entrée" was ordered, called "freshly ground tofu," Yiwu screamed for the guards to help. Like many prison memoirs, guards differ in their temperament and proclivity to violence. It was Officer Wen in this case, and he was indifferent, telling Yiwu to mind his own business. But because Wen and Yiwu also had a private chat, Yiwu was momentarily given a level of respect by the other inmates.

Yiwu's relationship with the various chiefs often took on this strange pattern of abuse followed by Yiwu's outburst or challenge, leading to a level of understanding or a draw between them. Wang Er, for example, could be vicious, raping other male inmates like Big Mouth[53] and ensuring the initiation protocol of new inmates (torture) was prescribed and followed. After one inmate lied about his gang membership to prevent such initiation, Wang Er later had him dipped "in the toilet pit to eat feces" as a punishment.[54] This same Wang Er could also talk philosophically with Yiwu and even orchestrated other prisoners to fulfill Yiwu's work quota so Yiwu could read in his cell.[55]

While prisoner-on-prisoner violence was severe (and supported by the system) the guards and interrogators could also be merciless. Officer Yu's abuse of Yiwu was highlighted above. Another guard called Pervert Liu handcuffed three prisoners together as a "sadistic" joke, knowing one prisoner was prone to epileptic seizures.[56]

Yiwu among Christians and Buddhists

While witness testimony can point to the failures of faith, it also illustrates hope and fidelity by those who strive to embody their beliefs to the end. It challenges the history of the oppressor and those in power. Yiwu interviews many such people in *God is Red*. Wu Yongsheng, born in 1928, tells Yiwu of the state-sponsored persecution against Christians, banning religious activities, closing churches, and seizing Church property: "It was a treat just to move our lips and shape the name of God."[57] The Com-

52. Ibid., 98.
53. Ibid., 244.
54. Ibid., 257.
55. Ibid., 219.
56. Ibid., 224.
57. Yiwu, *God is Red*, 47; see also ibid., 108. For the devastation and deaths caused

munist party not only murdered people who held onto their religious faith but spread lies about those beliefs. Yiwu admits to Zhang Yinxian, a Catholic nun then over 100 years of age, that when he grew up in the 1960s he was repeatedly told that Catholic nuns were Western spies who did horrible things to Chinese children.

Anecdotally, as a Catholic fed up with Christian missionary scandals and interfaith blundering, I had grown very leery of evangelizing in its old-fashioned guise, even under politically correct pretense: but *God Is Red* thunders why the message of Christ needs to be heard and promulgated in contexts where it has been unjustly disparaged, silenced, and persecuted. Shahe tells Yiwu: "It is the job of historians and writers to uncover the historical truth and explain it to the public."[58] Yiwu, an atheist, is doing precisely that.

Sister Yinixian further sets the record straight on the Communist government's narrative: "Lies. Lies. At public denunciation meetings during the Cultural Revolution, we were accused of murdering orphans. They said the priests were vampires."[59] Instead the nuns and priests worked to save babies and children left to die by their poor families who could no longer feed them. Two hundred children were adopted in this way by the nuns who became full-time nannies. Those already dead or whose health could not recover were buried in a Catholic gravesite, since demolished. The gravesite sat next to a Protestant cemetery, also destroyed in the attempt to obliterate any trace of Christianity.[60] "Those poor babies!" the sister exclaimed. In telling her story to Yiwu, who then dutifully published it, the lives of those children are, in a small way, restored. But so much damage was done. Sister Zhang, then "going on 101" relentlessly petitioned the government to restore all the Church's confiscated property."[61]

Solidarity of Witnesses

During Yiwu's interviews of others, he rarely speaks of his own suffering and struggle; of the similar torture and degradation he had to endure. In

---

from Mao's reign before, during, and after the Cultural Revolution, see Chang and Halliday, *Mao*. See also Wu, *Bitter Winds*; Gyatso, *Fire under the Snow*; and Tang, *Half a Walnut Tree*, 34–50.

58. Yiwu, *God is Red*, 212.
59. Ibid., 15.
60. Ibid., 16.
61. Ibid., 27.

November of 2002, he met Tian Zhiguang, who was cold and hungry, but seeking to get some compensation from the government for illegal imprisonment and the torture inflicted upon him. Yiwu led him into a restaurant to get him food and listen to his story. Zhiguang described different hellish techniques of prisoner-on-prisoner violence that were inflicted on him, like "granting the knighthood" in which a prisoner had to lay naked on the ground and had other inmates stomp and spit on him. Then two big chamber pots were put on top of Zhiguang. This torture was called: "tortoise carrying the shitload." Any movement caused urine to gush on top of him. Then inmates would sit on the toilet, crushing Zhiguang as they defecated or urinated. When hearing about the horrific story, Yiwu casually replies: "I've been in jail once and know something about initiation rituals. But I've never heard about the ceremony you told me. I guess prisoners are getting more creative when it comes to torturing people."[62] Nor will Yiwu correct them if they casually mention "you would not understand."

Another moving encounter was during a discussion with Yuan Xiangchen, a well-known Christian from the underground Christian community in Beijing whose own father was horrifically abused and mistreated during the Cultural Revolution. When Yiwu acknowledged that he had been in jail but could not understand someone refusing to sign a confession against one's faith if that meant freedom, Xiangchen replied:

"But you wouldn't chop off your right hand and swear never to write again, would you?" Yiwu answers emphatically "Of course not." And Xiangchen continues: "It's the same principle. My father would not betray his faith, because it was his life. When a person loses his life, then what does he have left for his family?"[63] As Wenguang Huang, the translator of Yiwu's books into English, presciently remarks: "Liao saw parallels in the perseverance by Chinese Christians with his own fight for the freedom to write and travel."[64]

In the spring of 2003, Yiwu interviewed 103-year-old Buddhist abbot Master Deng Kuan. During the Cultural Revolution Master Kuan was deemed a rich monk and a "capitalist roader,"[65] tortured and paraded

---

62. Yiwu, *Corpse Walker*, 259
63. Yiwu, *God is Red*, 167.
64. Huang, "Translator's Note," xiii.
65. A derogatory (and never fully defined) term in Maoist thought referring to someone with Western or capitalist leanings, affiliations, or stature who is perceived to be against socialist aims and programs. See Jian, Song, and Zhou, *Historical Dictionary*

in his village. He remained a testament to humility, integrity, and peace, even instructing his fellow monks to be kind to rats, who are also cold.[66] Despite his previous maltreatment, Master Kuan even felt compassion for those who tortured him, also practically noting: "When you start to blame and hate people, retribution will befall you."[67]

He died in 2005, having outlived all the horrors of Maoist China from the failed land reforms that had people resort to cannibalism to the utter uselessness of the Great Leap Forward in which trees were stripped from hills and any scrap metal (including cooking pots) was smelted for usable steel—all to no avail. Master Kuan was often brutalized and tormented, hung from a ceiling until he passed out, his right arm dislocated. He cites Buddha as the source of his survival. "I would never have survived this difficult period had it not been for my belief in Buddha."[68] During that time, Master Kuan was prevented from any outward show of Buddhist faith and resigned himself to suffer these indignities and torture to prevent the suffering from being unleashed on someone else: "Deep in my heart, I never give up hope in the benevolence of Buddha."[69]

Hope?

In memoirs like Yiwu's, hope, let alone meaningful portraits of humility, are rare. While sweeping the corridors of the jail as a prescribed task, Yiwu and some male inmates momentarily hear women's voices. They had stumbled into a section of the jail where women were held. All those days and nights lusting and dreaming—and here were real, live women. They could not quite be seen clearly behind the jail door, but there was a slot for food deliveries, so glimpses could be had. The women were begging for food. Their needs were clear. The men vied and pushed for a peak and immediately began bartering, though. They had different needs.

Some men were slapped or burned with cigarettes for demanding to see or touch the women's vaginas. One inmate was rewarded after handing in three buns of bread. A guard then came and reprimanded the men and chastised Yiwu in particular for mixing in with that sort. While

---

of the Chinese Cultural Revolution, 27–28.

66. Yiwu, *Corpse Walker*, 83.
67. Ibid., 91.
68. Ibid., 80.
69. Ibid., 81.

Yiwu tried to explain he was not involved like the others, the guard strode away and left Yiwu momentarily alone, reflecting on the role and cost of one's dignity in prison. The starving and desperate female inmates were still there, behind the door. "While I stood there trying to pull myself together," Yiwu wrote, "a pretty face peeked out of the food delivery window. 'Do you have buns?' said a soul-grabbing voice. 'You can look at my pussy for one bun . . . for two you can touch.'"[70]

If there is any hope, any salvaging piece to recall it is in Yiwu's commitment to speak the truth and allow other victims a platform for their forgotten lives to be retold and their unjust humiliations and punishments to be remembered. Yiwu's life is given some meaning after an encounter with an inmate named Sima, a "former" Buddhist monk "and the prison's oldest inmate" at 84.[71] Sima teaches Yiwu to play the bamboo flute, something Yiwu cherishes to this day. Sima's story is also humbling for us all. After horrific torture and interrogations, he simply told his persecutors: "'I have committed sins. So have you. We are all sinful.' The courts sentenced him to life imprisonment."[72] Sima's lessons and wisdom not only gave Yiwu hope but helped him after he was locked in an underground, dark, cramped, dank cell, shackled—for two weeks.[73] Yiwu imagined playing the flute and practiced the rhythmic breathing he was taught. Sadly, their relationship slowly faded away once Yiwu was back in his regular cell, and after they had a few more lessons. Sima even seemed to stop playing the flute all together. But then, on the day Yiwu was released from prison, Sima played one more final tune. "The tune floated out and over the mountain-high walls. Tears welled in [Yiwu's] eyes."[74] In such a place, that was as close to a happy ending one could find.

We, Too, Are the Torturers

As a child of the Cold War, Russia was the enemy. We—America—were the universal good guys. We safeguarded freedom and democracy.[75] As

70. Yiwu, *For a Song*, 138.
71. Ibid., 370.
72. Ibid, 370.
73. Ibid., 373.
74. Ibid., 380.

75. For a philosophical account sceptical of democracy, see Brennan, *Against Democracy*; for a historical account, see Cartledge, *Democracy*; and Runciman, *How Democracy Ends*; for a a helpful geopolitical overview, see Marshall, *Prisoners of Geography*.

one American interrogator told Mauritanian national, Mohamedou Ould Slahi, in the midst of the torture center that is Guantánamo: "The US is the greatest country in the world; we would rather forgive than punish."[76] That interrogator, like me, was too enmeshed in general ignorance, inexperience, and fear to confront hard truths. That we, too, are not just capable of evils, but commit them.[77]

As the Holocaust was my main foray into witness testimony, one can, perhaps, understand why an us/them language was reinforced. They (Nazis) were the ones who tortured, murdered, denied the torture, and kidnapped people without trial and evidence. As I read about other mass atrocities and genocides, it was the Russians or Chinese; Latin American paramilitary groups in El Salvador and Guatemala, or South American juntas in Argentina; the North Koreans; the Khmer Rouge; the Hutus in Rwanda or the Tutsis in Burundi; wars in Angola, the Congo, Sierra Leone, Uganda, Sudan; endless wars with them killing children and torturing and desecrating bodies; the Balkans, with claims of Europe's backyard, but still a (false) sense of them with their centuries-old ethnic affiliations and loyalty and revenge pacts;[78] and then the suicide bombers of Sri Lanka and the Muslim fundamentalists: them. I read of prisoner abuse, and denial of evidence, torture, executions, withholding of evidence, and more denial, and justifications of nationalism, peace, democracy, stability, or claimed superiority. I could shake my head in disgust at them: at those people, those countries, and what they did to those poor victims. I was proud if America was granted credit in halting such abuse, or if the victim or witness now lived in America or hoped to someday.

Then there was Abu Ghraib; the images and the accounts of torture; the Torture Memo; WikiLeaks; and so-called torture lite. US government officials caught in a web of lies and justifications no different than despotic regimes—from them.[79] The accounts of our soldiers, men and

76. Slahi, *Guantánamo Diaries*, 311.

77. See Fair, *Consequences*; Hafetz, *Obama's Guantánamo*; and Boumediene and Idir, *Witnesses of the Unseen*.

78. See Maass, *Love Thy Neighbor*, 273–74; Demick, *Besieged*, 19; Vulliamy, *War is Dead*; and Borger, *Butcher's Trail*. My visit to Mostar and Sarajevo in the summer of 2018 was both illuminating and humbling. My Sarajevo host, Admir, had told me of his family members murdered in the Serbian bombing of the Sarajevo fruit market during the infamous siege—while his wife's family and village in Foča were destroyed by Serbian paramilitaries. The "crime"? They were Bosnian Muslims. Yet, Admir and his wife try to teach their kids about the basic goodness of all human beings regardless of race or religion.

79. See Danner, *Torture and Truth*; Mayer, *Dark Side*; Filkins, *Forever War*;

women who grew up in my country, who predominantly practiced my Christian faith, seemed no different than guards in the gulags. Not them, but us, doing and denying and abusing; just like them, just like us. While searching for the truth about his relatives murdered during the Holocaust, Daniel Mendelsohn was distraught by how acts of torture committed by US soldiers in Iraq resembled those of the Nazis against Jews in his family's Ukrainian town of Bolechow. Both the American soldiers in 2001 and the Nazis in 1941 forced their prisoners to undress naked and form a human pyramid as one mode of torture, with the Nazis ultimately murdering all their captives.[80] Us and them.

Then there was a memoir, written in 2005 but not published until almost a decade later, its words blackened by the US censor, in some cases, entire pages,[81] Mohamedou Ould Slahi's *Guantánamo Diary*. There really was no us/them. We were them/they were us. In Jane Mayer's *The Dark Side*, we read a forensic account of how and why US government officials orchestrated and legalized sanctioned torture. A secret US military base in Baghdad had visible warnings reminding soldiers not to leave any physical trace of abuse on prisoners: "No Blood, No foul." As Mayer writes: "Soldiers stationed there told human rights workers that they witnessed detainees being stripped, beaten, covered in mud, drenched in freezing water, and made to stand all night in front of air conditioners. One was made to drink urine."[82] More and more damning evidence was eventually made public by objectors, journalists, and survivors of the abuse and torture. September 11th, 2001, could have been the epochal, transformative, geopolitical moment of the twenty-first century. I say this without hubris and well-trodden American provincialism, but in hopeful communion with the loss of 2,996 people in the attacks. For a brief moment, the world seemed to unite with the loss and pain of America. With its technological power, wealth, and reach, such a foundation could have supported unimaginably good deeds. It could have shown the world how best to respond to such vile and detestable acts: perhaps in forgiveness, contrition and self-evaluation, reminiscent of the Amish who famously responded to the murder of ten school girls in their community in Nickel Mines, Pennsylvania, on 2 October 2006.[83]

WikiLeaks, *WikiLeaks Files*; Cole, *Torture Memos*; Wolfendale, "Myth of 'Torture Lite,'" 47–61; and Danner, "Rumsfeld."

80. Mendelsohn, *The Lost*, 406.
81. Slahi, *Guantánamo Diaries*, 56–59.
82. Mayer, *Dark Side*, 250. See also ibid., 26, 165, and 309.
83. Shapiro, "Amish Forgive School Shooter"; Schiavenza, "In Charleston."

A similar response (with measures of increased security and seeking prosecution of the guilty) could have brought my fellow privileged Americans in deeper connection with the suffering victims of our world. Instead, this status as victim was not used for empathy or compassion towards others who have suffered unjustly, perhaps from American bombs, strikes, land and oil grabs, or divine beliefs. It was undertaken in the name of power and revenge and "never again." Slahi, of course, was one of the victims of the anti-terrorism response. And it is that response which reveals why that devastatingly tragic violence was instead misused and misinterpreted. Nearly twenty years after the attacks, the world is not a better or safer place.[84] Causes have not been assessed and any complicity has not been accepted. Hundreds of thousands of lives have since been lost through the wars in Afghanistan and Iraq and the spiralling debacles and tragedies, especially of Syria, but also Pakistan, Yemen, Libya, and Egypt.[85]

After being away from New York since high school, my wife and I returned in 2001 to live in the first floor of what had been my Sligo-born grandma and Tipperary-born grandpa's house on 21–52 35th Street in Astoria. That house was the first one I had been brought to after my birth and would be the one our first child lived in.

On September 11th, I was in Boston as I commuted there each week to attend graduate school at Boston College. Running late to teach a class at Lasell College, I tried to call my Department Chair and tell her from a pay phone in a T Station in Quincy. I couldn't hear because the TV was on in the waiting room and it was loud. I almost said, "Can you turn that down, please?" Eventually, I accepted that those planes crashing into the WTC and the collapse of the Towers and the murder of those people were real. In Manhattan a few days later, a city under siege, I walked around downtown, staring at the faces of the missing plastered on the wall outside St. Vincent Hospital or on lampposts or walls of the subway. The missing. Downtown, at what would be called Ground Zero, the sky still bellowed with smoke.

In the car, I listened to WFAN, normally about my favorite sports teams, but instead, like everyone else, could only hear and talk about the victims and the state of the city and the country. We had been attacked. Senseless destruction and senseless loss of life.

84. See, however, Pinker, *Better Angels of Our Nature*; and in terms of our impact on the planet, Kolbert, *Sixth Extinction*.

85. Crawford, *Accountability for Killing*.

At my mother's elementary school in Manhasset, NY, some classes had numerous kids who lost at least one parent. At a restaurant one night with my mother, I watched as she consoled one of those families. Loss, shock, and emptiness were constant threats, though in general spirits were friendly—save for some ugly incidents against innocent Middle Eastern men, whether Muslim or Sikh.

Wasn't it understandable to ensure such an attack would not happen again, to seek some form of justice? But at what cost to others?

Mohamedou Ould Slahi: 15 Years for Justice

The Periodic Review Board (deciding prisoner cases in Guantánamo Bay Prison) finally recommended in July of 2016 that Mohamedou Ould Slahi be transferred out of Guantánamo. He was sent home to Mauritania on 14 October 2016. His nightmarish descent into prison torture, false charges, abuse, denial of rights, being held without formal prosecution, and denial of outside contact had begun in November 2001. As Kafka's *The Trial* opens: "Someone must have been telling lies about Joseph K., for without having done anything wrong, he was arrested one fine morning."[86]

Slahi's story resembles Kafka's Joseph K.'s in certain regards, but fortunately he was not murdered "like a dog,"[87] though he admits, like Winston in Orwell's *1984*, of being broken.[88] Slahi was not a political activist at the time of his arrest. He was a computer technician, though one with past links to fighting in Afghanistan at a time when the US supported such jihads against Russia.

In late September of 2001 he had been detained by the Mauritanian government, of which he was a citizen, and questioned whether he was involved in the Millennium Plot. The FBI also questioned him, but he was released. In November 2001, Slahi was asked to again meet with Mauritanian officials. He complied and went willingly, presuming it was another mix-up or minor matter. Instead, he was flown in a CIA rendition plane[89] to Amman, Jordan, where he was interrogated for almost eight months. On July 19, 2002, he was "stripped, blindfolded, diapered, shackled and

---

86. Kafka, *Trial*, 1.
87. Ibid., 229.
88. Orwell, *1984*, 245.
89. Clark and Black, "Black Sites," 20–25; also Coll, *Directorate S*.

flown to the US military's Bagram Air Base in Afghanistan."[90] After two weeks of further interrogation, he and thirty-four other prisoners were flown to Guantánamo. He was abused and tortured through special government protocols "approved by Defense Secretary Donald Rumsfeld. Mohamedou's torture include[d] months of extreme isolation, a litany of physical, psychological, and sexual humiliations; death threats to his family; and a mock kidnapping and rendition."[91]

Slahi began the book that would be called *Guantánamo Diary* in the Summer of 2005. His aim was to present his case fairly to deserve a just hearing and "open a torture and war crimes investigation."[92] He was placing his hope that the American people, if more apprised of the situation, would not want it to continue.[93]

Are the American people ready for such truths, ready to face difficult questions? Are they ready to really see what is committed in their name? In Kabul, Afghanistan, in the summer of 2012, reporter J. Malcolm Garcia interviewed twenty-three-year-old, US-trained Afghani policeman Mohamad Doad. They were in Kabul's Orthopedic Center in the paraplegic ward. Doad had been eradicating poppy fields made for heroin and opium when the Taliban shot him in the back and left him for dead. He was medevacked by US soldiers, but Garcia writes that now "Plastic leg braces with Velcro straps straighten legs so thin I wonder if he had polio. Soiled Mickey Mouse socks donated by some humanitarian group and much too big for his feet droop over his toes."[94]

Doad tells Garcia he hates Americans and will kill American forces if he recovers, that he only became a policeman because he needed the 66 USD a month, and will only speak to Garcia to remember his face so he can kill him, too, one day. He tells Garcia that he saw coalition forces murder three families.

Surrounding Doad are other patients, their bodies looking as if they had been mauled, wounds sticking to sheets, fetid and abscessing. The smell is noxious. Garcia feels ill. He groans: "Oh, Jesus," and covers his nose and mouth.

Doad sneers.

90. Siems, "A Timeline of Detention," x.
91. Ibid., x.
92. Slahi, *Guantánamo Diaries*, 369–70.
93. Ibid., 339.
94. Garcia, *What Wars Leave Behind*, 197.

"Fuck America," he says.[95]

Such is the ground we do not want to see.

Slahi's complete manuscript was not permitted to be published until almost a decade later and only after government officials censored his text with more than 2,500 black-bar redactions.[96] If not for the tireless aid of Larry Siems and other human rights lawyers, little of Slahi's words and story would have been known. With their advocacy, some of that public discussion Slahi envisioned is taking place. I include analysis of the work in this chapter in the hope of advancing the discussion and bringing it further to light.

Before I touch upon some key passages and scenes, let me add my visceral, unedited reactions as I was reading the book, scribbled, as we often do, in the margins or opening and back pages.

"This book makes me want to cry," I wrote. "I just want it over. This is for democracy? For freedom? For the good of the American people? Me? My children? The guards here in the book are out of Wiesel, Levi, Solzhenitsyn, Partnoy, Hungada or Yiwu. But they are my people, acting in the name of my government, on behalf of American citizens like me (see 257)."

Upon going to page 257, we read of Slahi's thoughts on Arabs working for the US government to torture or abuse prisoners so Americans can claim innocence. We read from Slahi: "I felt ashamed that my people were being used for this horrible job by a government that claims to be leader of the democratic free world, a government that preaches against 'dictatorships' and 'fights' for human rights and sends its children to die for that purpose. What a joke this government makes of its own people!"[97]

In another comment in the margins, I wrote: "Rage. You want to hit back at them: at the guards. The American guards. At us. You want to strike at yourself. And leering behind it, government officials in their suits and million dollar business deals. You are grateful hell exists." After finishing the book, a bit exhausted and bleary-eyed, I hastily wrote on the last page: "30 April 2015 (Flight back from Malta): Required reading for all Americans. 10 years. This was written 10 years ago. What has happened since to him? 10 years plus 5 years. 15 years. Disgraceful shameful

---

95. Ibid., 198–99.

96. The October 2017 edition (Fully Restored Version, hereafter FRV) restored the censored material. Where applicable, footnotes will include the restored words or phrases and the page number in the restored version, cited with the abbreviation FRV.

97. Slahi, *Guantánamo Diaries*, 257.

demoralizing discrediting deplorable disheartening." Which words can even trace such shame, culpability, and guilt?

Dear Reader

Like Jane Eyre telling us that she married Rochester,[98] Slahi addresses us as Dear Reader—but under very different circumstances. "You, Dear Reader, could never understand the extent of the physical, and much more the psychological, pain people in my situation suffered, no matter how hard you even try to put yourself in another's shoes."[99]

Slahi is referring to a particular incident of torture after the usual curses and threats and being forced—so Siems surmises as the details are redacted—to stand in a stooped position while being shackled by his wrists to the floor.[100] Such an agonizing position causes severe back pain, among other injuries.[101] Not believing his innocence, the interrogators again insisted on Slahi admitting guilt, though not specifying the charge or crime. Then two female US soldiers took off some of their clothes and began to force themselves on him; speaking sexually and crudely to him and fondling him. Slahi writes: "What many ▬▬ don't realize is that men get hurt the same as women if they're forced to have sex."[102] Men raped and sexually violated are a special group of "hidden victims."[103] Slahi is clear that no one took his clothes off as he prayed and tried to ignore what the women were doing as their superiors watched. But things only escalated.

"'Stop the fuck praying! You're having sex with American ▬▬ and you're praying? What a hypocrite you are!' said ▬▬ angrily, entering the room."[104] For continuing to pray Slahi was banned from doing so for a year and prevented from fasting during Ramadan in November

---

98. Brontë, *Jane Eyre*, 509.

99. Slahi, *Guantánamo Diaries*, 231–32. See also 225; and Améry, *At the Mind's Limits*, 36.

100. Editor's footnote in Slahi, *Guantánamo Diaries*, 230.

101. Scarry, *Body in Pain*.

102. Slahi, *Guantánamo Diaries*, 230; (women: FRV, 226).

103. Stemple, "Hidden Victims."

104. Slahi, *Guantánamo Diaries*, 231; (whores: FRV, 228; S. F. C. Shally: FRV, 228).

2003. Responding to his hunger strike, ▬▬▬ said: "You're not gonna die, we're gonna feed you up your ass."[105]

The problem, as Slahi noted, was not just admitting his guilt, but in concocting a fake story convincing enough and with details he could maintain during interrogations. "'We're going to do this with you every single day, day in, day out, unless you speak about ▬▬▬ and admit to your crimes,' said ▬▬▬."[106] Slahi even asked the other guards later why they were mistreating him and preventing him from praying, another violation of international law. According to Slahi, the guards admitted fear at being transferred if they disobeyed orders. One even said: "I can go to hell for what I have done to you."[107] Slahi then refers to similar comments by Germans in WWII. He had studied and worked in Germany for a number of years and spoke German fluently. At one point, while interrogated by a German-speaking American who said "▬▬▬, Wahrheit macht frei, the truth sets you free," Slahi narrates that "Arbeit didn't set the Jews free."[108] Holocaust denial among many Muslims has been on the rise in recent years: his awareness of the Shoah is another element of Slahi's intellect and openness that is riveting and deeply appealing.

Following further sessions of torture, Slahi writes: "When I got to know ▬▬▬ more and heard him speaking I wondered, How could such a man as smart as he was possibly accept such a degrading job, which is surly going to haunt him the rest of his life?"[109] Such empathy and awareness of the others around him—even his perpetrators (which I do not cite here as Stockholm syndrome)—is another appealing trait of Slahi. He even understands and respects America's need to protect itself—just not the extent of injustice towards others that such protection supposedly demanded.

American Guards and the Qur'an

Another disturbing area in Slahi's account was the guards' interpretations of the Qur'an and their hostility to Slahi praying. Slahi was later told by a fellow prisoner, an Algerian Sheikh, to pray in one's heart under those

---

105. Ibid., 231; (SSG Mary: *FRV*, 228).
106. Ibid., 232; (Abdulmalek: *FRV*, 229; SSG Mary: *FRV*, 229).
107. Ibid., 234.
108. Ibid., 15; (Michael faced me and said: *FRV*, 14).
109. Ibid., 234; (Mr. X: *FRV*, 231).

conditions.[110] In one torture session, a guard punched Slahi in the mouth for praying: "Stop praying, Motherfucker, you're killing people." A further barrage of blows followed. Slahi thinks he eventually passed out.[111] Although the Qur'an was usually available to most prisoners, Slahi notes the guards treated it irreverently, tossing it like any other book. Because he knew the Qur'an by heart and didn't want the word of God disrespected, he didn't ask for one.[112] As most guards were Christian, Slahi even engaged in dialogue. One guard explicitly tried to convert him, but Slahi was just happy for someone to talk to and so give himself more time to go to the bathroom (guards had to observe prisoners at all times).[113] As Slahi had read the Bible, he was the perfect dialogue partner, unlike his "shallow" Christian counterparts. Another guard was confused about Christianity but would not accept his girlfriend's desire to convert to Islam. Slahi said it should be up to her as Americans are supposed to support freedom of religion.[114]

A discussion with an American Christian interrogator was more productive. This soldier knew the Bible and responded to Slahi's request to get him one. They spoke about a range of theological issues, especially on salvation, divorce and the Bible, Christology, and the Trinity. The interrogator said you needed to believe in Jesus for salvation or Slahi would go to hell and that good deeds were not enough. He sincerely wanted to save Slahi's soul, ironic in light of the torture inflicted on mostly Muslim prisoners by mostly Christian guards. When the interrogator asked about Islam's view of a Christian being saved, Slahi answered that you have to accept Muhammad as the last of the prophets and be a good Muslim—otherwise you go to hell. At the same time, Slahi kept repeating the need to ask God for forgiveness. The interrogator even asked if Slahi was trying to convert him. When Slahi admitted his intention, the interrogator adamantly responded that he could never be converted. The interrogator was also flummoxed as his theological acumen was no match for Slahi's probing questions on Christological and Trinitarian belief.[115]

---

110. Ibid., 216; see also 241 and 265.
111. Ibid., 252.
112. Ibid., 17.
113. Ibid., 12–13.
114. Ibid., 335.
115. Ibid., 355–58.

Recall the American guards' fanatical hostility against Islam when Slahi prayed. Such scenes eerily resembled Russian gulag guards or Nazis mocking their victims' beliefs. After another torture session in which Slahi prayed aloud to Allah for peace and aid, one guard mocked his prayers: "There is no Allah. He let you down!"[116] Other guards blared the US national anthem into Slahi's cell telling him to "Stop the fuck praying, you're insulting my country!"[117] Hours and hours.

Slahi's loyalty and commitment to Allah and his courageous prayer life resembles the best of any story of Christian martyrdom.

In his memoir Slahi comes across as a generous, clever, sociable, prayerful, interesting, funny, intelligent, honest, and forgiving individual. "I believed excessively in conspiracy theories," Slahi writes, "—though maybe not so much as the US government does."[118] In another passage, he describes a Mauritanian folktale about a man who fears roosters and is trying to convince a rooster he is not corn. The psychiatrist tells the man it is obvious he is not "a tiny ear of corn" but the man replies that he knows he is a man but it is the psychiatrist's job to convince the rooster of that truth. "The man was never healed, since talking with a rooster is impossible. End of story." Slahi adds: "For years I've been trying to convince the US government that I am not corn."[119]

The fact he succeeds in creating such an appealing portrait despite the conditions in which he wrote the book is all the more impressive. Many guards seem to take to him and share their feelings and apologize for his treatment. "'I hope you get released,' said ▬▬▬ genuinely."[120] Most readers were no doubt happy when this finally happened in 2016. In early March of 2017, he was interviewed for *60 Minutes*. "They broke me," Slahi said in regards to US torture.[121] Sadly, President Trump has not only refused to condemn torture, but has praised its (discredited) efficacy as part of US policy, showing no lessons were learned.

---

116. Ibid., 245.

117. Ibid., 246. See also ibid., 264–65 and 286.

118. Ibid., 79.

119. Ibid., 73.

120. Ibid., 313; (SSG Mary: *FRV*, 308); see also his exchange with a Mauritanian guard (2015 version, 130), and his hug and goodbye to an FBI agent, ibid., 210. See also Thanegi, *Nor Iron Bars a Cage*, 61 and 68.

121. See: http://www.cbsnews.com/news/ex-gitmo-detainee-on-torture-they-broke-me/.

Witness for the Witnesses

The two accounts above were composed by witnesses who experienced torture and witnessed other degrading treatment. More importantly, they are able to testify and narrate their thoughts, wounds, and nightmares—and the words, spoken and unspoken, of their fellow inmates. Most victims are unable to articulate their views and ordeals themselves, either because they are murdered, too deeply traumatized and scarred, or unable or unwilling to relate their accounts. This last reason could be due to a number of factors: sometimes it's still not safe to reveal their stories, they lack the contacts, opportunities, or medium, or do not consider their stories worthy of hearing or feel unable and unskilled to do so.

In many of these cases, a witness to the witness can inspire, aid, co-write, or stand-in as the proxy-witness. In Liao Yiwu we had an almost ideal witness, but even those whose bodies and minds have been spared such blows can become a voice and advocate for victims. Here, too, the literature in the field is rich and multifaceted. Journalists, NGO field workers, aid workers, photojournalists, doctors, trauma experts, forensic anthropologists, peace keepers, human rights activists, peacebuilders, missionaries—all have published and testified to their experiences in war-torn countries, refugee camps, dilapidated shanty towns, slums, favelas, and inner-city ghettoes.[122] Their aims are to raise awareness and sometimes include suggestions on how readers can aid victims from the conflicts covered.[123]

Deaths by Eviction in Milwaukee

What Katherine Boo refers to as sabotage against moral action, let alone human dignity,[124] pervades Matthew Desmond's painstakingly accurate and brutally unvarnished portrayal of the effects and causes of eviction on the poor in Milwaukee. Across America, millions of people are evicted every year because they can't afford the rent.[125] In Milwaukee, while black women make up only 9 percent of the population, they endure 30 percent

---

122. See Norridge, "Professional Witnessing in Rwanda," 129–43; di Giovanni, *Morning They Came For Us*; in a natural disaster, see Parry, *Ghosts of the Tsunami*.

123. Shannon, *Mama Koko*, 191–92.

124. Boo, *Behind the Beautiful Forevers*, 254.

125. Desmond, *Evicted*, 4. See also Greenberg, "Tenants Under Siege."

of its evictions. As Desmond pithily writes: "Poor black men were locked up. Poor black women were locked out."[126]

In poignant but soul-crushing accounts of individuals and families struggling to find and maintain some stable place to live, Desmond tracks how fragile are the lives enveloped in the squalor of low-paying jobs, addiction, surrounding violence, family abuse, poor education, and general apathy. Children in particular suffer; they see, hear, and experience things they shouldn't; and their parents, usually just a mom, seem helpless as their sinking world sinks further and further down the abyss and muck. "It can't get no worser,"[127] Arlene, a single mother of two boys (Jori, 13, and Jafaris, 5) moans. In and out of dilapidated, roach-filled apartments and homeless shelters, she tries to make it through another day as the 88th landlord turns down her request, if not plea, for tenancy. But of course, it does get worse, worser and worser, her younger children absorbing and collecting all the rejections, sordid cursing and desperation, the hopelessness of it all—having to transfer repeatedly to different schools, having all their possessions sent to storage and then removed when the bills couldn't be paid. Losing everything. Rent could take up 88 percent of her monthly 626-dollar welfare check.[128]

"Children didn't shield families from eviction," Desmond notes, "they exposed them to it."[129] In the case of Arlene and her boys, one eviction was caused by a snowball fight. Jori and a cousin threw a snowball at a passing car. The driver got out of his car, chased them into the house and kicked the door, breaking the lock. The landlord promptly evicted the family, out into the cold. Arlene knew any protest would just mean the sheriff. All their stuff would be either dumped on the curb or locked in storage—and eventually given away if payments weren't maintained.

Even joy is more fleeting for the poor. Though it was Christmastime, it did not mean any reprieve from an eviction or court. Out by the first or a summons and fine. Then there was Little, a cat Arlene and her kids were given and had come to love.[130] In the midst of countless evic-

---

126. Ibid., 98. See also Butler, *Chokehold*. Marc Lamont Hill writes that "black women and girls are disproportionately arrested (compared to their White and Black male counterparts) for minor crimes" (*Nobody*, 64).

127. Desmond, *Evicted*, 289.

128. Ibid., 3. See also Goldstein, *Janesville*; and Morduch and Schneider, *Financial Diaries*.

129. Desmond, *Evicted*, 287.

130. Ibid., 55.

tions, it was inevitable the cat would be left behind. Fortunately, a former neighbor, Trish, agreed to take care of Little. This meant the boys could reunite with Little from time to time. And one day, just when Arlene was thinking she was cursed—"can't win for losing"—she asked Trish if they could move in to her place. She agreed. The boys scurried up to Trish's house, looking for their cat. "But Little was dead. A car had ground him into the pavement."[131] Jori tried not to cry but the anger swelled. He saw a mannequin head in Trish's apartment and kept pounding and punching the face until the adults yelled at him to stop.

Conditions at Trish's, as with all the other places, were desultory. The threat of homelessness, constant money struggles for basic needs, and lack of legitimate and consistent ways to make money left few viable options.

Trish turned tricks for extra cash and the kids were witnesses to the random men coming and going. "In crowded houses, there were no separate places, and children quickly learned the ways of adults."[132] Poverty exacerbated tensions and fights.

Soon, Arlene and the boys would have to leave. Worse, Arlene suspected Trish called CPS on her. All Arlene had were her boys. So what to do now?

Desmond, a sociologist at Harvard, had followed the lives of Arlene and others living in and out of trailer parks, homelessness, and temporary shelters in Milwaukee in a period from May 2008 to December 2009. Eviction was a "process" according to Desmond that "bound poor and rich people together in mutual dependence and struggle."[133] The difference is that the poor needed the rich to live as the wealthy owned the access to basic needs, shelter the most obvious. The rich could sever ties with the poor and still live—just not as lavishly. Fear and the pangs of hunger and hopelessness limited any stable solidarity: "There was always something worse than the trailer park, always room to drop lower."[134]

Desmond presents an impassioned and solid case that housing, the right to safe, stable, and functioning shelter, is a "fundamental need," especially for children, and should be a fundamental, universal right. He calls for the implementation of a "universal housing voucher."[135] Evic-

131. Ibid., 288.
132. Ibid., 289.
133. Ibid., 317.
134. Ibid., 182.
135. Ibid., 307–9.

tions tear holes in families and communities, perpetuating the suffering. As he writes: "Eviction is a cause, not just a condition, of poverty."[136] High eviction rates often lead to increase in crime[137] and exacerbate the racial and class divides in America. Women abused by their partners could be evicted if they call 911 and the police come, deemed a nuisance. Some landlords will blame the woman if the man returns—even against her will.[138] When Arlene was living with a woman named Crystal, Crystal called 911 when the screams in the apartment above were unbearable. The landlord evicted the assaulted woman—and Crystal, Arlene, and her boys. Choiceless choices abounded.

Evicted touched too close to home. I have a PhD and a permanent university job and extended family abroad who can help—but our economic lives can still seem precarious. I think almost every day about how much the landlord will raise the rent again—and what we will do with no money to move, no cheaper place nearby. Thank God there is some government support here in Ireland, especially monthly child benefit. Yes, *Evicted* cut too close—and I am privileged. How those parents and families endure; how can they not snap? "It can't get no worser."

Genocide in Sri Lanka

It can get worse, though. Rohini Mohan's *The Season of Trouble: Life Amid the Ruins of Sri Lanka's Civil War* enters into a world of senseless, systematic violence. Mohan is a journalist based in Bangalore, India. In the book, she focuses on three individuals from two families upended by the civil war and its aftermath in Sri Lanka, which lasted twenty-six years (officially ending in May 2009) and cost more than 100,000 lives. In recent years there has been much momentum in establishing an account of a government-led genocide against the Tamil people in the North and East of the country. The report of the *People's Tribunal on Sri Lanka* from 2013 not only accuses the Sri Lankan government of genocide, but also contends that the "UK, the USA and India are guilty of complicity in genocide."[139]

---

136. Ibid., 299.
137. Ibid., 298.
138. Ibid., 192.
139. *People's Tribunal on Sri Lanka*, 5.2.4. See also Fernando, *Religion, Conflict and Peace in Sri Lanka*.

TESTIMONIES, WITNESSING, AND MORAL FAILURE 213

The book's three main characters, whose real names Mohan altered because of the ongoing security failures in Sri Lanka, are Mugil, a Tamil mother and former Tamil Tiger child soldier; Indra, a middle-aged Tamil woman who anguishes and doggedly labors for the health and freedom of her son; and Sarva, Indra's child, who was kidnapped and tortured by government forces for his brief stint in the Tigers[140] and who later tries to escape Sri Lanka, first for America, and then for England as a refugee.

Mugil considers her joining of the Tigers as voluntary, though she was around thirteen. Soon after her indoctrination and initial training, Mugil was forced to execute three government soldiers by a commander who at "perhaps twenty-one" was much older than her.[141] She served in the Tigers for seven years until she was injured from shrapnel wounds and was discharged. Becoming a mother and seeing the moral breakdown of the Tigers and the failure of the movement, she eventually focuses on her civilian life and survival. Atrocities on both sides left her with few options. In September 2008, she witnessed government forces rape and murder five young Tamil guards of twelve or thirteen years of age. Mugil had been hiding in a Mango tree but was without her T-56 assault rifle. She had hoped someone would intervene. "But below her only a smouldering garden shed stood mute witness."[142] She could hear their cries but could do nothing. Hours later she woke up. "Below her the carnage was over. Five naked girls, their bodies twisted in the last minutes of struggle, lay still in the mud."[143] She saw these girls as forced participants in the Tigers, unlike her, though such distinctions could be debated.

After surviving evacuation of her homeland in the Vanni (Northern Sri Lanka) and various government attacks on fleeing civilians, Mugil desperately sought refuge in a military-run camp at Manik Farm, then divided into eight zones, with Zone 2 (Ramanathan Zone) the most populated at 76,000 people amidst squalid and unsanitary conditions. Barbed wire surrounded the camps. Mugil's husband, Divyan, held by government forces and abused, was not released until January of 2012, two-and-a-half years later. Her father died of malnutrition and diarrhea. Eventually she and her children were bussed out of the camp and dropped

---

140. Mohan, *Season of Trouble*, 43 and 46.
141. Ibid., 33.
142. Ibid., 23. See also 233, where the euphemism "slept next to her" really means rape.
143. Ibid., 39.

off at Point Pedro. She was forbidden to return to where she grew up and lived in the Vanni.

Mugil ends up squatting in another family's house with her children, and life begins to return to some semblance of stability. She visits her husband in prison but their face-to-face contacts are limited. Once he is finally released, prospects for work for Tamils remain almost non-existent. While Mugil settles into family and civilian life, her brother, Prashant, imprisoned, and while under torture, reveals her sister's previous Tiger affiliation. Mugil is arrested and her fate is left unresolved—like the situation in the country for many Tamils.

For our contexts, while Buddhist faith and practice helped survivors like Chinese Master Deng Kuan, in the context of Sri Lanka, Buddhist radicals inflicted violence and retribution on the Enemy, usually Hindu Tamils but also Muslims and Christians.[144] In 1972 Buddhism was named the official religion of Sri Lanka, and according to Mohan, the State's most important role was protecting that faith.[145] For Western readers jaded by Christian or Muslim perpetrators of violence, here there are references to Buddhist monks or "hard-line" Buddhist extremists attacking mosques or Muslim-owned shops and malls.[146] Divyan, the husband of Mugil, witnesses the following scene as reported by Mohan, after visiting Mugil in prison: "There were around fifty people, most of them male and dressed in white. Some wore T-shirts displaying the words NO HALAL within a crossed red circle. Leading them were a half-dozen saffron-clad Buddhist monks."[147] One voice in particular stood out, a Buddhist monk of about 40: "His eyes popped, and spit sprayed from his mouth as he bellowed. When he punched the air above him, the rage seemed to shoot from his feet up to his clenched fist."[148]

Also of note are the NGOs and faith-based groups who work for peace and justice in Sri Lanka. After Indra's son Sarva is released from prison through the unrelenting work of Indra and NGO intervention, his life and safety remain at risk. While from a Hindu family, he is sheltered predominantly in Christian churches, moved from one to another as the threat of danger struck.[149] Sarva is also blessed with a number of aid

144. Yiwu, *Corpse Walker*, 75.
145. Mohan, *Season of Trouble*, 352.
146. Ibid., 239, 315, and 326. See also Kneale, *Atheist's History of Belief*, 155.
147. Mohan, *Season of Trouble*, 349.
148. Ibid., 349–50.
149. Ibid., 207–10.

workers who take on his case and provide a safe context for him to give witness to the tortures that were inflicted upon him by government interrogators, soldiers, and other prisoners (for being a Tamil). Isabel, a case worker for NGO Nonviolent Peaceforce in Sri Lanka, was exemplary, carefully listening to Sarva's story, showing honest disgust and worry at the details, and reassuring and consoling him.[150]

Poetry of Witness in Rwanda

In poet Laura Apol's *Requiem, Rwanda*, readers are confronted with the poetry of witness—but at multiple and interlacing levels. In the process of witnessing, survivors are given space to narrate and occupy what often is unnameable or indescribable—or what is a surfeit of loss, anguish, and trauma. The listener witnesses the words, gestures, and silences of the survivor—and the survivor witnesses the attention, presence, responses, and interjections of the listener. It is, at least, a two-way form of communication and dialogue.

What makes *Requiem, Rwanda* particularly interesting is the various angles or features of the text: from Apol's brief but helpful history of the Rwandan genocide, to her essay on the process or role of the poetry of witness and how she came to write these poems, not to mention the copious notes she supplies to the poems and essays. All these features form her testimony and are meant to be read and re-read in tandem. Here remembering and witnessing are juxtaposed with truth-seeking and clarity: these are poems meant to move but also inform; to disturb but also enlighten. In the context of what is often deemed beyond words, amidst trauma and the murder of almost a million people, Apol seeks to provide reflections and insights for some means of understanding, at first for herself, but then also for her Rwandan friends, and readers in general.

Apol sought critique and validation that the poems she wrote are truthful and accurate from the perspectives of Rwandan survivors of the 1994 genocide and other acts of mass violence. In one instance, Apol even omitted a poem from the collection because of objections from some of her Rwandan readers and colleagues. Such back-and-forth dialogue and critique is a crucial component of any process of becoming an authentic witness for and to the witnesses.

150. Ibid., 184–85.

Apol had first travelled to Rwanda twelve years after the genocide against the Tutsis as part of a small team of educators seeking to establish writing-through-trauma programs.[151] Such programs intended to work with a group of Rwandan survivors of the genocide to engage with the writing and narrative process for healing. Working through the jumble and unformed ideas of loss and despair, the hope was that formed words and expressions could offer safety and control in an otherwise chaotic and despondent mass of sordid and overwhelming memories and nightmares. The deeper hope was that such individuals could then use these techniques to teach their fellow Rwandans, and especially the youth who may have been too young to recall conscious details or who grew up after the void of the genocide, but still suffered trauma.[152]

Apol's initial visit to Rwanda spurred others, first focused on follow-up sessions with those involved in the program—and then shifted to her own witnessing to the witnesses through poems about her experiences in Rwanda and with those she met, mentored, and befriended. Weaved throughout Apol's collection are the realities of post-genocide Rwanda, from an outside observer who painstakingly acknowledges her privilege and otherness as a white woman from Midwest America ("this is no place for me").[153] In this regard there is much apology and justification—how can such a person after a few visits more than a decade after the genocide write for and about Rwandan victims? Apol is clear that while this is a valid question, justifying or answering it is not the aim of her work—though she is a witness, just as the people of Rwanda witnessed her as she lived, worked, taught, travelled, observed, and wrote while in their presence.

---

151. For victim-centered approaches to the Rwandan genocide, see Gourevitch, *We Wish to Inform You*; Hatzfeld's trilogy and follow-up on Rwanda: *Strategy of Antelopes*; *Machete Season*; *Life Laid Bare*; and *Blood Papa*. For comparative analysis, see Kiernan, *Blood and Soil*; Goldhagen, *Worse Than War*; Frey, *Genocidal Temptation*; Neuffer, *Key to My Neighbor's House*; de Waal, "Genocidal Warfare in North-east Africa," 529–49; and Fitzpatrick, *Political Reconciliation in Rwanda and Timor-Leste*. For a memoir that advocates total forgiveness, see Ilibagiza, with Erwin, *Left to Tell*. For critiques of the ethical use and teaching of testimony in the context of the Rwandan genocide, see Taylor, Sollange, and Rwigema, "Ethics of Learning," 88–118.

152. Okeowo, *Moonless, Starless Sky*, 140–47; Okeowo here is referring to a child suffering from "intergenerational trauma" in Uganda.

153. Apol, "Rift," in *Requiem, Rwanda*, 26; see also "Epilogue; Writer as Witness," in ibid., 86–89.

In the poetry of witness, especially as formulated by Carolyn Forché, the poet as witness to the trauma and violence of others or self, bears difficult, hidden, and subsumed truths within their poetry, testifying to what those in power seek to deny, annul, or redact. Essential for Forché is the impact this witnessing has on readers.[154] In a Levinasian sense, it is a call of witness to our infinite responsibility for the Other. We as readers are obligated to seek justice and healing upon hearing such poetry-as-witness, which for Levinas is an obligation that not only precedes our hearing but our existence. Forché adds: "When we read the poem as witness, we are marked by it and become ourselves witnesses to what it has made present before us . . . Witness begets witness."[155]

Forché's poem "The Colonel" is foundational in the poetry of witness (she also refers to it as a documentary poem, stating the date, May 1978 and the site: San Salvador).[156] Such witnessing by poets is widely represented in Forché's edited collection *Against Forgetting: Twentieth Century Poetry of Witness* and the follow-up collection edited with Duncan Wu, *Poetry of Witness: The English Tradition 1500-2001*. Both anthologies have set the standard and ground for this important field.[157] While Apol parallels such examples, she also intersects and aligns with the poetry of witness for her search to remember, her testifying, and her challenge to readers never to forget.

Apol is a witness to the witnesses, even if "coming to write as a 'witness' more than a decade post-genocide."[158] Like Desmond and Mohan's work, such is still an important link in the chain of a poetry of witness, bringing the silence of the victims and the perversions of the perpetrators to contemporary listeners who hear and hopefully respond. Even after the violence and trauma, Apol recognizes that such witnessing is not easy. Referring to one survivor noticeably scarred and wounded from a machete, she writes in "Rift": "I cannot look; I cannot look / away."[159] This tension and obligation of looking and not looking is also present in "Mother of God," in which Apol sees such testimony as the courage to observe and face, even as the images grow more gruesome and hideous:

154. Forché, "Reading the Living Archives," 21.
155. Ibid., 26.
156. See Forché. *Country Between Us*, 16.
157. Forché, *Against Forgetting*; and Forché and Wu, *Poetry of Witness*. See also Milosz, *Witness of Poetry*; and Rowland, *Poetry as Testimony*.
158. Apol, *Requiem, Rwanda*, 93 n.7.
159. Ibid, 27.

the raping of a woman, carrying her baby on her back, with a spear all the way through her skull. The baby nailed to the woman: both left for dead in the church. Apol reflects on a statue of Mary looking down at the victims: "Mother of God— / speak to me of crucifixion / and I will tell you about the human body / becoming a cross. / I will ask you what can save / or be saved / when we choose not to look, / hear the story, weep, and forget, when we refuse to inhabit these bones."[160] Theologian Mario Aguilar calls such scenes "a hermeneutics of bones at the periphery"[161]—though Aguilar hopes such can be a sign of God's presence among the broken and slain, for Jesus was also battered and broken. In Apol's poems, such hopes are often ambiguous. Survivor Cassius Niyonsaba, then twelve, witnessed the massacres in the church in Nyamata, saw little children burned alive by the *interahamwe*. "There was a strong smell of meat, and of petrol," he tells Jean Hatzfeld.[162] He should have died from a machete blow to the head. When he grows up, he tells Hatzfeld, he "will never enter another church."[163]

Poetry after Kibuye

Christian imagery, texts, history, complicity, and failures play a recurring role in Apol's poems here, fitting for a country predominantly Christian at the time of the genocide.[164] That the work is called *Requiem, Rwanda* is also apt (though Apol never explains her use of the Latin term).[165] A requiem is a mass for the dead and for the repose of souls: and there are so many souls at stake. While traditionally we would think of the victims—and perhaps Apol has them in mind—it is not the purported souls of the victims at stake. Sometimes we refer to the scarring of souls or lost souls in the context of victimization, but morally, such language is a further means of victimization. Or is it meant simply as a phrase: a soul as a person; or the soul of the country? Is this a grieving and mass for the

---

160. Ibid., 20–21. In "Witness," Apol writes: "I write your story / on bones" (25).
161. Aguilar, *Theology, Liberation*, 10.
162. Hatzfeld, *Into the Quick*, 5.
163. Ibid., 9.
164. See Rittner, Roth, and Whitworth, *Genocide in Rwanda*.
165. In response to an email I sent, Apol wrote: "when I give talks, I do explain the title. Requiem actually means rest. That's why the Prologue ends the way it does—wishing rest not only for the dead (as is usual for a requiem) but for the living as well." September 11, 2017.

soul of Rwanda—or even of Africa? Or is it more appropriate to speak of the soul of the First World in their role and negligence in the origins and spread of the genocide? How many souls are tainted, thus?

And what of the perpetrators? Do souls even pertain then—and would we even want a mass for such people, smeared in others' blood and sinews, unblotted, unwashed, unrepentant?

Apol's collection is divided into four parts: *Indroit, Lacrimosa, Sanctus, Benedictus*: all Latin words linked to the requiem mass or the Eucharistic prayer in the Catholic mass: offering rich religious symbolism and reflection but also raising more ethical questions. If the Church and Christianity failed so colossally in Rwanda, then does employing Christian religious terms still imply space and means for Christianity as healing and the frame for meaning and closure? Surely, Apol is not using these terms in solely an ironic sense?

Indroit is the opening part of the Eucharistic celebration in the mass, its etymology from *introitus*, "entrance"). It thus is an apt start to the work, with the opening poem delving into origins, titled: "Genesis: The Source of the Nile." The poem is not only referring to false historical claims of Rwanda as the source for the Nile but seeking to explain the origins of the country through the prism of biblical language, tainted with genocidal urgings, a false myth and a false return. The bodies of Tutsis were dumped in the Nyabarongo River to flow to Ethiopia, from where extremist Hutus claimed the Tutsis originated, claiming they were not true Rwandans. "So many ways to be wrong"[166] as the poem's refrain echoes. In the *Indroit*, believers pray for eternal rest. For the victims, and especially the living, so much more is needed than rest: justice.[167]

Dies Irae—The Day of Wrath—is the heading for the first group of poems, nine in all. It is a Latin hymn that forms part of the Requiem mass, with disputed origins from the seventh to the fourteenth century. Such a day of wrath, the hymn sings, will turn the world to ash. The violence is fitting here, and these nine poems, many reflecting on sites of mass atrocity, do indeed speak of bones, blood, and ash. "Early April in Rwanda" depicts banal scenes of normality: a woman cooking beans, a man sharpening his machete for farm and field work; but hinting at more macabre uses. April was the start of the genocide and so marks the traditional period of Rwanda's yearly commemorations.

166. Apol, *Requiem, Rwanda*, 3–5.
167. Ibid., xx. See also Hatzfeld, *Strategy of Antelopes*, 18.

"Six Seconds" refers to the average time it takes to chop and slice a human being. "Even the Land did not escape" reverberates with other atrocities: how human on human violence also violates the world around us: blood seeping into fields, murdered bodies slumping or dumped into rivers. Here it is not just human beings who witness, but also the grass and the rocks.[168] Various poems in Apol's collection portray sites of mass atrocities at churches. For many victims, churches no longer comfort: they are signs and places of cruelty, mutilation, godlessness, and despair. Such is compounded by tales of priests complicit in the genocide and a Church hierarchy who did little, who contributed to the killing, who failed to anticipate or check signs of its rising, or responded too late once so many had been murdered. Apol touches upon many of these notions, often with bitter irony. In "Genocide Site 1: Nyamata Church," there is blood sprayed on the altar—but no sacrifice—only murder. Eucharistic imagery points to the innocent people slaughtered: "Broken bodies, shed blood, / but not those of a Savior— / not in this Golgotha, this God- / forsaken, place of the skull."[169] In the notes, Apol reminds us that 10,000 people were murdered at this site.[170]

In "Genocide Site 2: Ntarama Church," the Sermon on the Mount (and Plain) is juxtaposed with narrative details of individuals seeking sanctuary in the church, bringing with them what they had—glasses, toys, clothes—but their bodies rendered into corpses, into mere bones, now tenderly sorted by survivors and those seeking to honor the dead. Apol notes that "The church *is* sanctuary now; it holds once more its silence, holds its prayers."[171] But she ends the poem with a rooster's crow: betrayal. Five thousand individuals died here. The site is also now a memorial.

Treachery continues in "Eucharist," which Apol notes "has always been about betrayal."[172] Judas was said to sell Jesus for thirty silver pieces as some priests sold out the Tutsis. Of course the Eucharist should be about table fellowship and community. But what fellowship can there be with a priest jeering the Tutsis crouched in churches (this one at Nyange) as his Hutu comrades burn and slash; the church ruined; believ-

---

168. Apol, *Requiem, Rwanda*, 13.

169. Ibid., 15. Nyamata means "place of milk" so the poem is explaining how a site of life is contaminated by genocide.

170. Ibid., 63.

171. Ibid., 16–17.

172. Ibid., 18.

ers murdered; while "the priest resurrected himself / in Europe, where the church universal / took him in."[173] We are reminded of Nazis protected by churches, often in South America. The priest Apol alludes to is Father Athanase Seromba, sentenced to life imprisonment in Benin. Apol's poem and the second part of the collection closes with allusions of Exodus and the drowning at the Red Sea, but also promises and a dove, normally a symbol of hope and peace.

Lacrimosa, Latin for "weeping," is the title of the third section. It not only can refer to Mary, as the Mother of Sorrows, but is part of the *Dies Irae* sequence in the Requiem mass, with the lines: "Lacrimosa dies illa" which refers to the judgment of the guilty and asks God for mercy. The opening phrase here refers to weeping for that day of judgment. We again have some ambiguity and discomfort if the victims are deemed guilty.[174] Must we hope for mercy for the killers and perpetrators, especially the most heinous and self-serving of them? Do we want to grant such killers "eternal rest" in heaven?

The poems comprising this section are predominantly about the witnessing of others or Apol's witnessing of their testimony; in fact, the poem titled "Witness" opens up the section. At times Apol feels helpless and can only listen ("The Lives of Others"). In this sense, the poems describe or paint pictures: of Glori who is enraged at the Westerners who fled with their dogs while abandoning Tutsi children ("Left"); to Louise who finally has some peace after a proper burial of her loved ones, 16 years later ("Dry Bones"—also note the reference to Ezekiel in the poem's title and epitaph); to Samuel who eventually saved some Tutsi children who kept imploring him for shelter ("Samuel and the Boys"); to Alphonse, a Hutu who says he was unjustly accused of a murder that occurred after the genocide while he claims he saved lives during it ("Confession"). To Alphonse, killers walk free who confess serious crimes during *gacaca* hearings,[175] while he had no such possibility and so remained in prison. Other portraits are not named: of a girl writing about her family's massacre, haunted by links of the color pink, once her favorite color but now tarnished by images of roses in the family yard or a flower on her sister's

---

173. Ibid., 18.

174. See Admirand, *Mass Atrocity*, chapter 4. On Rwanda's moral failures in Congo, see Berwouts, *Congo's Violent Peace*, 73–88.

175. For more on *gacaca*, see Thomson and Nagy, "Law, Power, and Justice," 11–30; and Pozen, Neugebauery, and Ntaganira, "Assessing the Rwanda Experiment," 31–52.

sandals ("Pink"); to a survivor finally returning fifteen years later to the house in Remera where she and her family hid during the genocide and leaving with a cutting from a rose bush that her mom had planted, but the stem is "all thorns, no rose."[176] Even with hints of new beginnings, the pain and prick of the past cannot be left behind.

Thirteen poems as portraits—along with observations of post-genocide Rwanda—comprise the fourth section, *Sanctus*, Latin for "holy" and part of the Roman Catholic mass, said or sung before the Eucharistic Prayer. One poignant portrait is "Meeting François in Heaven" in which Apol sees the machete scar on a waiter's ear and wants to "Caress it like a healer. / Ease it like a mother."[177] Apol also witnesses a Western journalist (in the notes listed as *New York Times* reporter Stephen Kinzer)[178] break down and cry while at a bar.

He is initially described in flip flops eating and drinking while typing away. Apparent aloofness belied deep sadness for the suffering witnessed ("At the Hotel Bar"). So much is not what you expect. We read of Apol's unease at the sight of a farmer with a machete ("Watching a Man Cut the Grass"); and we hear of Rwandans supporting Haiti after the 2010 earthquake ("Rwanda Stands Up for Haiti: January 2010"). Recall Maimonides's comment on the importance of giving to others in chapter 1. Such giving for Rwandans was not only a sign of their restoration but a testament for the need to speak up when others are in distress.

The final poem in the section "Language Lessons," opens with an epitaph from Paul Celan, whose Holocaust poem "Todesfuge" echoes in the final poem of the book, "Milkfugue." Celan is an interesting and complex Holocaust poet to highlight. The epitaph states that only language is reachable; but Celan's work is rendered more by darkness and opacity—the opposite of much of Apol's work here, though Michael Hamburger notes that Celan insists he was not a "hermetic poet."[179]

An aside: In 2001, while a graduate student in a class taught by the late Elie Wiesel, I had to present on the poetry of Celan. I claimed there was a hidden shred of hope and light in Celan's work, arguing for his attempt to be understood despite the trauma and ineffability of the Shoah. Wiesel listened attentively, smiled, complimented what I had written,

---

176. Apol, *Requiem, Rwanda*, 34.
177. Ibid., 46.
178. Ibid., 66.
179. Hamburger, "Introduction," 24. See also Spadaro, "Can only religious believers write poems that are prayers?," 61–62; and Mikics, *Who Was Jacques Derrida?*, 189.

and said: "Peter, I agree 99 percent except for Celan." He continued: "I, too, had those same thoughts, and so in Paul Celan's apartment in Paris in 196–" (the actual date escapes me) "I asked him such questions and for such clarity, but he could not answer them, did not answer them." In the marginalia of my copy of *Poems of Paul Celan,* scribbled around the poem "Psalm," I wrote the following while Wiesel was speaking: "Wiesel: 'Celan didn't want to be understood; it is possible he did not want to be understood.'" At the time I had no strong rebuttal, and still don't today.

"In Language Lessons," there are images of despair: of killers haunted by what they did; of Clinton's State Department press spokesperson, Christine Shelly, who painfully avoided the term "genocide" in the infamous press conference of June 10, 1994. But hope still predominates, especially in the stanza of the wedding of two survivors, Mukundwa ("Beloved") and Hakizimana ("God saves") which Apol attended as an adopted family member. The collection of poems is also dedicated to Joseph, whose mother and grandmother were survivors of the genocide. "Though he is only six," Apol writes, "Joseph is the reason for this book— the Joseph whose artwork smiles at me each morning from my desk, and all the Josephs growing up, or never to grow up, in Rwanda."[180]

Just as one poem was contained in the opening section, one poem closes the final section, *Benedictus,* which is the second part of the *sanctus* in the mass, meaning blessed. It also refers to the song of Zechariah in Luke 1:68 in which Zechariah, John the Baptist's father, has his voice restored after agreeing with his wife Elizabeth that the child will be called John. It's thus a song of thanksgiving and of a voice healed, hopeful images to close the work, though its links with Celan's famous poem dampen any unrealistic optimism. While Celan's poem is inundated by death and the drinking of death—"wir trinken und trinken"—milk symbolically entails life and death in Rwanda; milk as the gift of life, nourishment, and strength, linked with wedding ceremonies in the exchange of milk; but also the poisoning of kings and queens by milk[181]—the jarring apposition of Milkfugue and Todesfugue is fitting.

---

180. Apol, *Requiem, Rwanda,* xiii.
181. Ibid., 61–62; and notes, 68–70.

Conclusion

The texts highlighted in this chapter do not incriminate every religion, institution, or people, but I challenge any group to unequivocally deny Alexander Solzhenitsyn's challenge: "And just so we don't go around flaunting too proudly the white mantle of the just, let everyone ask himself: If my life had turned out differently, might I not have become just such an executioner?";[182] or as Svetlana Alexievich records in *Second-Hand Time*: "It's not just Stalin and Beria, it's also our neighbour Yuri and beautiful Aunt Olga."[183] This is not to claim everyone will become an executioner, as Wiesel and Levi have adamantly rebuked.[184] But witness testimonies reveal how the majority of us, along with our countries, faith systems, and ideologies, have failed. With a broad brush, we can say that America's democracy failed post 9/11; the Catholic Church failed in Rwanda; Buddhism failed in Sri Lanka. This is not to deny successes, but even in celebrations one cannot forget losses and culpability.

Science, socialism, democracy, technology, Christianity, Islam, Buddhism, America, China, India—who can claim clean hands? In this chapter, I have chosen recent texts of witnessing that also exhibit high artistic and moral merit—and if expanding that list with other worthy titles, who would be left standing as innocent, free of blemish, and morally integral and wholly sound?

Witness testimonies' most important challenge is to urge us to respond and seek justice and healing for victims, calling for ethical renewal and commitment to prevent such violence from repeating. They also probingly and categorically humble. In reading witness testimonies or in listening to survivors, we are confronted with moral failures, negligence, hypocrisy, and frailty. Face-to-face with a Yiwu, Arleen, Slahi, Juri, Mugil, and the unnamed mother and baby nailed to death in a Rwandan church, we stammer; look away; bite our tongues; or perhaps want to console or heal; to pray; to remedy. However, and whether, we respond, we are touched, wounded, humbled.

Few can candidly claim exemption. With a tarnished historical record, awareness of the gifts and sacredness of the Other, the call for forgiving and forgiveness becomes eminent. To such thoughts, we turn in our closing chapter.

---

182. Solzhenitsyn, *Gulag Archipelago*, 75.
183. Alexievich, *Second-Hand Time*, 62.
184. Levi, *Drowned and Saved*, 48–49; and Wiesel, *Sea Is Never Full*, 347.

8

Yielding with the Other
Forgiveness, Justice, Love

Prologue: Elephantine Forgiveness

Off to the zoo, I feel like a little kid. My older daughter asked if she could come. I impishly said it was for work (for this book, actually). A few weeks back, I had contacted Gerry Creighton, the Dublin Zoo Operations Manager. I told him about this project, and specifically, this chapter on forgiveness. Based on his extensive work with elephants and chimpanzees, I was curious about his views on animal forgiveness and reconciliation. He agreed to meet me, so now I am waiting at a bus stop near Parnell Square to take the 46A to Phoenix Park, one of Europe's largest urban parks.

I'm standing across from the Rotunda Hospital, founded in 1745, and of which John Banville quips: "Was ever a maternity hospital more aptly named?"[1] As if on cue, a pregnant woman comes out to smoke a cigarette. This is a chapter on our need for forgiveness, after all.

Once on the bus, we pass the supposedly haunted, Black Church, St. Mary's, with its four jagged, limestone spire-sticks slicing into the air. Apparently, the devil can be called forth if you walk around it counterclockwise three times at midnight.[2] Fortunately, the bus moves on without incident, past the Berkeley Pub on Mount Joy Street, and then, at Arran Quay Ward, The Irish Volunteer Monument, Phibsboro. On a limestone plinth is a soldier who stands for those members of the Dublin Brigade of the Irish Volunteers who fought and died during the Easter

---

1. Banville, *Time Pieces*, 182.
2. Whitney, *Hidden City*, 93–94.

Rising (1916) and the War of Independence (1919–21). Daffodils bob in proximity behind it. On the opposite side of the street is the Riverrun Garden, alluding to the opening of *Finnegan's Wake:* "from swerve of shore to bend of bay."[3]

On North Circular Road, we pass Spirasi, a haven and help for traumatized refugees and migrants, run by the Spiritan Fathers. In the distance soars the obelisk, The Wellington Monument of Phoenix Park. Before reaching our destination, we turn into a string of council housings and flats, the O'Devaney Gardens, boarded up and desolate, trash everywhere, graffiti slithering on all the doors—some doorways still having clothes lines with various articles drying in the intermittent sun. The site is slated for "regeneration." A mostly barren field nearby has two scrawny horses slinking about. The bus pulls away and stops a few minutes' walk from the entrance to the park. I soon enter the gates. Heading towards the Garda headquarters, I view lakes and trees, playgrounds, and sports fields. I'm on my way to lions, tigers, and bears (oh my).

Having accounted for how I journeyed to the zoo, let me now lay out the terrain of this chapter, which will focus primarily on forgiveness. Seeing forgiveness as another humbler, I will argue that where possible, we need to admit how our failures demand showing repentance, seeking forgiveness, and extending such forgiveness to others.

I will first tease out some of the key questions hovering and immersed in the contentious notion of forgiveness and then provide some definitions and flesh to the term, also explaining what I do not mean or intend by it. In the midst of this process and along the forgiveness continuum, lie grounds for further humbling. Particularly relevant is the relationship between forgiveness and justice.

The limits of forgiveness will also be addressed; likewise, on the squalor and dread of the unforgivable—as possibility or reality.[4] Is forgiveness, should forgiveness, always be sought and demanded? I don't really know—pulled by many sound voices on various sides—but I do know we are all in need of forgiveness, which first entails accepting responsibility for what we have done, or not done.

After an overview of forgiveness in a range of traditions, I will reflect on the reality of love as a humbler. Again, for all who love, which is

---

3. Joyce, *Finnegan's Wake*, 3.
4. Hatzfeld, *Into the Quick*, 27.

to say the human and non-human, love humbles.⁵ And it does so in ways that continue to amaze and transfix us. Whether as torrent, flash flood, or slow, steady droplets, love can erode or cleanse mountain chains of excessive pride, certitude, and irresponsibility.

We will then enter the zoo.

Questionable Forgiveness

Forgiveness's reputation has only increased with time. Philosopher Charles Griswold writes: "Forgiveness is said to do it all: it is the cure for wrongs both personal and political, the road to eternal salvation, and the secret to mental and physical health."⁶ This chapter may be a little guilty in extending the hype, but enough doubt and questioning are filtered through to debunk any forgiveness-elixir. Some traditions pride themselves on the ability and propensity to forgive. This sounds like a little humility is in order.

Before we proceed further, it will be helpful to highlight some salient questions hovering on the idea, practice, and process of forgiveness. Consider, for example, the following:

1. Is forgiveness merely renouncing revenge or must it entail some form of reconciliation?
2. Does forgiveness discount any need for justice or punishment?
3. Are there gradations of forgiveness or a decisive moment where forgiveness can be unequivocally pronounced?
4. If forgiveness is a process, is it ever completed? Does it need to be?
5. What does it mean to say an act is unforgivable? Do such pronouncements condemn the individual who has committed such an act? Is he or she, then, beyond saving or redemption?
6. Who can and who should not forgive: only the victims, or can second or third parties forgive, too? If so, under which circumstances or criteria? Can someone apologize for a victim? Can the dead be forgiven? Should the unrepentant?
7. Are there some acts that even God should not—or cannot—forgive?

---

5. King, *How Animals Grieve*, 10.
6. Griswold, "Preface," xi.

8. If an act is unforgivable, is it unethical to forgive such an act or such a perpetrator? For the sake of the victim or victims, must a perpetrator—even if he or she seems to show genuine repentance—never have this act forgiven? Does the victim always have the final say in these matters?

9. Must we forgive? Is it unethical not to forgive? If so, how do such arguments relate to belief in life after death and the existence of what has traditionally been called hell? Is everyone saved (i.e., universal salvation)?

10. Does forgiveness always heal and a refusal to forgive wound and harm?

This chapter cannot satisfactorily answer all these questions. Such would be the height of hubris. The concept of forgiveness calls first for seeing our own brokenness and failures. Simultaneously, forgiveness tries to re-evaluate and assess wrongs committed against ourselves and seeks wisdom and answers for what can best heal those fractures and wounds. It refuses to partake in revenge, though not necessarily the implementation of state justice or the possibility for cathartic if not redemptive punishment.[7] Forgiveness should be guided by the universal dignity of the human person and by human rights discourse. The victim thus ideally leaves room, no matter how sparse or unlikely, for one day seeing the offender beyond that damning label.

Note also that forgiveness is a decision, a choice. In deciding to forgive, there is an acknowledgment that not forgiving was also a viable option. As the narrator asks in Anthony Trollope's opening novel of the Palliser Series: "But can you forgive her, delicate reader?"[8] Even with the choice to forgive comes continual re-evaluation with no guarantee that old memories, fears, and resentment will not linger or return. Emphasizing forgiveness as a process and decision highlights the need for commitment, and facing struggles and doubt. It must also withstand the counter-pull of vengeance or isolation, even if only latent at some unconscious level. Lastly, forgiveness as denial, as a turning away ("have a good life far from here") is nowhere near reconciliation—which is a denser path. Reconciling is praised, but not fully advocated here. Humility must also be realistic. Though in truth, following the humblers advocated in

---

7. See, for example, Eisenbrandt, *Assassination of a Saint*.
8. Trollope, *Can You Forgive*, 398.

this book, in theory, can create a space for reconciling—while helping to limit and avoid what spurs and causes our failures and foibles.

Before expanding on various roads of and to forgiveness, a comment on one I unapologetically shun. While reading Peter Brown's *The Ransom of the Soul: Afterlife and Wealth in Early Western Christianity* I was struck—and appalled—by references to "the half-ascetic, courtly lifestyle" of the Merovingian Court, where "Ceremonious and scrupulous, [Courtiers] variably addressed each other as peccator—as 'fellow sinners.'"[9] It was a daily outpouring, tenaciously outlined, especially by the earlier influence of Augustine, of everyone's sinfulness. Also influential was "the Irish and British practice of regular confession, followed by 'tariffed,' that is by minutely calibrated, penance for each sin."[10] Such sin-keeping is not on order here. While specificity and context matter, we start at a more fundamental recognition that we all have caused harm to others and have been harmed in turn. Seeking and accepting forgiveness are roles and acts only unknown to the tyrant, demagogue, egotist, and newborn. The point is to know and believe this fallibility, not to be necessarily auditor-like in keeping accounts. Nor am I advocating total forgiveness, for everywhere, everywhen, everyone.

Forgivenesses?

"If forgiveness is difficult to give and to receive," Paul Ricoeur remarks: "it is just as difficult to conceive."[11] Part of the difficulty lies in many interrelated terms. Elizabeth A. Cole, for example writes: "Apology, forgiveness, reparations, restitution, truth-telling, acknowledgement, restorative and retributive justice, trust, repair, reconciliation: How do these processes relate to one another, how do they differ, and how do they operate at different social levels, from individuals to polities? Are they all even appropriate as responses to different types of wrongdoing?"[12] There are not only different conceptions of forgiveness, but different levels of forgiveness that would expect to be addressed or solved in various ways. How I seek forgiveness from my wife for some "minor" but typically self-centered action differs from a leader of a country making an apology

---

9. Brown, *Ransom of the Soul*, 194.
10. Ibid., 191.
11. See Ricoeur, *Memory, History, Forgetting*, 457–506.
12. Cole, "Apology," 421.

to the survivors of some historical state-injustice committed a century in the past, to a genocidal perpetrator seeking forgiveness from family members of his victims.

Anthony Bash wonders if it makes more sense to write and refer to "forgivenesses."[13] He also wants to specify thick or thin descriptions of forgiveness.[14] Others may speak of expansive or negotiated forgiveness,[15] among other qualifiers or descriptions. In the *Gospel in Solentiname*, Armando and Cesar proclaim that forgiveness is revolutionary,[16] especially in regards to economic debts and burdens in a revolutionary context. Linked here is the notion of the forgiving of debts with sins.[17] Is there anything forgiveness is not?

I will keep forgiveness in the singular, but only shying from Bash's idea because of its semantic awkwardness. There is a plurality to conceptions of forgiveness and this should be praised, not lamented.

Many philosophical accounts of forgiveness build on a key sermon of Joseph Butler, which situates forgiveness as an overcoming of resentment. Butler defines two kinds: "hasty and sudden, or settled and deliberate."[18] At issue is not why a flash of revenge arose in the mind, but how we reply and respond to that urge. Another issue is the relationship of forgiveness and reconciliation. Theologian Didier Pollefeyt succinctly writes: "forgiveness is the ability to recognize the space between what someone is and what he or she can be and between persons and their history, and to open for them a space, a future, not *in spite* of their history of evil but *beyond* that history."[19]

Forgiveness should give hope for the perpetrator to have a type of rebirth, but reconciliation or relationship between victim and perpetrators cannot be universalized or demanded. For example, I was again mopey the other day, not handling some basic, but still disappointing news in any calm, dignified way. I cursed, sulked, exuding negativity. My wife bore the emotional brunt of it. Seeking healthy release on the soccer pitch, I instead yelled and cursed that night at a teammate. Such can be

13. Bash, "Forgiveness," 142.
14. Ibid., 143.
15. Mellor, Di Bretherton, and Firth, "Aboriginal and Non-Aboriginal Australia," 11.
16. Cardenal, *Gospel in Solentiname*, 372.
17. See Anderson, *Sin*.
18. Butler, "Sermon VIII."
19. Pollefeyt, "Forgiveness after the Holocaust," 67.

reconciled, forgiven—even while less has also ruptured, as the little can build until everything breaks. Some acts preclude any hope of reconciliation, even if forgiveness is offered or extended, perhaps unconditionally, perhaps because the victim just needs a release, a wash-away, or must be undertaken for pragmatic reasons of survival. Such forgiveness is closer to not wanting harm to befall the other, and would not be a rich or thick conception of forgiveness. It may even be exemplary under the contexts. Rwandan genocide survivor Edith Uwanyiligira told reporter Jean Hatzfeld in 2000 that she was ready to forgive because she is carrying these haunted memories and pain and wants her body to be at peace. "Even though I do not believe their soothing words, I must sweep fear far away from me."[20]

The Forgiveness Project is notable in working through some of these entanglements. Desmond Tutu writes that it "has shown us that true greatness is found in humility and compassion."[21] Founded initially as an exhibition of stories on forgiveness, "The F Word Exhibition" has since spiralled into a global movement and project from the vision of its founder, Marina Cantacuzino. Refreshingly, she harbors no goal of containing forgiveness as a concept, noting her understanding of it is elusive and respects diverse views.[22] Cantacuzino also made sure that from its inception the "stories were not excessively faith-focused because there seemed a need to free forgiveness from the straightjacket of religion to make it accessible to people of all faiths as well as those of none."[23] Forgiveness is too important and layered to be owned and restrained by any culture or religious faith.

For philosopher Avishai Margalit, forgiveness can be a "policy" which is voluntary and demands a decision, or it entails a change of heart which is not voluntary.[24] In this change of heart, reaching forgiveness involves a long process "of mastering anger and humiliation."[25] Successful forgiveness does not forget the offense but "overcome[s] the resentment that accompanies it."[26] It shares elements with both types of forgiveness

20. Hatzfeld, *Into the Quick*, 126.
21. Tutu, "Foreword," in Cantacuzino, xi.
22. Cantacuzino, *Forgiveness Project*, 2.
23. Ibid., 11.
24. Margalit, *Ethics of Memory*, 203.
25. Ibid., 204.
26. Ibid., 208.

that Margalit depicts—or rather acknowledges that some deciding and some sense of struggling to overcome hatred are needed. Forgiveness as a process must continually confront waves of returning negative feelings and emotions.[27] For Desmond Tutu, it is not a matter of trying to forget the wrong, but calling upon compassion, tolerance, and patience to work through and to "let go of the negative feelings."[28] Just as the Dalai Lama urges that compassion is most beneficial to those giving compassion, Tutu makes the same claims for forgiveness. "It is practical politics."[29] This is part of the reason for his refrain: "There is no future without forgiveness."[30]

Anna Floerke Scheid's five points of forgiveness are particularly useful, which I paraphrase as follows:

1. Victims are the priority in any discussion of forgiveness.

2. Victims can initiate and offer forgiveness regardless of the role, intention or state of the perpetrator, whether living or dead.

3. Forgiveness does not depend on the actions of a perpetrator which then may demand forgiveness. Such freedom should empower victims to choose the path best for them.

4. Forgiveness does not demand expectation of any meaningful relationship with the perpetrator (sometimes, though, geographical proximity prioritizes some kind of interaction).

5. Forgiveness is a "lifetime process to which victims may have to recommit themselves regularly."[31]

The key refrain here is the focus on the needs and healing of the victims. A victim-centered approach is the most reasonable and appropriate, though a few further distinctions are needed. First, the label of victim does not preclude the label perpetrator in another context. Second, no victims have carte blanche to say or do whatever they want because they have been wronged. Sadly, many victims were or become perpetrators. Third, where a crime is excessive or a perpetrator is unrepentant, I agree with Claudia Card who questions the wisdom of forgiving in such

---

27. Scheid, *Just Revolution*, 111.
28. Tutu, "Foreword" in Henderson, xii.
29. Wiesenthal, *Sunflower*, 268.
30. Tutu, *No Future without Forgiveness*.
31. Scheid, *Just Revolution*, 111.

contexts even if there is no "logical incoherence in doing so."[32] Fourth, on the question of victims' obligations to seek justice, I remain undecided. Do victims have some sense of responsibility or obligation[33] to testify about their suffering as a means to bring perpetrators to justice, even if the final say on forgiveness should remain with the victims? The aims would be to give voice to the voiceless, restore honor to the dead, and prevent recurring injustice. Testifying in some cases, however, remains unsafe for victims so cannot be obligatory.

To sum up: forgiveness is an ongoing process, decision, and commitment, which tries to leave space between the perpetrator (a fellow human being) and the perpetrator's action (or inaction) of wrong-doing, and calls for justice and renewal while hoping the perpetrator can become committed to working for justice and renewal. Not surprisingly, humility is an important facet of forgiveness in achieving such aims.

The Symbiosis of Humility and Forgiveness[34]

A lack of humility often means a propensity to injure, a refusal to forgive, a predisposition to feel wronged, and equating justice with individual desires. Unhealthy or excessive humility can invoke a suspension of justice or is blind for the need of justice. Some broken victims do not even recognize their victimhood. Others believe they do not deserve justice. Either seeking martyrdom or equating justice as selfishness, they silently fester or proudly relinquish any claim. Yet forgiveness, humility, and justice are deeply interwoven.[35] Humility can moderate a justice too severe or a forgiveness too unquestioning.

Such a notion is tied to the idea that all are sinners (fallible and prone to injure)—or could be, which is all the more humbling. This path encourages compassion for perpetrators (even as the victim's state and recovery is rightly prioritized) while also portraying some form of fair, humane punishment as a symbol and educative path towards moral and civic renewal. That many prisons are destructive of personal growth is a

32. Card, *Atrocity Paradigm*, 180.

33. Booth, *Communities of Memory*, 138. See also Sacks, *Dignity of Difference*, 190; and MacIntyre, *After Virtue*, 130.

34. See Zhang et al., "Intellectual Humility and Forgiveness of Religious Conflict," 255–62.

35. Peterson, "Is Forgiveness Possible?," 184. See also Worthington, "Unforgiveness, Forgiveness, and Reconciliation," 181.

related, but still distinctive, issue on how punishment should be cathartic—or restorative, as I note further below.

In the context of peacebuilding amidst and after war and conflict, John Paul Lederach highlights the need for a deep vulnerability, which requires sincerity and humility. For Lederach, "humility [is] a combination of attitude and relational stance that remains permanently open to learning and insight, and regards the other as holding the potential for sharing wisdom."[36] We have highlighted this role of humility in the chapters on pluralism and interfaith dialogue.[37] Forgiveness not only humbles, but humility leads to a sharper awareness of the need for forgiveness, a keener quest for truth.[38] Such a conception of justice is closest to what is referred to as restorative justice. As John Braithwaite remarks: "reconciliation and restorative justice can only be combined in a spirit of humility."[39]

Forgiveness with/as Restorative Justice

Forgiveness and justice are often portrayed as clashing, but this need not be so. Forgiveness may foreswear revenge and harm, but justice should not be about revenge or inflicting senseless injury. In forgiving someone, do I not then remove the weight of punishment? Bash claims "there cannot be forgiveness with justice because the fact there has been moral wrong is irreversible."[40] Katharina von Kellenbach, moreover, avers: "Peace depends on justice, and reconciliation requires truth. Forgiveness that compromises the dignity and integrity of victims is a pretence."[41] We are again somewhat mired in how we interpret forgiveness. Is forgiveness relinquishing any form of punishment? Cannot some punishment be conducive to healing and forgiveness for the victim, the perpetrator, and even society?

36. Lederach, "Spirituality and Religious Peacebuilding," 558.
37. Ibid., 559. See also Lederach, "Five Qualities of Practise in Support of Reconciliation Processes," 198–99.
38. Foulcher, *Reclaiming Humility*, 83.
39. Braithwaite, "Traditional Justice," 214.
40. Bash, "Forgiveness," 145.
41. Kellenbach, *Mark of Cain*, 198; for peacemaking amidst violence in the context of world religions, see Omar and Duffey, *Peacemaking*; and Schmid, *Religion, Conflict, and Peacemaking*.

Trying to distinguish itself from other models of justice—namely, procedural, retributive, judicial, distributive, and transitional—proponents of restorative justice contend that its focus on the relational renders the most flexible, holistic, and integrative type of justice. Here the relational refers not only to frayed relations between the victim and perpetrator, but the ongoing roles and relations within the community, the State, and the International Community on account of the present or past rupture. As Pollefeyt remarks: "Justice entails public recognition of the evil done to the victims and their descendants. It requires efforts to restore their dignity and also identification of the perpetrators. Forgiveness presupposes justice."[42] Thus, healing needs to occur at all these levels with a vision focused on the long-term common good. Amidst such degradation and loss, what are the best methods to establish and—more importantly—maintain peace and to rebuild what is broken and lost?

The "bottom line of restorative justice," according to Ched Myers and Elaine Enns, is that "there is no victim whose pain does not deserve attention, and no offender who is beyond redemption."[43] Its victim-centered approach attempts to find a balance between justice and reconciliation in the context of war, atrocities, and peace-building. Punishment is seen as a part of the process of restoration and reconciling.[44] In theory, could this state be reached without punishment of a perpetrator? Perhaps, but a perpetrator's recognition of the consequences of his decision to commit wrong includes societal responses to deter future crimes. Punishment, even as part of reparation, can be viewed in this light, working through and atoning for grave errors and crimes. Christopher Marshall has called this "restorative punishment."[45] The idea is that perpetrators can be restored to what they once were or could become with aid, education, and trust. But the journey will be long, and jail time, community service, civic restrictions (within the bounds of human rights), and participation in educational workshops may be part of the rehabilitation. As Daniel Philpott adds: "When a victim wills punishment, she asserts that the hard treatment of punishment is also required to defeat the perpetrator's

---

42. Pollefeyt, "Forgiveness after the Holocaust," 57. See also Pollefeyt, "Ethics, Forgiveness, and the Unforgivable," 122.

43. Myers and Enns, *Ambassadors of Reconciliation*, 63. See also Holmgren, *Forgiveness and Reconciliation*, 277–78.

44. Pope, "Role of Forgiveness," 187.

45. Marshall, *Beyond Retribution*, 131–39.

injustice."⁴⁶ Can perpetrators see castigation in a similar light? Unfortunately, few of us reach a point where we validate the punishment we receive. Too often perpetrators believe they are innocent, framed, or justified in what they did. In the context of forgiveness, perpetrators would need to acknowledge their culpability and responsibility, and with that, the consequences that often entail punishment. The punishment should also provide avenues for perpetrators to come to this position.

Of the relationship between justice and forgiveness, Philpott teases various interrelated formulations, stating: "the meaning of reconciliation is quite close to the meaning of justice."⁴⁷ Referring to biblical traditions and Islam, he contends that justice in those traditions means restorative justice: meaning relational, righteousness, and righting relationship.⁴⁸ Elsewhere, he writes that "forgiveness instantiates justice"⁴⁹ and that "forgiveness is not contrary to justice but rather reflective of it if justice means restoration of right relationship."⁵⁰ Is this feasible? Echoing Pope Francis's decree in August 2018,⁵¹ forgiveness cannot condone any form of capital punishment, but could it sanction life imprisonment without parole? Here we need to examine the severity of the crime (and bear in mind the conditions of imprisonment). Can mercy, let alone, forgiveness, have any relevance with atrocious crimes and their magnitude?

In *Dives in Misericordia*, John Paul II proclaims: "True mercy is, so to speak, the most profound source of justice."⁵² Mercy is not about blanket amnesty or seeking to excuse or ameliorate deserved punishment, but guides and judges the punishment that is meted out to ensure the proper means and aim are in the best relational interests of the victim, perpetrator, and society. It seeks to overcome any primal urge for pure revenge or inflicting of pain and harm. "Properly understood," John Paul II writes: "justice constitutes, so to speak, the goal of forgiveness."⁵³ The key is how the terms are understood, not a straight-forward matter.

---

46. Philpott, "Justice of Forgiveness," 413.
47. Philpott, "Reconciliation," 97.
48. Philpott, "Justice of Forgiveness," 403.
49. Ibid., 403. See also de Lange, "Room for Forgiveness?," 175.
50. Philpott, "Justice of Forgiveness," 400. See also Philpott, "What Religion Offers," 152.
51. Povoledo and Goodstein, "Pope Francis Declares."
52. John Paul II, "Dives in Misericordia," §14.
53. Ibid., §14.

Thus concludes my contribution to forgiveness as an elixir. Now to some of its difficult realities and limitations, and why elixirs (whether as forgiveness or alchemy or humility) never work as advertised.

The Limits of Forgiveness

Forgiveness is often misunderstood and so has plenty of detractors. As with humility, some of these detractors also raise valid points. Writing the foreword to Thomas Brudholm's *Resentment's Virtue*, Jeffrie Murphy contests the notion that "forgiveness is always a virtue, that all resentments are unhealthy, and that all relationships are worth restoring."[54] In the contexts of forgiveness and mass atrocity, Brudholm suggests that high hopes like reconciliation can be replaced with more pragmatic notions of "coexistence."[55] His point is not to shun victims who have chosen to forgive but to "to say that—sometimes—the preservation of outrage or resentment and the refusal to forgive can be the reflex expression of a moral protest and ambition that are as permissible and admirable as the willingness to forgive or forgiveness proper."[56] For Brudholm, Jean Améry is a virtuous example of someone refusing to forgive.

Améry warns against any temptation to "lazily and cheaply forgive" or to give in to societal pressure to forgive. He would deem both immoral.[57] While time may theoretically heal, to renounce one's moral claims to what was wrong when no justice has been rendered is at the heart of what is immoral. Society wants to move forward or hang onto the hope of not repeating the crime. "But," as Améry writes: "my resentments are there in order that the crime[s] become a moral reality for the criminal, in order that he be swept into the truth of his atrocity."[58] Sadly, genocidal perpetrators often sleep soundly, while their living victims languish in despondency and fear.

Debates are ongoing here. Renée Jeffrey cites Case 001 against Kaing Guek Eav, alias Dutch, chairman of the notorious Toul Sleng Prison, before the Extraordinary Chambers in the Court of Cambodia. As part of the proceedings, Dutch re-visited the prison site and encountered three

54. Murphy, "Foreword," ix.
55. Brudholm, *Resentment's Virtue*, 172.
56. Ibid., 171.
57. Améry, *At the Mind's Limits*, 72.
58. Ibid., 70.

of the seven survivors. He sought forgiveness from them and in other contexts during the legal trial. As Jeffrey states: "Not one of the 22 civil parties who testified before the ECC offered forgiveness."[59] Again, is forgiveness necessary for the victim's well-being and inner-peace, and if not, should it still be promoted, requested, or expected from outside parties, let alone perpetrators?[60]

"Too often in church circles, for example," Myers and Enns rightly warn, "abused wives have been exhorted to 'just forgive' their husbands, which only functions to perpetuate the cycle of violation."[61] Need for such pragmatism and sensitivity towards victims is illustrated in the story of another centenarian Christian nun interviewed by Liao Yiwu in 2003. She first described how the Chinese Communist government persecuted and destroyed fellow Christians and her church. When asked about forgiveness by Liao Yiwu: "she jumped up from her seat and stamped her feet emphatically. 'No, certainly not! They still occupy our church property! I refuse to die! I will wait until they return everything back to the church!'"[62] In contexts of ongoing and unaddressed historical, systemic abuse, the nun's response is heroic and understandable. As theologian Stephen Pope writes, in the context of mass atrocities, "Sometimes, refusing to reconcile can be a condition of security, self-respect, and even mental health."[63]

Ma Thanegi tells of an incident from Yangon's Insein Prison when a former Military Intelligence Officer, who had arrested a number of political prisoners, was sentenced for corruption, and placed in the same prison of his victims. He anticipated harsh treatment but encountered widespread kindness and forgiveness. They even taught him how to meditate. "He burst into tears at their welcome, is now meditating diligently, and in turn is forgiving of his captors."[64]

Forgiveness in harsh, Darwinian conditions can also be a sign of weakness, a virtual death sentence. Regarding the notorious prison camps of North Korea, Shin In Guen told Blaine Harden that after he had escaped from North Korea he had heard about the concept of forgiveness

59. Jeffery, "Forgiveness Dilemma," 44.

60. See Saunders, "Questionable Associations," 119–41. See also Stover, *Witnesses*, 95.

61. Myer and Enns, *Ambassadors of Reconciliation*, 66.

62. Yiwu, *God is Red*, xxi.

63. Pope, "Role of Forgiveness," 178.

64. Thanegi, *Nor Iron Bars a Cage*, 9.

in church in South Korea but was confused by the term. "To ask for forgiveness in Camp 14, he said, was 'to beg not to be punished.'"[65]

The Possibility and Reality of the Unforgivable

The unforgivable: crimes of such cruelty and severity that we feel only outrage and shock, unless sadly, the unforgivable becomes routine, and so im-possible.[66] Tragically, we do not have to look long for what many would deem "unforgivable acts." While there is often a certain level of subjectivity in labelling an act as unforgivable, there may be cases that transcend cultures or times. And then there can be no cheap forgiveness or cheap reconciliation.[67] Every response has a sharp cost. The cases and contexts are severe, demoralizing, and noxious. Cries, loss, and clashes abound.

Griswold writes that "The issue of 'unforgivability' arises with respect to levels of evil that elicit resentment so deep as to be accompanied by rage, indeed outrage."[68] Examining a fictional example of such outrage, Jeffrie Murphy turned to the case of the General in *The Brothers Karamazov* who sends the hounds after a poor innocent serf-boy to be devoured and torn to shreds while his mother was forced to look on.[69] For Murphy, the challenge of forgiveness is to inquire whether it would "all things considered" even be possible to forgive such a supposed "moral monster"? Murphy maintains the importance of still recognizing the humanity in such perpetrators who still have human dignity and rights.[70] He links this idea to "the virtue of moral humility"—a recognition that we all can fail and may be in need of forgiveness, not to mention our inability to truly know another. He also holds the possibility that we may not forgive people for unforgivable actions.[71]

---

65. Harden, *Escape from Camp 14*, 11. For an update on the controversy in the book, see Lee, "True Lies." For other survivor accounts from North Korean gulags, see Lee, *Eyes of the Tailless Animals*; Chol-Hwan, *Aquariums of Pyongyang*; and Kim, *Long Road Home*.
66. Derrida, "To Forgive," 48.
67. Volf, "Forgiveness," 34; and Sobrino, "Christianity and Reconciliation," 80.
68. Griswold, *Forgiveness*, 91.
69. Dostoyevsky, *Brothers Karamazov*, 236.
70. Murphy, "Case of Dostoevsky's General," 193.
71. Ibid., 208.

What to do, then, about Joshua Milton Blahyi (General Butt Naked), a warlord in Liberia who lead child soldiers with promises that bullets wouldn't wound them? He professed to have killed at least 20,000 people, but has since claimed to have found Jesus and is determined to show his repentance and conversion. "Everything I was doing was devilish, was wrong, was inhuman."[72] Cannibalism and human sacrifice were some of those crimes. Most disturbingly, according to his memoir, his supposed Saul-to-Paul conversion was right after he and his soldiers murdered a three-year-old child by opening the little girl's back and plucking out her heart as part of some ritual.

Blahyi claims he "negotiated" with the mother to give him the child. He and his soldiers, after killing the girl, then began to eat her heart. When finished, he ordered his soldiers to go to the river to bring back water to wash his hands. Jesus then appeared to him. The voice said: "My son, why are you enslaving yourself?" The figure was all light and ten feet tall. They exchanged words and the voice ended with the ominous words: "repent and live—or refuse and die."[73] Going into battle, Blahyi alleges his weapons malfunctioned, he got shot, and had to retreat for the first time. There are so many elements to the vision that are disturbing—beginning with the fate of the murdered girl and her coerced mother. Why would this voice only come after the murder—and why when there were no witnesses? The child soldiers were also in desperate need of encountering such a presence—even if it seemed no different than any other warlord with its threats.

When the Truth and Reconciliation Commission was established after the Liberian civil war ended in 2003, Blahyi publically confessed his sins. He now preaches salvation and healing and runs a home to help former child soldiers. He seems to be doing fine, with book deals, media presence, and films, but questions about his many victims, including the child soldiers he employed, seem minimized. Is it possible to forgive such a man—and are his actions even genuine? What is unforgivable seems to touch not only upon the helplessness of humanity to heal or prevent such trauma and loss, but the impotence of God as well. Ironically, God is rendered powerless, even within his supposed encounter with the warlord—at what seemed to be an opportune time for Blahyi, after most of

---

72. Tabor, "Greater the Sinner."

73. Blahyi, *Redemption*, 108.

the damage was done, and the need for a different persona and act was required. Yes, I'm skeptical.⁷⁴

In Simon Wiesenthal's *The Sunflower*, a dying Nazi named Karl asks Wiesenthal, then an Auschwitz concentration camp inmate, for forgiveness simply because Wiesenthal is a Jew. In his memoir, Wiesenthal requested responses on whether he was right to withhold forgiveness. A number of replies endorsed the unforgivable and are worth highlighting here.

1. Sidney Shachnow, a fellow Holocaust survivor, responds: "[Karl] allowed himself to be changed into a foul beast who did the unforgivable . . . What he did was the ultimate and irreversible denial of his humanity."⁷⁵

2. Survivor Dith Pran remarks: "As a witness to and survivor of the Cambodian killing fields, I could never forgive or forget what the top leadership of the Khmer Rouge has done to me, my family, or friends. It's impossible."⁷⁶ He does distinguish between the leaders whom he would never forgive and their pawns.⁷⁷

3. Cynthia Ozick challenges: "Forgiveness can brutalize."⁷⁸ Ozick is not wrong, of course. Humility, too can brutalize. Is it real, mature forgiveness if it brutalizes, though? She continues: "forgiveness is pitiless. It forgets the victim. It negates the right of the victim to his own life. It blurs over suffering and death. It drowns the past. It cultivates sensitiveness toward the murderer at the price of insensitiveness toward the victim."⁷⁹

4. Rabbi Arthur Hertzberg contends: "The crimes in which this SS man had taken part are beyond forgiveness by man, and even by God, for God Himself is among the accused."⁸⁰

---

74. As of August 2018, it is still possible he may be prosecuted. See Azango, "Liberia."
75. Wiesenthal, *Sunflower*, 242.
76. Ibid., 230.
77. Ibid., 232.
78. Ibid., 215.
79. Ibid., 217.
80. Ibid., 167.

5. In Nazi architect Albert Speer's response, he thanks Wiesenthal for showing him respect as a fellow human but is clear that he can never forgive himself let alone expect a victim to forgive him.[81]

Taking a different approach, Jesuit theologian Theodore M. Hesburgh responds that the call to forgive, even the apparently unforgivable, can serve "as a surrogate for our almighty and all-forgiving God."[82] These are potent and hopeful words—but they remain suggestion, not mandate.

There is no right to forgiveness. Whenever I read or reflect upon testimonies of horrific torture and mutilation inflicted on human beings (or non-human species), it seems inhuman to maintain some form of emotional equilibrium and demand just the facts. Are there not some acts that are so heinous—such as genocide—that whoever commits them is tainted by the unforgivable? If so, does this mean that no matter what steps or attempts a perpetrator makes towards repentance, it will never be sufficient? Are such individuals therefore no longer recognizably human and so undeserving of forgiveness? Or is the fact that they can't be forgiven somehow embedded in their being human (the unforgivable has little meaning attached to a poisonous snake or hurricane that causes pain, or even death). Rwandan genocide survivor Sylvie Umubyeyi remarks: "there is no forgiving the White who let the killers do their work. There is no forgiving the Hutu who massacred. There can be no forgiving he who watched as his neighbour opened girls' bellies and killed the baby inside before their eyes. It is useless wasting words talking to him about it. Only justice can forgive."[83] Justice as retributive is clearly advocated.

Innocent Rwililiza, a teacher whose wife and son were murdered in the Rwandan genocide, speaks of "humanitarian organizations importing forgiveness to Rwanda, and they wrap in lots of dollars to win us over.... But when we talk among ourselves, the word forgiveness has no place; I mean that's oppressive ... It's outside of nature." [84] Here, the State and global community pressure victims to forgive as the outside world wants results and to move on. Forgiveness seems a way to do so.

Lawrence Langer writes: "I have never encountered a single Holocaust testimony supporting the conclusion that compassion for those

---

81. Ibid., 246.
82. Ibid., 169.
83. Hatzfeld, *Quick of Life*, 171.
84. Hatzfeld, *Strategy of Antelopes*, 18.

guilty of mass murder is 'deeply therapeutic and restorative.'"[85] Langer's observations carry heavy weight. If the victims should have the final say in these matters, and the evidence suggests a general skepticism about forgiveness, does this mean forgiveness advocates should be humbled and chastened in their approach or should they insist on forgiveness as a bitter, but needed remedy?

Backing up Langer's observations, Holocaust survivor William Benson remarks: "I teach my children, you never forgive, you never forget. And they should teach their children about Germany never to forget, never to forgive, never as long as our children can teach their children and keep on teaching their children. I don't want them to forgive, ever. This is something you don't forgive."[86]

In the section "Useless Knowledge" in Charlotte Delbo's potent Holocaust trilogy is the poem: "Prayer to the Living / To Forgive Them for Being Alive." Delbo is watching people pass her by on the street, those presumably untouched by the horrors of the war, and she wants them to live life because so many, so many have perished. She cries: "how / will you ever be forgiven / by those who died / so that you may walk by / dressed in all those muscles."[87] Her plea is for them to do something meaningful with their lives—even if it is to "learn a dance step"—because otherwise the death of so many millions, who wanted to live so desperately, would be even more senseless than their loss already is. It would be unforgivable for those of us gifted with life to keep squandering it—and with such "sparkling indifference."[88]

All Religions and Cultures Praise Forgiveness, Right?

I do not want the following sections to be one group screaming loudly and exuberantly that they are the paragons of forgiveness, but can it be taken for granted that every major faith views forgiveness as a virtue, if not a moral obligation? Must the Jew, the Muslim and all the others forgive? And on what basis can atheists forgive?

---

85. Langer, *Using and Abusing the Holocaust*, 91.
86. Johnson and Reuband, *What We Knew*, 7.
87. Delbo, *Auschwitz and After*, 229–30.
88. Hunter, *End We Start From*, 37. Hunter is referring to the stars amidst the calamity depicted in her novel.

Hopefully the sections above have showcased how much more complicated, nuanced, and careful we need to be treading here, but let's take a deeper look at specific religious and secular contexts.

Classical World

Forgiveness was a questionable trait in the ancient world, meant principally between equals.[89] Most ancient Greek philosophical schools took little interest in it.[90] Examining the *Iliad* and *Antigone*, Page duBois contends the "archaic Greek world did not know empathy or forgiveness"[91] and that forgiveness could not be prized in a culture that puts a premium on heroic accomplishments in war and a need to avenge the dead. Du Bois concludes that forgiveness is not a "universal human quality" and that examining the ancient world "demonstrates [forgiveness's] fragility and its precarious status as a product of centuries of cultural labor."[92]

In such contexts, the great and powerful should not be bothered by actions of so-called inferiors. Can a slave matter to its master, a defeated enemy to its vanquisher? Achilles could eventually accept Agamemnon's half-hearted apology. The king needed Achilles for the war and Achilles wanted revenge for the death of Patroclus. In the nineteenth century, Nietzsche scorned the power of forgiveness, dredging up the image of humility like a worm. For the powerful cannot recall such a sleight, and so can "shake off with a single shrug a collection of worms that in others would dig itself in."[93]

Indigenous Forgiveness

Indigenous traditions have endured genocidal and systemic repression, murder, and destruction of bodies, texts, cultures, and rituals. In February of 2016, Pope Francis asked for forgiveness from the Mexican indigenous people (while also challenging them to seek forgiveness from those

---

89. Schreiter, "Practical Theology of Healing," 390.
90. See Konstan, "Assuaging Rage," 17 and 20.
91. duBois, "Achilles, Psammentius, and Antigone," 31.
92. Ibid., 47.
93. Nietzsche, *Genealogy of Morals*, 21; see also Blustein, *Forgiveness and Remembrance*, 23–30.

they wronged, too).[94] Despite the legitimate reasons to seek vengeance and reprisals against their oppressors, the dominant trope spread among indigenous traditions is compassion. Eleazar López Hernández notes: "The reconciliation and forgiveness that we indigenous peoples champion implies rebuilding the harmony we have lost—with God, with the earth, with the people, with our dead or ancestors."[95] Legitimate reasons, though, remain for any hesitation for blanket forgiveness. Wrongs have not been addressed and the history of colonial treatment of indigenous peoples has entailed mostly lies and broken promises. A wait-and-see approach remains fair and reasonable.

Confucianism

According to Kwong-loi Shun, "Forgiveness is not idealized in Confucian thought" and "there is no [early Chinese] concept close to that of forgiveness."[96] According to Shun, the Confucian emphasis as victim is to focus on any deficiencies in oneself and one's response to the wrong in relation to ethical standards in society and not show resentment against the other as a means of self-protection.[97] Qualities of *ren* and *li*, while following the Middle Way, would also be expected. The *junzi* (Gentleman) or *sheng* (sage) here is also somewhat similar to Nietzsche's *übermensch* in not allowing external factors to unjustly weigh on him (there is a wide gap between the sage and the common man). Confucius, however, parts widely from Nietzsche in following benevolence as his guide. As we read in *The Analects*: "The gentleman is easy of mind, while the small man is always full of anxiety."[98] And most importantly: "Make it your guiding principle to do your best for others and to be trustworthy in what you say. Do not accept as friend anyone who is not good as you. When you make a mistake do not be afraid of mending your ways."[99] Forgiveness is not explicit here, but between acknowledging legitimate ignorance (as noted in chapter 1), in trying to do what is best for the other as exemplified in

---

94. Kearns, "Pope in Mexico."
95. Hernández. "Perspective from Central America," 43.
96. Shun, "Resentment and Forgiveness," 13.
97. Ibid., 34.
98. Confucius, *Analects*, VII.37 (91).
99. Ibid., IX.25 (99).

the silver rule,¹⁰⁰ and admitting mistakes and aiming to avoid repeating them, we are well immersed in a thick conception of forgiveness. When turning to the more positive portrayal of human nature in Mencius,¹⁰¹ the importance of forgiveness can also be advocated. Note as well that in the rival school of Mohism, Master Mo's (Mo Zi's) promotion of universal love would also be deeply congruent with an ethic of forgiveness.¹⁰²

Hinduism

Forgiveness also pervades Hinduism, especially as read through the spiritual and political life of Gandhi as his grandson Rajmohan Gandhi notes.¹⁰³ Gandhi's commitment to *ahimsa* and *satyagraha* deeply parallels and intertwines with what are sometimes perceived as Western notions of forgiveness and reconciliation.¹⁰⁴ As Alan Hunter contends, forgiveness, close to *ksama* in Sanskrit, was not a major feature in classical Hindu texts, but there are extended discussions of forgiveness in the *Mahabharata* and *Ramayana*.¹⁰⁵ The former, as Hunter reminds us, even has a "hymn to forgiveness," with lyrics like "forgiveness is Brahma [God]; forgiveness is truth."¹⁰⁶ As part of *samsara*, vengeance need not have the final say as what was destructive in one life may still have the opportunity for peace in the next life. Forgiveness is that eventual lasting peace.¹⁰⁷

Buddhism

Two different notions in Buddhism compose what we may deem forgiveness in the Western tradition: "The first notion is the renouncing of anger and resentment toward the offender ... the second notion is the removal of an expectation of retribution."¹⁰⁸ Forbearance along with empathy

---

100. Ibid., XV.24 (135).
101. Mencius, *Mencius,* 164–65.
102. See Master Mo, *Master Mo,* 75–90.
103. Rajmohan Gandhi, "Perspective," 106–8.
104. da Silva, "Through Nonviolence to Truth," 305–27.
105. Hunter, "Forgiveness," 36.
106. Ibid., 37.
107. Ibid., 41.
108. Paz, Neto, and Mullet, "Forgiveness," 292.

and compassion move to the core of an essence of forgiveness. However, without concern about ultimate truth or reality, as Joseph O' Leary reminds us, the "concept of forgiveness may seem at first sight remote from the concerns of Buddhism." The biblical concepts of divine atonement, grace, forgiveness, and reconciliation would not seem to be of major relevance. Anger and resentment, which would need to be surmounted for forgiveness to occur, are also delusions in themselves that should be overcome as undue attachment. Thus, victims who have been deeply wronged would also be disillusioned if fixated on the crimes suffered.[109] In Mahayana Buddhism, as O'Leary points out, forgiveness, as practiced by the *bodhisattva*, is also a gift to the offender. The forgiveness offered is unconditional and absolute. For the *bodhisattva* any offense is an opportunity to "practise forgiveness." In the Middle Way, of neither emptiness nor substantialism, rooted in our inter-being (co-dependent arising), forgiveness is both necessary and superfluous. As O'Leary explains: "The self now is not the self then or in the future." Especially lacking any commitment to a permanent self, for the Buddhist, as Matthieu Ricard notes, "forgiveness is always possible and one should always forgive."[110]

In his daily meditation practice, the Dalai Lama envisions receiving the suffering of others, but then visualizes sending forth compassion and forgiveness. "I pay special attention to the Chinese—especially those doing terrible things to the Tibetans. So, as I meditate, I breathe in all their poisons—hatred, fear, cruelty. Then, I breathe out. And I let all the good things come out, like compassion, forgiveness."[111] Chan writes that the Dalai Lama forgives the Chinese "with no reservations."[112] He contends that anger, "a destructive emotion," only causes pain to himself and impedes the full focus and attention needed in the Tibetan "struggle for freedom," while forgiveness produces calmness and the attention needed in that struggle.[113] The Dalai Lama also likes to cite the experiences of a fellow monk, Lopom-la, for whom forgiveness helped while being tortured by the Chinese.[114] When hearing about such abject stories, the Dalai Lama tries to see the perpetrators as fellow human beings who don't

109. O' Leary, "Buddhism and Forgiveness."
110. Wiesenthal, *Sunflower*, 235.
111. Dalai Lama and Chan, *Wisdom of Forgiveness*, 74; see also Dalai Lama and Chan, *Wisdom of Compassion*, 91.
112. Dalai Lama and Chan, *Wisdom of Forgiveness*, 21.
113. Ibid., 47.
114. Ibid., 48.

want violence. He then reflects on how they chose this path, often from propaganda. Such awareness spurs a response of compassion and forgiveness.[115] Recall the example of Buddhist Master Deng Kuan.[116] Master Deng had suffered horrifically at the hands of the Chinese Communists, especially during the Cultural Revolution. Yet he deemed forgiveness a required response of Buddhists, noting he would in turn suffer if he were to retain hatred.

Humanist Forgiveness

Philosopher Ramin Jahanbegloo, imprisoned unjustly in Iran, does not consider himself a religious man, but contends: "I believe my responsibility to the other is not lived primordially as being accused or accusing, but as an act of forgiveness."[117] He opposes vengeance and believes working non-violently for change is the best path for all of us.

In his reply to critics of his well-received 2007 book on forgiveness, Charles Griswold comments: "My analysis is framed as secular,"[118] and contends there is no need to look into religious conceptions—just as such would not be needed in examining the nature of justice. According to Griswold, six conditions should be met for the offended party to renounce "resentment, or at least, [give] up the judgment that the wrongdoer warrants continued resentment."[119] These would apply to religious and nonreligious victims.

1. The offender must take responsibility for her actions.
2. The offender must renounce and condemn the wrong actions she committed.
3. The offender must "experience and express regret" for inflicting harm on the victim.
4. The offender must work to oppose the person she had been who committed such acts and to become someone who promotes peace, in word and deed.

---

115. Ibid., 111.
116. Yiwu, *Corpse Walker*, 91.
117. Jahanbegloo, *Time Will Say Nothing*, 209–10.
118. Griswold, "Forgiveness, Secular and Religious," 311.
119. Griswold, *Forgiveness*, 49.

5. The offender must empathize with the victim, seeking to understand the victim's perspective, and the harm the offender caused.[120]

6. The offender must, as clearly as possible, offer a true narrative and context for why and how she committed this offence, answering questions the injured party asks, such as "who is this person, such that she could have injured me thus? Such that she warrants forgiveness?"[121]

Griswold's six points are not meant in any order and are presented as part of an ideal case, but they are helpful barometers of assessing whether offenders are genuine in their sense of repentance and whether forgiveness should be granted.

Humanist philosopher Andrew Fiala, moreover, contends: "Humanists generally reject the theological standpoint and its revaluation of values. And when humanistic moral traditions permit forgiveness, it is often not the preferred option in a system that values justice. At best humanistic forgiveness is based on pragmatic interests—psychological or emotional needs—and not on a radical revaluation of values."[122] Most humanists reject any duty to forgive "because they reject the basic ground upon which such a duty can be established."[123] Fiala continues: "A humanistic approach recognizes the genuine difficulty of linking justice and forgiveness in a world without God."[124]

This is a crucial point as a rejection of any divinity (and so any possibility for divine justice) heightens the meaning of injustice in this world, the only world where injustice can be addressed, no matter how inadequately. Perhaps, theists can take a certain chance in forgiving because it seems required of them in this life and does not preclude what justice may befall the perpetrator in the afterlife. There is a type of risk here for theists, but notice it is sugar-coated with benefits to the self in this life emotionally (and in moral standing in the next). Atheists have no such incentive to forgive and cannot rely on any meta-form of justice. It would be wrong to delay justice as punishment or condemnation especially because there is no post-mortem existence.

---

120. Ibid., 50–51.
121. Ibid., 51.
122. Fiala, "Radical Forgiveness," 494–95.
123. Ibid., 496.
124. Ibid., 499.

I would contend that taking life is always a loss (even if only as a waste of what could have been a rewarding life), and while forgiving must be weighed against other virtues and values, there could still be strong reason, without God, to forego vengeance and violence. I don't see how retaining hatred can be healthy—but working for redemption and prevention of similar crimes—which entails memory and justice—would seem a more holistic and healthy path. Andrew Fiala notes that fellow "humanists can learn from Christians to see the value of forgiveness."[125] This is promising, but in returning the compliment, I would contend that knowing there will be no divine post-mortem judgment, punishment, or justice, atheists who promote forgiveness, once again humble theists.

Eva Mozes Kor and her twin sister Miriam were among the "Mengele twins" experimented upon in Auschwitz. When Eva was confronted with an opportunity to meet one of the doctors involved in the horrific experiments, she eventually reached a place ready to forgive, even meeting the doctor along with their grandchildren at the site of the torture chambers. Her motive was not religious as she stressed to Michael Henderson: "My forgiveness has nothing to do with God. Or religion; it has to do with our ability to heal ourselves by forgiving. I believe that people do not have to believe in God to forgive.'"[126]

All one needs is empathy, or even just to feel pain and acknowledge such pain. As Daniel Philpott comments: "To be sure, secular versions lack the divine justification and enablement offered by religious rationales. But the potential of secular justification makes the possibility all the stronger that forgiveness can come to play a constructive role in global politics."[127]

Judaism

According to Rabbi Dratch, "The classical Jewish approach emphasizes repentance, not forgiveness."[128] However, Jews are still encouraged to forgive, when and where possible. They are told not to bear grudges or take revenge (Lev 19:18). The Day of Atonement is marked every year

---

125. Ibid., 504.

126. Henderson, *No Enemy to Conquer*, 87–88. See also Cantacuzino, *Forgiveness Project*, 44–47.

127. Philpott, "Reconciliation, Politics, and Transitional Justice," 349.

128. Dratch, "Forgiving the Unforgivable?," 32.

for Jews to reflect upon whom they have wronged and to address such infractions and make amends. Sins committed against fellow human beings (*beyn adam l'adam*) must be dealt with differently than sins towards God (*beyn adam le makom*), though both are also linked as man is made in God's image. Alan L. Berger and David Patterson write: "Only the person sinned against can forgive the sinner, and only God can forgive the trespasses against the divine. Consequently the Jewish understanding of forgiveness requires a personal, one-to-one encounter."[129] They cite this as one of the differences in understanding about forgiveness between Jews and Christians.

As David Blumenthal notes, repentance (*teshuvah*), according to most Jewish sages, "requires five elements: recognition of one's sins as sins (*hakarát ha-chét*), remorse (*charatá*), desisting from sin (*azivát ha-chét*), restitution where possible (*peira'ón*), and confession (*vidúi*)."[130] These notions bear similarities with Griswold's secular approach.

Blumenthal also highlights three types of forgiveness in Judaism: "The most basic kind of forgiveness is 'forgoing the other's indebtedness' (*mechilá*)." According to Blumenthal, this is like a pardon which a criminal receives after signs of repentance and undergoing fair trial. The debt of what is owed is met but there is no reconciliation, as such. Without the perpetrator making restitution and amends as signs of repentance, forgiveness is not demanded or expected. Repentance must be sincere. *Selichá* is the second type of forgiveness. Blumenthal calls this "an act of the heart. It is reaching a deeper understanding of the sinner." Yet he is clear that such is not reconciliation, but a more profound understanding by the victim that the perpetrator is also human and frail and so "deserving of sympathy." With some crimes, victims are not expected or even encouraged to reach this kind of forgiveness. "There is no legal obligation," as Mark Dratch stresses.[131] Lastly, *Kappará* or "purification" (*tahorá*) is the third type of forgiveness, deemed atonement. "Kappara is the ultimate form of forgiveness, but it is only granted by God. No human can 'atone' the sin of another; no human can 'purify' the spiritual pollution of another."[132]

---

129. Berger and Patterson, *Jewish Christian Dialogue*, 134–35.

130. Blumenthal. "Forgiveness and Repentance," 75–81. See also Magonet, *Rabbi Reads*, 72–76.

131. Dratch, "Forgiving the Unforgivable?," 27.

132. Blumenthal, "Forgiveness and Repentance," 75–81.

Biblical stories are replete with the call to return to God after sins and failing, from individuals like David (2 Sam 12:113) to the Israelites as a people (Ezek 14:6). Citing Pesahim 54a and Psalms 9:1–2, Dratch remarks: "So essential is forgiveness for the very survival of humanity and of human society that it is one of seven things that were created even before the world was created."[133] In the Book of Jonah, God sends a reluctant prophet to the Ninevites telling them to repent or be destroyed (3:4). The Ninevites listen to Jonah's half-hearted warning. They repent (3:10). But ironically, as some rabbis were later to note, such a people become instrumental in the destruction of Jerusalem.

Other, more ambiguous examples may come to mind, such as the flood (Gen 6:9–9:17), Sodom and Gomorrah (Gen 19), the destruction at Ai (Josh 8), and the punishment of the Israelites after their doubt in the wilderness of Par'an at Ka'desh (Num 14). Nevertheless, God is deemed merciful and there are rituals and feast days to provide or promise the means of atonement, or performing *teshuvah* (repentance or return).

As Reuven Hammer notes regarding a rabbinic commentary on Exodus 20:7, "Judaism affirms that no matter what the sin, reconciliation with God is always possible."[134] God, too, is urged to pardon. Elie Wiesel tells the story of the Hasid Levi-Yitzhak of Berditchev. A father of six children came to him acknowledging he was unable to pray, being so full of sadness and anger after the sudden loss of his wife and home. The rebbe asked if the man had his prayer book, but this too was destroyed in the fire. So the rebbe requested a helper to bring another prayer book and asked the man if he would then pray. Still weeping, the man said he would. The rebbe asked if he would forgive God, and the man said he must as it was Yom Kippur. Moved, Levi-Yitzhak was said to "roar" to God: "Well, then it is up to You to do the same . . . You, too must forgive!"[135]

While Judaism advocates interpersonal forgiveness as a one-to-one encounter, this may not always be possible. Maimonides explained there are various rituals or liturgical acts one can perform to show *teshuvah* even if one does not know whom one offends or whether the victim is alive. Of utmost importance is for the person guilty to show true repentance. In *The Laws of Repentance*, Maimonides states one of the best

---

133. Dratch, "Forgiving the Unforgivable?," 22.
134. Hammer, *Classic Midrash*, 157.
135. Wiesel, *Souls on Fire*, 88.

testaments to true repentance is when a person finds himself in the same situation to sin but refuses to commit the wrongful deed again.[136] Such repentance entails regret for what he has done, verbally confessing his wrong, and calling God as a witness for his oath on future ethical living. Mere words without testimonial action are not enough. Maimonides also provides additional examples of repentance beyond the requirement of making restitution to the victim (or the victim's family, pacifying the soul of the deceased), which includes charity, living modestly and humbly, even changing one's name and place where one lives as a further distance from past sinful choices.[137]

Some sins, though, are unforgivable. In the Talmud, Abuyah (Aher) was even prevented from repenting.[138] While Maimonides elsewhere also seems to hold out for the power of repentance for many sins,[139] among those he lists that deny the life to come include: murderers, gossipers, apostates, heretics, and deniers of the Torah.[140]

More recently, consider Elie Wiesel's remarks at the commemoration of the fiftieth anniversary of the liberation of Auschwitz where he implores: "God of forgiveness, do not forgive those who created this place. God of mercy, have no mercy on those who killed Jewish children here . . . God of compassion, have no compassion for those who had none."[141]

It is a jarring juxtaposition of terms, calling upon a God of compassion not to show compassion. But in the context of genocide, when does compassion for the perpetrator become another wound to the victim? As Peter Haas remarks: "There is no mechanism within Jewish law for extending forgiveness to perpetrators who did not, and cannot repent."[142]

Christianity

Christians begin with Jesus as a paragon of forgiveness. Hannah Arendt, though Jewish, even claimed Jesus "was the discoverer of the role of

136. Maimonides, "Laws of Repentance," 109 (2.2); and Yoma 86b. See also Haas, "Forgiveness, Reconciliation, and Jewish Memory," 5–15.
137. Maimonides, "Laws of Repentance," 111 (2.4).
138. Dratch, "Forgiving the Unforgivable?," 29.
139. Maimonides, "Laws of Repentance," 129 (3.14).
140. Ibid., 119 (3.6).
141. Wiesel, *Sea is Never Full*, 194.
142. Haas, "Forgiveness, Reconciliation, and Jewish Memory," 14.

forgiveness in the realm of human affairs."¹⁴³ Such, however, is to discount the Jewish tradition that Jesus was reared in—not to mention its occurrence in other contexts.¹⁴⁴ Yet, without desire to be mired in another uniqueness (or originator) argument, it is safe to say how Jesus profoundly contributed to our understanding of forgiveness by both his words and deeds. While challenging Arendt's claim, Bash still contends that "Jesus holds the pivotal place in the development of forgiveness in Western thought, culture, and ethics."¹⁴⁵ Naysayers who bring up outlier passages like Jesus using a whip in the temple (John 2:15) or saying he came to bring a sword and not peace (Matt 10:34) cannot cohesively claim such are normative statements for Jesus. A Christian could quip: Jesus forgives you, and the words would have bite. Indeed, it would seem beyond the point of pedantry to try to disunite Jesus and his call for forgiveness.

Principally, there is Jesus's comment, while being tortured and dying on the cross, "Father, forgive them; for they do not know what they are doing" (Luke 23:34) and his instruction to the disciples that one must forgive beyond what is expected, seventy times seven (Matt 18:22). Did Jesus's forgiveness always entail an unconditional offer? Yes and No. Clearly, with this forgiveness came an expectation of sinning no more, as he told the Samaritan woman at the well (John 4:4-26; see also John 8:11). Others promised change after Jesus's reaching out: recall Zacchaeus the tax collector who promised to make amends for his corruption and thievery (Luke 19:8).

Jesus, moreover, stressed that his mission was to the poor and outcasts, the sick and the sinners—those who needed him for healing (Mark 2:17). I again agree with Bash: "To argue that Christianity applauds, endorses, and promotes forgiveness for the unrepentant is, in my view, theologically misguided—and often pastorally naïve, simplistic, and dangerous."¹⁴⁶ Those who want to be Christ-like would seem to continue such a tradition, applying forgiveness that expects concrete repentance. There is one instance of the unforgivable mentioned by Jesus—those who blaspheme against the Holy Spirit (Matt 12:31). Such is both broad and undeveloped to lead to more confusion than help. A possible example

---

143. Arendt, *Human Condition*, 238.

144. Bash, "Did Jesus Discover Forgiveness?," 382.

145. Ibid., 396.

146. Bash, "Forgiveness," 137. See also Knust, "Jesus' Conditional Forgiveness," 183.

is when Christopher Columbus swore by the Holy Spirit that he would subdue the natives of the Americas. Linking or calling upon the Holy Spirit in one's subduing of innocent people would certainly come close to the unforgivable.

In the call for turning the other cheek, Walter Wink and others have shown that it is a form of non-violent resistance.[147] While I note Jean Hampton's remark that Jesus is "frequently an angry man,"[148] it also testifies to Jesus's passion for mercy and justice for all. As noted above, "The process of forgiving does not exclude hatred and anger."[149] While hatred may go too far, such anger is rooted for example in theological protest that itself is founded on love of God and love of neighbor.[150] Forgiveness (with justice) should be at the heart and soul of Christian belief and practice.

Islam

Islam shares much with Judaism's view of forgiveness in terms of its practicality and earthy focus. As with Jews, Muslims turn to God asking for forgiveness multiple times each day, and there is a distinction between interpersonal sins and sins committed against God.[151] Conditions for forgiveness include fear that Allah may not forgive, shame at what one has done, signs of repentance, and after requesting forgiveness, the repentant must promise to "mend his ways."[152] Like Judaism, in Islam forgiveness is not always demanded, but is viewed as a more noble, moral choice, and so deserving of award (2:178). Such a predisposition to forgive is deemed an especially fruitful step towards peace and reconciliation in society.[153] There is understanding when individuals choose justice and punishment of an offender after a wrong committed, but believers should dwell on God as compassionate and merciful (67:2), especially in light of human sinfulness. As S. Ayse Kadayifci-Orellana writes: "*Afe* (forgiveness) is an-

147. Wink, *Powers That Be*, 98–111.

148. Murphy and Hampton, *Forgiveness and Mercy*, 12.

149. Tutu, "Foreword," xii. See also Thomas, "Evil and Forgiveness," 123.

150. See Admirand, *Mass Atrocity*, 169–84 and 295–300.

151. Abu-Nimer and Nasser, "Forgiveness in the Arab and Islamic Contexts," 476 and 478.

152. Ibid., 477.

153. Ridgeon, "War and Peace in Islam," 174; see also Esposito and Yilmaz, "Islam and Peacebuilding," 15–32.

other critical principle of Islamic peacebuilding. As an act of goodness (*ihsan*) and the basis for reconciliation, Islam urges believers to forgive those who have wronged them to re-establish harmony. Forgiveness is closely related to the Islamic values of *rahmah* (compassion) and *rahim* (mercy)."[154]

Allah is thus perfect compassion and mercy. The surah, Ghafir ("The Forgiver) would be one of the prominent titles of Allah. Its opening calls Allah: "Forgiver of Sins and Acceptor of repentance, severe in punishment, infinite in bounty" (40:2).

The unforgivable, though, lurks in the Qur'an, and as with all faiths, a lot depends on context and interpretation. Some Qur'anic passages include as the unforgivable worship of other gods (4:116); those who "disbelieve, bar others from God's path, and die as disbelievers" (47:34); or those who reject their faith and turn away from God (shirk; 4:137); and those who "have disbelieved and do evil" (4:167). The latter comment is in the context of the People of the Book and earlier prophets sent to them, calling them to desist from Trinitarian worship and clarify that Jesus is only a Prophet (4:171).

Would a Christian holding such beliefs be unforgivable, so that God will not "guide them to any path except that of Hell, where they will remain forever—this is easy for God" (4:169)? The refrain is that forgiveness is always there before the Day of Judgment, if only one would turn to God. All people have been sent messengers to hear of the way—and even those who only fear God in private will still be forgiven (67:12).

In addition to the Qur'an, Muslims also turn to the life and sayings of the Prophet Muhammad to navigate their way amidst the call for justice and the hope of mercy. For Muslims, Muhammad is a paragon of compassion and forgiveness. Numerous stories depict Muhammad granting and showing forgiveness in difficult and traumatic cases. In one hadith, 'Ali reports Muhammad saying that God at sunset during the month of Sha'ban (right before Ramadan) inquires: "Is there no one who asks forgiveness so that I may forgive him?" Here God is eager, taking the initiative to encourage the sinner to repent.[155] When Muhammad prayed, moreover, he would always ask for God's forgiveness three times. He was forgiving of others and also taught others to be forgiving. When his wife Aisha was slandered by Abdullah bin Ubayy bin Salul, Muhammad urged

---

154. Kadayifci-Orellana, "Peacebuilding in the Muslim World," 444.
155. Quoted in Renard, *Seven Doors to Islam*, 14.

her to trust in God and seek God's forgiveness if the rumor was true. Aisha, citing the example of Yusef (Joseph), was later vindicated when Muhammad received a revelation confirming her innocence.

Also cited is Muhammad's forgiveness of his enemies. At Ta'if, they hurled stones at him but he forgave. So, too, did he forgive those who attacked him in Hudybiyya, and when they were later captured by Muhammad's followers, he still insisted they go free. In another case, Hind bint 'Utbah, a woman, desecrated the bodies of slain Muslims, including Muhammad's uncle, Hamza. In time, Muhammad even forgave her. Eventually she was overcome by his kindness and became a Muslim.[156]

Mohammad Hassan Khali retells the well-known hadith in the Sahih al-Bukhari of "a prostitute who used her shoe to collect water for a dog on the verge of death," for which God forgave her sins.[157] Khali also analyses who likely ends up in hell, whether hell is eternal, and whether purification and saving can even occur in hell. Al-Ghazālī, for example, contends that God will pardon most Christians because they may never have properly heard the truth of Islam and that even Trinitarian belief may not necessarily be considered *shirk,* though other interpretations are less inclusive. Khali informatively adds how some contemporary Muslims "have averred that God may even save those People of the Book and other non-Muslims who do find the Islamic message compelling yet choose to remain within their religious traditions."[158]

Examples of forgiveness are also seen in Prophet Muhammad's treatment of those Meccans who had forced Muhammad and his followers into exile. After returning in victory to Mecca, he explained why he should practice forgiveness, again citing the case of Yusef as his example, according to the Sufi ascetic and sheikh.[159] Such is not surprising as Yusef (Joseph) is a model of forgiveness for Judaism, Christianity, and Islam.[160]

---

156. For examples, see Abu-Nimer and Nasser, "Forgiveness in the Arab and Islamic Contexts," 478–79.
157. Khalil, "Divine Forgiveness in Islamic Scripture and Thought," 84.
158. Ibid., 86.
159. Renard, *Seven Doors to Islam,* 263.
160. See Admirand, "'Scripture Speak[ing] Fictitious Words.'"

Conclusion: Humbled by Forgiveness, Justice, Love

Levinas has warned us: "A world where forgiveness is almighty becomes inhuman."[161] Why?—because then there is no justice or mercy for the victims and the oppressed, it weakens human responsibility, rendering further injustice likely.[162] In rushing to forgiveness, as Jon Sobrino warns, we can undermine and threaten the role of truth and justice. There can be no lasting forgiveness that bypasses truth and justice.[163] As Jean Baptiste Munyankore tells Jean Hatzfeld in regards to her Hutu neighbors in Rwanda who came to ask forgiveness: "I listened so that they would go away sooner and leave me with my grief. As they left, those people topped off the visit by saying they had done me a great kindness by failing to catch me in the marshes. I pretended to be grateful."[164]

Summing up these reflections in a chapter titled "Bargaining for Forgiveness" in *Machete Season*, Hatzfeld comments: "We can see, then, that the survivors and the killers do not show the same understanding of forgiveness or pardon, and that itself, may make forgiveness impossible."[165]

Saying sorry, and sometimes accepting another's repentant words or actions, can be penetratingly humbling.[166] It sears and stings. It exposes our hypocrisies, shaming and embarrassing us. It is a reminder of our fallibility and faults. Where deep wrongs lie, it resembles chasms and gulfs; retching and miasma. But sometimes, sometimes, it lightens, restores, and croons renewal. In *Vanity Fair*, Thackeray spoke of "the uninteresting forgiveness of Miss Crawley."[167] Forgiveness may be many things, but uninteresting it is not.

Seeking and accepting justice: this too humbles. So much is at stake. Rwandan genocide survivor Berthe Mwanankabandi remarks that "being just is inhuman."[168] To kill all the killers would lead to another genocide; to

---

161. Quoted in Pollefeyt, "Forgiveness after the Holocaust," 55. See also Levinas, *Difficult Freedom*.

162. Pollefeyt, "Forgiveness after the Holocaust," 55–56.

163. Sobrino, "Christianity and Reconciliation," 82.

164. Hatzfeld, *Strategy of Antelopes*, 85.

165. Hatzfeld, *Machete Season*, 197.

166. Desmond Tutu notes how humbling it was to hear victims of apartheid forgive their oppressors in the TRC in South Africa. Quoted in Dalai Lama and Chan, *Wisdom of Forgiveness*, 67.

167. Thackeray, *Vanity Fair*, 178.

168. Hatzfeld, *Strategy of Antelopes*, 130.

punish them all would be impossible, and pardoning is "unthinkable."[169] True justice is light-years beyond us—always insufficient in this life: the wrongs too incisive; too many lost lives gone forever. Often, justice can only mock more than it heals. Yet, it can still be worth the scars and stumbles. In its incompletion, as well as its triumphs, it bears the mark and stain of humanity's essence and striving.

Love, beyond which life has little meaning or purpose, humbles in modes that border the wordless and flirt with the miraculous. Love is in many ways one long letter of forgiveness. It holds in its sway humility, justice, and forgiveness—and all which can heal, grow, and flourish. Love is the source and end for all that unites. We should all seek a love, as Thomas Hardy writes, which "is strong as death—that love which many waters cannot quench, nor the floods drown, beside which the passion usually called by its name is evanescent as steam."[170]

This work, which paints a picture of our mutual frailty, ignorance, and sins, is ultimately geared and calibrated by love—if not hope, which like faith, can be a certain kind of abiding love. It's rooted in a healthy love of self that wants to present as real and unadorned a portrait as possible, demanding a truth and humility that shuns neither deserved praise nor blame. Love is transparency as much as translucence. It reveals and allows revealing. Love is revelation for all creeds and ways of life. Love also is light that must slip and slither in the night. Love must be a different kind of "darkness visible."[171]

Love is the good, the Aristotelian end, the God of Aquinas, the shaky beginning that is also a finality, in this way an Alpha and Omega. Everywhere it is the same: one loves because there is no other choice, no other option, and when this is no longer believed, life is over, becomes an endless succession of Mondays and Tuesdays, of midnights and middays, and woe to us all, woe to us all. Yes, love is obstinate, demanding, often refusing to renounce when all sight is obscured and all words are daggers. It ascends like helium, but can burst into flames as well. It can also heal, regenerate like a starfish mercilessly cut by wanton boys. Rooted in the body, it tendrils through the mind and heart to reach forth to unknown depths and ticklish heights, saving the stranger in a burning fire, feeling pain for another's loss that moves beyond the acute. Love can even

---

169. Ibid., 130.
170. Hardy, *Madding Crowd*, 314.
171. Milton, *Paradise Lost*, I.63; see also Forché and Wu, *Poetry of Witness*, 136.

deaden itself because the feelings are so intense; loving so much one lets go, for the good of the one loved, released like a balloon in a child's hand, peptides in the synapses. Another image: a father holding his freezing son's "feet against his stomach to warm them."[172] Such parental love is one instance of many. All love humbles.

But more importantly, love giggles and graces, caresses and creates. It flirts, if not embodies, divinity. Humbling faiths, then, is only a first, stumbling step. Without love, it is mere pandering and desiccation, a wasting away. The demand, the need, the impossible step is loving what is so different and challenging within, so seemingly incongruent and puzzling without.

All of us, in some way, are culpable and negligent at various points in our lives. In this sense, as Pollefeyt notes: "forgiveness is a transmoral act of love."[173] This should not be revelation. Yes, this book has showcased models and lenses to propel us to recognize and acknowledge the moral failure of our religious and philosophical systems and institutions, spilling over into national, ethnic, and other identities. In showing the failure of what makes and forms who we are as individuals, it also touches on our own fallibility and culpability. Again, this was not meant in a spirit of breaking and grinding—we are formed of the dust of the earth (*humi*), but also of the stars (*stellarum*).[174] We can still feel aglow in joy, success, striving, and companionship. Humility, too, must be humbled at times, the stars never too far out of our reach. Ambition, striving, greatness, excellence—these are not being combatted here, but why and how we do so, and the language and after-effects in the journey and completion.

Accepting and recognizing our brokenness and frailty should also be freeing. Trying to convince ourselves and one another that we are the best or perfect and they are wrong, unsaved, or mad is a weighty, burdening load. There are different kinds of brokenness: minor and major, and all gradations in-between. Yes, some are demoralizing, drowning; back-broke. Then there is a brokenness traversed by beauty, a half-moon, resting ethereally in the night-time sky. Brokenness, read as imperfection, more importantly as seeking wholeness, is a common feature of all of us. We are blank slates without our scars. Perhaps, the minimally

---

172. McCarthy, *The Road*, 36.

173. Pollefeyt, "Forgiveness after the Holocaust," 61.

174. David Hinton remarks that in Chinese folklore, human beings were said to be descended from dragons ("Introduction" to *I Ching*, vii). Who wouldn't want to be descended from dragons?

broken seek to aid the devastatingly broken—but all are broken. Once this is seen, there is no need for tallies or *peccator* addresses. The aim is restoration and continual renewal, fashioning moments, even structures, for laughter, lightness, love.

"If forgiveness was a color," Cantacuzino reflects, "for me it would be grey, the color of compromise and conciliation, and because it sits between the two extremes of black and white."[175] Russian poet and gulag survivor Irina Ratushinskaya wrote that grey is the color of hope.[176] Humility is grey, too—maybe more grey than forgiveness. Justice (with or without the blindfold) is also grey—but what about love? Love has to have some grey, of white and black, too—all colors, really: a rainbow. Forgiveness, definitely, is grey.

Now perhaps the most difficult question of all: what of self-forgiveness? Martha Nussbaum warns that such "an obsessive inward process" can be "stifling" and "impede outward looking concerns and activities."[177] It is more healthy to focus on "the welfare of others" and not "one's guilty conscious."[178] Likewise, as my wife astutely reminds me, "Self-forgiveness is the most important life skill you can possibly have. You can't move on, change, grow, learn, or evolve without it—you'll be stuck in the past, just stuck. And how do you really forgive others if you can't forgive yourself?"

She's right, too (as usual). Why is it so easy to tell others: "Don't beat yourself up. Let it go," when the same issue pulls you down like millstones pressing on your neck, your heart, sinking; like a horde of zombies clawing and scraping within, without?

In "Here's Not Here," the best episode of *The Walking Dead* television series, there's this wonderful dialogue between Morgan Jones, who is traumatized by the losses he has suffered and the cost of survival, and Eastman, who has his own demons, but has come to see how to endure, how to find some peace, and so helps bring Morgan back to who he was, who he is.

> Morgan: So you have to care about yourself.
>
> Eastman: You have to believe your life is precious, that all life is precious.

175. Cantacuzino, *Forgiveness Project*, 24.
176. Ratushinskaya, *Grey is the Color*.
177. Nussbaum, *Anger and Forgiveness*, 132.
178. Ibid., 134.

> Morgan: You have to redirect those thoughts, the history that tells you otherwise.
>
> Eastman: What we've done, we've done.
>
> Morgan: We evade it by moving forward with a code to never do it again.
>
> Eastman: To make up for it.
>
> Morgan: To still accept what we were.
>
> Eastman: To accept everyone.
>
> Morgan: To protect everyone.
>
> Eastman: And in doing that, protect yourself.
>
> Morgan: To create peace.[179]

Zombie apocalypse notwithstanding (!), that is really the hope for all of us: "to create peace." Humility is just a path, a means, a way, but it fails or subverts if it doesn't create peace, instill love, render justice. Acceptance is part of that path: accepting what we are, what we were, and providing some space for what we can be, too. It is an acceptance that carries over to others. But it starts with the self, and here such self-forgiveness, such self-love, are gifts, perhaps from others, perhaps from God, ideally from yourself. Those who have accepted such gifts need to seek those who haven't; to create peace.

With peace (and not zombies) in our hearts, we can return to the zoo, as promised. I close this chapter with non-human signs and examples of forgiveness to prevent any monopolistic claim by any human groups. Awareness of failures can liberate and purify our convictions and identities as we seek to exhibit repentance and provide hope and reason to be forgiven. Such may never fully transpire, and yet, as believer or non-believer, atheist or theist, and yes, bonobo or elephant, we labor on, strengthened and emboldened in our quests and hopes: renewal, rebirth, restoration.

Epilogue: Back to the Zoo: Non-Human, Animal Forgiveness

In my focusing on forgiveness, it is humbling, perhaps comforting, to be reminded that such a need or desire transcends not only any so-called

---

179. *Walking Dead*, "Here's Not Here." Their interaction is inspired by Morihei Ueshiba's *The Art of Peace*.

religious-secular divide, but plays out beyond the strictly human realm. Forgiveness is not just owned by Christians or homo sapiens in general. We are not unique because we forgive and seek forgiveness; nor because we love. And yet, nothing is more imperative or needed. "In other species, particularly in primates," Caitlin O'Connell writes, "reconciliation has been exhibited after a discrete aggressive act."[180] In the field of primatology, wide reports show how mountain gorillas, bonobos, and chimpanzees may kiss, hold out their hands, or embrace after a conflict.[181] Michael McCullough calls these "forgiving-esque" acts, noting how "goats, sheep, dolphins, and hyenas all tend to reconcile after conflicts (rubbing horns, flippers, and fur are common elements of these species' reconciliation gestures)."[182]

O'Connell, an expert on elephants, writes: "In these situations, after an aggressive act, such as a shove away from the best drinking position, the aggressor might place his trunk in the mouth of the one that was displaced, almost as an apology."[183] Carl Safina reports that elephant experts acknowledge how elephants often use a mediator to solve some problems among them. The mediator, sometimes one of the aggrieved elephants, the matriarch, or a close relative "approaches the conflicting elephants . . . and, while standing head to head, rumbles while head-raising and ear-lifting and reaching toward the other with an outstretched trunk in an affiliative gesture."[184] Most telling, Lawrence Anthony praised the elephant named ET, for "Somewhere along the way she had recovered her life and in the process taught me how to forgive, as she had forgiven humans for the horrors they had visited on her own family before she came to us."[185] ET's entire family had been shot or sold by human hunters, but she still found the courage and trust to accept Anthony's overtures. She could have written off the human race. But she forgave.

We need not belabor the point. The need and call for forgiveness is wider and further-reaching than most of us can imagine. Even as we struggle to quantify or specify moral motives and nuance to non-human species' apparent acts of forgiveness, the resemblance seems more than

180. O'Connell, *Elephant Don*, 45.
181. De Waal and Pokorny, "Primate Conflict," 22.
182. McCullough, *Beyond Revenge*, 120. See also Crane, *Beastly Morality*.
183. O'Connell, *Elephant Don*, 45.
184. Safina, *Beyond Words*, 76. See also the anecdote in Montaigne, *Essays*, II:12 (356).
185. Anthony, with Spence, *Elephant Whisperer*, 365.

uncanny. From this observation, various threads have been woven—some contending forgiveness is an evolutionary by-product and needs no God or religion to form and develop; others contend its role in evolution underlies a merciful God behind creation. Neither path must be the exclusive destination here, because either way, the importance and universal role (if not qualified need) of forgiveness is stressed.

Did my visit to the zoo corroborate or challenge some of the above claims?

Nearing the entrance to Dublin Zoo, I walk-up towards Alan, a security guard: "Hi, I'm here to see Gerry Creighton."

He asks for my name. I tell him. "Not a name you hear every day." I nod in agreement. "Gerry Creighton over," Alan speaks into his radio.

"He's not in today," a voice crackles back. Alan smiles and repeats what he had heard to me. I momentarily get ready to insist there must be some mistake. "He's just messing." Almost immediately, as if by teleportation, Gerry appears smiling, hand out to shake. We proceed to walk a few steps to a rail overlooking a lake. Across it is an island for monkeys hopping and clinging about branches. I barely notice them, fumbling for my journal and pen trying to record whatever Gerry says. He has short-cropped red hair, a mischievous, but warm smile. I am immediately at ease. "Thirty-five years" he tells me he has been here, even longer when you consider his father worked at the zoo as well. He jokes that he "spends more time with the animals here than with his family at home."

I divulge to Gerry that my kids like his zoo better than the Bronx Zoo, but not to tell my father that (who hopefully won't read these lines). Of course, everything is perspective—a key idea in our discussions here. New Yorkers naturally think Manhattan (others, Brooklyn!) is the best city in the world (and as a New Yorker, I don't necessarily disagree). But then you see other ways of life, maybe complementary, or competing—or just not applicable: a different kind of beauty or wisdom. The human or non-human discussion can be akin to that.

Gerry is rightly proud of Dublin Zoo's recent accomplishments, growth, and developments. He has staff train elephants to become used to vet access, trying to make any interruption into their normal lives as stress-free as possible. They advocate "protective consent." Animals should have a choice as much as possible—outside emergency situations. The zoo does a range of studies comparing life in the wild and life in zoos: locomotion studies, sleep studies, the amount of food elephants forage in the zoo as opposed to the wild. Gerry happily says it's comparable at the Dublin Zoo. Sleep studies showed elephants sleep standing up when they're not feeling safe (or for only short naps), so every night, staff create a mound of sand for them to lay on. Sound sleep improved. Just like a well-rested human is a happy human, the same would go for elephants, too. "The need," Gerry says, "is to foster an approach that is species specific," encouraging "natural family dynamics." The zoo he inherited was a Victorian zoo, and it has come a long way. Ideally, I think we wouldn't have zoos, but that is a sensitive discussion for another day. Circuses come up later in the conversation, about how "dreadful" it was for elephants. Fortunately, elephants are no longer part of the Ringling Brothers circus.

And what of animal forgiveness? I ask Gerry whether he thinks it makes sense to speak of forgiveness in animals. He does not hesitate, emphasizing and extending the word: "Ab-so-lute-ly." But crucial to this idea is how most humans and non-human animals communicate. We tend to rely on verbal language while nonhuman animals use a lot of body language, body posture, and various tactile methods to signal and symbolize meaning.

Gerry then speaks of elephants and the "dynamics of the herd" and "survival instinct." Forgiveness makes sense in such a dynamic. They all "look after one another" and "invest a huge amount of time in one another." The mother-daughter bond is for life. He notes how in observing elephants, these signs of forgiveness between them are very visible. After there are disputes among them, the "elephants embrace each other." They're very tactile. There's a "vocalization of acceptance. Their body language carries 'acceptance.'" They may sleep together. Such forgiveness is "in the best interests of the herd." There is a lot of "in-house discipline," an expected "code of conduct."

He observes similar signs among chimpanzees and ape societies. There may be a dominant male or one trying to push his way, a violent outburst, fighting for mating rights. But then they'll groom one another, and "clearly embrace each other." Or, a silverback gorilla will approach a young male acting up, put his hand on his shoulder—boom!—and the message is sent.

In elephants, when young bulls test limits, the matriarch steps in. Gerry also mentions the case of a herd of males in Africa whose mothers were poached and they suffered from juvenile delinquency, always ready to fight. They had not received any parental education, didn't know what to do. They even tried to mate rhinos. No big matriarch around to "put manners into them."

I smile, writing away.

Their "emotional awareness," he continues, "is incredible. They exhibit empathy, display love. They manipulate you, charm you." He mentions the documented case of a young chimpanzee who lost his mother and father but an alpha male provided the food to help the baby live, even slept next to the young male to protect him—"It can be like the school yard otherwise and if you have no one behind you—bullying is common." This shows that animals are individuals. In an elephant herd, there are extroverts and introverts, elephants who like other elephants and elephants who don't—and so on.

While critics may call this anthropomorphism, it has value to help you understand, he explains. It's "where you start." I nod in agreement. He jokes that just as he sees a human parent holding a child who is upset or who may have wandered off, he sees a mother elephant reaching out a trunk to comfort one of the babies who may also have wandered too far away. The parental instinct.

I ask him about any cases of non-human animals forgiving any member of his staff. He says he doesn't allow staff members to sedate the animals they work with using a dart gun when such has to be done for medical reasons. He doesn't want that to interfere with the relationship. So he'll take the gun. He'll then stay away from the chimpanzees for at least a week and then come back offering grapes and apples but also respecting distance. Once they relax and touch him, he knows all's ok again.

I turn the conversation to the area of the unforgivable.

Apes will seek revenge if someone in their group is murdered by another. If they succeed, they may celebrate the death of the victim, mutilate the carcass. Chimpanzees hunt in search of members of another group with the intention of killing any they can. It's a type of, well, "guerrilla warfare." Chimpanzees will organize a hunt—it takes planning with members playing different roles like spotter, blocker, or ambusher. They do the same seeking to capture and kill colobus monkeys.

I then ask what we can learn from these animals on forgiveness.

"They understand the benefits of living cohesively. There's no self-agenda, but the benefits of mutual respect for one another." He pauses, reflects. "There's such a purpose in everything they do. And biological cooperation: they don't isolate anyone."

Winding the interview down, I ask him what discovery or finding about non-human animals does he foresee in the not too distant future.

He immediately replies "greater expansion of animal rights, especially of apes; more welfare guidelines, which are needed." He stresses a greater need to be concerned about animal happiness. He also says that "Elephants will be the new orcas."

Finally, and perhaps a bit sheepishly, I ask him about humility and the wild. Are animals humble? Or does humility even makes sense in the wild? And I try to present what I mean by humility—an awareness of your proper place and stature, neither denigrating nor inflating.

He laughs. And I realize it was probably a silly question. "They don't repress development. And humility in the wild would be seen as a weakness. Nature doesn't allow for weakness. Life is perilous. It's about survival repertoire, and to show toughness and defend turf and so on."

More for humility to be humbled about.

I thank Gerry and we shake hands. He makes sure I have his phone and email and to call if we need to follow-up or I have a question. He encourages me to take a stroll around the zoo and points me in the direction of the elephants. He doesn't have to ask twice.

So I head for the section called Kazianga Forest, modelled after the forest in Northeast India along the Brahmaputra River in Assam. I can hear elephant trumpeting, but can see nothing amidst all the shrubbery and trees. I pass a waterfall and a further clump of trees.

Then I see them.

"This is their home," a sign reads, "you are welcome guests."

I just stare and occasionally jot notes—otherwise I'm no different than the kids pointing and laughing. Look at that one taking mud from her trunk and splattering it on herself. Calves tug and bump and push each other. Messing around—elephantine horseplay—of some sorts. I notice a slight incline of mud and one calf in particular likes to knock the others down it. So playful, rambunctious—I think of my kids. No feelings seem hurt, though. And they all lumber off together, leaving scant space between them. They bump, push, and wrestle some more, mouths agape, trunks entangled in trunks.

Conclusion

Mutual Stumbling, Together: Embracing Brokenness, Doubt, Dialogue

In 1391, pogroms swept through Spain and devastated the Jewish population.[1] In Valencia, where I am now heading by train from Alicante, Jewish life was eradicated. No synagogues remain. After the expulsion of Jews in 1492, little to nothing was left. Tomorrow I plan to see Sagunt (formerly Monteverde), once a thriving Jewish medieval community. Today only an expert can unearth those remains from the layers of history since built upon Jewish lives and rubble. Yet I hope to visit as a means of facing and expiation, and if possible, dialogue. But again, how do I dialogue with the unavenged dead?

Brokenness, doubt, dialogue: such is the subtitle of the book and the journey traversed in these pages. Within it, my faith has been riddled with doubts and plagued with brokenness, hovering between the humbled and the humiliated.

In the introduction I sang of the dream and the dread. I was a bit coy about the latter, selecting a safe place to reflect, ensconced in the beauty of a riad in Fes, Morocco. In transit now on a REF intercity train, all seems blur and velocity. So much passes without knowledge or connection: ruined castles on layers of mountains, stretches of olive trees, lines of orange groves, endless space and blue sky. The dread, my dread, remains. I fear saying it here, naming it, the stench of failure, the burden of being unheard, unheeded, ignored. Maybe I still think I can outrun or outwit the dread. It follows, though, and perhaps must follow any journey into beliefs, hopes, affinities, and dreams. The dread, and perhaps even its fruition, is part of the humbling.

First, the brokenness. Humility is a broken virtue, which is part of its appeal, but also its venom. Without healthy pride, humility can lull its victims into states of stupor and sloth; paralysis—morally, socially,

---

1. See Schama, *Story of the Jews*, 374–421

emotionally. But even in its brokenness, humility can be a salve for healing. This work, again, is not about crushing and razing identity and belief, but moderating or challenging them in some contexts, rejoicing in others. It seeks balance through honest self-critique, dialogue, and encounter. If the zealous still imbibe a deep and vibrant love for all, then humbling is to channel that passion to insure a holy aim and goal. Again, some of the humbled need to be raised aloft, humility banished. In others, humility needs to be pumped into our systems like oxygen in a spaceship. Beyond that lies only the black hole of humiliation, and there we ought not tread. Though tempting, we should not coerce the unyieldingly triumphant to be humbled. Only life can, and failing that, death. I do not just speak of people, but civilizations, gods, religions, worldviews, churches. Nor am I undermining the fervent call to combat injustice and furnish peace—but means and ends matter.

Thus, a spunky humility or a humbled pride was advocated here.[2] I rebel against language that stresses our nothingness, or is uncompromising about it, especially in the context of God. Why would a God of Love intend or create us to be nothing, or merely to see ourselves as such? Some say that is the only path to reach greatness, and humility is often the means to do so. Perhaps, but it need not be the only way. Deprecating ourselves, according to Henri J. M. Nouwen, is "to deny God's first love for [us]."[3] The key is not simply to avoid denigrating our values, hopes, or dreams, but to test and evaluate how they impact, and whether they heal, others. We are all broken in some way, all in need of menders. We all are haunted by past and present failures, even unnamed future ones. Tinges of regret and disappointments: who is not burdened by them?

Our society and the ideological battles among religions are obsessed with being different, unique, and special. While I am partial to Peter Phan and Thich Nhat Hanh's critiques of uniqueness,[4] I have already expressed my hesitation to dismiss Christ's theological uniqueness. If Christ is not theologically or soteriologically unique, does not Christianity falter? To cross that Rubicon with John Hick and fellow radical pluralists seems to close off viable options. What's left? Phan, for example, writes of an interfaith Christology, which entails Christian and non-Christian pre-

---

2. I thus agree with Hans Rosling's claim that "Most important of all, we should be teaching our children humility and curiosity" (*Factfulness*, 269)—though I would also add compassion.

3. Nouwen, *Return of the Prodigal Son*, 107.

4. See Phan, *Being Religious Interreligiously*; and Hanh, *Living Buddha*.

sentations and understandings of Jesus, ideally made collaboratively.[5] I agree with Phan that in our pluralist world, such a Christology provides the promises of great depth and breadth. It is a method I have always employed in my Christology module. And yet . . .

Am I unable to release such theological uniqueness out of genuine faith and respect to uphold Christ's dignity, or is it complacent, misplaced, or egotistical faith? Difference can matter, but as St. Bernard notes, often this seeking of difference is a matter of show, making sure others know, for example, that a monk is fasting beyond the norm, while the others nibble and munch.[6] I fear every aspect of my faith is humbled, nibbled, and munched. Can this be a hopeful sign, a painful glimpse into something deeper?

In this work I emphasized why we are broken, because our beliefs, or non-beliefs, our belongings and identities, remain flawed, myopic, self-absorbed, unredeemed. Various lenses rendered such faults all too clearly, from:

1. The depth, nuances, and imperfections of humility and pride in various world faiths, philosophies, and disciplines (chapters 1 and 2);

2. The reality of religious pluralism (chapter 3);

3. The face-to-face encounter of interreligious dialogue, especially Jewish-Christian dialogue (chapter 4);

4. The secular, sacred encounter and dialogue that highlights deep overlap and bridges in our public and private spheres and promotes (as a Catholic theologian) the value of secular morality and humility (chapter 5);

5. The tomes and voices of history and memory (especially as analyzed through contemporary African-American voices from Bryan Stevenson to Ta-Nehisi Coates (chapter 6);

6. The horrors endured and depicted in testimonies of mass atrocities (chapter 7), from the painful songs of poet Liao Yiwu in Chinese prisons to the blows inflicted on Mohamedou Ould Slahi by my fellow Americans in Guantánamo;

---

5. Phan, *Joy of Religious Pluralism*, 92–96.
6. Bernard of Clairvaux, "On the Steps of Humility and Pride," 142.

7. The universal need for forgiveness and justice (chapter 8), and that best humbler of all—love.

Despite my failures and doubts, my brokenness and stammering, I love. It is a love still yearning, mere bulb or seed, too often selfish, immature, conditional, petty. Yet, in my sincerity to love, there opens a space for another to love me. And here especially there is humbling. For is not love "the secret of destiny, the key to life"?[7] Again, all this talk of humbling is really talk of love. Love humbles because it names and sees brokenness and frailty and still loves. I don't love my wife, kids, or parents because they're perfect. Nor do they love me based on some such empyrean state. Indeed, the deeper the love, the more aware we are of the brokenness and imperfections, reasons not to love. And yet, love we do, and love we must. Self-love is built this way, and perhaps, a human, all too human, love of God, too.

All of these lenses individually humble, and together they push us to the brink and reality of brokenness.

But only to a point. Amidst and aware of this brokenness, or sensing it, doubt swirls and typhoons within and around us. We doubt our foundations, upbringing, values, our once exclusive, solid grip on truth, salvation, liberty, or anarchy—like the blind men and the elephant parable.

Yes, doubt can empower, but it often degrades, angst-ridden. We hear the refrain "not to doubt," and I can piously chime such a hymn, but I still doubt. Some doubts are not freeing: the dread that can hover around me I wish on no one. Such humiliates, silences, and disempowers. It whispers of failures and lack of worth, of wasted journeys and hollow, vacuous beliefs.[8] Yet this work was not supposed to be "about ruin."[9]

My ultimate hope, my faith, is that doubt and humility will allay or prevent strands of violence, dismissal, moral blindness. Seeing flaws within myself, my faith, and nationality should orient me towards listening and learning. Yes, too often, doubt propels lashing out, attacking from fear and uncertainty crouched as faith. It would not be doubt without these rancid possibilities, just as humility would be something else if not for its negative pulls and stomps. But there is neither legitimate faith nor healthy self-love without doubt and humility.

---

7. Hugo, *Les Misérables*, 770.
8. See Tan, *The Red Tree*.
9. Akkad, *American War*, 6. Akkad's narrator is clear about his story, though.

CONCLUSION 273

This is all part of the dialogue, the dream and the dread, doubt and certitude, humility and pride. The dialogue is the conversation, the movement towards love, goodness, and beauty. It is the dialogue that can unite us, in our brokenness, through our doubts, and amidst those elephantine dreams.

Thus, humbling faith can unite all because it can be an act of solidarity and moral growth. As theists, nontheists, or atheists, steeped in certitude and a sense of our superior ways, we can recognize our gaps—those failures, misconceptions, and self-delusions in our convictions and interpreted evidence. Is any person, ideology, or institution left standing, sacrosanct and sanctimonious, after the roads we have traversed in this book? The hope is such awareness can breed change and transform how we describe ourselves and one another, especially in our teaching, learning, personal interactions, writing, speaking, or prayer. Such changes can also transform others who can now see a greater possibility for mutually mature hospitality, searching, and questioning. If they are honest and alert, they will examine their own certainties, and they, too, can be humbled.

And so, still on my journey—our journey—seeking and unearthing some riddles, solving a few, but encountering and struggling with others, we persevere. Humbling faith is not something that ever really ends. It expands, corrects, becomes fine-tuned, nuanced, humbled. It becomes our way and our horizon: a journey of mutual stumbling, together.

In transit: Alicante to Valencia

Bibliography

Abela, Joseph S. *Malta: A Brief History*. Malta: BDL Publishing, 2014.
Abelard, Peter. *Ethical Writings*. Translated by Paul Vincent Spade. Indianapolis: Hackett, 1995.
Abu-Nimer, Mohammad, and Ilham Nasser. "Forgiveness in the Arab and Islamic Contexts: Between Theology and Practise." *Journal of Religious Ethics* 41 (September 2013) 474–94.
Acemoglu, Daron, and James A. Robinson. *Why Nations Fail: The Origins of Power, Prosperity, and Poverty*. New York: Crown, 2012.
Actis, Munu, Cristina Aldini, Liliana Gardella, Miriam Lewin, and Elisa Tokar. *That Inferno: Conversations of Five Women Survivors of an Argentine Torture Camp*. Translated by Gretta Siebentritt. Nashville: Vanderbilt University Press, 2006.
Admirand, Peter. *Amidst Mass Atrocity and the Rubble of Theology: Searching for a Viable Theodicy*. Eugene, OR: Cascade, 2012.
———. "Dialogue in the Face of a Gun? Interfaith Dialogue and Limiting Mass Atrocities." *Soundings: An Interdisciplinary Journal* 99 (2016) 267–90.
———. "Dirt, Collapse, and Eco-responsibility: 'Natural' Evils and the Eager Longing for Eco–justice." *Worldviews: Global Religions, Culture, and Ecology* 15 (2011) 1–24.
———. "Embodying an 'Age of Doubt, Solitude, and Revolt': Christianity Beyond 'Excarnation' in *A Secular Age*." *The Heythrop Journal* 51 (2010) 905–20.
———. "Healing the Distorted Face: Doctrinal Reinterpretation(s) and the Christian Response to the Other." *One in Christ* 42 (2008) 302–17.
———. "How Pope Francis can Purify the Church despite a Dirty War." *SEARCH: A Church of Ireland Journal* 36 (Autumn 2013) 163–78.
———. "Landmines and Vegetables: The Hope and Perils of Recent Jewish Critiques of Christianity." In *Pathways for Interreligious Dialogue*, edited by Vladimir Latinovic, Gerard Mannion, and Peter Phan, 81–96. New York: Palgrave, 2016.
———, ed. *Loss and Hope: Global, Interreligious, and Interdisciplinary Perspectives*. London: Bloomsbury Academic, 2014.
———. "Mission in Remission: Mission and Interreligious Dialogue in a Postmodern, Postcolonial Age." *Concilium: International Review of Theology* (2011) 95–104.
———. "No Dialogue without Hope: Interfaith Dialogue and the Transformation of a Virtue." In *Hope in All Directions*, edited by Geoffrey Karabin, chapter 1. Oxford: Interdisciplinary, 2014.
———. "Overcoming 'Mere Oblivion': Mission Encountering Dialogue. A Reflection in Five Acts." *SEARCH: A Church of Ireland Journal* 34 (2011) 30–38.
———. "Rifts, Trust, and Openness: John Paul II's Legacy in Catholic Intra-and-Inter-Religious Dialogue." *Journal of Ecumenical Studies* 47 (Fall 2012) 555–75.

———. "'Scripture Speak[ing] Fictitious Words': Yusef as a Model for Interfaith Reconciliation." *Revista Dionysiana* 4 (2010) 1–15.

———. "Seeking Humility and Self-Critique: A Christological Analysis of *A Common Word*." In *The Future of Interfaith Dialogue: Muslim-Christian Encounters through A Common Word*, edited by Yazid Said and Lejla Demiri, 144-61. Cambridge, UK: Cambridge University Press, 2018.

———. "Should we still teach a beautiful novel by a racist author?" *International Journal of Ethics Education* (2017) 1–14. https://link.springer.com/article/10.1007/s40889-017-0042-2.

———. "The Ethics of Displacement and Migration in the Abrahamic Faiths: Enlightening Believers and Aiding Public Policy." *Journal of Ethnic and Migration Studies* 40 (2014) 671–87.

———. "The Pedophile Scandal and Its (Hoped-for) Impact on Catholic Intra- and Interreligious Dialogue." In Admirand, *Loss and Hope*, 123–36.

———. "'Traversing Towards the Other' (Mark 7:24–30): The Syrophoenician Woman Amidst Voicelessness and Loss." In *The Bible: Culture, Community, and Society*, edited by Angus Paddison and Neil Messer, 157–70. London: T. & T. Clark, 2013.

———. "Why Liberation Theology Should Be Taught in Catholic Secondary Schools." *International Studies in Catholic Education* 10 (2018) 156–69.

Afsaruddin, Asma, "Finding Common Ground: 'Mutual Knowing,' Moderation and the Fostering of Religious Pluralism." In Heft, Firestone, and Safi, *Learned Ignorance*, 67–86.

Agee, James, and Walker Evans. *Let Us Now Praise Famous Men*. Boston: Mariner, 2001.

Aguilar, Mario I. *Pope Francis: His Life and Thought*. Cambridge, UK: Lutterworth, 2014.

———. *Theology, Liberation, and Genocide: A Theology of the Periphery*. London: SCM, 2009.

Akkad, Omar El. *American War*. New York: Knopf, 2017.

Alexander, Michelle. *The New Jim Crow: Mass Incarceration in the Age of Colorblindness*. Revised edition. New York: New Press, 2012.

Alexievich, Svetlana. *Second-Hand Time*. Translated by Bela Shayevich. London: Fitzcarraldo Editions, 2016.

Al-Khalili, Jim, ed. *Aliens: Science Asks: Is There Anyone Out There?* London: Profile, 2016.

Allen, John L., Jr. *The Future Church: How Ten Trends Are Revolutionizing the Catholic Church*. New York: Random House, 2010.

Allinson, Robert Elliott. "Hillel and Confucius: The Prescriptive Formulation of the Golden Rule in the Jewish and Chinese Confucian Ethical Traditions." *Tao* 3 (2003) 29–41.

Amaladoss, Michael. "The Pluralism of Religions and the Significance of Christ." In *Asian Faces of Jesus*, edited by R. S. Sugirtharajah, 85–103. Maryknoll, NY: Orbis, 1993.

Ambar, Saladin. *American Cicero: Mario Cuomo and the Defense of American Liberalism*. Oxford: Oxford University Press, 2018.

Ammaniti, Niccolò. *Anna*. Edinburgh: Canongate, 2017.

Améry, Jean. *At the Mind's Limits: Contemplations by a Survivor on Auschwitz and Its Realities*. Translated by Sidney Rosenfeld and Stella P. Rosenfeld. Bloomington: Indiana University Press, 1994.

Ammerman, Nancy. "Response by Nancy Ammerman: Modern Altars in Everyday Life." In Berger, *Many Altars of Modernity*, 94–110.
Anderson, Carol. *White Rage: The Unspoken Truth of Our Racial Divide*. New York: Bloomsbury, 2017.
Anderson, Gary A. *Sin: A History*. New Haven: Yale University Press, 2009.
Anderson, Perry. *The Origins of Postmodernity*. London: Verso, 1998.
Andrić, Ivo. *The Bridge over the Drina*. Translated by Lovett F. Edwards. London: Harvill, 1995.
Angell, Roger. "Back to School." *The New Yorker*, September 10, 2015. http://www.newyorker.com/news/sporting-scene/back-to-school.
Anthony, Lawrence, with Graham Spence. *The Elephant Whisperer: My Life with the Herd in the African Wild*. London: Pan, 2010.
Antony, Louise M. "Introduction." In *Philosophers without God: Meditations on Atheism and the Secular Life*, edited by Louise M. Antony, ix–xiv. Oxford: Oxford University Press, 2007.
Apess, William. "An Indian's Looking Glass for the White Man." In *The Heath Anthology of American Literature*, Vol. 1, 4th edition, edited by Paul Lauter, 1398–1403. Boston: Houghton Mifflin, 2001.
Apol, Laura. *Requiem, Rwanda*. East Lansing: Michigan State University Press, 2015.
Aquinas, Thomas. *Summa Theologiae*. Translated by The Fathers of the English Dominican Province. http://www.newadvent.org/summa/.
Arendt, Hannah. *The Human Condition*. Chicago: University of Chicago Press, 1958.
Aristotle. *Nichomachean Ethics*. In *Introduction to Aristotle*, edited by Richard McKeon, 298–543. New York: Modern Library, 1947.
Armstrong, Karen. *The Bible: The Biography*. London: Atlantic, 2008.
Aronson, Ronald. *Living without God: New Directions for Atheists, Agnostics, Secularists, and the Undecided*. Berkeley: Counterpoint, 2008.
Arthur, Wallace. *Life through Time and Space*. Cambridge, MA: Harvard University Press, 2017.
Augustine. *Confessions*. Translated by Henry Chadwick. Oxford: Oxford University Press, 1992.
———. *On Christian Doctrine*. Translated by D. W. Robertson Jr. New York: Macmillan, 1958.
———. *The City of God*. Translated by Henry Bettenson, edited by David Knowles. Middlesex: Penguin, 1980.
Aurelius, Marcus. *Meditations*. Translated by Maxwell Staniforth. Middlesex: Penguin, 1983.
Austen, Jane. *Pride and Prejudice*. London: Penguin, 2008.
Aydin, Mahmut. "Islam in a World of Diverse Faiths: A Muslim View." In Leukel and Ridgeon, *Islam and Inter-faith Relations*, 33–54.
Azango, Mae. "Liberia: Former Fierce Warlord, 'Butt Naked', Now Humanitarian, Likely to Face War Crimes Prosecution?" *Front Page Africa*, August 14, 2018. https://frontpageafricaonline.com/liberia-war-crimes-trial/liberia-former-fierce-warlord-butt-naked-now-humanitarian-likely-to-face-war-crimes-prosecution/.
Bailey, Kenneth E. *Jesus Through Middle Eastern Eyes: Cultural Studies in the Gospels*. London: SPCK, 2008.
Baker, Joseph O., and Buster G. Smith. *American Secularism: Cultural Contours of Nonreligious Belief Systems*. New York: New York University Press, 2015.

Balagangadhara, S. N., and Jakob De Roover. "The Dark Hour of Secularism: Hindu Fundamentalism and Colonial Liberalism in India." In Ghosh, *Making Sense of the Secular*, 111–30.

Baldwin, James. *The Evidence of Things Not Seen*. New York: Henry Holt, 1995.

———. *The Fire Next Time*. New York: Vintage, 1993.

Banville, John. *Time Pieces: A Dublin Memoir*. Dublin: Hatchette, 2016.

Baptist, Edward E. *The Half Has Never Been Told: Slavery and the Making of American Capitalism*. New York: Basic, 2016.

Barbieri, William A., Jr., ed. *At the Limits of the Secular: Reflections on Faith and Public Life*. Grand Rapids: Eerdmans, 2014.

———. "The Post–Secular Problematic." In Barbieri, *At the Limits of the Secular*, 129–61.

Barnstone, Tony, and Chou Ping, eds. *The Anchor Book of Chinese Poetry: From Ancient to Contemporary. The Full 3000-Year Tradition*. New York: Anchor, 2005.

Bash, Anthony. "Did Jesus Discover Forgiveness?" *Journal of Religious Ethics* 41 (2013) 382–99.

———. "Forgiveness: A Re-appraisal." *Studies in Christian Ethics* 242 (2011) 133–46.

Batnitzky, Leora. "On the Suffering of God's Chosen: Christian Views." In *Christianity in Jewish Terms*, edited by Frymer-Kensky, et al., 203–29. Boulder, CO: Westview, 2000.

Battlestar Galactica. "Daybreak: Part 2 and 3." Directed by Michael Rymer. Written by Ronald D. Moore. SyFy. March 20, 2009.

Bauer, Yehuda. *Rethinking the Holocaust*. New Haven: Princeton University Press, 2001.

Beard, Mary. *Confronting the Classics: Traditions, Inventions, and Innovations*. London: Profile, 2014.

Beattie, Tina. "Maternal Well-Being in Sub-Saharan Africa: From Silent Suffering to Human Flourishing." In *The Church We Want: African Catholics Look to Vatican III*, edited by Agbonkhianmeghe E. Orobator, 175–88. Maryknoll, NY: Orbis, 2016.

Becker, Karl Joseph, and Ilaria Morali, eds. *Catholic Engagement with World Religions: A Comprehensive Study*. Maryknoll, NY: Orbis, 2010.

———. "Conclusion: Looking Forward and Backward." In Becker and Morali, *Catholic Engagement with World Religion*, 509–11.

Bellos, David. *The Novel of the Century: The Extraordinary Adventure of Les Misérables*. New York: Farrar, Straus and Giroux, 2017.

Benedict. *The Rule of St. Benedict*. Edited by Timothy Fry. New York: Vintage, 1998.

Benedict XVI. *Porta Fidei*. October 11, 2011. http://w2.vatican.va/content/benedict-xvi/en/motu_proprio/documents/hf_ben-xvi_motu-proprio_20111011_porta-fidei.html.

Bennhold, Katrin. "Women Travel Migrant Trail Rife with Risk." *The New York Times*. January 3, 2016. A1.

Berger, Alan L., ed. *Post-Holocaust Jewish-Christian Dialogue: After the Flood, before the Rainbow*. Lanham, MD: Lexington, 2014.

———, ed. *Trialogue and Terror: Judaism, Christianity, and Islam after 9/11*. Eugene, OR: Cascade, 2012.

Berger, Alan L., and David Patterson, with David P. Gushee, John T. Pawlikowski, and John K. Roth. *Jewish-Christian Dialogue: Drawing Honey from the Rock*. St. Paul, MN: Paragon House, 2008.

Berger, Peter. *The Many Altars of Modernity: Toward a Paradigm for Religion in a Pluralist Age*. Boston: De Gruyter, 2014.
Bergoglio, Jorge Mario, and Abraham Skorka. *On Heaven and Earth: Pope Francis on Faith, Family and the Church in the Twenty-first Century*. New York: Image, 2013.
Berg-Sørensen, Anders, ed. *Contesting Secularism: Comparative Perspectives*. Surrey: Ashgate, 2013
Berkovits, Eliezer. *Essential Essays on Judaism*. Edited by David Hazony. Jerusalem: Shalem, 2003.
Bernard of Clairvaux. "On the Steps of Humility and Pride." In *Bernard of Clairvaux: Selected Works*, 99–143. Translated by G.R. Evans. New York: Paulist, 1987.
Bersnak, P. Bracy. "The Magnanimity and Humility of St. Ignatius Loyola." *Crisis Magazine*. July 29, 2013. http://www.crisismagazine.com/2013/the-magnanimity-and-humility-of-st-ignatius-loyola.
Berthrong, John. "Christian-Confucian Dialogue." In Cornille, *Wiley-Blackwell Companion to Inter-Religious Dialogue*, 296–310.
Berwouts, Kris. *Congo's Violent Peace: Conflict and Struggle since the Great African War*. London: Zed, 2017.
Betts, Dwayne. "The Stoop Isn't the Jungle." *Slate,* July 10, 2014. http://www.slate.com/articles/news_and_politics/jurisprudence/2014/07/alice_goffman_s_on_the_run_she_is_wrong_about_black_urban_life.html.
Bhagavad-Gita. Translated by Barbara Stoler Miller. New York: Bantam, 1986.
Bhargava, Rajeev. "How Should States Deal with Deep Religious Diversity? Can Anything Be Learned from the Indian Model of Secularism?" In *Rethinking Religion and World Affairs*, edited by Timothy Samuel Shah, Alfred Stepan, and Monica Duffy Toft, 73–84. Oxford: Oxford University Press, 2012.
———. "Multiple Secularisms and Multiple Secular States." In Berg-Sørensen, *Contesting Secularism*, 17–41.
Biggar, Nigel, and Linda Hogan, eds. *Religious Voices in Public Places*. Oxford: Oxford University Press, 2009.
Bilgrami, Akeel, ed. *Beyond the Secular West: Religion, Culture, and Public Life*. New York: Columbia University Press, 2016.
Bissell, Tom. *Apostle: Travels among the Tombs of the Twelve*. London: Faber & Faber, 2017.
Blahyi, Joshua. *The Redemption of an African Warlord: The Joshua Blahyi Story: A Modern Day Conversion from Saul to Paul*. Shippensburg, PA: Destiny Image, 2013.
Blake, William. *The Poems of William Blake*. Edited by John Sampson. London: Senate, 1995.
Blessing, Kimberly A. "Atheism and the Meaningfulness of Life." In Bullivant and Ruse, *Oxford Handbook of Atheism*, 104–18.
Bloom, Paul. *Against Empathy: The Case for Rational Compassion*. New York: HarperCollins, 2017.
Bloxham, Donald, and A. Dirk Moses, eds. *The Oxford Handbook of Genocide Studies*. Oxford: Oxford University Press, 2013.
Blumenthal, David R. "Forgiveness and Repentance." *Crosscurrents* (Spring 1988) 75–81.
Blustein, Jeffrey. *Forgiveness and Remembrance: Remembering Wrongdoing in Personal and Public Life*. Oxford: Oxford University Press, 2014.

———. *The Moral Demands of Memory*. Cambridge, UK: Cambridge University Press, 2008.
Boase, Roger. "Ecumenical Islam: Muslim Response to Religious Pluralism." In Boase, *Islam and Global Dialogue*, 247–65.
———, ed. *Islam and Global Dialogue: Religious Pluralism and the Pursuit of Peace*. Surrey, UK: Ashgate, 2010.
Boehm, Barbara Drake, and Melanie Holcomb, eds. *Jerusalem 1040–1400: Every People Under Heaven*. New York: Metropolitan Museum of Art, 2016.
Boff, Clodovis. "Saint Thomas Aquinas and the Theology of Liberation: A Letter to a Young Theological Student." *New Blackfriars* 65.773 (November 1984) 458–71.
Bolick, Kate. "All the Single Ladies." *Atlantic*, September 30, 2011. https://www.theatlantic.com/magazine/archive/2011/11/all-the-single-ladies/308654/.
Boo, Katherine. *Beyond the Beautiful Forevers: Life, Death, and Hope in a Mumbai Undercity*. New York: Random House, 2012.
Booth, James W. *Communities of Memory: On Witness, Identity, and Justice*. Ithaca, NY: Cornell University Press, 2006.
Borger, Julian. *The Butcher's Trail: How the Search for Balkan War Criminals Became the World's Most Successful Manhunt*. New York: Other Press, 2017.
Borges, Jorge Luis. "Funes the Memorious." In *Labyrinths: Selected Stories and Other Writings*, edited by Donald A. Yates and James E. Irby, 59–66. New York: New Directions, 1964.
Boschki, Reinhold. "Teaching through Words. Teaching through Education: Education after (and about) Auschwitz." In Katz and Rosen, *Elie Wiesel*, 243–54.
Boswell, Matthew. "Beyond Autobiography: Hybrid Testimony and the Art of Witness." In Kilby and Rowland, *Future of Testimony*, 144–59.
Boteach, Schmuley. *Kosher Jesus*. Jerusalem: Gefen, 2012.
Boumediene, Lakhdar, and Mustafa Ait Idir. *Witnesses of the Unseen: Seven Years in Guantanamo*. Stanford: Stanford University Press, 2017.
Bowden, John. "Religious Pluralism and the Heritage of the Enlightenment." In Boase, *Islam and Global Dialogue*, 13–20.
Bowels, Paul. *Travels: Collected Writings 1950–93*. London: Sort of Books, 2010.
Bowker, John. *Why Religions Matter*. Cambridge, UK: Cambridge University Press, 2015.
Boyarin, Daniel. "Hellenism in Jewish Babylonia." In *The Cambridge Companion to the Talmud and Rabbinic Literature*, edited by Charlotte E. Fonrobert and Martin S. Jaffee, 336–63. Cambridge, UK: Cambridge University Press, 2007.
———. *The Jewish Gospels: The Story of the Jewish Christ*. New York: New Press, 2012.
Boyd, Craig A. "Pride and Humility: Tempting the Desire to Excellence." In *Virtues & Their Vices*, edited by Kevin Timpe and Craig A. Boyd, 245–66. Oxford: Oxford University Press, 2014.
Boys, Mary C. "This I Believe." In Berger, *Trialogue and Terror*, 121–33.
Brackley, Dean. *The Call to Discernment in Troubled Times: New Perspectives on the Transformative Wisdom of Ignatius of Loyola*. New York: Crossroad, 2004.
Braithwaite, John. "Traditional Justice." In Llewellyn and Philpott, *Restorative Justice, Reconciliation, and Peace Building*, 214–39.
Brennan, Jason. *Against Democracy*. Princeton: Princeton University Press, 2016.
Brombert, Victor. *Musings on Mortality: From Tolstoy to Primo Levi*. Chicago: University of Chicago Press, 2013.

Bronner, Ethan. "Mourning Victims, Sikhs Lament Being Mistaken for Radicals or Militants." *The New York Times*, August 6, 2012. http://www.nytimes.com/2012/08/07/us/sikhs-mourn-victims-and-lament-post-9-11-targeting.html?_r=0.

Brontë, Charlotte. *Jane Eyre*. London: Penguin, 2006.

Brown, Peter. *The Ransom of the Soul: Afterlife and Wealth in Early Western Christianity*. Cambridge, MA: Harvard University Press, 2015.

Browning, Christopher R. *Ordinary Men: Reserve Police Battalion 101 and the Final Solution in Poland*. New York: Harper, 1998.

———. *Remembering Survival: Inside a Nazi Slave-Labor Camp*. New York: Norton, 2011.

Bruce, Steve. *Secularization*. Oxford: Oxford University Press, 2011.

Brudholm, Thomas. *Resentment's Virtue: Jean Améry and the Refusal to Forgive*. Philadelphia: Temple University Press, 2009.

Brueck, Laura R. *Writing Resistance: The Rhetorical Imagination of Hindi Dalit Literature*. Dehli: Primus, 2017.

Brusatte, Steve. *The Rise and Fall of the Dinosaurs*. London: Macmillan, 2018.

Bucko, Adam, and Rory McEntee. *The New Monasticism: An Interspiritual Manifesto for Contemplative Living*. Maryknoll, NY: Orbis, 2015.

Buell, Lawrence. *The Dream of the Great American Novel*. Cambridge, MA: Harvard University Press, 2014.

Bullivant, Stephen. *Faith and Unbelief*. Norwich, UK: Canterbury, 2012.

Bullivant, Stephen, and Michael Ruse. "Introduction." In Bullivant and Ruse, *Oxford Handbook of Atheism*, 1–7.

———, eds. *The Oxford Handbook of Atheism*. Oxford: Oxford University Press, 2013.

Burdon, Christopher. "William Blake." In *The Oxford Handbook of English Literature and Theology*, edited by Andrew W. Hass, David Jasper, and Elisabeth Jay, 448–64. Oxford: Oxford University Press, 2009.

Burrell, David B. "Aquinas and Islamic and Jewish Thinkers." In *The Cambridge Companion to Aquinas*, edited by Norman Kretzmann and Eleonore Stump, 60–84. Cambridge, UK: Cambridge University Press, 2009.

Burrows, William R. *Jacques Dupuis Faces the Inquisition: Two Essays by Jacques Dupuis on Dominus Iesus and the Roman Investigation of His Work*. Eugene, OR: Pickwick, 2012.

Bushlack, Thomas J. *Politics for a Pilgrim Church: A Thomistic Theory of Civic Virtue*. Grand Rapids: Eerdmans, 2015.

Butler, Joseph. "Sermon VIII. Upon Resentment and Forgiveness of Injuries—Matt.5:43–44." *Project Canterbury*. http://anglicanhistory.org/butler/rolls/08.html.

Butler, Paul. *Chokehold: Policing Black Men*. New York: New Press, 2017.

Button, Mark E. "'A Monkish Kind of Virtue?' For and Against Humility." *Political Theory* 33 (2005) 840–68.

———. *Political Vices*. Oxford: Oxford University Press, 2016.

Buxbaum, Yitzhak. *The Life and Teachings of Hillel*. Lanham, MD: Rowman and Littlefield, 2004.

Byrd, Jodi A. "American Indian Transnationalisms." In *The Cambridge Companion to Transnational American Literature*, edited by Yogita Goyal, 174–189. Cambridge, UK: Cambridge University Press, 2017.

Calhoun, Craig, Mark Juergensmeyer, and Jonathan VanAntwerpen, eds. *Rethinking Secularism*. Oxford: Oxford University Press, 2011.
Campbell, Joseph. *The Hero with a Thousand Faces*. Princeton: Princeton University Press, 1973.
Camus, Albert. *The Plague*. Translated by Stuart Gilbert. New York: Vintage, 1991.
Cantacuzino, Marina. *The Forgiveness Project: Stories for a Vengeful Age*. London: Jessica Kingsley, 2016.
Caputo, John D, and Michael Scanlon, eds. *God, the Gift and Postmodernism*. Bloomington: Indiana University Press, 1999.
———, eds. *Questioning God*. Bloomington: Indiana University Press, 2001.
Card, Claudia. *The Atrocity Paradigm: A Theory of Evil*. Oxford: Oxford University Press, 2002.
Cardenal, Ernesto. *The Gospel in Solentiname*. Translated by Donald D. Walsh. Maryknoll, NY: Orbis, 2010.
Cargill, C. Robert. *Sea of Rust: A Novel*. New York: Harper Voyager, 2018.
Carr, Garrett. *The Rule of the Land: Walking Ireland's Border*. London: Faber & Faber, 2017.
Carroll, Anthony, and Richard Norman, eds. *Religion and Atheism: Beyond the Divide*. London: Routledge, 2017.
Carson, Clayborne, and Kris Shepard, eds. *A Call to Conscience: The Landmark Speeches of Martin Luther King Jr.* New York: Warner, 2002.
Carter, Forrest. *The Education of Little Tree*. Albuquerque: University of New Mexico Press, 1993.
Cartledge, Paul. *Democracy: A Life*. Oxford: Oxford University Press, 2018.
Caruth, Cathy. *Unclaimed Experience: Trauma, Narrative, and History*. Baltimore: Johns Hopkins University Press, 1996.
Casanova, José. "The Secular, Secularizations, Secularisms." In Calhoun, Juergensmeyer, and VanAntwerpen, *Rethinking Secularism*, 55–74.
Casas, Bartolomé de Las. *A Short Account of the Destruction of the Indies*. Edited and Translated by Nigel Griffin. London: Penguin, 1992.
Cassian, John. *The Institutes*. Translated by Edgar S. Gibson. http://www.osb.org/lectio/cassian/inst.
Cavanaugh, William T. "The Invention of the Religious-Secular Distinction." In Barbieri, *At the Limits of the Secular*, 105–28.
———. *The Myth of Religious Violence: Secular Ideology and the Roots of Modern Conflict*. Oxford: Oxford University Press, 2009.
Cea, J. Abraham Vélez de. "The Buddha and the Dalai Lama on Religious Pluralism." In Phan and Ray, *Understanding Religious Pluralism*, 46–65.
Celan, Paul. *Poems of Paul Celan*. Translated by Michael Hamburger. New York: Persea, 1995.
Cervantes, Miguel de. *Don Quixote*. Translated by Edith Grossman. New York: HarperCollins, 2003.
Chambers, Becky. *Record of a Spaceborn Few*. New York: Harper Voyager, 2018.
Chang, Jung, and Jon Halliday. *Mao: The Unknown Story*. London: Jonathan Cape, 2005.
Chappel, James. *Catholic Modern: The Challenge of Totalitarianism and the Remaking of the Church*. Cambridge, MA: Harvard University Press, 2018.

Chazan, Robert. *From Anti-Judaism to Anti-Semitism: Ancient and Medieval Constructions of Jewish History.* Cambridge, UK: Cambridge University Press, 2016.
Cheetham, David, Douglas Pratt, and David Thomas, eds. *Understanding Interreligious Relations.* Oxford: Oxford University Press, 2013.
Chelius, Judith, ed. *Feminist Interpretations of Saint Augustine.* University Park, PA: Penn State University Press, 2007.
Chief Seattle. "Speech of Chief Seattle." In *The Heath Anthology of American Literature,* Vol. 1, 4th Edition, edited by Paul Lauter, 1418–22. Boston: Houghton Mifflin, 2001.
Chol-Hwan, Kang. *The Aquariums of Pyongyang: Ten Years in the North Korean Gulag.* Translated by Yair Reiner. New York: Basic, 2000.
Christian Scholars Group on Christian-Jewish Relations. "A Sacred Obligation: Rethinking Christian Faith in Relation to Judaism and the Jewish People." September 1, 2002. http://www.jcrelations.net/en/?id=986.
Chuang Tzu. *The Book of Chuang Tzu.* Translated by Martin Palmer, Elizabeth Breuilly, Chang Wei Ming, and Jay Ramsay. London: Penguin, 2006.
Churchill, Ward. "I am Indigenist." In *Readings in Indigenous Religions,* edited by Graham Harvey, 275–309. London: Continuum, 2002.
Chvala-Smith, Anthony J. "Augustine of Hippo." In Pui-lan, Compier, and Rieger, *Empire,* 79–93.
Cicero, Marcus Tullius. "Against Lucius Sergius Catalina 1–4." In *Selected Political Speeches,* 71–145. Translated by Michael Grant. London: Penguin, 1989.
———. *On Duties.* Translated by M. T. Griffin and E. M. Atkins. Cambridge, UK: Cambridge University Press, 1991.
Clark, Edmund, and Crofton Black. "Black Sites." *FT Weekend Magazine.* March 19, 2016, 20–25.
Clayton, Philip. "The Religious Spinoza." In *The Persistence of the Sacred in Modern Thought,* edited by Chris L. Firestone and Nathan A. Jacobs, 66–86. Notre Dame: University of Notre Dame Press, 2012.
Clunas, Craig. *Art in China.* 2nd edition. Oxford: Oxford University Press, 2009.
Coates, Ta-Nehesi. *Between the World and Me.* New York: Spiegel & Grau, 2015.
———. "Nonviolence as Compliance." *Atlantic,* April 27, 2015. http://www.theatlantic.com/politics/archive/2015/04/nonviolence-as-compliance/391640/.
———. "The Black Family in the Age of Mass Incarceration." *Atlantic.* October 2015. https://www.theatlantic.com/magazine/archive/2015/10/the-black-family-in-the-age-of-mass-incarceration/403246/.
———. "The Case for Reparations." *Atlantic.* June 2014. https://www.theatlantic.com/magazine/archive/2014/06/the-case-for-reparations/361631/.
———. *We Were in Eight Years in Power: An American Tragedy.* New York: One World, 2017.
Cobb, John B., Jr. "Rethinking Christian Faith in the Context of Religious Diversity." In *The Dialogue Comes of Age: Christian Encounters with Other Traditions,* edited by John B. Cobb Jr. and Ward M. McAfee, 9–40. Minneapolis: Fortress, 2010.
Cohen, Charles L., Paul F. Knitter, and Ulrich Rosenhagen, eds. *The Future of Interreligious Dialogue: A Multireligious Conversation on Nostra Aetate.* Maryknoll, NY: Orbis, 2017.

Coker, Christopher. *Men at War: What Fiction Tells Us about Conflict from the Iliad to Catch-22*. Oxford: Oxford University Press, 2014.
Cole, David, ed. *Torture Memos: Rationalizing the Unthinkable*. New York: The New Press, 2009.
Cole, Elizabeth A. "Apology, Forgiveness, and Moral Repair." *Ethics and International Affairs* 22 (Winter 2008) 421–28.
Coll, Steve. *Directorate S: The CIA and America's Secret Wars in Afghanistan and Pakistan, 2001–2016*. New Dehli: Allen Lane, 2018.
Comins, Neil F. *The Traveler's Guide to Space: For One-Way Settlers and Round-Trip Tourists*. New York: Columbia University Press, 2017.
Commission for Religious Relations with the Jews. "'The Gifts and the Calling of God Are Irrevocable' (Rom 11:29): A Reflection on the Theological Questions Pertaining to Catholic-Jewish Relations on the Occasion of the 50th Anniversary of 'Nostra Aetate' (No. 4)." December 10, 2015. http://www.vatican.va/roman_curia/pontifical_councils/chrstuni/relations-jews-docs/rc_pc_chrstuni_doc_20151210_ebraismo-nostra-aetate_en.html.
Committee on Doctrine and Committee on Ecumenical and Interreligious Affairs. "A Note on Ambiguities Contained in 'Reflections on Covenant and Mission.'" USCCB. June 18, 2009. http://www.ccjr.us/dialogika–resources/themes–in–todays–dialogue/conversion/559–usccb–09june18.
Confucius. *The Analects*. Translated by D. C. Lau. London: Penguin, 1979.
Congregation for the Doctrine of the Faith. *Doctrinal Note on Some Aspects of Evangelization*. December 3, 2007. http://www.vatican.va/roman_curia/congregations/cfaith/documents/rc_con_cfaith_doc_20071203_nota-evangelizzazione_en.html,
———. *Dominus Iesus*. August 6, 2000. http://www.vatican.va/roman_curia/congregations/cfaith/documents/rc_con_cfaith_doc_20000806_dominus-iesus_en.html.
Connolly, William E. *Why I Am Not a Secularist*. Minneapolis: University of Minnesota Press, 1999.
Contreras, Randol. *The Stickup Kids: Race, Drugs, Violence, and the American Dream*. Berkeley: University of California Press, 2013.
Cook, Joan E. *Hear, O Heavens and Listen, O Earth: An Introduction to the Prophets*. Collegeville, MN: Liturgical, 2006.
Cook, Michael J. *Modern Jews Engage the New Testament: Enhancing Jewish Well-Being in a Christian Environment*. Woodstock, VT: Jewish Lights, 2008.
Cooper, Julie E. *Secular Powers: Humility in Modern Political Thought*. Chicago: The University of Chicago Press, 2013.
Cornille, Catherine. "Conditions for Inter-Religious Dialogue." In Cornille, *Wiley-Blackwell Companion to Inter-Religious Dialogue*, 20–33.
———. "Multiple Religious Belonging." In Cheetham, Pratt, and Thomas, *Understanding Interreligious Relations*, 324–40.
———. *The Im-Possibility of Interreligious Dialogue*. New York: Herder & Herder, 2008.
———, ed. *The Wiley-Blackwell Companion to Inter-Religious Dialogue*. Oxford: Wiley–Blackwell, 2013.
Cornille, Catherine, and Jillian Maxey, eds. *Women and Interreligious Dialogue*. Eugene, OR: Wipf and Stock, 2013.

Coronil, Fernando. "Latin American Postcolonial Studies and Global Decolonization." In Lazarus, *Cambridge Companion to Postcolonial Literary Studies*, 221–40.
Corrington, Gail. "Anorexia, Asceticism, and Autonomy: Self-Control as Liberation and Transcendence." *Journal of Feminist Studies in Religion* 2 (Fall 1986) 51–61.
Cosgrove, Elliot, ed. *Jewish Theology in Our Time: A New Generation Explores the Foundations & Future of Jewish Belief*. Woodstock, VT: Jewish Lights, 2010.
Courtine-Denamy, Sylvie. *Three Women in Dark Times: Edith Stein, Hannah Arendt, Simone Weil*. Translated by G. M. Goshgarian. Ithaca: Cornell University Press, 2000.
Coward, Howard, ed. *Hindu-Christian Dialogue: Perspectives and Encounters*. Maryknoll, NY: Orbis, 1990.
Cowen, Rob. *Common Ground*. London: Willmill, 2016.
Crane, Jonathan K., ed. *Beastly Morality: Animals as Ethical Agents*. New York: Columbia University Press, 2016.
Crane, Tim. *The Meaning of Belief: Religion from an Atheist's Point of View*. Cambridge, MA: Harvard University Press, 2017.
Crawford, Neta C. *Accountability for Killing: Moral Responsibility for Collateral Damage in America's Post-9/11 Wars*. Oxford: Oxford University Press, 2013.
Crosthwaite, Alejandro. "Thomas Aquinas on Servitude." In Floyd-Thomas and De La Torre, *Beyond the Pale*, 33–40.
Crownshaw, Rick. "A Natural History of Testimony?" In Kilby and Rowland, *The Future of Testimony*, 161–76.
Crownshaw, Rick, Jane Kilby, and Antony Rowland. "Preface." In Crownshaw, Kilby, and Rowland, *Future of Memory*, ix–xiii.
Cruz, Juana Inés de la. *Poems, Protest, and a Dream*. Translated by Margaret Sayers Peden. New York: Penguin, 1997.
Csikszentmihalyi, Mark A. "The Golden Rule in Confucianism." In Neusner and Chilton, *Golden Rule*, 157–69.
Cubilié, Anne. *Women Witnessing Terror: Testimony and the Cultural Politics of Human Rights*. New York: Fordham University Press, 2005.
Cunliffe, Barry. *Europe Between the Oceans, 9000 BC—AD 1000*. New Haven: Yale University Press, 2008.
Cunningham, Philip A. *Seeking Shalom: The Journey to Right Relationship Between Catholics and Jews*. Grand Rapids: Eerdmans, 2015.
Cunningham, Philip A., Norbert J. Hofmann, and Joseph Sievers, eds. *Christ Jesus and the Jewish People Today: New Explorations of Theological Interrelationships*. Grand Rapids: Eerdmans, 2011.
Curzor, Harold J. *Aristotle and the Virtues*. Oxford: Oxford University Press, 2012.
D'Costa, Gavin. *Christianity and World Religions: Disputed Questions in the Theology of Religions*. Oxford: Wiley-Blackwell, 2009.
———, ed. *Christian Uniqueness Reconsidered: The Myth of a Pluralistic Theology of Religions*. Maryknoll, NY: Orbis, 1990.
———. "Reflections on the Philosophical Presuppositions of the Pluralist Theology of Religions." In Becker and Morali, *Catholic Engagement with World Religions*, 329–44.
———. *The Meeting of Religions and the Trinity*. Maryknoll, NY: Orbis, 2000.
Dacey, Austin. *The Secular Conscience*. Amhherst, NY: Prometheus, 2008.

Dalai Lama. *Beyond Religion: Ethics for a Whole World.* Boston: Houghton Mifflin Harcourt, 2011.
———. *The Good Heart: A Buddhist Perspective on the Teachings of Jesus.* Edited by Robert Kiely. Translated by Geshe Thupten Jinpa. Somerville, MA: Wisdom, 1998.
———. *The Universe in a Single Atom: The Convergence of Science and Spirituality.* New York: Morgan Road, 2005.
———. *Toward a True Kinship of Faiths: How the World Religions Can Come Together.* New York: Doubleday Religion, 2010.
Dalai Lama, with Franz Alt. *An Appeal to the World: The Way to Peace in a Time of Division.* New York: William Collins, 2017.
Dalai Lama, and Victor Chan. *The Wisdom of Compassion.* New York: Riverhead, 2012.
———. *The Wisdom of Forgiveness: Intimate Conversations and Journeys.* New York: Riverhead, 2005.
Daley, Brian E. "The Pursuit of Excellence and the 'Ordinary Manner': Humility and the Jesuit University." In *For That I Came: Virtues and Ideals of Jesuit Education*, edited by William J. O'Brien, 11–35. Washington, DC: Georgetown University Press, 1997.
———. "'To Be More Like Christ': The Background and Implications of 'Three Kinds of Humility.'" *Studies in the Spirituality of Jesuits* 27 (January 1995) 1–39.
Dallmayr, Fred. *Being in the World: Dialogue and Cosmopolis.* Lexington: University Press of Kentucky, 2013.
Dalyrimple, William. *From the Holy Mountain: A Journey Among the Christians of the Middle East.* New York: Henry Holt, 1999.
Danner, Mark. "Rumsfeld: Why We Live in His Ruins." *The New York Review of Books.* February 6, 2014. http://www.nybooks.com/articles/archives/2014/feb/06/rumsfeld-why-we-live-his-ruins/.
———. *Torture and Truth: America, Abu Ghraib, and the War on Terror.* New York: New York Review, 2004.
Darwin, Charles. *The Origen of Species.* First Edition. London: Penguin, 1985.
da Silva, Anthony. "Through Nonviolence to Truth: Gandhi's Vision of Reconciliation." In Helmick and Petersen, *Forgiveness and Reconciliation*, 305–27.
Davies, Brian. "The New Atheism: Its Virtues and its Vices." *New Blackfriars* 92.1037 (January 2011) 18–34.
Davies, Norman. *Europe: A History.* Oxford: Oxford University Press, 1996.
Dawkins, Richard. *The God Delusion.* Boston: Houghton Mifflin, 2006.
Day, Abby. *Believing in Belonging: Belief & Social Identity in the Modern World.* Oxford: Oxford University Press, 2011.
Day, Dorothy. *The Long Loneliness.* New York: HarperOne, 1997.
Delbo, Charlotte. *Auschwitz and After.* Translated by Rosete C. Lamont. New Haven: Yale University Press, 1995.
Delio, Ilia. *The Emergent Christ: Exploring the Meaning of Catholic in an Evolutionary Universe.* Maryknoll, NY: Orbis, 2011.
Deloria, Vine, Jr. "Indigenous Peoples." In *The Blackwell Companion to Religious Ethics*, edited by William Schweiker, 552–59. Oxford: Blackwell, 2008.
Demick, Barbara. *Besieged: Life Under Fire on a Sarajevo Street.* London: Granta, 2012.
Deneyer, Simon. "On Tiananmen Square anniversary, detentions in China and candlelight vigil in Hong Kong." *The Washington Post.* June 4, 2017. https://www.washingtonpost.com/news/worldviews/wp/2017/06/04/on-tiananmen-square-

anniversary-detentions-in-china-and-candlelight-vigil-in-hong-kong/?utm_term=.933f6ad06362.
Derrida, Jacques. "To Forgive: The Unforgivable and the Imprescriptible." In Caputo, Dooley and Scanlon, *Questioning God*, 21–51.
Desmond, Matthew. *Evicted: Poverty and Profit in the American City*. London: Allen Lane, 2016.
De Waal, Frans. *Are We Smart Enough to Know How Smart Animals Are?* New York: Norton, 2016.
De Waal, Frans and Jennifer J. Pokorny. "Primate Conflict and Its Relation to Human Forgiveness." In *Handbook of Forgiveness*, edited by Everett L. Worthington Jr., 17–32. New York: Routledge, 2005.
Dickens, Charles. *Bleak House*. New York: Signet, 1980.
———. *David Copperfield*. London: Penguin, 2004.
Dietrich, Donald J. "Globalization, Human Rights, and the Catholic Response." In Berger, *Trialogue and Terror*, 134–49.
Donaldson, Laura E. and Kwok Pui-lan, eds. *Postcolonialism, Feminism, & Religious Discourse*. New York: Routledge, 2002.
Doniger, Wendy. *The Hindus: An Alternative History*. New York: Penguin, 2009.
Dostoyevsky, Fyodor. *The Brothers Karamazov*. Translated by Constance Garnett. New York: Signet, 1986.
Dratch, Mark. "Forgiving the Unforgivable? Jewish Insights into Repentance and Forgiveness." In *Forgiveness and Abuse: Jewish and Christian Reflections*, edited by Marie M. Fortune and Joretta L. Marshall, 21–36. New York: Routledge, 2009.
Driver, Julia. "Modesty and Ignorance." *Ethics* 109 (July 1999) 827–34.
Dube, Musa W. *Postcolonial Feminist Interpretations of the Bible*. St. Louis: Chalice, 2000.
duBois, Page. "Achilles, Psammentius, and Antigone: Forgiveness in Homer and Beyond." In Griswold and Konstan, *Ancient Forgiveness*, 31–47.
Du Bois, W. E. B. *The Souls of Black Folk*. New York: Dover, 1994.
Duck, Waverly. *No Way Out: Precarious Living in the Shadow of Poverty and Drug Dealing*. Chicago: University of Chicago Press, 2015.
Dunbar-Ortiz, Roxanne. *An Indigenous People's History of The United States*. Beacon, 2015.
Duneier, Mitchell. *Ghetto: The Invention of a Place. The History of an Idea*. New York: Farrar, Straus, and Giroux, 2016.
Dupré, Louis. "The Dialectic of Faith and Atheism in the Eighteenth Century." In Himes and Pope, *Finding God in All Things*, 39–52.
Dupuis, Jacques. *Christianity and the Religions: From Confrontation to Dialogue*. Translated by Philip Berryman. Maryknoll, NY: Orbis, 2003.
———. *Toward a Christian Theology of Religious Pluralism*. Maryknoll, NY: Orbis, 2001.
Durham, E. Cole, Jr., and Elizabeth A. Clark. "The Place of Religious Freedom in the Structure of Peacebuilding." In Omer, Appleby, and Little, *The Oxford Handbook of Religion, Conflict, and Peacebuilding*, 281–306.
Düwell, Marcus, Jens Braarvig, Roger Brownsword, and Dietmar Mieth, eds. *The Cambridge Handbook of Human Dignity: Interdisciplinary Perspectives*. Cambridge, UK: Cambridge University Press, 2014.

Dworkin, Ronald. *Religion without God*. Cambridge, MA: Harvard University Press, 2013.
Dyson, Michael Eric. *Tears We Cannot Stop: A Sermon to White America*. New York: St. Martin's, 2017.
Eagleton, Terry. *Culture and the Death of God*. New Haven: Yale University Press, 2014.
Eck, Diana L. "Is Our God Listening? Exclusivism, Inclusivism, and Pluralism." In Boase, *Islam and Global Dialogue*, 21–49.
Eckhart, Meister. *Selected Writings*. Translated by Oliver Davies. London: Penguin, 1994.
Edin, Kathryn, and Timothy J. Nelson. *Doing the Best I Can: Fatherhood in the Inner City*. Berkeley: University of California Press, 2013.
Edin, Kathryn J., and H. Luke Shaefer. *$2.00 a Day: Living on Almost Nothing in America*. New York: Houghton Mifflin, 2016.
Edmonds, David. *Would You Kill the Fat Man? The Trolley Problem and What Your Answer Tells Us about Right and Wrong*. Princeton: Princeton University Press, 2015.
Einstein, Albert. *Ideas and Opinions*. Translated by Sonja Bargmann. New York: Crown Trade, 1982.
Eiseley, Loren. *All the Strange Hours: The Excavations of a Life*. New York: Scribner's, 1975.
———. *Darwin and the Mysterious Mr. X*. New York: Harvest, 1981.
———. *The Firmament of Time*. New York: Atheneum, 1960.
———. *The Immense Journey: An Imaginative Naturalist Explores the Mysteries of Man and Nature*. New York: Vintage, 1959.
———. *The Night Country*. New York: Simon & Schuster, 1971.
———. *The Star Thrower*. New York: Harvest, 1979.
———. *The Unexpected Universe*. New York: Hardcourt, Brace, and World, 1969.
Eisenbrandt, Matt. *Assassination of a Saint: The Plot to Murder Óscar Romero and the Quest to Bring His Killers to Justice*. Oakland: University of California Press, 2017.
Ellacuría, Ignacio. "Utopia and Prophecy in Latin America." Translated by James R. Brockman. In Ellacuría and Sobrino, *Mysterium Liberationis*, 289–328.
Ellacuría, Ignacio and Jon Sobrino, eds. *Mysterium Liberationis: Fundamental Concepts of Liberation Theology*. Maryknoll, NY: Orbis, 1993.
Elliot, George. *Middlemarch*. Herfordshire, UK: Wordsworth, 2000.
Ellison, Ralph. *Invisible Man*. New York: Vintage, 1980.
Epstein, Greg. *Good Without God: What a Billion Nonreligious People Do Believe*. New York: HarperCollins, 2010.
Esposito, John L., and Ihsan Yilmaz. "Islam and Peacebuilding: The Gülen Movement in Global Action." In Marsden, *Ashgate Companion to Religion and Conflict Resolution*, 15–32.
Etinson, Adam, ed. *Human Rights: Moral or Political?* Oxford: Oxford University Press, 2018.
Fair, Eric. *Consequences: A Memoir*. New York: Holt, 2016.
Fallada, Hans. *Nightmare in Berlin*. Translated by Allan Blunden. London: Scribe, 2016.
Farley, Margaret. *Just Love: A Framework for Christian Sexual Ethics*. London: Continuum, 2012.
Farrelly, Maura Jane. *Anti-Catholicism in America, 1620-1860*. Oxford: Oxford University Press, 2018.

Fasching, Darrell J. *The Ethical Challenge of Auschwitz and Hiroshima: Apocalypse or Utopia?* Albany: State University of New York Press, 1993.

Feinstein, Edward, ed. *Jews and Judaism in the 21st Century: Human Responsibility, the Presence of God, and the Future of the Covenant.* Woodstock, VT: Jewish Lights, 2007.

Feirstein, Daniel. "National Security Doctrine in Latin America: The Genocide Questions." In Bloxham and Moses, *Oxford Handbook of Genocide Studies*, 489–508.

Felman, Shoshana and Dori Laub. *Testimony: Crises of Witnessing in Literature, Psychoanalysis, and History.* New York: Routledge, 1992.

Fernando, Jude Lal. *Religion, Conflict and Peace in Sri Lanka: The Politics of Interpretation of Nationhoods.* Münster: Lit Verlag, 2013.

Fiala, Andrew. "Radical Forgiveness and Human Justice." *Heythrop Journal* 53 (2012) 494–506.

Field, David N. "On (Re)Centering the Margins: A Euro-African Perspective on the Option for the Poor." In Rieger, *Opting for the Margins*, 45–69.

Filkins, Dexter. *The Forever War.* New York: Vintage, 2009.

Finkel, Evgeny. *Ordinary Jews: Choice and Survival during the Holocaust.* Princeton: Princeton University Press, 2017.

Finlayson, Clive. *The Humans Who Went Extinct: Why Neanderthals Died Out and We Survived.* Oxford: Oxford University Press, 2009.

Firestein, Stuart. *Failure: Why Science Is So Successful.* Oxford: Oxford University Press, 2016.

Fitzpatrick, Breda. *Political Reconciliation in Rwanda and Timor-Leste.* Master's thesis, Mater Dei Institute of Education, 2014.

Fletcher, Jeannine Hill. "Women in Inter-Religious Dialogue." In Cornille, *Wiley-Blackwell Companion to Inter-Religious Dialogue*, 168–83.

Flores, Nichole M. "When Discourse Breaks Down: Race and Aesthetic Solidarity in the US Catholic Church." In *Polarization in the US Catholic Church: Naming the Wounds, Beginning to Heal*, edited by Mary Ellen Konieczny, Charles C. Camosy, and Tricia C. Bruce, 101–10. Collegeville, MN: Liturgical, 2016.

Floyd-Thomas, Stacey M., and Miguel A. De La Torre, eds. *Beyond the Pale: Reading Ethics from the Margins.* Louisville: Westminster John Knox, 2011.

Flynn, Kieran. *Islam in the West: Iraqi Shi'i Communities in Transition and Dialogue.* Oxford: Peter Lang, 2013.

Forché, Carolyn, ed. *Against Forgetting: Twentieth-Century Poetry of Witness.* New York: Norton, 1993.

———. "Reading the Living Archives: The Witness of Literary Art." In Forché and Wu, *Poetry of Witness*, 17–26.

———. *The Country Between Us.* New York: Harper & Row, 1981.

Forché, Carolyn, and Duncan Wu, eds. *Poetry of Witness: The English Tradition 1500–2001.* New York: Norton, 2014.

Fonrobert, Charlotte Elisheva. "Regulating the Human Body: Rabbinic Legal Discourse and the Making of Jewish Gender." In *The Cambridge Companion to The Talmud and Rabbinic Literature*, edited by Charlotte Elisheva Fonrobert and Martin S. Jaffee, 270–94. Cambridge, UK: Cambridge University Press, 2007.

Forman, James, Jr. *Locking Up Our Own: Crime and Punishment in Black America.* New York: Farrar, Straus and Giroux, 2018.

Formisano, Ronald P. *Plutocracy in America: How Increasing Inequality Destroys the Middle Class and Exploits the Poor*. Baltimore: John Hopkins University Press, 2015.

Foster, Charles. *Being a Beast: Adventures Across the Species Divide*. New York: Picador, 2017.

Foulcher, Jane. *Reclaiming Humility: Four Studies in the Monastic Tradition*. Collegeville, MN: Liturgical, 2015.

Francis of Assisi, and Clare of Assisi. *Francis and Clare: The Complete Works*. Translated by Regis J. Armstrong and Ignatius C. Brady. New York: Paulist 1982.

Francis, Gavin. *Adventures in Human Being*. London: Welcome Collection, 2016.

Francis. "Homily of Pope Francis." March 28, 2013. http://w2.vatican.va/content/francesco/en/homilies/2013/documents/papa-francesco_20130328_messa-crismale.html.

———. *Laudato si'*. May 24, 2015. http://w2.vatican.va/content/francesco/en/encyclicals/documents/papa-francesco_20150524_enciclica-laudato-si.html.

Francisco, Jose Mario C. "Migration and New Cosmopolitanism in Asian Christianity." In Wilfred, *Oxford Handbook of Christianity in Asia*, 575–92.

Franklin, Benjamin. *The Autobiography of Benjamin Franklin*. Mineola, NY: Dover Thrift, 1996.

Frankopan, Peter. *The Silk Roads: A New History of the World*. London: Bloomsbury, 2016.

Frazier, Jessica. "Hinduism." In Bullivant and Ruse, *Oxford Handbook of Atheism*, 367–79.

Frede-Wenger, Britta. "'Good' Friday After Auschwitz?" In *Fire in the Ashes: God, Evil, and the Holocaust*, edited by David Patterson and John K. Roth, 137–49. Seattle: University of Washington Press, 2005.

Fredriksen, Paula. *Augustine and the Jews: A Christian Defense of Jews and Judaism*. New York: Doubleday, 2008.

———. "Paul, Practical Pluralism, and the Invention of Religious Persecution." In Phan and Ray, *Understanding Religious Pluralism*, 87–118.

Freud, Sigmund. *The Future of an Illusion*. Translated by James Strachey. New York: Norton, 1989.

Frey, Robert S, ed. *The Genocidal Temptation: Auschwitz, Hiroshima, Rwanda, and Beyond*. Dallas: University Press of America, 2004.

Froese, Paul, and Christopher Bader. *America's Four Gods: What We Say about God—and What That Says about Us*. Updated Edition. Oxford, Oxford University Press, 2015.

Fry, Jason. "Welcome Home." *Faith and Fear in Flushing*. September 27, 2015. http://www.faithandfearinflushing.com/2015/09/27/welcome-home/.

Frymer-Kensky, Tikva, David Novak, Peter Ochs, David Fox Samuel, and Michael A. Signer, eds. *Christianity in Jewish Terms*. Boulder, CO: Westview, 2000.

Fulkerson, Mary McClintock. "Feminist Theology." In Vanhoozer, *Cambridge Companion to Postmodern Theology*, 109–25.

Fullam, Lisa. "Teresa of Avila's Liberative Humility." *Journal of Moral Theology* 3 (2014) 175–98.

Gale, Alastair. "North Korean Defectors Recount Ordeals." *The Wall Street Journal*, June 24, 2015. https://www.wsj.com/articles/north-korean-defectors-recount-ordeals-1435162847.

Gandsman, Ari. "The Ex-Disappeared in Post-Dictatorship Argentina: The Work of Testimony and Survival at the Margins." In *Beyond Testimony and Trauma: Oral History in the Aftermath of Mass Violence*, edited by Steven High, 31–55. Vancouver: The University of British Columbia Press, 2015.
Gandhi, Mohandas K. *An Autobiography: The Story of My Experiments with Truth*. Boston: Beacon, 1957.
Gandhi, Rajmohan. "Perspective: The Righteous Chariot." In Henderson, *No Enemy to Conquer*, 106–8.
Garcia, J. Malcolm. *What Wars Leave Behind: The Faceless and the Forgotten*. Columbia: University of Missouri Press, 2014.
Gebara, Ivone. *Out of the Depths: Women's Experience of Evil and Salvation*. Translated by Ann Patrick Ware. Minneapolis: Fortress, 2002.
Gebara, Ivone, and María Clara Bingemer. *Mary: Mother of God, Mother of the Poor*. Translated by Philip Berryman. Maryknoll, NY: Orbis, 1989.
Gerges, Fawaz A. *ISIS: A History*. Princeton: Princeton University Press, 2016.
Ghosh, Ranjan, ed. *Making Sense of the Secular: Critical Perspectives from Europe to Asia*. New York: Routledge, 2013.
Gest, Justin. *The White Working Class*. Oxford: Oxford University Press, 2018.
Gilkey, Langdon. "Plurality and its Theological Implications." In *The Myth of Christian Uniqueness: Toward a Pluralistic Theology of Religions*, edited by John Hick and Paul F. Knitter, 37–50. Maryknoll, NY: Orbis, 1987.
Gillis, Chester. *Pluralism: A New Paradigm for Theology*. Leuven, BE: Peeters, 1998.
Giovanni, Janine di. *The Morning They Came For Us: Dispatches from Syria*. New York: Liverright, 2016.
Glass, Charles. *Syria Burning: A Short History of a Catastrophe*. London: Verso, 2016.
Gleiser, Marcelo. *The Island of Knowledge: The Limits of Science and the Search for Meaning*. New York: Basic, 2015.
Glover, Jonathan. *Humanity: A Moral History of the Twentieth Century*. London: Pimlico, 2001.
Glowacka, Dorota. *Disappearing Traces: Holocaust Testimonials, Ethics, and Aesthetics*. Seattle: University of Washington Press, 2012.
Gobodo-Madikizela, Pumla. *A Human Being Died that Night: A South African Story of Forgiveness*. Boston: Houghton Mifflin, 2003.
Godfrey-Smith, Peter. *Other Minds: The Octopus, The Sea, and the Deep Origins of Human Consciousness*. New York: Farrar, Straus, and Giroux, 2016.
Goff, Lisa. *Shantytown, USA: Forgotten Landscapes of the Working Poor*. Cambridge, MA: Harvard University Press, 2016.
Goffman, Alice. "A Reply to Professor Lubet's Critique." http://www.ssc.wisc.edu/soc/faculty/docs/goffman/A%20Reply%20to%20Professor%20Lubet.pdf.
———. *On the Run: Fugitive Life in an American City*. Chicago: University of Chicago Press, 2014.
Goldenberg, Myrna, and Rochelle L. Millen, eds. *Testimony, Tensions, and Tikkun: Teaching the Holocaust in Colleges and Universities*. Seattle: University of Washington Press, 2007.
Goldhagen, Daniel Jonah. *Worse Than War: GENOCIDE, ELIMINATIONISM, AND THE ONGOING ASSAULT ON HUMANITY*. NEW YORK: PUBLIC AFFAIRS, 2009.
Golding, William. *The Lord of the Flies*. New York: Penguin, 1954

Goldman, David P. "Christianity and Myth: Why There's No Jewish Narnia." *First Things*. March 5, 2010. http://www.firstthings.com/blogs/firstthoughts/2010/03/christianity-and-myth-why-theres-no-jewish-narnia.

Goldman, Samuel. *God's Country: Christian Zionism in America*. Philadelphia: University of Pennsylvania Press, 2018.

Goldstein, Amy. *Janesville: An American Story*. New York: Simon & Shuster, 2017.

Gonzalez, Michelle A. "Sor Juana Inés de la Cruz (1651–1695)." In Pui-lan, Compier, and Rieger, *Empire and the Christian Tradition*, 229–42.

——. "Who is Americana/o? Theological Anthropology, Postcoloniality, and the Spanish-Speaking Americas." In Keller, Nausner, and Rivera, *Postcolonial Theologies*, 58–78.

Goodwin, Allison A. "Right View, Red Rust, and White Bones: A Reexamination of Buddhist Teachings on Female Inferiority." *Journal of Buddhist Ethics* 19 (2012) 198–343.

Gopnik, Adam. "Bigger then Phil: When Did Faith Start to Fade?" *The New Yorker*. February 17, 2014. http://www.newyorker.com/magazine/2014/02/17/bigger-phil.

Gould, Stephen Jay. *The Richness of Life: The Essential Stephen Jay Gould*. Edited by Steven Rose. New York: Norton, 2007.

Gourevitch, Philip. *We Wish to Inform You That Tomorrow We Will Be Killed With Our Families: Stories From Rwanda*. New York: Farrar, Straus, and Giroux, 1998.

Graber, Jennifer. *The Gods of Indian Country: Religion and the Struggle for the American West*. Oxford: Oxford University Press, 2018.

Grann, David. *Killers of the Flower Moon: Oil, Money, Murder and the Birth of the FBI*. New York: Doubleday, 2017.

Greenberg, Irving. "Cloud of Smoke, Pillar of Fire: Judaism, Christianity and Modernity after the Holocaust." In *Auschwitz: Beginning of a New Era? Reflections on the Holocaust*, edited by Eva Fleischner, 7–55. New York: Ktav, 1977.

——. "Dialectic Living and Thinking: Wiesel as Storyteller and Interpreter of the Shoah." In Katz and Rosen, *Elie Wiesel*, 173–89.

——. *For the Sake of Heaven and Earth: The New Encounter between Judaism and Christianity*. Philadelphia: Jewish Publication Society, 2004.

——. "Judaism and Christianity: Covenants of Redemption." In Frymer-Kensky, Novak, Ochs, Samuel, and Signer, *Christianity in Jewish Terms*, 141–58.

Greenberg, Irving, Edward Feinstein, and Harold M. Schulweis. "On Orthodox and Non–Orthodox Judaism." In Feinstein, *Jews and Judaism in the Twenty-First Century*, 121–26.

——. "On the Meaning of Pluralism." In Feinstein, *Jews and Judaism in the Twenty-First Century*, 149–54.

——. "On the Role of Denominations." In Feinstein, *Jews and Judaism in the 21st Century*, 113–20.

Greenberg, Michael. "Tenants Under Siege: Inside New York City's Housing Crisis." *The New York Review of Books*, August 17, 2017. http://www.nybooks.com/articles/2017/08/17/tenants-under-siege-inside-new-york-city-housing-crisis/.

——. "We're Not Going to Stand for This Anymore." *The New York Review of Books*, December 16, 2014. http://www.nybooks.com/daily/2014/12/16/new-york-after-eric-garner/.

Greenspan, Henry. "Survivors' Accounts." In Hayes and Roth, *The Oxford Handbook of Holocaust Studies*, 441–27.

Gregory, Brad. *The Unintended Reformation*. Cambridge, MA: Harvard University Press, 2012.

Grem, Darren E. *The Blessings of Business: How Corporations Shaped Conservative Christianity*. Oxford: Oxford University Press, 2016.

Grey, Thomas. "Elegy Written in a Country Churchyard." *Thomas Grey Archive*. http://www.thomasgray.org/cgi-bin/display.cgi?text=elcc.

Griswold, Charles L. *Forgiveness: A Philosophical Exploration*. Cambridge, UK: Cambridge University Press, 2007.

———. "Forgiveness, Secular and Religious: A Reply to My Critics." *American Catholic Philosophical Association, Proceedings of the ACPA* Vol. 82 (2009) 303–13.

———. "Preface." In Griswold and Konstan, *Ancient Forgiveness*, x–xv.

Griswold, Charles L., and David Konstan, eds. *Ancient Forgiveness: Classical, Judaic, and Christian*. Cambridge, UK: Cambridge University Press, 2012.

Groppe, Elizabeth. "After Augustine: Humility and the Search for God in Historical Memory." In Heft, Firestone, and Safid, *Learned Ignorance*, 191–209.

Gülen, Fethullah. "Tawadu. Humility." *The Fountain Magazine* 77 (September-October 2010). http://www.fountainmagazine.com/Issue/detail/Humility-Tawadu.

Guo, Jian, Yongyi Song, and Yuan Zhou. *Historical Dictionary of the Chinese Cultural Revolution*. Historical dictionaries of ancient civilizations and historical eras 17. Lanham, MD: Scarecrow, 2006.

Gutschow, Kim. *Being a Buddhist Nun: The Struggle for Enlightenment in the Himalayas*. Cambridge, MA: Harvard University Press, 2004.

Gyatso, Palden. *Fire under the Snow: Testimony of a Tibetan Prisoner*. Translated by Tsering Shakya. London: Harvill, 1997.

Gyger, Pia. "The Religions and the Birth of a New Humanity." In May, *Pluralism and the Religions*, 90–96.

Haas, Peter J. "Forgiveness, Reconciliation, and Jewish Memory after Auschwitz." In Patterson and Roth, *After-Words*, 5–15.

Habermas, Jürgen. "Religion in the Public Sphere." *European Journal of Philosophy* 14 (April 2006) 1–25.

Hafetz, Jonathan, ed. *Obama's Guantánamo: Stories from an Enduring Prison*. New York: New York University Press, 2016.

Hamburger, Michael. "Introduction." In Celan, *Poems of Paul Celan*, 19–34.

Hammer, Joshua. "The Imperilled Bloggers of Bangladesh." *The New York Times Magazine*, January 3, 2016. https://www.nytimes.com/2016/01/03/magazine/the-price-of-secularism-in-bangladesh.html?mcubz=0.

Hammer, Reuven, ed. *The Classic Midrash: Tannaitic Commentaries on the Bible*. Translated by Reuven Hammer. New York: Paulist, 1995.

Hanh, Thich Nhat. *Going Home: Jesus and Buddha as Brothers*. New York: Riverhead, 1999.

———. *Interbeing: Fourteen Guidelines for Engaged Buddhism*. Berkeley, CA: Parallax, 1987.

———. *Living Buddha, Living Christ*. New York: Riverhead, 1995.

Harari, Yuval Noah. *Sapiens: A Brief History of Humankind*. London: Vintage, 2014.

Harden, Blaine. *Escape from Camp 14: One Man's Remarkable Odyssey from North Korea to Freedom in the West*. London: Mantle, 2012.

Hardy, Thomas. *Far from the Madding Crowd*. Herfordshire: Wordsworth Classics, 2000.
Hartman, Geoffrey H. "Introduction: Darkness Visible." In *Holocaust Remembrance: The Shapes of Memory*, edited by Geoffrey H. Hartman, 1–22. Oxford: Blackwell, 1994.
Hatzfeld, Jean. *Blood Papa: Rwanda's New Generation*. Translated by Joshua Jordan. New York: Farrar, Straus and Giroux, 2018.
———. *Life Laid Bare: The Survivors in Rwanda Speak*. Translated by Linda Coverdale. New York: Other Press, 2007.
———. *Machete Season: The Killers in Rwanda Speak*. Translated by Linda Coverdale. New York: Picador, 2006.
———. *The Strategy of Antelopes: Rwanda after the Genocide*. Translated by Linda Coverdale. London: Serpent's Tail, 2009.
Hayes, Peter, and John K. Roth, eds. *The Oxford Handbook of Holocaust Studies*. Oxford: Oxford University Press, 2012.
Hazony, Yoram. *The Philosophy of Hebrew Scripture*. Cambridge, UK: Cambridge University Press, 2012.
Heft, James L. "Ignorance: An Introduction." In Heft, Firestone, and Safid, eds., *Learned Ignorance*, 1–19.
Heft, James L., Reuven Firestone, and Omir Safid, eds. "Epilogue: The Purpose of Interreligious Dialogue." In Heft, Firestone, and Safi, *Learned Ignorance*, 300–311.
Hegel, G. W. F. *Reason in History*. Translated by Robert S. Hartman. Indianapolis: BobbsMerrill, 1980.
Helmick, Raymond, and Rodney Petersen, eds. *Forgiveness and Reconciliation*. Philadelphia: Templeton Foundation, 2002.
Helmreich, William B. *The New York Nobody Knows: Walking 6,000 Miles in the City*. Princeton: Princeton University Press, 2013.
Henderson, Michael. *No Enemy to Conquer: Forgiveness in an Unforgivable World*. Waco, TX: Baylor University Press, 2009.
Hennessy, Kate. *Dorothy Day: The World Will Be Saved by Beauty: An Intimate Portrait of My Grandmother*. New York: Scribner, 2017.
Herbert, Frank. *Dune*. London: Hodder, 2005.
Hernández, Eleazar López. "A Perspective from Central America." In *Reconciliation in a World of Conflicts, Concilium* no. 5, edited by Luis Carlos Susin and María Pilar Aquino, 42–45. London: SCM, 2003.
Heuer, Kenneth, ed. *The Lost Notebooks of Loren Eiseley*. Boston: Little Brown, 1987.
Hibbard, Scott. "Religions, Nationalism, and the Politics of Secularism." In Omer, Appleby, and Little, *Oxford Handbook of Religion, Conflict, and Peacebuilding*, 100–123.
Hick, John. "The Next Step beyond Dialogue." In Knitter, *Myth of Religious Superiority*, 3–12.
Hick, John, and Paul F. Knitter, eds. *The Myth of Christian Uniqueness: Toward a Pluralistic Theology of Religions*. Maryknoll, NY: Orbis, 1987.
Hill, Johnny Bernard. "Thomas Aquinas." In Floyd-Thomas and De La Torre, *Beyond the Pale*, 55–62.
Hill, Marc Lamont. *Nobody: Casualties of America's War on the Vulnerable, from Ferguson to Flint and Beyond*. New York: Atria, 2016.

Himes, Michael J., and Stephen J. Pope, eds. *Finding God in All Things: Essays in Honor of Michael J. Buckley, S.J.* New York: Crossroads, 1996.
Hinton, David. "Introduction." In *I Ching,* vii–xix.
Hinton, Elizabeth. *From the War on Poverty to the War on Crime: The Making of Mass Incarceration in America.* Cambridge, MA: Harvard University Press, 2016.
Hitchens, Christopher. *God is not Great: How Religion Poisons Everything.* New York: Twelve, 2007.
Hobbes, Thomas. *Leviathan.* Cambridge, UK: Cambridge University Press, 1996.
Hochbaum, Nora, and Florencia Battiti. *Monumento a Las Victimas del Terrorismo de Estado Parque de la Memoria.* Consejo de Gestión Parque de la Memoria Buenos Aires, 2010.
Hochschild, Adam. *King Leopold's Ghost: A Story of Greed, Terror, and Heroism in Colonial Africa.* London: Papermac, 2000.
Hoffman, Eva. *After Such Knowledge: Memory, History, and the Legacy of the Holocaust.* New York: PublicAffairs, 2004.
Holland, Nancy J. *Ontological Humility: Lord Voldemort and the Philosophers.* Albany: State University of New York Press, 2013.
Hollenbach, David. "Human Dignity in Catholic Thought." In Düwell, Braarvig, Brownsword, and Mieth, *The Cambridge Handbook of Human Dignity,* 250–59.
Holyoake, George Jacob. *The Principles of Secularism.* 3rd Rev. ed. 1871. Project Guttenberg. http://onlinebooks.library.upenn.edu/webbin/gutbook/lookup?num=36797.
Holzer, Harold, and the New York Historical Society. *The Civil War in 50 Objects.* New York: Viking, 2013.
Homerin, Th. Emil. "The Golden Rule in Islam." In Neusner and Chilton, *The Golden Rule,* 99–115.
Hooks, Bell. *Bone Black: Memories of Girlhood.* New York: Holt, 1996.
Holmgren, Margaret R. *Forgiveness and Reconciliation: Responding to Wrongdoing.* Cambridge, UK: Cambridge University Press, 2013.
Houser, R. E. "The Virtue of Courage (IIa IIae, qq.123–140)." In *The Ethics of Aquinas,* edited by Stephen J. Pope, 304–20. Washington, DC: Georgetown University Press, 2002.
Howard, Thomas Albert. *God and the Atlantic: America, Europe, and the Religious Divide.* Oxford: Oxford, University Press, 2011.
Hsün Tzu. *Hsün Tzu: Basic Writings.* Translated by Burton Watson. New York: Columbia University Press, 1996.
Huang, Wenguang. *The Little Red Guard: A Family Memoir.* New York: Riverhead, 2013.
———. "Translator's Note." In Yiwu, *God is Red,* vii–xiv.
Hugo, Victor. *Les Misérables.* Translated by Julie Rose. New York: The Modern Library, 2009.
Hume, David. *An Enquiry Concerning the Principles of Morals: A Critical Edition.* Edited by Tom L. Beauchamp. Oxford: Oxford University Press, 2006.
Hunter, Alan. "Forgiveness: Hindu and Western Perspectives." *Journal of Hindu-Christian Studies* 20 (2007) 35–42.
Hunter, Megan. *The End We Start From.* London: Picador, 2017.
I Ching: The Book of Change. Translated by David Hinton. New York: Farrar, Straus, and Giroux, 2015.

Ignatieff, Michael. *The Ordinary Virtues: Moral Order in a Divided World*. Cambridge, MA: Harvard University Press, 2017.
Ignatius of Loyola. *St. Ignatius' Own Story as told to Luis Gonzalez de Camara*. Translated by William J. Young. Chicago: Loyola University Press, 1980.
———. *The Spiritual Exercises of Saint Ignatius*. Translated by Anthony Mottola. New York: Image, 1989.
Ilibagiza, Immaculée, with Steve Erwin. *Left to Tell: Discovering God Amidst the Rwandan Holocaust*. Carlsbad, CA: Hay House, 2006.
Irwin, Lee. "Freedom, Law, and Prophecy: A Brief History of Native American Resistance." In *Native American Spirituality: A Critical Reader*, edited by Lee Irwin, 295–316. Lincoln, NE: University of Nebraska Press, 2000.
———. "Native American Spirituality: An Introduction." In *Native American Spirituality: A Critical Reader*, edited by Lee Irwin, 1–8. Lincoln, NE: University of Nebraska Press, 2000.
Isbell, Lynne A. *The Fruit, The Tree, and the Serpent: Why We See So Well*. Cambridge, MA: Harvard University Press, 2009.
Isenberg, Nancy. *White Trash: The 400-Year Untold History of Class in America*. New York: Penguin, 2017.
Iyengar, Rishi. "Tens of Thousands Gather in Hong Kong to Remember the 1989 Tiananmen Massacre," *Time Magazine*, June 4, 2015. http://time.com/3908678/tiananmen-massacre-26th-anniversary-hong-kong-china-vigil-victoria-park/.
Jacobs, Steven Leonard. "'Can We Talk?': The Jewish Jesus in a Dialogue between Jews and Christians." *Shofar* 3 (Spring 2010) 135–48.
Jahanbegloo, Ramin. *Time Will Say Nothing: A Philosopher Survives an Iranian Prison*. Regina, CA: University of Regina Press, 2014.
Jakelić, Slavica. "Secular-Religious Encounters as Peacebuilding." In Omer, Appleby, and Little, *The Oxford Handbook of Religion, Conflict, and Peacebuilding*, 124–45.
Jalabi, Afra. "Walking on Divine Edge: Reading Notions of Arrogance and Humility in the Qur'an." In Heft, Firestone, and Safid, *Learned Ignorance*, 170–88.
James, Henry. *The Portrait of a Lady*. Oxford: Oxford University Press, 1998.
Jeffery, Renee. "The Forgiveness Dilemma: Emotions and Justice at the Khmer Rouge Tribunal." *Australian Journal of International Affairs* 691 (2015) 35–52.
Jenkins, Philip. *The Lost History of Christianity: The Thousand-Year Golden Age of the Church in the Middle East, Africa, and Asia—And How it Died*. New York: Harper, 2009.
Jisheng, Yang. *Tombstone: The Great Chinese Famine, 1958–1962*. Translated by Stacy Mosher and Jian Guo. New York: Farrar, Straus and Giroux, 2013.
John Paul II. "Address to Representatives of the Jewish Community in Mainz, West Germany." November 17, 1980. https://w2.vatican.va/content/john-paul-ii/en/speeches/1980/november.index.2.html.
———. "Dives in Misericordia." November 30, 1980. http://w2.vatican.va/content/john-paul-ii/en/encyclicals/documents/hf_jp-ii_enc_30111980_dives-in-misericordia.html.
———. *Evangelium Vitae*. March 25, 1995. http://w2.vatican.va/content/john-paul-ii/en/encyclicals/documents/hf_jp-ii_enc_25031995_evangelium-vitae.html.
———. "Old Testament Essential to Know Jesus." April 23, 1997. http://www.ewtn.com/library/PAPALDOC/JP2PBC.htm.

Johnson, Eric A., and Karl-Heinz Reuband. *What We Knew: Terror, Mass Murder, and Everyday Life in Nazi Germany. An Oral History.* Cambridge, MA: Basic, 2006.
Johnson, Ian. *The Souls of China: The Return of Religion after Mao.* New York: Pantheon, 2017.
Jordan, Mark D. "Thomas Aquinas, 1225–1274." In Pui-lan, Compier, and Rieger, *Empire and the Christian Tradition*, 153–66.
Joyce, James. *Finnegan's Wake.* New York: Penguin, 1999.
Juergensmeyer, Mark, Dinah Griego, and John Soboslai. *God in the Tumult of the Global Square: Religion in Global Civil Society.* Oakland: University of California Press, 2015.
Kadayifci-Orellana, S. Ayse. "Peacebuilding in the Muslim World." In Omer, Appleby, and Little, *The Oxford Handbook of Religion, Conflict, and Peacebuilding*, 430–69.
Kafka, Franz. *The Trial.* Translated by Willa and Edwin Muir. New York: Schocken, 1995.
Kalimtzis, Kostas. *An Inquiry into the Philosophical Concept of Scholê: Leisure as a Political End.* London: Bloomsbury Academic, 2017.
Kant, Immanuel. *The Metaphysics of Morals.* Translated by Mary Gregor. Cambridge, UK: Cambridge University Press, 1996.
Kärkkäinen, Veli-Matti. *Christology: A Global Introduction.* Grand Rapids: Baker Academic, 2003.
Kassabova, Kapka. *Border: A Journey to the Edge of Europe.* London: Granta, 2017.
Katz, Steven T., and Alan Rosen, eds. *Elie Wiesel: Jewish, Literary, and Moral Perspectives.* Bloomington: Indiana University Press, 2013.
———, eds. *Obliged by Memory: Literature, Religion, Ethics.* Syracuse: Syracuse University Press, 2006.
Kearns, Rick. "Pope in Mexico: Asks Indigenous for Forgiveness." *Indian Country*, February 19, 2016. http://indiancountrytodaymedianetwork.com/2016/02/19/pope-mexico-asks-indigenous-forgiveness-163487.
Kellenbach, Katharina von. *The Mark of Cain: Guilt and Denial in the Post-War Lives of Nazi Perpetrators.* Oxford: Oxford University Press, 2013.
Keller, Catherine, Michael Nausner, and Mayra Rivera. "Introduction." In Keller, Nausner, and Rivera, *Postcolonial Theologies*, 1–19.
———, eds. *Postcolonial Theologies: Divinity and Empire.* St. Louis: Chalice, 2004.
Kerr, Fergus. "Thomas Aquinas." In *The Medieval Theologians*, edited by G. R. Evans, 211–20. Oxford: Blackwell, 2001.
———. *Twentieth-Century Catholic Theologians.* Malden, MA: Blackwell, 2008.
Kessler, Ed. *Jesus: Pocket Giants.* Stroud, UK: History Press, 2016.
Keys, Mary M. "A 'Monkish Virtue' Outside the Monastery: On the Social and Civic Value of Humility." Working paper submitted to the Religion and Culture Web Forum, University of Chicago, May 2004, 1–14. https://divinity.uchicago.edu/sites/default/files/imce/pdfs/webforum/062004/monkish%20virtue.pdf.
Khalidi, Tarif, ed. *The Muslim Jesus: Sayings and Stories in Islamic Literature.* Translated by Tarif Khalidi. Cambridge, MA: Harvard University Press, 2003.
Khalil, Mohammad Hassan. "Divine Forgiveness in Islamic Scripture and Thought." In *Sin, Forgiveness, and Reconciliation: Christian and Muslim Perspectives*, edited by Lucinda Mosher and David Marshall, 83–89. Washington, DC: Georgetown University Press, 2016.

Kiel, Paul. "Debt and the Racial Wealth Gap." *The New York Times,* January 3, 2016. https://www.nytimes.com/2016/01/03/opinion/debt-and-the-racial-wealth-gap.html?mcubz=0.

Kiernan, Ben. *Blood and Soil: A World History of Genocide and Extermination from Sparta to Darfur.* New Haven: Yale University Press, 2007.

Kilby, Jane, and Antony Rowland, eds. *The Future of Testimony: Interdisciplinary Perspectives on Witnessing.* New York: Routledge, 2014.

Kim, Yong, with Suk-Young Kim. Translated by Suk-Young Kim. *Long Road Home: Testimony of a North Korean Camp Survivor.* New York: Columbia University Press, 2009.

Kimelman, Reuven. "Wiesel and the Stories of the Rabbis." In Katz and Rosen, *Elie Wiesel,* 38–48.

King, Barbara J. *How Animals Grieve.* Chicago: University of Chicago Press, 2013.

King, Jay Caspian. "Our Demand is Simple: Stop Killing Us." *The New York Times Magazine,* May 10, 2015. https://www.nytimes.com/2015/05/10/magazine/our-demand-is-simple-stop-killing-us.html?mcubz=0.

King, Ursula. "Feminism: The Missing Dimension in the Dialogue of Religions." In May, *Pluralism and the Religions,* 40–55.

King, Ursula, and Tina Beattie, eds. *Gender, Religion and Diversity: Cross-Cultural Perspectives.* London: Continuum, 2005.

Kitcher, Philip. *Life after Faith.* New Haven: Yale University Press, 2014.

Klancer, Catherine Hudak. "How Opposites Should Attract: Humility as a Virtue for the Strong." *The Heythrop Journal* 53 (2012) 662–77.

Knafo, Saki. "A Black Police Officer's Fight Against the N.Y.P.D." *The New York Times Magazine.* February 18, 2016. https://www.nytimes.com/2016/02/21/magazine/a-black-police-officers-fight-against-the-nypd.html?mcubz=0.

Kneale, Matthew. *An Atheist's History of Belief.* London: Vintage, 2014.

Knitter, Paul. "Inter-religious Dialogue and Social Actions." In Cornille, *Wiley-Blackwell Companion to Inter-Religious Dialogue,* 133–48.

———. "Responsibilities for the Future: Toward an Interfaith Ethic." In May, *Pluralism and the Religions,* 75–89.

———, ed. *The Myth of Religious Superiority: A Multifaith Exploration.* Maryknoll, NY: Orbis, 2005.

———. "The Transformation of Mission in the Pluralist Paradigm." In *Pluralist Theology: The Emerging Paradigm. Concilium,* edited by Luiz Carlos Susin, Andrés Torres Queiruga, and José María Vigil. London: SCM, 2007.

———. "Toward a Liberation Theology of Religions." In Hick and Knitter, *The Myth of Christian Uniqueness,* 178–200.

———. *Without Buddha I Could not be a Christian.* London: Oneworld, 2017.

Kolbert, Elizabeth. *The Sixth Extinction: An Unnatural History.* New York: Picador, 2015.

Knust, Jennifer Wright. "Jesus' Conditional Forgiveness." In Griswold and Konstan, *Ancient Forgiveness,* 177–94.

Kogan, Michael S. *Opening the Covenant: A Jewish Theology of Christianity.* Oxford: Oxford University Press, 2008.

Konstan, David. "Assuaging Rage: Remorse, Repentance, and Forgiveness in the Classical World." In Griswold and Konstan, *Ancient Forgiveness,* 17–30.

Kosicki, Piotr H., ed. *Vatican II Behind the Iron Curtain*. Washington, DC: The Catholic University of America Press, 2016.

Krajewski, Stanislaw. "A Meditation on Intellectual Humility, Or On a Fusion of Epistemic Ignorance and Covenantal Certainty." In Heft, Firestone, and Safid, *Learned Ignorance*, 241–56.

Kristjánsson, Kristján. "Liberating Moral Traditions: Saga Morality and Aristotle's Megalopsychia." *Ethical Theory and Moral Practice* 1 (1998) 397–422.

Krom, Michael P. "Modern Liberalism and Pride: An Augustinian Perspective." *The Journal of Religious Ethics* 35 (September 2007) 453–77.

Kruse, Kevin M. *One Nation Under God: How Corporate America Invented Christian America*. New York, Basic, 2015.

Kugel, James L. *How to Read the Bible: A Guide to Scripture Then and Now*. New York: Free Press, 2007.

Kujawa-Holbrook, Sheryl A. *God Beyond Borders: Interreligious Learning among Faith Communities*. Eugene, OR: Wipf and Stock, 2014.

Küng, Hans. "Global Ethic: Development and Goals." In *War and Peace in World Religions*, edited by Perry Schmidt-Leukel, 183–98. London: SCM, 2004.

Lane, Christopher. *The Age of Doubt: Tracing the Roots of Our Religious Uncertainty*. New Haven: Yale University Press, 2013.

Lane, Dermot A. *Stepping Stones to Other Religions: A Christian Theology of Inter-Religious Dialogue*. Dublin: Veritas, 2011.

Lang, Berel. "Evil Inside and Outside History: The Post-Holocaust vs. the Postmodern." In *Evil after Postmodernism: Histories, Narratives, Ethics*, edited by Jennifer L. Geddes, 11–23. London: Routledge, 2001.

Langer, Lawrence. *Holocaust Testimonies: The Ruins of Memory*. New Haven: Yale University Press, 1991.

———. *Using and Abusing the Holocaust*. Bloomington: Indiana University Press, 2006.

Langton, Rae. *Kantian Humility: Our Ignorance of Things in Themselves*. Oxford: Oxford University Press, 2001.

Lao-Tzu. *Tao Te Ching*. Translated by D. C. Lau. London: Penguin, 1963.

Lapp, Cynthia. "Balancing Power and Humility: Feminist Values in Mennonite Ministry." In *New Feminist Christianity: Many Voices, Many Views*, edited by Mary E. Hunt and Diann L. Neu, 254–60. Woodstock, VT: Skylight Paths, 2010.

Larson, Edward J., and Michael Ruse. *On Faith and Science*. New Haven: Yale University Press, 2017.

Lawrence, D. H. *Sons and Lovers*. New York: Viking, 1973.

Lawrence, David Peter. "Buddhist-Hindu Dialogue." In Cornille, *Wiley-Blackwell Companion to Inter-Religious Dialogue*, 187–203.

Lazarus, Neil, ed. *The Cambridge Companion to Postcolonial Literary Studies*. Cambridge, UK: Cambridge University Press, 2004.

Lear, Jonathan. *Radical Hope: Ethics in the Face of Cultural Devastation*. Cambridge, MA: Harvard University Press, 2006.

Leask, Ian, et al., eds. *The Taylor Effect: Responding to a Secular Age*. Cambridge, UK: Cambridge Scholars, 2010.

Lederach, John Paul. "Five Qualities of Practise in Support of Reconciliation Processes." In Helmick and Petersen, *Forgiveness and Reconciliation*, 193–203.

———. "Spirituality and Religious Peacebuilding." In Omer, Appleby, and Little, *The Oxford Handbook of Religion, Conflict, and Peacebuilding*, 541–68.

Lederach, John Paul, and Angela Jill Lederach. *When Blood and Bones Cry Out: Journeys through the Soundscape of Healing and Reconciliation.* Oxford: Oxford University Press. 2010.

Lee, Soon Ok. *Eyes of the Tailless Animals: Prison Memoirs of a North Korean Woman.* Translated by Bahn-Suk Lee and Jin Young Choi. Bartlesville, OK: Living Sacrifice, 1999.

Lee, Sophia. "True Lies," *World.* February 20, 2015. http://www.worldmag.com/2015/02/true_lies/page1.

Legenhausen, Muhammad. "A Muslim's Non-Reductive Religious Pluralism." In Boase, *Islam and Global Dialogue,* 51–73.

Lepore, Jill. *The Secret History of Wonder Woman.* Melbourne: Scribe, 2016.

Levenson, Jon D. *Inheriting Abraham: The Legacy of the Patriarch in Judaism, Christianity, and Islam.* Princeton: Princeton University Press, 2012.

Levi, Primo. *The Drowned and the Saved.* Translated by Raymond Rosenthal. New York: Vintage, 1989.

———. *The Periodic Table.* Translated by Raymond Rosenthal. New York: Schocken, 1995.

Lévinas, Emmanuel. *Difficult Freedom: Essays on Judaism.* Translated by Seán Hand. Baltimore: John Hopkins University Press, 1990.

———. "Judaism and Kenosis." In *In the Time of Nations.* Translated by Michael B. Smith, 101–18. London: Continuum, 2007.

Levine, Amy-Jill. *The Misunderstood Jew: The Church and the Scandal of the Jewish Jesus.* New York: Harper, 2007.

Levine, Amy-Jill, and Marc Zvi Brettler. "The Editors' Preface." In Levine and Brettler, *The Jewish Annotated New Testament,* xi–xiii.

———, eds. *The Jewish Annotated New Testament.* Oxford: Oxford University Press, 2011.

Levoy, Jill. *Ghettoside: A True Story of Murder in America.* London: Vintage, 2015.

Leys, Ruth. *Trauma: A Genealogy.* Chicago: Chicago University Press, 2000.

Lewis, Nancy. "Extensive Forensic Testing Slows Release of Autopsy Reports." *The Washington Post.* May 30, 1997. https://www.washingtonpost.com/archive/local/1997/05/30/extensive-forensic-testing-slows-release-of-autopsy-results/e504dba4-c43a-476f-906a-c91436f3a5a8/.

Lewis, Ralph. *Finding Purpose in a Godless World: Why We Care Even If the Universe Doesn't.* Amherst, NY: Prometheus, 2018.

Lewis-Krauss, Gideon. "The Trials of Alice Goffman." *The New York Times Magazine,* January 12, 2016. http://www.nytimes.com/2016/01/17/magazine/the-trials-of-alice-goffman.html.

Leydesdorff, Selma. *Surviving the Bosnian Genocide: The Women of Srebrenica Speak.* Translated by Kay Richardson. Bloomington: Indiana University Press, 2011.

Lightman, Alan. *Searching for Stars on an Island in Maine.* London: Corsair, 2018.

Lim, Louisa. *The People's Republic of Amnesia: Tiananmen Revisited.* Oxford: Oxford University Press, 2015.

Lin, Jing, and Yingji Wang. "Confucius' Teaching of Virtues and Implication on World Peace and Peace Education." In *Religion, Spirituality and Peace Education,* edited by Jing Lin, John P. Miller, and Edward J. Brantmeier, 3–17. Charlotte, NC: Information Age, 2010.

Linderman, Frank B. *Plenty-Coups: Chief of the Crows.* Lincoln, NE: Bison, 2002.

———. *Pretty-shield: Medicine Woman of the Crows*. Lincoln, NE: Bison, 2003.
Li Po. "On Yellow-Crane Tower, Farewell to Meng Hao-Jan Who's Leaving for Yang-Chou." Translated by David Hinton. In Weinberger, *New Directions Anthology of Classical Chinese Poetry*, 83.
Livio, Mario. *Brilliant Blunders: From Darwin to Einstein—Colossal Mistakes by Great Scientists That Changed Our Understanding of Life and the Universe*. New York: Simon & Schuster, 2013.
Llewellyn, Jennifer J., and Daniel Philpott, eds. *Restorative Justice, Reconciliation and Peacebuilding*. Oxford: Oxford University Press, 2014.
Lloyd, Vincent W. *Religion of the Field Negro: On Black Secularism and Black Theology*. New York: Fordham University Press, 2018.
Lloyd, Vincent W., and Andrew Prevo, eds. *Anti-Blackness and Christian Ethics*. Maryknoll, NY: Orbis, 2017.
Long, Jeffery D. "Hinduism and the Religious Other." In Cheetham, Pratt, and Thomas, *Understanding Interreligious Relations*, 37–63.
Loomba, Ania. *Colonialism/Postcolonialism*. London: Routledge, 1998.
López, Antonio. "Divine Revelation." In Becker and Morali, *Catholic Engagement with World Religions*, 230–43.
Lopez, Donald S., ed. *Buddhist Scriptures*. London: Penguin, 2004.
Lower, Wendy. *Hitler's Furies: German Women in the Nazi Killing Fields*. London: Chatto & Windus, 2013.
Loy, David. "Wei-Wu-Wei: Nondual Action." *Philosophy East and West* 35 (January 1985) 73–86.
Lubet, Steven. "Alice Goffman's Denial of Murder Conspiracy Raises Even More Questions." *The New Republic*, June 3, 2015. https://newrepublic.com/article/121958/sociologist-alice-goffman-denies-murder-conspiracy-run.
———. "Ethics on the Run." *The New Rambler*, September 24, 2015. http://newramblerreview.com/book-reviews/law/ethics-on-the-run.
Lynch, Tom, and Susan Naramore Maher, eds. *Artifacts and Illuminations: Critical Essays on Loren Eiseley*. Omaha: University of Nebraska Press, 2012.
Maass, Peter. *Love Thy Neighbor: A Story of War*. New York: Vintage, 1997.
MacCulloch, Diarmaid. *The Reformation: A History*. Penguin: New York: 2005.
MacFarquhar, Larissa. *Strangers Drowning: Voyages to the Brink of Moral Extremity*. London: Allen Lane, 2015.
MacGregor, Neil. *A History of the World in 100 Objects*. London: Allen Lane, 2010.
MacIntyre, Alasdair. *After Virtue*. 2nd Edition. Notre Dame: University of Notre Dame Press, 2003.
Maclure, Jocelyn, and Charles Taylor. *Secularism and Freedom of Conscience*. Translated by Jane Marie Todd. Cambridge, MA: Harvard University Press, 2011.
MacMillan, Margaret. *Dangerous Games: The Uses and Abuses of History*. New York: Modern Library, 2009.
Madigan, Daniel. "Saving *Dominus Iesus*." In Heft, Firestone, and Safid, *Learned Ignorance*, 257–77.
Magonet, Jonathan. *A Rabbi Reads the Psalms*. Updated Edition. London: SCM, 2004.
Mahmood, Saba. *Religious Difference in a Secular Age: A Minority Report*. Princeton: Princeton University Press, 2015.
Mahon, Peter. *Posthumanism: A Guide for the Perplexed*. London: Bloomsbury, 2017.

Maier, Charles S. "A Surfeit of Memory? Reflections on History, Melancholy and Denial." *History and Memory* 5 (Fall–Winter 1993) 136–52.

Maimonides. "Laws of Repentance." In *Maimonides-Essential Teachings on Jewish Faith and Ethics: The Book of Knowledge and the Thirteen Principles of Faith*, edited and translated by Marc D. Angel. Woodstock, VT: SkyLight Paths, 2012.

———. *Mishneh Torah, Shoftim, Laws of Kings and Their Wars*. Translated by Eliyahu Touger. *Chabad.org*. http://www.chabad.org/library/article_cdo/aid/1188343/jewish/Melachim-uMilchamot.htm.

Mallet, Victor. *River of Life, River of Death: The Ganges and India's Future*. Oxford: Oxford University Press, 2017.

Mann, Charles C. *1491: New Revelations of the Americas Before Columbus*. New York: Vintage, 2006.

Mann, Thomas. *Buddenbrooks*. Translated by John E. Woods. New York: Knopf, 1994.

Margalit, Avishai. *The Ethics of Memory*. Cambridge, MA: Harvard University Press, 2002.

Marsden, Lee, ed. *The Ashgate Companion to Religion and Conflict Resolution*. Surrey, UK: Ashgate, 2012.

Marshall, Christopher. *Beyond Retribution: A New Testament Vision for Justice, Crime, and Punishment*. Grand Rapids: Eerdmans, 2001.

Marshall, Tim. *Prisoners of Geography*. Rev. and expanded ed. London: Eliot and Thompson, 2016.

Martin, James. "Fr. James Martin on the Humor of St Teresa of Ávila." *Order of Carmelites*. October 13, 2013. http://www.carmelites.net/news/the-humor-of-st-teresa-of-avila/.

———. "His Way of Proceeding." *America Magazine*, April 29, 2013. http://americamagazine.org/issue/article/his-way-proceeding.

———. *The Jesuit Guide to (Almost) Everything: A Spirituality for Real Life*. New York: HarperOne, 2012.

Masson, Jeffrey Moussaieff, and Susan McCarthy. *When Elephants Weep: The Emotional Lives of Animals*. New York: Delta, 1996.

Master Mo. *The Book of Master Mo*. Translated by Ian Johnston. London: Penguin, 2014.

Marx, William. *The Hatred of Literature*. Translated by Nicholas Elliot. Cambridge, MA: Harvard University Press, 2018.

Matthäus, Jürgen, ed. *Approaching an Auschwitz Survivor: Holocaust Testimony and its Transformations*. Oxford: Oxford University Press, 2009.

May, John D'Arcy, ed. *Pluralism and the Religions: The Theological and Political Dimensions*. London: Cassell, 1998.

———. *Transcendence and Violence: The Encounter of Buddhist, Christian and Primal Traditions*. New York: Continuum, 2003.

May, Todd. *A Significant Life: Human Meaning in a Silent Universe*. Chicago: University of Chicago Press, 2015.

Mayer, Jane. *The Dark Side: The Inside Story of How the War on Terror Turned Into a War on American Ideals*. New York: Anchor, 2009.

McBride, James. *The Color of Water: A Black Man's Tribute to His White Mother*. New York: Riverhead, 1996.

McCarthy, Cormac. *The Road*. New York: Vintage, 2006.

McCullough, Michael. *Beyond Revenge: The Evolution of the Forgiveness Instinct*. San Francisco: Jossey-Bass, 2008.

McDaniel, Jay Byrd. *Gandhi's Hope: Learning from Other Religions as a Path to Peace.* Maryknoll, NY: Orbis, 2005.
McDonald-Gibson, Charlotte. *Cast Away: Stories of Survival from Europe's Refugee Crisis.* London: Portobello, 2017.
McEvoy, James Gerard. *Leaving Christendom for Good: Church-World Dialogue in a Secular Age.* Lanham, MD: Lexington, 2014.
McGregor, Jena. "The Next Dalai Lama Could Be a Woman." *The Washington Post.* June 17, 2013. http://www.washingtonpost.com/blogs/on-leadership/wp/2013/06/17/the-next-dalai-lama-could-be-a-woman/.
McInerney, Joseph J. *The Greatness of Humility: St. Augustine on Moral Excellence.* Eugene, OR: Pickwick, 2016.
McMaster, Johnston. *A Word Between Us: Ethics in Interfaith Dialogue.* London: Centre for Hizmet Studies, 2015.
McMullin, Ernan. "Evolutionary Contingency and Cosmic Purpose." In Himes and Pope, *Finding God in All Things,* 140–61.
Meier, Christian. *A Culture of Freedom: Ancient Greece and the Origins of Europe.* Translated by Jefferson Chase. Oxford: Oxford University Press, 2011.
Mellor, David, Di Bretherton, and Lucy Firth. "Aboriginal and Non-Aboriginal Australia: The Dilemma of Apologies, Forgiveness, and Reconciliation." *Peace and Conflict Journal of Peace Psychology* 13 (2007) 11–36.
Melville, Herman. *Moby-Dick.* Herfordshire: Wordsworth, 2002.
Menchú, Rigoberta. *I, Rigoberta Menchú, An Indian Woman in Guatemala.* Edited by Elisabeth Burgos-Debray. Translated by Ann Wright. London: Verso, 1984.
Mencius. *Mencius.* Translated by D. C. Lau. London: Penguin, 2004.
Mendelsohn, Daniel. *The Lost: A Search for Six of Six Million.* London: Harper, 2007.
Mendham, Matthew. "Rousseau's Discarded Children: The Panoply of Excuses and the Question of Hypocrisy." *History of European Ideas* 41 (2015) 131–52.
Meredith, Martin. *The Fate of Africa: A History of Fifty Years of Independence.* New York: Public Affairs, 2005.
Merrigan, Terrence, and John Friday, eds. *The Past, Present, and Future of Theologies of Interreligious Dialogue.* Oxford: Oxford University Press, 2017.
Merton, Thomas. *Seeds of Contemplation.* London: Catholic Book Club, 1950.
Meszler, Joseph B. "Where Are the Jewish Men? The Absence of Men from Liberal Synagogue Life." In *New Jewish Feminism: Probing the Past, Forging the Future,* edited by Rabbi Elyse Goldstein, 165–74. Woodstock, VT: Jewish Lights 2008.
Metz, Johann Baptist. "Facing the World: A Theological and Biographical Inquiry." *Theological Studies* 75 (March 2014) 23–33.
———. *Faith in History and Society: Toward a Practical Fundamental Theology.* Translated and edited by J. Matthew Ashley. New York: Herder & Herder, 2007.
———. "The Future in the Memory of Suffering." Translated by John Griffiths. In Johann-Baptist Metz and Jürgen Moltmann, *Faith and the Future: Essays on Theology, Solidarity, and Modernity.* Nijmegen, NL: The Concilium Foundation, 1995, 3–16.
Michel, Thomas. "Religious Pluralism in Islam." In Phan and Ray, *Understanding Religious Pluralism,* 170–85.
Millies, Steven P. *Good Intentions: A History of Catholic Voters' Road from Roe to Trump.* Collegeville, MN: Liturgical, 2018.

Mikics, David. *Who Was Jacques Derrida? An Intellectual Biography*. New Haven: Yale University Press, 2009.
Millbank, John. "The End of Dialogue." In D'Costa, *Christian Uniqueness Reconsidered*, 174–91.
Milosz, Czeslaw. *The Witness of Poetry*. Cambridge, MA: Harvard University Press, 1984.
Min, Anselm K. "Loving Without Understanding: Raimon Panikkar's Ontological Pluralism." *International Journal for Philosophy of Religion* 68 (2010) 59–75.
Mittleman, Alan L. *A Short History of Jewish Ethics*. Oxford: Wiley-Blackwell, 2012.
Moffic, Evan. "A Progressive Reform Judaism." In Cosgrove, *Jewish Theology in Our Time*, 56–62.
Mohan, Rohini. *The Season of Trouble: Life Amid the Ruins of Sri Lanka's Civil War*. London: Verso, 2014.
Montaigne. *The Complete Essays of Montaigne*. Translated by Donald M. Frame. Stanford: University of Stanford Press, 2016.
Moore, Natalie Y. *The Southside: A Portrait of Chicago and American Segregation*. New York: St. Martin's, 2016.
Moore, Rowan. *Why We Build: Power and Desire in Architecture*. New York: Harper Design, 2013.
Morduch, Jonathan, and Rachel Schneider. *The Financial Diaries: How American Families Cope in a World of Uncertainty*. Princeton: Princeton University Press, 2017.
Morris, Heather. *The Tattooist of Auschwitz*. London: Zaffre, 2018.
Morrison, Toni. *Beloved*. New York: Plume, 1987.
———. *Sula*. New York: Penguin, 1982.
Moskowitz, Peter. *How to Kill a City: Gentrification, Inequality, and the Fight for the Neighborhood*. New York: Nation, 2017.
Moyaert, Marianne. "Interreligious Dialogue." In Cheetham, Pratt, and Thomas, *Understanding Interreligious Relations*, 193–217.
Murphy, Jeffrie G. "Foreword." In Brudholm, *Resentment's Virtue*, ix–xii.
———. "The Case of Dostoevsky's General: Some Ruminations on Forgiving the Unforgivable." In *Punishment and the Moral Emotions: Essays in Law, Morality, and Religion*, 181–214. Oxford: Oxford University Press, 2014.
Murphy, Jeffrie G., and Jean Hampton. *Forgiveness and Mercy*. Cambridge, UK: Cambridge University Press, 1998.
Myers, Ched. *Binding the Strong Man: A Political Reading of Mark's Story of Jesus*. Anniversary Edition. Maryknoll, NY: Orbis, 2008.
Myers, Ched, and Elaine Enns. *Ambassadors of Reconciliation: New Testament Reflections on Restorative Justice and Peacemaking*, vol. 1. Maryknoll, NY: Orbis, 2009.
Nabokov, Vladimir. *Speak, Memory*. New York: Knopf, 1999.
Narchison, J. Rosario. "Theological Education for Pluralism in India." In May, *Pluralism and the Religions*, 59–74.
National Conference of US Catholic Bishops. *Economic Justice for All: A Pastoral Letter on Catholic Social Teaching and the U.S. Economy*. Washington, DC: NCCC, 1996.
Neihardt, John G. *Black Elk Speaks: Being the Life Story of a Holy Man of the Oglala Sioux*. New York: Pocket, 1972.
Nelson, Daniel M. "The Virtue of Humility in Judaism: A Critique of Rationalist Hermeneutics." *The Journal of Religious Ethics* 13 (1985) 298–311.

Newbigin, Lesslie. *A Word in Season: Perspectives on Christian World Mission*. Grand Rapids: Eerdmans, 1994.

Neufeldt, Ronald. "Hindu Views of Christ." In Coward, *Hindu-Christian Dialogue*, 162-75.

Neuffer, Elizabeth. *The Key to My Neighbor's House: Seeking Justice in Bosnia and Rwanda*. New York: Picador, 2001.

Neusner, Jacob. *A Rabbi Talks with Jesus*. Rev. ed. Montreal: McGill-Queen's University Press, 2007.

Neusner, Jacob, and Bruce Chilton, eds. *The Golden Rule: The Ethics of Responsibility in World Religions*. London: Continuum, 2008.

Nguyen, Viet Thanh. *Nothing Ever Dies: Vietnam and the Memory of War*. Cambridge, MA: Harvard University Press, 2016.

Nielsen, Kai. "Ethics without Religion." In *Exploring the Philosophy of Religion*, edited by David Stewart, 361-69. Englewood Cliffs, NJ: Prentice Hall, 1992.

Nietzsche, Friedrich. *Beyond Good and Evil*. Translated by R. J. Hollingdale. London: Penguin, 1990.

———. *On the Genealogy of Morals*. Translated by Walter Kaufmann. New York: Vintage, 1989.

———. *The Anti-Christ*. Translated by R. J. Hollingdale. Middlesex: Penguin, 1978.

———. *The Gay Science: With a Prelude in Rhymes and an Appendix of Songs*. Translated by Walter Kaufmann. New York: Vintage, 1974.

———. *Thus Spoke Zarathustra: A Book for None and All*. Translated by Walter Kaufmann. New York: Penguin, 1978.

———. *Twilight of the Idols*. Translated by R. J. Hollingdale. Middlesex: Penguin, 1978.

Nixon, Nicholas. "Modesty, Snobbery, and Pride." *The Journal of Value Inquiry* 39 (2005) 415-29.

Nora, Pierre. "Les Lieux de Mémoire." Translated by Marc Roudebush. *Representations*, No. 26, Special Issue: "Memory and Counter-Memory." (Spring 1989) 7-24.

Norenzayan, Ara. *Big Gods: How Religion Transformed Cooperation and Conflict*. Princeton: Princeton University Press, 2013.

Norridge, Zoe. "Professional Witnessing in Rwanda." In Kilby and Rowland, *The Future of Testimony*, 129-43.

Nostra Aetate, Declaration on the *Relation* of the *Church* to *Non-Christian Religions*. October 28, 1965. http://www.vatican.va/archive/hist_councils/ii_vatican_council/documents/vat-ii_decl_19651028_nostra-aetate_en.html.

Nouwen, Henri J. M. *The Return of the Prodigal Son: A Story of Homecoming*. London: Darton, Longman, & Todd, 1998.

Nussbaum, Martha. *Anger and Forgiveness: Resentment, Generosity, Justice*. Oxford: Oxford University Press, 2016.

O'Connell, Caitlin. *Elephant Don: The Politics of a Pachyderm Posse*. Chicago: University of Chicago Press, 2015.

O'Leary, Joseph. "Buddhism and Forgiveness." Joseph O'Leary Homepage, July 10, 2005. http://josephsoleary.typepad.com/my_weblog/2005/07/.

O'Malley, John W. "Jesuit History: A New Hot Topic." *America*, May 9, 2005. http://americamagazine.org/issue/530/article/jesuit-history-new-hot-topic.

O'Neill, Kevin Lewis. "Anthropology and Genocide." In Bloxham and Moses, *The Oxford Handbook of Genocide Studies*, 182-97.

Okeowo, Alexis. *A Moonless, Starless Sky: Ordinary Women and Men Fighting Extremism in Africa*. London: Corsair, 2017.
Ohnuma, Reiko. "The Story of Rupavati: A Female Past Birth of the Buddha." *Journal of the International Association of Buddhist Studies* 23 (2000) 103–46.
Omar, Irfan A., and Michael K. Duffey, eds. *Peacemaking and the Challenge of Violence in World Religions*. Malden, MA: Wiley Blackwell, 2015.
Omer, Atalia, R. Scott Appleby, and David Little, eds. *The Oxford Handbook of Religion, Conflict, and Peacebuilding*. Oxford: Oxford University Press, 2015.
"Orthodox Rabbinic Statement on Christianity." CJCUC. December 3, 2015. http://cjcuc.com/site/2015/12/03/orthodox-rabbinic-statement-on-christianity/.
Orwell, George. *1984*. New York: Signet, 1981.
Osnos, Evan. "Tiananmen Square, Beijing: In Search of Heavenly Peace." In *City Squares: Eighteen Writers on the Spirit and Significance of Squares around the World*, edited by Catie Marron, 151–65. New York: HarperCollins, 2016.
Osterhammel, Jürgen. *The Transformation of the World: A Global History of the Nineteenth Century*. Translated by Patrick Camiller. Princeton: Princeton University Press, 2014.
Ou, Amy Y., et al., "Humble Chief Executive Officers' Connections to Top Management Team Integration and Middle Managers' Responses." *Administrative Science Quarterly* 59 (March 2014) 34–72.
Ozick, Cynthia. "The Rights of History and the Rights of Imagination." In Katz and Rosen, *Obliged by Memory*, 3–18.
Panikkar, Raimundo. *The Intrareligious Dialogue*. New York: Paulist, 1978.
———. *Worship and Secular Man*. Maryknoll, NY: Orbis, 1973.
Pappas, Stephanie. "5 Reasons Women Trail Men in Science." *Live Science*, March 6, 2013. https://www.livescience.com/27682-women-men-science-gender-gap.html.
Pardue, Stephen T. *The Mind of Christ: Humility and the Intellect in Early Christian Theology*. London: Bloomsbury, 2013.
Parry, Richard Lloyd. *Ghosts of the Tsunami: Death and Life in Japan's Disaster Zone*. London: Jonathan Cape, 2017.
Partnoy, Alicia. *The Little School: Tales of Disappearance and Survival*. Translated by Lois Athey and Sandra Braunstein. San Francisco: Cleis, 1986.
Pascal, Blaise. *Penseés*. Translated by A. J. Krailsheimer. Middlesex: Penguin, 1970.
Patt-Shamir, Galia, and Ping Zhang. "A Confucian-Jewish Dialogue." In Cornille, *Wiley-Blackwell Companion to Inter-Religious Dialogue*, 450–67.
Patterson, David. "Life and Afterlife: Judaism's Contribution to the Jewish-Christian-Muslim Trialogue." In Berger, *Trialogue and Terror*, 37–50.
———. "The Ashen Earth: Jewish Reflections on our Relation to Nature in the Post-Holocaust Era." In *Holocaust and Nature*, edited by Didier Pollefeyt, 117–26. Wien, DE: LitVerlag, 2013.
———. "'Where is Your Brother?' Jewish Teachings on the 'Stranger.'" In *Encountering the Stranger: A Jewish-Christian-Muslim Trialogue*, edited by Leonard Grob and John K. Roth, 38–49. Seattle: University of Washington Press, 2012.
Patterson, David, and John K. Roth, eds. *After-Words: Post-Holocaust Struggles with Forgiveness, Reconciliation, Justice*. Seattle: University of Washington Press. 2004.
Paulson, Ronald. *Sin and Evil: Moral Values in Literature*. New Haven: Yale University Press, 2007.

Paz, Regina, Félix Neto, and Etienne Mullet. "Forgiveness: Similarities and Differences between Buddhists and Christians Living in China." *The International Journal for the Psychology of Religion* 14 (2007) 289–301.
Peace, Jennifer, Howe Or N. Rose, and Gregory Mobley. *My Neighbor's Faith: Stories of Interreligious Encounter, Growth, and Transformation*. Maryknoll, NY: Orbis, 2012.
Peelman, Achiel. "Native American Spirituality and Christianity." In Cornille, *Wiley-Blackwell Companion to Inter-Religious Dialogue*, 346–59.
People's Tribunal on Sri Lanka. http://www.ptsrilanka.org/.
Peterson, Rodney L. "Is Forgiveness Possible? Reconciliation as a Key Ecumenical Mandate." *The Ecumenical Review* 66 (July 2014) 177–90.
———. "What I Learned in Zenica about Forgiveness." In Peace, Rose, and Mobley, *My Neighbor's Faith*, 144–48.
Phan, Peter C. *Being Religious Interreligiously: Asian Perspectives on Interfaith Dialogue*. Maryknoll, NY: Orbis, 2004.
———. "Peacebuilding and Reconciliation: Interreligious Dialogue and Catholic Spirituality." In Schreiter, Appleby, and Powers, *Peacebuilding*, 332–65.
———. *The Joy of Religious Pluralism: A Personal Journey*. Maryknoll, NY: Orbis, 2017.
Phan, Peter C., and Jonathan Y. Tan. "Majority-Minority Dynamics." In Cheetham, Pratt, and Thomas, *Understanding Interreligious Relations*, 218–40.
Phan, Peter C., and Jonathan S. Ray, eds. *Understanding Religious Pluralism: Perspectives from Religious Studies and Theology*. Eugene, OR: Pickwick, 2014.
Phillips, D. Z. *The Problem of God and the Problem of Evil*. Minneapolis: Fortress, 2005.
Phillips, Nickie D., and Staci Strobl. *Comic Book Crime: Truth, Justice, and the American Way*. New York: New York University Press, 2013.
Phillips, Trevor. "Farewell to the Chief." *The Sunday Times Magazine*. January 15, 2017. 16–27.
Philpott, Daniel. "Reconciliation: A Catholic Ethic for Peacebuilding in the Political Order." In Schreiter, Appleby, and Powers, *Peacebuilding*, 92–124.
———. "Reconciliation, Politics, and Transitional Justice." In Omer, Appleby, and Little, *The Oxford Handbook of Religion, Conflict, and Peacebuilding*, 335–54.
———. "The Justice of Forgiveness." *Journal of Religious Ethics* 41 (2013) 400–416.
———. "What Religion Offers the Politics of Transitional Justice." In Shah, Stepan, and Toft, *Rethinking Religion and World Affairs*, 149–61.
Philpott, Daniel, and Timothy Samuel Shah, eds. *Under Caesar's Sword: How Christians Respond to Persecution*. Cambridge, UK: Cambridge University Press, 2018.
Piketty, Thomas. *Capital in the Twenty-First Century*. Translated by Arthur Goldhammer. Cambridge, MA: Harvard University Press, 2014.
Pilario, Daniel Franklin. "Revisiting Historiographies: New Trajectories for Asian Christianity." In Wilfred, *The Oxford Handbook of Christianity in Asia*, 539–57.
Pinckney, Darryl. "In Ferguson." *The New York Review of Books*, January 8, 2015. http://www.nybooks.com/articles/2015/01/08/in-ferguson/.
———. "The Afro-Pessimist Temptation." *The New York Review of Books*. June 7, 2018. https://www.nybooks.com/articles/2018/06/07/ta-nehisi-coates-afro-pessimist-temptation/.
Pinker, Steven. *Enlightenment Now: The Case for Reason, Science, Humanism, and Progress*. New York: Viking, 2018.

———. *The Better Angels of Our Nature: Why Violence Has Declined*. New York: Viking, 2011.
Pinnock, Sarah K., ed. *Facing Death: Confronting Mortality in the Holocaust and Ourselves*. Seattle: University of Washington Press, 2017.
Plaskow, Judith. *The Coming of Lilith: Essays on Feminism, Judaism, and Sexual Ethics, 1972–2003*. Edited by Donna Berman. Boston: Beacon, 2005.
Plato. "Euthyphro." Translated by F. J. Church; Revised translation by Robert D. Cumming, 1–20. In *Euthyphro, Apology, Crito*. Indianapolis: Bobbs-Merrill, 1956.
———. *Meno*. Translated by Benjamin Jowett. Indianapolis: Bobbs-Merrill, 1946.
———. "The Apology." Translated by F. J. Church; Revised translation by Robert D. Cumming, 21–49. In *Euthyphro, Apology, Crito*. Indianapolis: Bobbs-Merrill, 1956.
———. *The Laws*. Translated by Trevor J. Saunders. London: Penguin, 2004.
———. *The Republic*. Translated by Desmond Lee. London: Penguin, 2003.
Pollefeyt, Didier. "Christology After Auschwitz: A Catholic Perspective." In *Jesus Then & Now: Images of Jesus in History and Christology*, edited by Marvin Meyer and Charles Hughes, 229–48. Harrisburg: Trinity, 2001.
———. "Ethics, Forgiveness, and the Unforgivable after Auschwitz." In Pollefeyt, *Incredible Forgiveness*, 121–59.
———. "Forgiveness after the Holocaust." In Patterson and Roth, eds. *After-Words*, 55–80.
———, ed. *Incredible Forgiveness: Christian Ethics between Fanaticism and Reconciliation*. Leuven, BE: Peeters, 2004.
Pope, Stephen J. "Theological Anthropology, Science, and Human Flourishing." In *Questioning the Human: Toward a Theological Anthropology for the Twenty-First Century*, edited by Lieven Boeve, Yves De Maeseneer, and Ellen Van Stichel, 13–30. New York: Fordham University Press, 2014.
———. "The Role of Forgiveness in Reconciliation and Restorative Justice: A Christian Theological Perspective." In Llewellyn and Philpott, *Restorative Justice, Reconciliation, and Peace Building*, 174–96.
Porter, Bill. *Road to Heaven: Encounters with Chinese Hermits*. San Francisco: Mercury House, 1993.
Povoledo, Elisabetta. "Pope Appeals for More Interreligious Dialogue." *The New York Times*, March 22, 2013. http://www.nytimes.com/2013/03/23/world/europe/pope-francis-urges-more-interreligious-dialogue.html.
Povoledo, Elisabetta, and Laurie Goodstein. "Pope Francis Declares Death Penalty Unacceptable in All Cases." August 2, 2018. *The New York Times*. https://www.nytimes.com/2018/08/02/world/europe/pope-death-penalty.html.
Pozen, Joanna, Richard Neugebauery, and Joseph Ntaganira. "Assessing the Rwanda Experiment: Popular Perceptions of Gacaca in Its Final Phase." *The International Journal of Transitional Justice* 8 (2014) 31–52.
Pratt, Douglas. "Fundamentalism, Exclusivism, and Extremism." In Cheetham, Pratt, and Thomas, *Understanding Interreligious Relations*, 241–61.
———. *The Church and Other Faiths. The World Council of Churches. The Vatican and Interreligious Dialogue*. Bern: Peter Lang, 2010.
Preston, Louisa. *Goldilocks and the Water Bears: The Search for Life in the Universe*. London: Bloomsbury Sigma, 2016.

Puchner, Martin. *The Written World: How Literature Shaped History*. London: Granta 2017.
Pugliese, Marc A., and Alexander Y. Hwang, eds. *Teaching Interreligious Encounters*. Oxford: Oxford University Press, 2017.
Pui-lan, Kwok, ed. *Hope Abundant: Third World and Indigenous Women's Theology*. Maryknoll, NY: Orbis, 2010.
Pui-lan, Kwok, Don H. Compier, and Joerg Rieger, eds. *Empire and the Christian Tradition: New Readings of Classical Theologians*. Minneapolis: Fortress, 2007.
The Qur'an. Translated by M. A. S. Abdel Haleem. Oxford: Oxford University Press, 2010.
Rahner, Karl. *Foundations of Christian Faith: An Introduction to the Idea of Christianity*. London: Darton, Longman & Todd, 1978.
Ramadan, Tariq. *In the Footsteps of the Prophet: Lessons from the Life of Muhammad*. Oxford: Oxford University Press, 2007.
Rambachan, Anantanand. "Christian Influence on Hindu Spiritual Practice in Trinidad." In Coward, *Hindu-Christian Dialogue*, 207–14.
Rankin, Aidan. "Ahimsa: The Way of Humility." In *The Jain Path: Ancient Wisdom for the West*. Winchester, UK: O-Books, 2006, 193–222.
Raphael, Melissa *The Female Face of God in Auschwitz: A Jewish Feminist Theology of the Holocaust*. London: Routledge, 2003.
Ratushinskaya, Irina. *Grey is the Color of Hope*. Translated by Alyona Kojevnikov. Vintage: New York, 1989.
Ratzinger, Cardinal. *The Dialectics of Secularization: On Reason and Religion*. San Francisco: Ignatian, 2006.
Rawls, John. "The Idea of Public Reason Revisited." *The University of Chicago Law Review* 64 (Summer 1997) 765–807.
Rectenwald, Michael, Rochelle Almeida, and George Levine, eds. *Global Secularisms in a Post-Secular Age*. Boston: De Gruyter, 2017.
Reda, Mario. "Anorexia and the Holiness of Saint Catherine of Siena." Translated by Graeme Newman. *Journal of Criminal Justice and Popular Culture* 8 (2001) 37–47.
Redbanks, James. *The Shepherd's Life: A Tale of the Lake District*. London: Penguin, 2016.
Regan, Ethna. *Theology and the Boundary Discourse of Human Rights*. Washington, DC: Georgetown University Press, 2010.
Renard, John. *Seven Doors to Islam: Spirituality and the Religious Life of Muslims*. Berkeley: University of California Press, 1996.
Rich, Nathaniel. "Losing Earth: The Decade We Almsot Stopped Climate Change." *The New York Times Magazine*. August 1, 2018. https://www.nytimes.com/interactive/2018/08/01/magazine/climate-change-losing-earth.html.
Richards, Norvin. "Is Humility a Virtue?" *American Philosophical Quarterly* 25 (1998) 253–59.
Ricoeur, Paul. *Memory, History, Forgetting*. Translated by Kathleen Blamey and David Pellauer. University of Chicago Press, 2004.
Ridgeon, Lloyd. "War and Peace in Islam." In Perry Schmidt-Leukel, *War and Peace in World Religions*, 148–80.
Rieger, Joerg, "Introduction: Opting for the Margins in a Postmodern World." In Rieger, *Opting for the Margins*, 3–22.

———, ed. *Opting for the Margins: Postmodernity and Liberation in Christian Theology.* Oxford: Oxford University Press, 2003.

———. "Theology, Power of Margins in a Postmodern World." In Rieger, *Opting for the Margins*, 179–99.

Rios, Victor M. *Punished: Policing the Lives of Black and Latino Boys. New Perspectives in Crime, Deviance, and Law.* New York: New York University Press, 2011.

Rittner, Carol, John K. Roth, and Wendy Whitworth. *Genocide in Rwanda: Complicity of the Churches?* St. Paul: Paragon House, 2004.

Roberts, Jonathan, and Christopher Rowland. "William Blake." In *The Blackwell Companion to the Bible in English Literature*, edited by Rebecca Lemon, Emma Mason, Jonathan Roberts, and Christopher Rowland, 373–82. Malden, MA: Wiley-Blackwell, 2012.

Roberts, Robert C. *Spiritual Emotions: A Psychology of Christian Virtues.* Grand Rapids: Eerdmans, 2007.

Robinson, Randall. *The Debt: What America Owes to Blacks.* New York: Plume, 2001.

Rogers, Murray. "Hindu Influence on Christian Spiritual Practice." In Coward, *Hindu-Christian Dialogue*, 198–206.

Rose, Or N. "Spiritual Mappings: A Jewish Understanding of Religious Diversity." In Cosgrove, *Jewish Theology in Our Time*, 63–70.

Rosenfeld, Alvin H. "Améry, Levi, Wiesel: The Futility of Holocaust Testimony." In Katz and Rosen, *Elie Wiesel*, 220–32.

Rosenthal, Gilbert S., ed. *A Jubilee for All Time: The Copernican Revolution in Jewish–Christian Relations.* Eugene, OR: Pickwick, 2014.

———. "Salvation Jewish Style." In Berger, *Trialogue and Terror*, 23–36.

Rosin, Hannah. "The End of Men." *Atlantic*, June 8, 2010. http://www.theatlantic.com/magazine/archive/2010/07/the-end-of-men/308135/.

Rosling, Hans, with Ola Rosling and Anna Rosling Rönnlund. *Factfulness: Ten Reasons We're Wrong About the the World and Why Things Are Better Than You Think.* New York: Flatiron, 2018.

Roth, Harold D. *Original Tao: Inward Training (Nei-yeh) and the Foundations of Taoist Mysticism.* New York: Columbia University Press, 2004.

Roth, John K. *The Failures of Ethics: Confronting the Holocaust, Genocide and Other Mass Atrocities.* Oxford: Oxford University Press, 2015.

Rothberg, Michael. *Multidirectional Memory: Remembering the Holocaust in the Age of Decolonization.* Stanford: Stanford University Press, 2009.

Rousseau, Jean-Jacques. *Confessions.* Translated by Angela Scholar. Oxford: Oxford World's Classics, 2008.

Rowland, Antony. *Poetry as Testimony: Witnessing and Memory in Twentieth-century Poems.* New York: Routledge, 2014.

Rubin, Edward L. *Soul, Self, and Society: The New Morality and the Modern State.* Oxford: Oxford University Press, 2015.

Rubin, Sergio, and Francesca Ambrogetti. *Pope Francis: Conversations with Jorge Bergoglio: His Life in His Own Words.* New York: Putnam, 2013.

Rubio, Julie Hanlon. *Hope for Common Ground: Mediating the Personal and the Political in a Divided Church.* Washington, DC: Georgetown University Press, 2016.

Rudin, James. *Christians & Jews Faith to Faith: Tragic History, Promising Present, Fragile Future.* Woodstock: Jewish Lights, 2011.

Rumi. *The Essential Rumi*. Translated by Coleman Barks. New York: Quality Paperback Book Club. 1998.
Runciman, David. *How Democracy Ends*. New York: Basic Books, 2018.
Ruse, Michael. *Atheism: What Everyone Needs to Know*. Oxford: Oxford University Press, 2015.
Ruston, Roger. *Human Rights and the Image of God*. London: SCM, 2004.
Rutenberg, Jim. "A Dream Undone: Inside the 50-Year Campaign to Roll back the Voting Rights Act." *The New York Times Magazine*, August 2, 2015. https://www.nytimes.com/2015/07/29/magazine/voting-rights-act-dream-undone.html?mcubz=0.
Ryan, Alan. *On Politics*. London: Penguin, 2012.
Ryan, Phil. *After the New Atheist Debate*. Toronto: University of Toronto Press, 2014.
Sacks, Jonathan. *Future Tense: Jews, Judaism, and Israel in the Twenty-First Century*. New York: Schocken, 2009.
———. *The Dignity of Difference: How to Avoid the Clash of Civilizations*. Revised edition. London: Continuum, 2003.
Sadler, Gregory. "Anselm and the Seven Levels of Humility." http://gbsadler.blogspot.ie/2011/04/anselm-on-seven-levels-of-humility.html.
Safina, Carl. *Beyond Words: What Animals Think and Feel*. New York: Holt, 2015.
Sagan, Carl. *Billions & Billions: Thoughts on Life and Death at the Brink of the Millennium*. New York: Ballantine, 1997
Sallust. *The Jugurthine War / The Conspiracy of Catiline*. Translated by S. A. Handford. London: Penguin, 1963.
Samway, Patrick. *Flannery O'Connor and Robert Giroux: A Publishing Partnership*. Notre Dame: The University of Notre Dame Press, 2018.
Sands, Philippe. *East West Street: On the Origins of Genocide and Crimes against Humanity*. London: Weidenfeld & Nicolson, 2017.
Sarch, Alexander. "What's Wrong with Megalopsychia?" *Philosophy* 83 (2008) 231–53.
Saunders, George. *Lincoln in the Bardo*. London: Bloomsbury, 2018.
Saunders, Rebecca. "Questionable Associations: The Role of Forgiveness in Transitional Justice." *The International Journal of Transitional Justice* 5 (2011) 119–41.
Scalmer, Sean. "Mohandas Gandhi." In Marsden, *The Ashgate Research Companion to Religion and Social Conflict*, 337–52.
Scarry, Elaine. *The Body in Pain: The Making and Unmaking of the World*. New York: Oxford University Press, 1985.
Schaab, Gloria L. *The Creative Suffering of the Triune God: An Evolutionary Theology*. Oxford: Oxford University Press, 2007.
Schama, Simon. *The Story of the Jews: Finding the Word 1000 BCE – 1492 CE*. London: Vintage, 2014.
Scheid, Anna Floerke. *Just Revolution: A Christian Ethic of Political Resistance and Social Transformation*. Lanham, MD: Lexington, 2015.
Schiavenza, Matt. "In Charleston, Forgiveness Meets Hatred." *Atlantic*, June 20, 2015. http://www.theatlantic.com/national/archive/2015/06/charleston-dylann-roof-forgiveness-healing/396428/.
Schmid, Muriel, ed. *Religion, Conflict, and Peacemaking: An Interdisciplinary Conversation*. Salt Lake City: The University of Utah Press, 2018.
Schmidt, Michael. *The Novel: A Biography*. Cambridge, MA: Harvard University Press, 2014.

Schmidt-Leukel, Perry. "Christianity and the Religious Other." In Cheetham, Pratt, and Thomas, *Understanding Interreligious Relations*, 118–47.

———. *Religious Pluralism and Interreligious Dialogue: The Gifford Lectures—An Extended Edition*. Maryknoll, NY: Orbis, 2017.

———, ed. *War and Peace in World Religions*. Canterbury: SCM, 2004

Schmidt-Leukel, Perry, and Lloyd Ridgeon, eds. *Islam and Inter-faith Relations*. London: SCM, 2007.

Schreiter, Robert J. "A Practical Theology of Healing, Forgiveness, and Reconciliation." In Schreiter, Appleby, and Powers, *Peacebuilding*, 366–97.

Schreiter, Robert J., R. Scott Appleby, and Gerard F. Powers, eds. *Peacebuilding: Catholic Theology, Ethics, and Praxis*. Maryknoll, NY: Orbis, 2010.

Schuck, Michael J., and John Crowley-Buck, eds. *Democracy, Culture, Catholicism: Voices from Four Continents*. New York: Fordham University Press, 2016.

Schueler, G. F. "Why IS Modesty a Virtue?" *Ethics* 109 (July 1999) 835–41.

———. "Why Modesty Is a Virtue." *Ethics* 107 (April 1997) 467–85.

Schweizer, Bernard. *Hating God: The Untold Story of Misotheism*. Oxford: Oxford University Press, 2011.

Scruton, Roger. *Where We Are: The State of Britain Now*. London: Bloomsbury, 2017.

Sen, Amartya. "The Threats to Secular India." *The New York Review of Books*, April 8, 1993. http://www.nybooks.com/articles/archives/1993/apr/08/the-threats-to-secular-india/.

Senauke, Alan. *The Bodhisattva's Embrace: Dispatches from Engaged Buddhism's Front Lines*. Berkeley, CA: Clear View, 2010.

Shah, Timothy Samuel. "Secular Militancy as an Obstacle to Peacebuilding." In Omer, Appleby, and Little, *The Oxford Handbook of Religion, Conflict, and Peacebuilding*, 380–406.

Shah, Timothy Samuel, Alfred Stepan, and Monica Duffy Toft, eds. *Rethinking Religion and World Affairs*. Oxford: Oxford University Press, 2012.

Shakespeare, William. *The Merchant of Venice*. In *The Riverside Shakespeare*, edited by G. Blakemore Evans, 250–85. Boston: Houghton Mifflin, 1974.

———. *The Tragedy of Romeo and Juliet*. In *The Riverside Shakespeare*, edited by G. Blakemore Evans, 1055–99. Boston: Houghton–Mifflin, 1974.

Shankman, Steven. *Other Others: Levinas, Literature, Transcultural Studies*. Albany: State University of New York Press, 2010.

Shannon, Lisa J. *Mama Koko and the Hundred Gunmen: An Ordinary Family's Extraordinary Tale of Love, Loss, and Survival in Congo*. New York: PublicAffairs, 2014.

Shanor, Karen, and Jagmeet Kanwal. *Bats Sing, Mice Giggle: Revealing the Secret Lives of Animals*. London: Icon, 2009.

Shapiro, Joseph. "Amish Forgive School Shooter, Struggle with Grief." *National Public Radio*, October 2, 2006. http://www.npr.org/templates/story/story.php?storyId=14900930.

Sharma, Arvind. "Can There Be More than One Kind of Pluralism?" In Knitter, *Myth of Religious Superiority*, 56–72.

Shelby, Tommie. *Dark Ghettoes: Injustice, Dissent, and Reform*. Cambridge, MA: Harvard University Press, 2016.

Shenker, Noah. *Reframing Holocaust Testimony*. Bloomington: Indiana University Press, 2015.

Sherratt, Yvonne. *Hitler's Philosophers*. New Haven: Yale University Press, 2013.
Sherwin, Byron. "'Who Do You Say That I Am?' (Mark 8:29): A New Jewish View of Jesus." In *Jesus through Jewish Eyes: Rabbis and Scholars Engage an Ancient Brother in a New Conversation*, edited by Beatrice Bruteau, 31–44. Maryknoll, NY: Orbis, 2003.
Shun, Kwong-loi. "Resentment and Forgiveness in Confucian Thought." *Journal of East-West Thought* 4 (December 2014) 13–35.
Siems, Larry. "A Timeline of Detention." In Slahi, *Guantánamo Diaries*, iv–x.
Sifton, John. *Violence All Around*. Cambridge, MA: Harvard University Press, 2015.
Signer, Michael A. "'Seeing the Sounds': Humility and the Process of Dialogue." In Heft, Firestone, and Safi, *Learned Ignorance*, 53–66.
Singer, Peter. "Taking Humanism Beyond Speciesism." *Free Inquiry* 24 (October/November 2004) 19–21.
Singh, Nidhi. *Japji Sahib: An Interpretation in Humility*. Independently Published, 2017.
Sirry, Mun'im. "'Compete with One Another in Good Works': Exegesis of Qur'an Verse 5.48 and Contemporary Muslim Discourses on Religious Pluralism." *Islam and Christian-Muslim Relations* 20 (2009) 423–38.
Skjaervo, Prods Oktor, ed. *The Spirit of Zoroastrianism*. Translated by Prods Oktor Skjaervo. New Haven: Yale University Press, 2012.
Skye, Lee Miena. "Australian Aboriginal Women's Christologies." In Pui-lan, *Hope Abundant*, 194–202.
Slahi, Mohamedou Ould. *Guantánamo Diaries*. Edited by Larry Siems. Edinburgh: Cannongate, 2015.
———. *Guantánamo Diaries: The Fully Restored Text*. Edited by Larry Siems. Edinburgh: Cannongate, 2017.
Slingerland, Edward. *Effortless Action: Wu-Wei as Conceptual Metaphor and Spiritual Ideal in Early China*. Oxford: Oxford University Press, 2003.
Smith, Buster G., and Joseph O. Baker. *American Secularism: Cultural Contours of Nonreligious Belief Systems*. New York: New York University Press, 2015.
Smith, James K. A. *How (Not) to Be Secular: Reading Charles Taylor*. Grand Rapids: Eerdmans, 2014.
Smith, Mark A. *Secular Faith: How Culture Has Trumped Religion in American Politics*. Chicago: Chicago University Press, 2015.
Smith, Mychal Denzel. *Invisible Man, Got the Whole World Watching*. New York: Nation, 2016.
Smith, Paul Chaat. *Everything You Know about Indians is Wrong*. Minneapolis: University of Minnesota Press, 2009.
Snyder, Timothy. *Bloodlands: Europe Between Hitler and Stalin*. London: The Bodley Head, 2010.
Sobrino, Jon. "Christianity and Reconciliation: The Way of Utopia." In *Reconciliation in a World of Conflicts*, Concilium no. 5, edited by Luis Carlos Susin and María Pilar Aquino, 80–90. London: SCM, 2003.
———. "Communion, Conflict, and Ecclesial Solidarity." Translated by Margaret D. Wilde. In Ellacuría and Sobrino, *Mysterium Liberationis*, 615–36.
———. *No Salvation Outside the Poor: Prophetic-Utopian Essays*. Maryknoll, NY: Orbis, 2008.
Solomon, Erika. "Syria: A Tale of Three Cities." *FT Weekend Magazine*, August 5, 2017, 12–21.

Solzhenitsyn, Aleksandr. *The Gulag Archipelago 1918–1956*. Translated by Thomas P. Whitney. London: Harvill, 1995.

Soulen, R. Kendall. "Israel and the Church: A Christian Response to Irving Greenberg's Covenantal Pluralism." In Frymer-Kensky, Novak, Ochs, Samuel, and Signer, *Christianity in Jewish Terms*, 167–74.

Spadaro, Antonio. "Poetry at the Threshold of Prayer." In *Poetry and Prayer: Power of the Word II*, edited by Francesca Bugliani Knox and John Took, 57–65. Surrey, UK: Ashgate, 2015.

Sparks, Elicka Peterson. *The Devil You Know: The Surprising Link between Conservative Christianity and Crime*. Amherst, New York: Prometheus, 2016.

Spinoza, Benedict. *Theologico-Political Treatise*. Translated by R. H. M. Elwes. New York: Dover, 1951.

———. *Ethics*. Translated by Edwin Curley. London: Penguin, 1996.

Stedman, Chris. *Faitheist: How an Atheist Found Common Ground with the Religious*. Boston: Beacon, 2012.

Stein, Arlene. *Reluctant Witnesses: Survivors. Their Children, and the Rise of Holocaust Consciousness*. Oxford: Oxford University Press, 2014.

Steinbeck, John. *East of Eden*. New York: Penguin, 2002.

Stemple, Laura. "The Hidden Victims of Wartime Rape." *The New York Times*, March 1, 2011. http://www.nytimes.com/2011/03/02/opinion/02stemple.html.

Steuber, Jason. *China: 3,000 Years of Art and Literature*. New York: Welcome, 2008.

Stevenson, Bryan. *Just Mercy: A Story of Justice and Redemption*. New York: Spiegal and Grau, 2014.

Stolberg, Sheryl Gay, and Richard A. Oppel Jr., "Suspects in Gray Case: A Portrait in Miniature of the Baltimore Police." *The New York Times,* May 10, 2015, A25.

Stone, Dan. "Beyond the Mnemosyne Institute: The Future of Memory after the Age of Commemoration." In Crownshaw, Kilby, and Rowland, *Future of Memory*, 17–36.

———. "History, Memory, Testimony." In Kilby and Rowland, *Future of Testimony*, 17–30.

Stout, Jeffrey. "2007 Presidential Address: The Folly of Secularism." *Journal of the American Academy of Religion* 76 (September 2008) 533–44.

———. *Democracy and Tradition*. Princeton: Princeton University Press, 2004.

Stover, Eric. *The Witnesses: War Crimes and the Promise of Justice in The Hague*. Philadelphia: University of Pennsylvania Press, 2007.

Straub, Thomas. *Hidden in the Rubble: A Haitian Pilgrimage to Compassion and Resurrection*. Maryknoll, NY: Orbis, 2010.

Sugirtharajah, R. S., *Jesus in Asia*. Cambridge, MA: Harvard University Press, 2018.

———., ed. *The Postcolonial Biblical Reader*. Oxford: Blackwell, 2006.

———. "The Syrophoenician Woman." *The Expository Times* 98 (1986) 13–15.

Suleiman, Susan Rubin. "Do Facts Matter in Holocaust Memoirs? Wilkomirski/Wiesel." In Katz and Rosen, *Obliged by Memory*, 21–42.

Sullivan, Michael. *The Three Perfections: Chinese Painting, Poetry, and Calligraphy*. New York: George Braziller, 1980.

Suzman, James. *Affluence Without Abundance: The Disappearing World of the Bushmen*. New York: Bloomsbury, 2017.

Swan, Laura. *The Forgotten Desert Mothers: Sayings, Lives, and Stories of Early Christian Women*. Mahwah, NJ: Paulist, 2001.

Swanepoel, Elizabeth. "Blossoms of the Dharma: The Contribution of Western Nuns in Transforming Gender Bias in Tibetan Buddhism." *Journal of Buddhist Ethics* 21 (2014) 569–99.
Sweeney, Eileen. "Vice and Sin (Ia IIae qq.71–89)." In *The Ethics of Aquinas*, edited by Stephen J. Pope, 151–68. Washington, DC: Georgetown University Press, 2002.
Swidler, Leonard. "Interreligious and Interideological Dialogue: The Matrix for All Systematic Reflection Today." In *Toward a Universal Theology of Religion*, edited by Leonard Swidler, 5–50. Maryknoll, NY: Orbis, 1987.
———. "The Dialogue Decalogue: Ground Rules for Interreligious, Intercultural Dialogue." http://globalethic.org/Center/decalog.htm.
———. "The History of Inter-Religious Dialogue." In Cornille, *Wiley-Blackwell Companion to Inter-Religious Dialogue*, 3–19.
Swindal, James. "Habermas, Religion, and a Postsecular Society." In *Christianity and Secular Reason: Classical Themes and Modern Developments*, edited by Jeffrey Bloechl, 217–38. Notre Dame: University of Notre Dame Press, 2012.
Tabor, Damon. "The Greater the Sinner: A Liberian Warlord's Unlikely Path to Salvation." *The New Yorker*, March 14, 2016. http://www.newyorker.com/magazine/2016/03/14/general-butt-naked-the-repentant-warlord.
Taliaferro, Charles. *The Golden Chord: A Short Book on the Secular and the Sacred.* Notre Dame: University of Notre Dame Press, 2013.
Tan, Shaun. *The Red Tree*. Sydney: Lothian, 2010.
Tang, Edmond. "Identity and Marginality—Christianity in East Asia." In Wilfred, *The Oxford Handbook of Christianity in Asia*, 80–97.
Tang, Quin Qing. *Half a Walnut Tree*. Christchurch, NZ: CHB, 2016.
Taylor, Charles. *A Secular Age*. Cambridge, MA: Harvard University Press, 2007.
———. "Western Secularity." In Calhoun, Juergensmeyer, and VanAntwerpen, *Rethinking Secularism*, 31–53.
Taylor, Lisa, Umwali Sollange, and Marie-Jolie Rwigema. "The Ethics of Learning from Rwandan Survivor Communities." In *Beyond Testimony and Trauma: Oral History in the Aftermath of Mass Violence*, edited by Steven High, 88–118. Vancouver: The University of British Columbia Press, 2015.
Taylor, Mark C. "Erring: A Postmodern Theology." In *From Modernism to Postmodernism: An Anthology*, edited by Lawrence E. Cahoone, 514–33. Oxford: Blackwell, 1996.
Taylor-Guthrie, Danielle, ed. *Conversations with Toni Morrison*. Jackson: University Press of Mississippi, 1981.
Telushkin, Joseph. *Hillel: If Not Now, When?* New York: Schocken, 2010.
Tennent, Timothy. *Invitation to World Missions: A Trinitarian Missiology for the Twenty-first Century*. Grand Rapids: Kregel, 2010.
Teresa of Ávila. *The Complete Works of Saint Teresa of Jesus*, vol. 3. Translated and edited by E. Allison Peers. London: Sheed & Ward, 1950.
———. *The Interior Castle*. Translated by Kieran Kavanaugh and Otilio Rodriguez. Mahweh, NJ: Paulist, 1979.
———. *The Life of Saint Teresa of Ávila by Herself*. Translated by J. M. Cohen. London: Penguin, 1957.
Tertullian. *The Prescription against Heretics*. Translated by Peter Holmes. http://www.tertullian.org/anf/anf03/anf03-24.htm#P3125_1133921.
Thackeray, William Makepeace. *Vanity Fair*. London: J. M. Dent, 1930.

Thanegi, Ma. *Nor Iron Bars a Cage*. San Francisco: Things Asian, 2013.
Thatamanil, John J. "Learning from (and Not Just about) Our Religious Neighbors: Comparative Theology and the Future of Nostra Aetate." In Cohen, Knitter, and Rosenhagen, *Future of Interreligious Dialogue*, 289–301.
The Walking Dead. "Here's Not Here." Directed by Stephen Williams. Written by Frank Darabont. AMC. November 1, 2015.
Thiemann, Ronald F. *The Humble Sublime: Secularity and the Politics of Belief*. London: I. B. Tauris, 2013.
Thomas, David. "Islam and the Religious Other." In Cheetham, Pratt, and Thomas, *Understanding Interreligious Relations*, 148–71.
Thomas, Laurence. "Evil and Forgiveness: The Possibility of Moral Redemption." In *Evil, Political Violence, and Forgiveness: Essays in Honor of Claudia Card*, edited by Andrea Veltman and Kathryn J. Norlock, 115–33. Lanham, MD: Lexington, 2009.
Thomas, R. S. *Selected Poems*. London: Penguin, 2004.
Thomson, Susan, and Rosemary Nagy. "Law, Power, and Justice: What Legalism Fails to Address in the Functioning of Rwanda's *Gacaca* Courts." *The International Journal of Transitional Justice* 5 (2011) 11–30.
Thoreau, Henry David. *Walden, or Life in the Woods*. New York: Dover, 1995.
Thubron, Colin. *Behind the Wall: A Journey Through China*. New York: HarperCollins: 1989.
Tillich, Paul. *Dynamics of Faith*. New York: HarperOne, 2009.
Tillinghast, Richard. *Finding Ireland: A Poet's Exploration of Irish Literature and Culture*. Notre Dame: University of Notre Dame, 2008.
Tinker, Tink. "American Indian Liberation: Paddling a Canoe Upstream." In *The Reemergence of Liberation Theologies: Models for the Twenty-First Century*, edited by Thia Cooper, 59–67. New York: Palgrave Macmillan, 2013.
Tolkien, J. R. R. *The Lord of the Rings: The Two Towers*. London: HarperCollins, 2012.
Tonnelat, Stéphane, and William Kornblum. *New Yorkers on the 7 Train*. New York: Columbia University Press, 2017.
Toumani, Meline. *There Was and There Was Not: A Journey Through Hate and Possibility in Turkey, Armenia, and Beyond*. New York: Metropolitan, 2014.
Tracy, David. *Dialogue with the Other: The Inter-Religious Dialogue*. Leuven, BE: Peeters, 1990.
———. "Fragments: The Spiritual Situation of Our Times." In Caputo and Scanlon, *God, the Gift, and Postmodernism*, 169–84.
———. "Kenosis, Sunyata, and Trinity: A Dialogue with Masao Abe." In *The Emptying God: A Buddhist-Jewish Christian Conversation*, edited by John B. Cobb Jr. and Christopher Ives, 135–54. Eugene, OR: Wipf and Stock, 2005.
———. *Naming the Present: God, Hermeneutics, and Church*. Maryknoll, NY: Orbis, 1994.
———. *Plurality and Ambiguity: Hermeneutics, Religion, Hope*. New York: Harper & Row, 1987.
———. "Religion in the Public Realm: Three Forms of Publicness." In Barbieri, *At the Limits of the Secular*, 29–50.
———. *The Analogical Imagination: Christian Theology and the Culture of Pluralism*. New York: Crossroads, 1998.

———. "The Christian Option for the Poor." In *The Option for the Poor in Christian Theology*, edited by Daniel G. Groody, 119–31. Notre Dame: University of Notre Dame Press, 2007.

———. "Western Hermeneutics and Interreligious Dialogue." In *Interreligious Hermeneutics*, edited by Catherine Cornille and Christopher Conway, 1–43. Eugene, OR: Cascade, 2010.

Trawick, Margaret. *Death, Beauty, Struggle: Untouchable Women Create the World*. Philadelphia: University of Pennsylvania Press, 2017.

Trezise, Thomas. *Witnessing Witnessing: On the Reception of Holocaust Testimony*. New York: Fordham University Press, 2013.

Trible, Phyllis, and Letty M. Russell. *Hagar, Sarah, and Their Children: Jewish, Christian, and Muslim Perspectives*. Louisville: Westminster John Knox, 2006.

Trollope, Anthony. *Can You Forgive Her?* Middlesex: London, 1972.

Turner, Denys. *Thomas Aquinas: A Portrait*. New Haven: Yale University Press, 2013.

Tutu, Desmond. "Foreword." In Cantacuzino, *Forgiveness Project*, xi–xii.

———. "Foreword." In Henderson, *No Enemy to Conquer*, xi–xiii.

———. *No Future without Forgiveness*. New York: Image, 2000.

Ueda, Shizuteru. "Jesus in Contemporary Zen." In *Buddhist Perceptions of Jesus*, edited by Perry Schmidt-Leukel, Gerhard Köberlin, and Thomas Josef Götz, 42–58. St. Ottilien, DE: Eos, 2001.

Unterman, Alan, ed. *The Kabbalistic Tradition*. London: Penguin, 2008.

The Upanishads. Translated by Juan Mascaró. London: Penguin, 1965.

Valkenberg, Pim. *Sharing Lights on the Way to God: Muslim-Christian Dialogue and Theology in the Context of Abrahamic Partnership*. Amsterdam: Rodopi, 2006.

Vainio, Olli-Pekka. *Disagreeing Virtuously: Religious Conflict in Interdisciplinary Perspective*. Grand Rapids: Eerdmans, 2017.

Vallely, Paul. *Pope Francis: Untying the Knots*. London: Bloomsbury, 2013.

Vanhoozer, Kevin J. "Scripture and Tradition." In Vanhoozer, *The Cambridge Companion to Postmodern Theology*, 149–69.

———, ed. *The Cambridge Companion to Postmodern Theology*. Cambridge, UK: Cambridge University Press, 2003.

Vance, J. D. *Hillbilly Elegy: A Memoir of a Family and Culture in Crisis*. New York: Harper, 2016.

Vaughan, Olufemi. *Religion and the Making of Nigeria*. Durham, NC: Duke University Press, 2016.

Volf, Miroslav. "Forgiveness, Reconciliation, and Justice: A Christian Contribution to a More Peaceful Social Environment." In Helmick and Petersen, *Forgiveness and Reconciliation*, 27–49.

———. *The End of Memory: Remembering Rightly in a Violent World*. Grand Rapids: Eerdmans, 2006.

von Brück, Michael. "A Theology of Multiple Religious Identity." In *Converging Ways: Conversion and Belonging in Buddhism and Christianity*, edited by John D'Arcy May, 181–206. St. Ottilien, DE: OS Klosterverlag, 2007.

———. "What do I Expect Buddhists to Discover in Jesus? 'Christ and the Buddha Embracing Each Other.'" In *Buddhist Perceptions of Jesus*, edited by Perry Schmidt-Leukel, Thomas Josef Götz, and Gerhard Köberlin, 158–75. St. Ottilien, DE: Eos, 2001.

Vulliamy, Ed. *The War is Dead, Long Live the War: Bosnia: The Reckoning.* London: Bodley Head, 2012.
Wagner, Roger, and Andrew Briggs. *The Penultimate Curiosity: How Science Swims in the Slipstream of Ultimate Questions.* Oxford: Oxford University Press, 2016.
Walsh, David. *The Luminosity of Existence.* Cambridge, UK: Cambridge University Press, 2008.
Warner, Michael, Jonathan VanAntwerpen, and Craig Calhoun, eds. *Varieties of Secularism in a Secular Age.* Cambridge, MA: Harvard University Press, 2013.
Wartofsky, Alona. "A Lesson in the Language of Grief." *The Washington Post*, November 14, 1996. https://www.washingtonpost.com/archive/lifestyle/1996/11/14/a-lesson-in-the-language-of-grief/b33d7240-3d38-407a-8d0c-5d91dd88f5e2/.
Watson, Peter. *The Age of Atheists: How We Have Sought to Live since the Death of God.* New York: Simon & Shuster, 2014.
Watterson, Bill. *Calvin and Hobbes.* March 6, 1991. http://www.gocomics.com/calvinandhobbes/1991/03/06.
Waxman, Zoë Vania. *Writing the Holocaust: Identity, Testimony, Representation.* Oxford: Oxford University Press, 2006.
Weber, Alison. *Teresa of Avila and the Rhetoric of Femininity.* Princeton: Princeton University Press, 1996.
Webster, John C. B. "Gandhi and the Christians: Dialogue in the Nationalist Era." In Coward, *Hindu-Christian Dialogue*, 80–99.
Weil, Simone. *The Simone Weil Reader.* Edited by George A. Panichas. New York: David McKay, 1977.
Weinberger, Eliot, ed. *The New Directions Anthology of Classical Chinese Poetry.* New York: New Directions, 2003.
Weissman, Debbie. *Memoirs of a Hopeful Pessimist: A Life of Activism through Dialogue.* Jerusalem: Ktav, 2017.
Whitehead, Colson. *The Underground Railroad.* London; Fleet, 2016.
Whitehead, Hal, and Luke Rendell. *The Cultural Lives of Whales and Dolphins.* Chicago: The University of Chicago Press, 2015.
Whitmore, Todd D. "Peacebuilding and its Catholic Partners: Justice, Human Rights, Development, and Solidarity." In Schreiter, Appleby, and Powers, *Peacebuilding*, 155–89.
Whitney, Karl. *Hidden City: Adventure and Explorations in Dublin.* Dublin: Penguin Ireland, 2014.
Wiesel, Elie. *And the Sea is Never Full: Memoirs, 1969–.* Translated by Marion Wiesel. New York: Knopf, 1999.
———. *Night.* Translated by Marion Wiesel. London: Penguin, 2006.
———. *One Generation After.* Translated by Lily Edelman and Marion Wiesel. New York: Schocken 2011
———. *Souls on Fire* and *Somewhere a Master.* Translated by Marion Wiesel. Middlesex: Penguin, 1984.
———. *Wise Men and Their Tales: Portraits of Biblical, Talmudic, and Hasidic Masters.* New York: Schocken, 2003.
Wiesenthal, Simon. *The Sunflower: On the Possibilities and Limits of Forgiveness.* Rev. ed. New York: Schocken, 1998.
Wieviorka, Annette. *The Era of the Witness.* Translated by Jared Stark. Ithaca: Cornell University Press, 2006.

WikiLeaks. *The WikiLeaks Files: The World According to US Empire*. London: Verso 2015.
Wilfred, Felix, ed. *The Oxford Handbook of Christianity in Asia*. Oxford: Oxford University Press, 2014.
Wilgoren, Debbi, and Avis Thomas-Lester, "Boy Found Dead in Filthy D.C. Closet." *The Washington Post*, June 8, 1996. https://www.washingtonpost.com/archive/local/1996/06/08/boy-found-dead-in-filthy-dc-closet/c235a25e-a014-4a7a-93b1-645f56a01b64/.
Wilhite, David E. "Augustine the African: Post-Colonial, Postcolonial, and Post-Postcolonial Readings." *Journal of Postcolonial Theory and Theology* 5 (July 2014) 1–34.
Williams, Anthony Marc. "Forgiveness, Resentment, and Intentional Agency." *Essays in the Philosophy of Humanism* Vol 19 (2011) 1–12.
Williams, Rowan. *Dostoevsky: Language, Faith and Fiction*. London: Continuum, 2009.
———. *Teresa of Avila*. London: Geoffrey Chapman, 1992.
Williams, Robert R. *Tragedy, Recognition, and the Death of God: Studies in Hegel and Nietzsche*. Oxford: Oxford University Press, 2012.
Williams, Trevor, and Trevor B. Milton. *The Con Men: Hustling in New York City*. New York: Columbia University Press, 2015.
Wilson, Bryan. "Secularization: The Inherited Model." In *The Sacred in a Secular Age*, edited by Phillip E. Hammond, 9–20. Berkeley: University of California Press, 1985.
Wink, Walter. *The Powers That Be: Theology for a New Millennium*. New York: Doubleday, 1999.
Wiseman, James, and Donald Mitchell, eds. *The Gethsemani Encounter: A Dialogue on the Spiritual Life by Buddhist and Christian Monastics*. New York: Continuum, 1999.
Wohlforth, Charles, and Amanda R. Hendrix. *Beyond Earth: Our Path to a New Home in the Planets*. New York: Pantheon, 2016.
Wohlleben, Peter. *The Hidden Life of Trees: What They Feel, How They Communicate*. Translated by Jane Billinghurst. Vancouver, BC: Greystones, 2016.
Wolfendale, Jessica. "The Myth of 'Torture Lite.'" *Ethics & International Affairs* 23 (Spring 2009) 47–61.
Woodbine, Onaje X. O. *Black Gods of the Asphalt: Religion, Hip-Hop, and Street Basketball*. New York: Columbia University Press, 2016.
Wooden, Cindy. "Pope, Rabbi Skorka join effort to promote friendship across faiths." *Crux*, June 16, 2017. https://cruxnow.com/global-church/2017/06/16/pope-rabbi-skorka-join-effort-promote-friendship-across-faiths/.
Woodhead, Linda. "Neither Religious Nor Secular: The British Situation and Its Implications for Religious-state Relations." In Berg-Sørensen, *Contesting Secularism*, 137–61.
Worthington, Everett L., Jr. "Unforgiveness, Forgiveness, and Reconciliation, and Their Implications for Societal Interventions." In Helmick and Petersen, *Forgiveness and Reconciliation*, 171–92.
Wright, Richard. *Native Son*. New York: Perennial, 1993.
Wu, Harry Hongada. *Bitter Winds: A Memoir of My Years in China's Gulag*. New York: John Wiley, 1994.

Yadlapati, Madhuri M. *Against Dogmatism: Dwelling in Faith and Doubt.* Champaign, IL: University of Illinois Press, 2013.
Yang, Guobin. *The Red Guard Generation and Political Activism in China.* New York: Columbia University Press, 2016.
Yao, Zhihua. "I Have Lost Me: Zhuangzi's Dream." *Journal of Chinese Philosophy* 40 (September/December 2013) 511–26.
Yarov, Sergey. *Leningrad 1941–1942: Morality in a City under Siege.* Translated by Arch Tait. Cambridge, MA: Polity, 2017.
Yerushalmi, Yosef Hayim. *Zakhor: Jewish History and Jewish Museum.* Seattle: University of Washington Press, 1996.
Yiwu, Liao. *For a Song and a Hundred Songs: A Poet's Journey through a Chinese Prison.* Translated by Wenguang Huang. Boston: New Harvest, 2013.
———. *God is Red: The Secret Story of How Christianity Survived and Flourished in Communist China.* Translated by Wenguang Huang. New York: HarperOne, 2011.
———. *The Corpse Walker: Real-Life Stories, China from the Bottom Up.* Translated by Wenguang Huang. New York: Anchor, 2009.
Young, James. *Writing and Rewriting the Holocaust and the Consequences of Narrative Interpretation.* Bloomington: Indiana University Press, 1990.
Young, Paul. *Frank Miller's Daredevil and the Ends of Heroism.* New Brunswick: Rutgers University Press, 2016.
Yu-Hsi, Chen. "The Buddhist Perception of Humility." *The International Network on Personal Meaning.* http://meaning.ca/archives/archive/art_buddhist-humility_C_Yu_Hsi.htm.
Zhang, Hansong, et al. "Intellectual Humility and Forgiveness of Religious Conflict." *Journal of Psychology and Theology* 43 (2015) 255–62.
Zhang, Qianfan. "Human Dignity in Classical Chinese Philosophy: The Daoist Perspective." *Journal of Chinese Philosophy* 40 (September/December 2013) 493–510.
Ziegler, Dominic. *Black River Dragon: A Journey down the Amur River between Russia and China.* New York: Penguin 2016.
Zim, Rivkah. *The Consolations of Writing: Literary Strategies on Resistance from Boethius to Levi.* Princeton: Princeton University Press, 2014.
Zimmerman, Jens. *Humanism and Religion: A Call for the Renewal of Western Culture.* Oxford: Oxford University Press, 2012.
Zinn, Howard. *A People's History of the United States of America.* New York: Perennial Classics, 2005.
Zuckerman, Phil. *Living the Secular Life: New Answers to Old Questions.* New York: Penguin, 2014.
Zuckerman, Phil and John Shook, eds. *The Oxford Handbook of Secularism.* Oxford: Oxford University Press, 2017.

Name Index

A Xia, 189–190
Abela, Joseph S., 149n1
Abelard, Peter, 105n41
Abu-Nimer, Mohammad, 255n151, 257n156
Acemoglu, Daron, 70
Actis, Munu, 186n15
Adkins, Peter, 12
Admirand, Peter, 35n92, 51n25, 61n92, 63n101, 64n105, 70n17, 86n103, 90n118, 97n5, 99n10, 104n40, 106n49, 108n57, 109n63, 112n77, 114n88, 124n36, 143n145, 151n4, 160n58, 182n3, 221n174, 255n150, 257n160
Afsaruddin, Asma, 90–91
Agee, James, 11
Aguilar, Mario, 218
Akkad, Omar El, 272n9
Aldini, Cristina, 186n15
Alexander, Michelle, 172–73, 177, 178
Alexievich, Svetlana, 224
Al-Ghazali, Copy diacritic in Word, 257
Allen, John L., Jr., 101n18
Allen, Woody, 141
Allinson, Robert Elliott, 58n69
Almeida, Rochelle, 127n49
al-Qurtubi, Muhammad b. Ahmad, 91
Amaladoss, Michael, 85n98
Ambar, Saladin, 173n108

Ambrogetti, Francesca, 107n55
Ambrose, 28
Améry, Jean, 205n99, 237
Ammerman, Nancy, 125
Anderson, Carol, 152n13
Anderson, Gary A., 230n16
Anderson, Perry, 161n63
Angell, Roger, 116
Anselm, 32
Anthony, Lawrence, 21n1, 263, 263n185
Antony, Louise M., 136
Apess, William, 59
Apol, Laura, 182, 215–223
Aquinas, 31–35, 44, 45, 53, 58, 91, 120
Arendt, Hannah, 253–54
Aristotle, 7, 32–34, 43, 91
Aronson, Ronald, 123, 126, 138n106, 143n145
Ashoka (Emperor), 160
Athanasius, 28
Augustine, 8, 28–31, 32
Aung Suu Kyi, 63
Aydin, Mahmut, 90
Azango, Mae, 241n74

Bacon, Francis, 158
Bader, Christopher, 126n47
Bailey, Kenneth, 27
Baker, Joseph, 126n47
Balagangadhara, S. N., 128n56
Baldwin, James, 151n8, 152, 154n20, 170n89, 172, 173, 177
Banville, John, 225

NAME INDEX

Baptist, Edward E., 177n136
Barbieri, William A., Jr., 124n36
Barnet, Mac, 96
Barnstone, Tony, 57n62
Bash, Anthony, 230, 234, 254
Basil of Caesarea, 28
Battiti, Florencia, 184n11
Bauer, Yehuda, 158, 159n50
Beard, Mary, 162n72
Beattie, Tina, 101n18, 160n57
Becker, Karl Joseph, 97n4
Benedict, St., 28n39, 32
Benedict of Nursia, 28
Benedict XVI, Pope, 84n85, 107, 113n86
Bennhold, Katrin, 158n45
Benson, William, 243
Berger, Alan L., 106n45, 111, 112, 113, 251
Berger, Peter, 124–25
Bergoglio, Jorge Mario, 35, 107n55
Berkovits, Eliezer, 134–35
Bernard of Clairvaux, St., 11, 271
Bersnak, P. Bracy, 35
Berthrong, John, 58n67
Berwouts, Kris, 221n174
Betts, Dwayne, 174
Bhargava, Rajeev, 127
Bilgrami, Akeel, 124n36
Bingemer, María Clara, 28n37
Bird, Larry, 166
Black, Crofton, 202n89
Black Elk, 62
Blahyi, Joshua Milton, 240–41
Blake, William, 9
Blessing, Kimberly A., 137n103
Bloom, Paul, 58n70
Blustein, Jeffrey, 152n9, 155n26, 155n27, 244n93
Boase, Roger, 90
Boehm, Barbara Drake, 100n16
Boff, Clodovis, 31n59
Bolick, Kate, 101n18
Boo, Katherine, 209
Booth, W. James, 155, 233n33
Borger, Julian, 199n78
Borges, Jorge Luis, 155n26
Boschki, Reinhold, 161n62

Boteach, Schmuley, 89n110, 111n67, 111n70, 113
Boumediene, Lakhdar, 199n77
Bowden, John, 69n13
Bowels, Paul, 141n127
Bowker, John, 117n3
Boyarin, Daniel, 78n57, 111n70
Boyd, Craig A., 34, 102n31
Boys, Mary C., 103, 107n53, 115n89
Braithwaite, John, 234
Brennan, Jason, 198n75
Bretherton, Di, 230n15
Brettler, Marc Zvi, 110, 110n65
Brombert, Victor, 143–44, 161n66
Brontë, Charlotte, 205n98
Brown, Michael, 178
Brown, Peter, 229
Browning, Christopher R., 182n2
Bruce, Steve, 85
Brudholm, Thomas, 237
Brueck, Laura R, 51n26
Bucko, Adam, 101n18
Buddha, 50
Buell, Lawrence, 170n88, 170n89
Bullivant, Stephen, 139n115, 142
Burrell, David B., 31n61, 106n45
Bushlack, Thomas J., 28n41
Butler, Joseph, 230
Butler, Paul, 210n126
Button, Mark E., 5, 8n34, 104n39
Buxbaum, Yitzhak, 91n125
Byrd, Jodi A., 60n83

Cabilla, Veronica Maria, 183
Calhoun, Craig, 124n36
Camus, Albert, 135, 144
Cantacuzino, Marina, 231, 261
Caputo, John D., 137n102
Card, Claudia, 232, 233n32
Cardenal, Ernesto, 27n35, 230n16
Carr, Garrett, 149n1
Carroll, Anthony, 124n38
Carson, Clayborne, 64n110
Cartledge, Paul, 198n75
Caruth, Cathy, 24n16, 180n1
Casas, Bartolomé de Las, 105n43
Cassian, John, 28
Cavanaugh, William T., 118, 123

Cea, J. Abraham Vélez de, 76, 86n101
Celan, Paul, 222–23
Chambers, Becky, 96n1
Chan, Victor, 247, 258n166
Chang, Jung, 195n57
Charles V (Spanish Emperor), 148
Chatterjee, Partha, 128
Chazan, Robert, 30n54
Chelius, Judith, 30n56
Chol-Hwan, Kang, 239n65
Chuang Tzu, 54–55, 57, 144n147
Churchill, Ward, 61
Chvala-Smith, Anthony J., 28n41
Cicero, 7–8, 29
Clark, Edmund, 202n89
Clark, Elizabeth A., 117n4
Clayton, Clayton, 138n108
Clement of Alexandria, 28
Coates, Ta-Nehisi, 177–78
Cobb, John B, Jr., 74n27, 79
Coker, Christopher, 154
Colaresi, Michael, 17
Cole, David, 200n79
Cole, Elizabeth A., 229
Coll, Steve, 202n89
Compier, Don H., 164n80
Comte, August, 119
Condorcet, Nicolas de, 119
Confucius, 245
Connolly, William E., 118, 122
Cook, Joan E., 158n48
Cook, Michael J., 105n41, 111, 113
Cooper, Julie, 137–38
Cornille, Catherine, 85n99, 100, 102n27, 103, 163n76
Coronil, Fernando, 163n78
Corrington, Gail, 44n130
Crane, Jonathan K., 263n182
Crane, Tim, 124n38
Crawford, Neta, 201n85
Creighton, Gerry, 225, 264–67
Crossan, John Dominic, 4–5
Crosthwaite, Alejandro, 31n58
Crownshaw, Rick, 157n39, 171n96, 180n1
Cruz, Juana Inés, de la, 42
Csikszentmihalyi, Mark A., 58n69

Cubilié, Anne, 158n44, 180n1
Cunliffe, Barry, 163n74
Cunningham, Philip A., 106n45, 111n66
Curzor, Harold J., 33n75

da Silva, Anthony, 246n104
Dacey, Austin, 121
Dalai Lama, 9, 45, 49n12, 51, 54, 64, 75–78, 79, 101n18, 127, 128, 132–33, 144, 232, 247–48, 258n166
Daley, Brian, 38
Dallmayr, Fred, 144n148
Dalyrimple, William, 87
Danner, Mark, 199n79, 200n79
Darwin, Charles, 12
Davies, Brian, 124n38
Davies, Norman, 159, 162
Dawkins, Richard, 14, 143
Day, Abby, 123
D'Costa, Gavin, 70–71, 76, 79–80, 86
De Roover, Jakob, 128n56
De Waal, Frans, 216n151, 263n181
Delbo, Charlotte, 178, 179n146, 243
Deloria, Vine, Jr, 61
Demick, Barbara, 199n78
Deneyer, Simon, 186n16
Derrida, Jacques, 239n66
Desmond, Matthew, 171n92, 182, 209–12, 217
Dickens, Charles, 22
Dietrich, Donald J., 81n81
Dith Pran, 241
Doad, Mohamad, 203
Donaldson, Laura E., 164n80
Doniger, Wendy, 48, 88, 128n56, 154
Dostoyevsky, Fyodor, 239n69
Dratch, Mark, 250, 251–52
Du Bois, W.E.B., 170
Dube, Musa W., 68n10, 164n80
duBois, Page, 244
Dubuc, Marianne, 96
Duck, Waverly, 175–76, 178
Duffey, Michael K., 234n41
Dunbar-Ortiz, 159n56
Duneier, Mitchell, 158n48

NAME INDEX

Dupré, Louis, 139
Dupuis, Jacques, 72, 80–81
Durham, E. Cole, Jr., 117n4
Dworkin, Ronald, 140, 141–42, 143n145
Dyson, Michael Eric, 165, 173n111

Eagleton, Terry, 13, 120n14, 130
Eck, Diana L., 82n82, 95, 102n30
Edin, Kathryn J., 37n97
Einstein, Albert, 13, 16, 141–42
Eiseley, Loren, 14, 56, 56n56, 92–94, 95, 144
Eisenbrandt, Matt, 228n7
Ellacuría, Ignacio, 36
Ellison, Ralph, 171
Enns, Elaine, 235, 238
Epstein, Greg, 134n90
Erasmus, 141n126
Erwin, Steve, 216n151
Esposito, John L., 255n153
Esselen, Christian, 121
Etinson, Adam, 134n89

Fair, Eric, 199n77
Fallada, Hans, 151n4
Fanon, Frantz, 163
Farley, Margaret, 29n46
Fasching, Darrell J., 162n69
Feinstein, Edward, 63n104, 66n2
Felman, Shoshana, 180n1
Fernando, Jude Lal, 59, 62, 212n139
Fiala, Andrew, 249–250
Field, David N., 162n72
Filkins, Dexter, 199n79
Finkel, Evgeny, 180n1
Finlayson, Clive, 12, 151
Firestein, Stuart, 14
Firestone, Reuven, 65
Firth, Lucy, 230n15
Fitzpatrick, Breda, 216n151
Fletcher, Jeannine Hill, 102
Floerke Scheid, Anna, 232
Flores, Nichole M., 178n140
Flynn, Kieran, 25
Fonrobert, Charlotte Elisheva, 101n18
Fonts, Claudia, 183

Forché, Carolyn, 217, 259n171
Forman, James, Jr., 173n108
Formisano, Ronald P., 152n13, 171n97
Fossati, Gaspare and Giuseppe, 87
Foster, Charles, 92n129
Foster, Darren, 167, 168, 169
Fote, Fortunato Leandro, 184
Foulcher, Jane, 32, 32n64, 77, 101n18, 234n38
Francis, Gavin, 63
Francis, Pope, 35, 36, 102, 107, 131, 182, 236, 244
Francisco, Jose Mario, 100n15
Franklin, Benjamin, 8
Frankopan, Peter, 160n60
Frazier, Jessica, 138n112
Fredriksen, Paula, 30n54, 67, 79
Freud, Sigmund, 24, 143
Frey, Robert S, 215n151
Friday, John, 99n8
Froese, Paul, 126n47
Fry, Jason, 147
Fulkerson, Mary McClintock, 161n67
Fullam, Lisa, 10, 40–41, 42n118, 44n127

Galen, Clemens August von, 126
Galileo, 13
Gandhi, Mahatma, 49–50, 64
Gandhi, Mohandas K., 152n11, 246
Gandhi, Rajmohan, 246
Gandsman, Ari, 183n8, 183n9
Garcia, J. Malcolm, 203
Gardella, Liliana, 186n15
Garner, Eric, 178
Gautama, Siddhartha, 52, 91
Gebara, Ivone, 28n37, 42n120, 63n103, 101n18, 163n75
Gellel, Adrian-Mario, 149n1
Gerges, Fawaz A., 157n36
Gest, Justin, 165n83
Gilkey, Langdon, 85n94
Gillis, Chester, 69, 71, 85
Giovanni, Janine di, 209n122
Glass, Charles, 131n72
Gleiser, Mario, 13

NAME INDEX   325

Glover, Jonathan, 161n66
Glowacka, Dorota, 180n1
Goff, Lisa, 170n91
Goffman, Alice, 173–75, 178
Goldenberg, Myrna, 180n1
Goldhagen, Daniel Jonah, 216n151
Golding, William, 134
Goldman, David P., 96n1
Goldstein, Amy, 210n128
Gonzalez, Michelle A., 162n72
Goodstein, Laurie, 236n51
Goodwin, Allison A., 54n43
Gould, Stephen Jay, 12
Gourevitch, Philip, 216n151
Graber, Jennifer, 60n87
Grann, David, 60n82
Gray, Freddie, 178
Greenberg, Irving, 39, 63, 66n2, 72–73, 89–90, 112, 125–26
Greenberg, Michael, 178n139, 209n125
Greenspan, Henry, 182n2
Gregory, Brad, 118–19
Gregory of Nyssa, 28
Grey, Thomas, 156n35
Griego, Dinah, 127n49
Griswold, Charles, 227, 239, 248–49
Groppe, Elizabeth, 28n38, 30n53
Gülen, Fethullah, 26
Gutiérrez, Fernando, 184
Gutíerrez, Gustavo, 144
Gutschow, Kim, 54
Gyatso, Palden, 195n57
Gyger, Pia, 92n127

Haas, Peter, 253
Habakkuk, Prophet, 27
Habermas, Jürgen, 118
Hafetz, Jonathan, 199n77
Halbwachs, Maurice, 157
Halliday, Jon, 195n57
Hamburger, Michael, 222
Hammer, Joshua, 135n95
Hammer, Reuven, 252
Hampton, Jean, 255
Hananiah, Joshua ben, 89
Hanh, Thich Nhat, 12, 51n28, 53n36, 270

Harari, Yuval Noah, 134n91, 135
Harden, Blaine, 238, 239n65
Hardy, Thomas, 259
Hartman, Geoffrey H., 155
Hatzfeld, Jean, 179n147, 216n151, 218, 219n167, 226n4, 231, 242n83, 242n84, 258
Heft, James, 65
Hegel, G.W.F., 159n53
Heidegger, Martin, 5
Henderson, Michael, 250n126
Hennessy, Kate, 150n3
Herbert, Frank, 96n1
Hernández, Eleazar López, 245
Hertzberg, Arthur, 241
Hesburgh, Theodore M., 242
Hibbard, Scott, 118
Hick, John, 80, 270
Hilary of Poitiers, 28
Hill, Johnny Bernard, 31n59
Hill, Marc Lamont, 178n140, 210n126
Himes, Michael J., 37n100
Hinton, David, 260n174
Hinton, Elizabeth, 172n107
Hirsch, Marianne, 157
Hobbes, Thomas, 137, 138
Hochbaum, Nora, 184n11
Hoffman, Eva, 157
Hofmann, Norbert J., 106n45
Holcomb, Melanie, 100n16
Holland, Nancy, 5
Hollenbach, David, 132
Holyoake, George Jacob, 121
Holzer, Harold, 158n47
Homerin, Th. Emil, 26, 90n118
hooks, bell, 171
Houser, R. E., 33, 34
Howard, Thomas Albert, 120n16, 121
Hsün Tzu, 59n78, 134
Huang, Wenguang, 188n22, 196, 196n64
Hugo, Victor, 3n5, 28n38, 28n39, 61n89, 100n17, 131n36, 131n73, 159n55, 182n4, 272n7
Hume, David, 8–9, 46, 131

Hunter, Alan, 246
Hunter, Megan, 243n88
Hurston, Zora Neale, 24
Hutton, James, 56

Idir, Mustafa Ait, 199n77
Ignatieff, Michael, 134n89
Ignatius, 35–39, 45
Ilibagiza, Immaculée, 216n151
Irwin, Lee, 60, 62n95
Isenberg, Nancy, 164n81
Iyengar, Rishi, 186

Jacobs, Steven Leonard, 112, 112n76
Jahanbegloo, Ramin, 248
Jakelić, Slavica, 128n56
Jalabi, Afra, 26, 90n118
James, Henry, 22n7
James I, King of Aragon, 105
Jeffrey, Renée, 237–38
Jenkins, Philip, 87
Ji, Arjan Dev, 47n4
Jian, Guo, 196n65
Jing Lin, 58
Jisheng, Yang, 189n26
John Paul II, Pope, 68n11, 106, 113n85, 236
Johnson, Eric A., 243n86
Johnson, Ian, 191n41
Jones, Prince Carmen, 178
Jordan, Mark D., 31, 31n60
Joyce, James, 226n3
Juergensmeyer, Mark, 127n49

Kadayifci-Orellana, S. Ayse, 255–56
Kafka, Franz, 202
Kaing Guek Eav, 237–38
Kanwal, Jagmeet, 92n127
Karamazov, Ivan, 69
Kärkkäinen, Veli-Matti, 133n86
Kassabova, Kapka, 100n15
Kearns, Rick, 245n94
Kellenbach, Katharina von, 234
Keller, Catherine, 163n79
Kerr, Fergus, 31n58, 133n86
Kessler, Ed, 110n65
Keys, Mary M., 31n62, 32
Khalidi, Tarif, 26

Khalil, Mohammad Hassan, 257
Kiel, Paul, 171n98
Kiernan, Ben, 216n151
Kilby, Jane, 157n39, 180n1
Kim, Yong, 239n65
Kimelman, Reuven, 25
King, Barbara J., 227n5
King, Jay Caspian, 178n141
King, Martin Luther, Jr., 64, 176
King, Ursula, 101n18, 102
Kinzer, Stephen, 222
Kitcher, Philip, 139n115, 140, 142–44
Klancer, Catherine Hudak, 10, 58
Knafo, Saki, 175n123
Kneale, Matthew, 214n146
Knitter, Paul, 68n9, 68n12, 74–75, 81, 185n13
Knust, Jennifer Wright., 254n146
Kogan, Michael S., 89n110, 107, 107n52, 112
Kolbert, Elizabeth, 201n84
Konstan, David, 244n90
Kor, Eva Mozes, 250
Kosicki, Piotr H., 106n46
Krajewski, Stanislaw, 24
Krom, Michael P., 32
Kruse, Kevin M., 119n12
Kuan, Deng, 196–97, 214, 248
Kugel, James, 21n1, 24
Kujawa-Holbrook, Sheryl A., 100n14
Küng, Hans, 79, 97

Landsberg, Alison, 157
Lane, Dermot A., 106, 133n86
Lang, Berel, 161
Langer, Lawrence, 157, 180n1, 182n5, 242–43
Lao Lai Tzu, 57
Lao Yang, 66, 95
Lao-Tzu, 55–56
Lapp, Cynthia, 10
Larrubia, Susana Alicia, 183
Laub, Dori, 180n1
Lawrence, D. H., 8n32, 28n36
Lawrence, David Peter, 48n6
Lear, Jonathan, 59n79

NAME INDEX

Leask, Ian, 124n36
Lederach, Jill, 28n37
Lederach, John Paul, 28n37, 234
Lee, Soon Ok, 239n65
Lee, Sophia, 239n65
Legenhausen, Muhammad, 79
Leisner, Karl, 126
Levi, Primo, 191, 224
Lévinas, Emmanuel, 24–25, 74–75, 130, 217, 258
Levine, Amy-Jill, 110, 110n65, 111n70
Levine, George, 127n49
Levi-Yitzhak of Berditchev, 252
Levoy, Jill, 175n123, 177n132
Lewin, Miriam, 186n15
Lewis, Nancy, 170n86
Lewis, Ralph, 142n140
Lewis-Krauss, Gideon, 174n120
Leydesdorff, Selma, 153n19
Leys, Ruth, 24n16
Li Po, 56–57
Lightman, Alan, 142n140
Lim, Louisa, 155, 186, 187n18
Linderman, Frank B., 59, 59n79
Linenthal, Edward, 157
Liu Shahe, 188, 195
Livio, Mario, 12, 56n55
Lloyd, Vincent, 127n49, 171n95
Long, Jeffrey D., 88
Loomba, Ania, 162n72
López, Antonio, 79n3
Lopez, Donald S., 52n32
Lower, Wendy, 158
Lubet, Steven, 174n120
Lyell, Charles, 56
Lynch, Tom, 92n128
Lyotard, Jean-François, 161

Maass, Peter, 199n78
MacCulloch, Diarmaid, 36
MacGregor, Neil, 99
MacIntyre, Alasdair, 6, 8, 233n33
Maclure, Jocelyn, 128–29
MacMillan, Margaret, 154, 159n54
Madan, T. N., 128
Madigan, Daniel, 84
Maggid of Mezeritch, 62

Maher, Susan Naramore, 92n128
Mahmood, Saba, 129n63
Maier, Charles S., 154n25
Maimonides, 39, 89n111, 91, 222, 252–53
Mallet, Victor, 51n26
Mao Zedong, 188
Margalit, Avishai, 157, 231–32
Marshall, Christopher, 235
Marshall, Tim, 198n75
Martin, James, 37n99, 42n121
Marx, Karl, 119
Marx, William, 54n45
Mary, mother of Jesus, 27–28
Matthäus, Jürgen, 180n1
Maxey, Jillian, 102n27
May, John D'Arcy, 60n82
May, Todd, 140
Mayer, Jane, 199n79, 200
McCarthy, Cormac, 260n172
McCullough, Michael, 263
McDaniel, Jay Byrd, 49n15, 79n59
McDonald-Gibson, Charlotte, 131n72
McEntee, Rory, 101n18
McEvoy, James Gerard, 79n60, 124n36
McGinn, Bernard, 31n58
McGraw, Tug, 116
McGregor, Jena, 54n42
McInerney, Joseph J., 10
McMaster, Johnston, 87n104
Meier, Christian, 163n74
Meiri, Menahem, 89n112
Mellor, David, 230n15
Menahem-Mendl of Kotzk, 23
Menchú, Rigoberta, 61–62
Mencius, 58n69, 59, 246
Mendelsohn, Daniel, 200
Mendham, Matthew, 138n109
Merrigan, Terrence, 99n8
Merton, Thomas, 33n76, 33n78
Meszler, Joseph B., 101n18
Metz, Johann Baptist, 153, 157
Mian Mir (Mohammed Muayyinul Islam), 47n4
Michel, Thomas, 90n115
Míguez, Pabló, 183

328 NAME INDEX

Mikics, David, 222n179
Millbank, John, 97n4
Millen, Rochelle L., 180n1
Millies, Steven P., 172n104
Milosz, Czeslaw, 217n157
Milton, John, 259n171
Milton, Trevor B., 152n12
Min, Anselm K., 78, 79, 80
Mitchell, Donald, 101n20
Mittleman, Alan L., 105n42
Mo Zi (Master Mo), 246
Moffic, Evan, 75n31
Mohan, Rohini, 182, 212–14, 217
Montaigne, 8, 8n32, 263n184
Moore, Natalie Y., 171n92
Morali, Ilaria, 97n4
Morduch, Jonathan, 210n128
Morrison, Toni, 170
Moses, 24
Moskowitz, Peter, 174n116
Moyaert, Marianne, 103–4
Muhammad, Prophet, 26–27
Mullet, Etienne, 246n108
Munyankore, Jean Baptiste, 258
Murphy, Jeffrie G., 237, 239, 255n148
Mwanankabandi, Berthe, 258
Myers, Ched, 235, 238
Myers, PZ, 124

Nabokov, Vladimir, 191
Nagy, Rosemary, 221n175
Nahman, Moshe ben (Nachmanides), 105
Narchison, J. Rosario, 127–28
Nasser, Ilham, 255n151, 257n156
Nausner, Michael, 163n79
Neihardt, John, 62, 62n95
Nelson, Daniel M., 10, 24
Neto, Félix, 246n108
Neufeldt, Ronald, 89n109
Neuffer, Elizabeth, 216n151
Neugebauery, Richard, 221n175
Neusner, Jacob, 111, 113
Newbigin, Lesslie, 78n58
Newton, Isaac, 13
Nguyen, Viet Thanh, 157
Nielsen, Kai, 135

Nietzsche, Friedrich, 9, 11, 130, 155, 244, 245
Nixon, Nicholas, 63
Niyonsaba, Cassius, 218
Nora, Pierre, 153
Norenzayan, Ara, 133n87
Norman, Richard, 124n38
Noroña, Hector Pablo, 183
Norridge, Zoe, 209n122
Nouwen, Henri J. M., 280
Ntaganira, Joseph, 221n175
Nussbaum, Martha, 261

Obama, Barack, 172n104
Obreque, Sauro Antonio, 183
O'Connell, Caitlyn, 263
Ogden, Schubert, 85
Ohnuma, Reiko, 52n32
Okeowo, Alexis, 216n152
O'Leary, Joseph, 247
Omar, Irfan A., 234n41
O'Neill, Kevin Lewis, 182n2
Oppel, Richard A., Jr., 178n141
Origen, 28
Orwell, George, 144, 191, 202
Osnos, Evan, 187n18
Osterhammel, Jürgen, 159
Ozick, Cynthia, 182n5, 241

Panikkar, Raimundo, 67, 79, 80, 100, 128, 144
Pappas, Stephanie, 102n28
Pardue, Stephen T., 28n38, 30n53, 114n87
Parry, Richard Lloyd, 209n122
Partnoy, Alicia, 183n8
Pascal, 11, 21n2, 45–46
Patterson, David, 75, 111, 112, 113, 161n61, 184n10, 251
Patt-Shamir, Galia, 58n73
Paul, St., 104, 107
Paulson, Ronald, 134n88
Paz, Regina, 246n108
Peace, Jennifer, 98n7
Peelman, Achiel, 60n85
Peterson, Rodney L., 233n35
Phan, Peter C., 79n59, 89, 152n11, 270–71

NAME INDEX   329

Phillips, D. Z., 143n145
Phillips, Trevor, 172n104
Philpott, Daniel, 87n104
Philpott, David, 235–36, 250
Piazza, Mike, 116
Piketty, Thomas, 47, 144
Pilario, Daniel Franklin, 158n42
Pinckney, Darryl, 177n136, 178n140
Ping, Chou, 57n62
Pinker, Steven, 134n90, 201n84
Pinnock, Sarah K., 144n147
Plaskow, Judith, 101n18
Plato, 7
Pokorny, Jennifer J., 263n181
Pollefeyt, Didier, 106n50, 230, 235, 258n161, 258n162, 260
Poorthuis, Marcel J.H.M., 106n45
Pope, Stephen J., 37n100, 45n144, 235n44, 238
Porter, Bill, 51, 66
Povoledo, Elisabetta, 107n54, 236n51
Pozen, Joanna, 221n175
Pratt, Douglas, 85–86, 105n41
Pretty-shield, 59
Prevo, Andrew, 171n95
Puchner, Martin, 119n13
Pui-lan, Kwok, 164n80
Puri, Jasbir Singh, 47n4

Que Yao, 193

Rahner, Karl, 133
Rambachan, Anantanand, 49
Rankin, Aidan, 47n4
Raphael, Melissa, 25
Ratushinskaya, Irina, 261
Rawls, John, 118, 129, 144
Rectenwald, Michael, 127n49
Reda, Mario, 44n130
Redbanks, James, 151n6
Regan, Ethna, 133n86
Renard, John, 256n155, 257n159
Reuband, Karl-Heinz, 243n86
Rex, Adam, 96
Rice, Tamir, 178
Rich, Nathaniel, 60n84
Richards, Norvin, 10–11

Ricoeur, Paul, 229
Ridgeon, Lloyd, 255n153
Rieger, Joerg, 82–83, 162n72, 164n80
Rios, Victor M., 176n125
Rittner, Carol, 218n164
Rivera, Joseph, 116n1
Rivera, Mayra, 163n79
Roberts, Robert C., 10
Robinson, James A., 70
Robinson, Randall, 177n136
Rogers, Murray, 48n7
Rorty, Richard, 132
Rose, Or N., 89, 98n7
Rosenfeld, Alvin, 182
Rosenthal, Gilbert S., 89n112, 108n58
Rosin, Hannah, 101n18
Rosling, Hans, 270n2
Roth, Harold D., 55n50
Roth, John K., 151n4, 161n61, 218n164
Rothberg, Michael, 157
Rousseau, Jean-Jacques, 137, 138
Rowland, Antony, 157n39, 180n1, 217n157
Rubin, Sergio, 107n55
Rubio, Julie Hanlon, 36n96
Rudin, Rabbi, 70, 111, 112n71
Rumi, 1
Rumsfeld, Donald, 203
Runciman, David, 198n75
Ruse, Michael, 16, 124n38, 139, 140, 142
Russell, Letty M., 164n80
Ruston, Roger, 105n44
Ruttenberg, Jim, 171
Rwigema, Marie-Jolie, 216n151
Rwililiza, Innocent, 242
Ryan, Alan, 122, 159n53, 160n59
Ryan, Mike, 169
Ryan, Phil, 132

Sacks, Jonathan, 16, 89, 92n127, 233n33
Sadler, Gregory, 32n66
Safina, Carl, 13, 263
Sagan, Carl, 14

Said, Edward W., 163
Samway, Patrick, 161n68
Saunders, George, 151n4
Saunders, Rebecca, 238n60
Scalmer, Sean, 64n109
Scanlon, Michael, 137n102
Scarry, Elaine, 205n101
Schaab, Gloria L., 120n15
Schaefer, H. Luke, 37n97
Schama, Simon, 269n1
Schiavenza, Matt, 200n83
Schmid, Muriel, 234n41
Schmidt-Leukel, Perry, 74n27, 81n78
Schneider, Rachel, 210n128
Schreiter, Robert J., 244n89
Schulweis, Harold M., 63n104, 66, 66n2
Schweizer, Bernard, 24n16
Scruton, Roger, 123n33
Seattle, Chief, 62
Sen, Amartya, 128
Sen, Keshab Chunder, 89
Senauke, Alan, 51n28
Seromba, Athanase, 221
Shachnow, Sidney, 241
Shah, Timothy Samuel, 87n104, 119n11, 137n102
Shakespeare, 23n11, 56, 56n56
Shannon, Lisa J., 209n123
Shanor, Karen, 92n127
Shapiro, Joseph, 200n83
Sharma, Arvind, 67, 78n56, 79
Shelby, Tommie, 173n108
Shelly, Christine, 223
Shen Zhou, 56
Shenker, Noah, 180n1
Shepard, Kris, 64n110
Sherwin, Byron, 112
Shin In Guen, 238–39
Shook, John, 117n3
Shun, Kwong-loi, 245
Siems, Larry, 203n90, 204, 205
Sievers, Joseph, 106n45
Sifton, John, 70n16
Singer, Peter, 135n96
Singh, Nidhi, 47n4
Sirry, Mun'im, 90n118

Skaggs, John, 175
Skjaervo, Prods Oktor, 47n4
Skorka, Abraham, 107, 107n55
Skye, Lee Miena, 60
Slahi, Mohamedou Ould, 182, 199, 200, 201, 202–8
Smith, Buster G., 126n47
Smith, James K. A., 124n36
Smith, Mark A., 136n100
Smith, Mychal Denzel, 172n104
Snyder, Timothy, 154, 184
Soboslai, John, 127n49
Sobrino, Jon, 22, 68, 83n84, 239n67, 258
Socrates, 7
Sollange, Umwali, 216n151
Solomon, Erika, 131n72
Solzhenitsyn, Alexander, 224
Soulen, R. Kendall, 79n60
Spadaro, Antonio, 222n179
Speer, Albert, 242
Spence, Graham, 21n1, 263n185
Spinney, Joseph, 165
Spinoza, Baruch, 8, 137, 138
Staples, Fiona, 96
Stedman, Chris, 124n38, 139–140
Stein, Arlene, 157, 158n43
Steinbeck, John, 11
Stemple, Laura, 205n103
Steuber, Jason, 56n60
Stevenson, Bryan, 176–77
Stier, Oren Baruch, 157
Stolberg, Sheryl Gay, 178n141
Stone, Dan, 153n19, 157, 182n2
Stout, Jeffrey, 137, 143
Stover, Eric, 180n1, 238n60
Sugirtharajah, R. S., 89n108, 160n58, 164n80
Suleiman, Susan Rubin, 182n5
Sullivan, Michael, 56n61
Suzman, James, 60n81
Swanepoel, Elizabeth, 54n43
Swidler, Leonard, 79, 100n7
Swindal, James, 131

Tabor, Damon, 240n72
Taliaferro, Charles, 28n40
Talib, Abi, Ali b., 91

NAME INDEX 331

Tan, Jonathan Y., 152n11
Tan, Shaun, 272n8
Tang, Edmond, 97n4
Tang, Quin Qing, 195n57
Tarfon, Rabbi, 25
Taylor, Charles, 118, 122–23, 124, 128–29, 143, 162
Taylor, Lisa, 216n151
Taylor, Mark, 162
Taylor-Guthrie, Danielle, 170n88
Telushkin, Joseph, 24, 78n57
Tennent, Timothy, 81n81
Teresa of Ávila, 40–46, 146n149
Tertullian, 120
Thackeray, William Makepeace, 11, 258, 258n167
Thanegi, Ma, 63, 208n120, 238
Thatamanil, John M., 53, 53n35
Thiemann, Ronald, 135n97, 138, 139n113
Thomas, Biggar, 171, 176
Thomas, David, 90n118
Thomas, Laurence, 255n149
Thomas, of Aquinas. *See* Aquinas
Thomas, R. S., 11
Thomas-Lester, 169n85
Thomson, Susan, 221n175
Tian Zhiguang, 196
Tillich, Paul, 13, 69n14
Tillinghast, Richard, 151n7
Tinker, Tink, 61
Tokar, Elisa, 186n15
Tolkien, J.R.R., 96
Torrano, Graciela Beatriz, 184
Toumani, Meline, 173n113
Tracy, David, 51n27, 84–85, 97, 129–130, 161, 163
Trawick, Margaret, 51n26
Trezise, Thomas, 180n1
Trible, Phyllis, 164n80
Trollope, Anthony, 228
Trump, Donald, 165, 171, 172n104, 208
Tu Fu, 56
Turner, Judith, 31n57
Tutu, Desmond, 231, 232, 255n149, 258n166

Ueda, Shizuteru, 108n57
Ueshiba, Morihei, 262n179
Umubyeyi, Sylvie, 242
Uwanyiligira, Edith, 231

Valkenberg, Pim, 97n3
Vallely, Paul, 35, 107n55
VanAntwerpen, Jonathan, 124n36
Vance, J.D., 165n83
Vanhoozer, Kevin J., 63
Vaughan, Brian K., 96
Vaughan, Olufemi, 127n49
Veblen, Thorstein, 119
Volf, Miroslav, 156n34, 239n67
von Brück, Michael, 64, 78n56
Vulliamy, Ed, 199n78

Walsh, David, 130n71
Ward, Eddie (pseudonym), 169
Warner, Michael, 124n36
Wartofsky, Alona, 170n86
Watson, Peter, 124
Watterson, Bill, 141n129
Waxman, Zoë Vania, 180n1
Weber, Max, 119
Webster, John C. B., 49n15
Weil, Simone, 45, 51n25
Weissman, Debbie, 102n28
Whitehead, Colson, 165n82
Whitney, Karl, 225n2
Whitworth, Wendy, 218n164
Wiesel, Elie, 22–23, 25, 62, 63, 161, 182, 222–23, 224, 252
Wiesenthal, Simon, 232n29, 241, 248n110
Wieviorka, Annette, 180n1
WikiLeaks, 200n79
Wilgoren, Debbi, 169–170
Wilhite, David E., 28n41, 30n56
Willaime, Jean-Paul, 121
Williams, Robert R., 32n66
Williams, Rowan, 97n5
Williams, Trevor, 152n12
Wink, Walter, 255n147
Wiseman, James, 101n20
Wohlleben, Peter, 22n4, 68n8
Wolfendale, Jessica, 200n79
Wood, Nancy, 157

Woodbine, Onaje X.O., 167n84
Wooden, Cindy, 107n56
Woodhead, Linda, 123
Worthington, Everett L., Jr., 233n35
Wright, Richard, 171n94
Wu, Duncan, 217, 259n171
Wu, Harry Hongada., 195n57
Wu Yongsheng, 194

Yadlapati, Madhuri M., 26, 48, 67n4
Yang (Chinese prisoner), 188n22
Yardley, Jim, 149n2
Yerushalmi, Yosef Hayim, 153n17
Yilmaz, Ihsan, 255n153
Yingji Wangwe, 58
Yiwu, Liao, 182, 187–198, 209, 214n144, 238, 248n116
Yongyi Song, 196n65

Young, James, 157, 180n1
Yuan Xiangchen, 196
Yuan Zhou, 196n65
Yu-Hsi, Chen, 53

Zelizer, Barbie, 157
Zhang, Hansong, 233n34
Zhang, Ping, 58n73
Zhang, Qianfan, 54–55, 57
Zhang Yinxian, 195
Zhu Xi, 58
Ziegler, Dominic, 57n63
Zim, Rivkah, 191n39
Zinn, Howard, 159n56
Zuckerman, Phil, 117n3, 121n24, 133n83, 136
Zusia, Rebbe, 23

Subject Index

action less action (*wu-wei*), 55, 57
African Americans
   civil rights, 171
   evictions of, 209–12
   imprisonment, 172–73, 176–77, 178
   police brutality and, 174–75, 178
   poverty, 175–76, 178
After the New Atheist Debate (Ryan), 132
Against Forgetting: Twentieth Century Poetry of Witness (Forché), 217
ahimsa, meaning of, 50–51
American Revolution, 119. *See also* United States
"Améry, Levi, Wiesel: the Futility of Holocaust Testimony" (Rosenfeld), 182
Amish community, 200
The Analects (Confucius), 57, 245–46
animal rights, 267
animals, forgiveness in, 262–66
animals, humility in, 267
anthropocentric belief, 123
Antigone (Sophocles), 244
anti-memory, 155
The Apology (Socrates), 7
apophatic theology, 137
Aquinas, 31–35
Argentina, 183–86
Argentina, Buenos Aires (state terrorism), 183–85
asceticism, 44, 53

At the Limits of the Secular: Reflections on Faith and Public Life (Tracy), 129
atheism
   companion of belief, 139
   ethics, 130–33, 140
   faitheists, 139–40
   forgiveness, 248–50
   humility, 134–38, 139–41
   religious atheists, 140, 141–44
   soft atheism, 143
   values, 133–34
atheist-theist dialogue. *See* secular-religious dialogue
A/Theology (Taylor), 162
atonement theory, 50
atrocities. *See* testimonies of mass atrocity
attachments, material, 36
Augustine, 28–30
Autobiography (Gandhi), 49

Baghdad, Iraq, torture in, 200
basketball coaching (author), 166–170
Battlestar Galactica (television series), 94–95
Beatitudes. *See* Sermon on the Mount
Beijing, (Tiananmen Square). China, 186–87, 188, 190
belief
   companion of atheism, 139
   ethics, 130–33
belief without belonging, 123

333

334 SUBJECT INDEX

Benedictus (Catholicism), 223
benevolence (ren), 58
Between the World and Me (Coates), 177
Beyond Religion (Dalai Lama), 78
Beyond Religion: Ethics for a Whole World (Dalai Lama), 127
Bhagavad Gita, 48–50, 55
bhakti yoga, 48
Billy Twitters and His Blue Whale Problem (Barnet and Rex), 96
Black Panther (comic book), 177
Bleak House (Dickens), 22
Bodhisattvas, 52
The Book of Chuang Tzu, 56–57
Bosnia, Sarajevo, (Serbian bombing of 1999), 199n78
brokenness
    causes of, 269–72
    forgiveness and, 228, 260–61
    humility in acknowledging, 126
    racism, 177
The Brothers Karamozov (Dostoyevsky), 239
Buddhism
    China, 196–97
    Engaged Buddhism, 51
    forgiveness, 246–48
    humility and, 51–54
    The Middle Way, Buddhism, 53, 91
    pluralism and, 76–78, 79
    Sri Lanka, 214
Buenos Aires, Argentina (state terrorism), 183–85

Calvin and Hobbes (Watterson), 141
Cambodia
    killing fields, 241
    Toul Sleng Prison, 237–38
Capital in the Twenty-First Century (Piketty), 144
Catholic Church
    China, 195
    historical development, 118–20
    in Ireland, 124
    in Malta, 148–49
    post-Vatican II, 120
    Rwandan genocide and, 219
    Second Ecumenical Council of the Vatican, 31
    social teaching, 132
CDF (Congregation for the Doctrine of the Faith), 84, 107
Charlottesville, VA (white supremacists rally), 171
chimpanzees, forgiveness and, 263, 265, 266
China
    Buddhism, 196–97
    Christianity, 194–96, 238
    forgiveness, 247–48
    prison abuses, 186–98
    testimonies of mass atrocity, 186–98
Christianity
    Aquinas, magnanimity, 31–35
    Augustine, 28–30
    in China, 194–96, 238
    forgiveness, 238, 253–55
    Gospels, humility and, 27–28
    of Guantánamo guards, 207
    historical development, 118–22
    humility and, 8
    Ignatian humility, 35–39
    interfaith presentation, 270–71
    Jewish view of Jesus, 111–14
    moral failure, 219
    Rwandan genocide and, 218–23
    Teresa of Ávila, 40–46
    on unbelief, 138–39
    views of interfaith dialogue, 103–4
Chuang-Tzu (story of), 54
church buildings, atrocities at, 220
The City of God (Augustine), 8, 30
civil rights, rollbacks, 171. See also racism
classics, dialogue with, 129–30
classism, 165–66
Communist Manifesto (Marx and Engels), 136
compassion
    as attribute of pluralism, 75–78

SUBJECT INDEX   335

practicality of, 133
Confessions (Augustine), 29–30
Confucianism
   forgiveness, 245–46
   humility and, 57–59
Congregation for the Doctrine of the Faith (CDF), 84, 107
contemplative prayer, 40
corporate culture, humility in, 5
The Corpse Walker: Real-Life Stories from the Bottom Up (Liao Yiwu), 187, 193–94
"Cosas del Rio" (Gutiérrez), 184
creation, God's presence in, 120, 130, 145–46

Dabru Emet (Jewish document), 109
death
   acceptance of, 143–44
   inequality in, 156–57
"The Declaration on the Rights of Indigenous Peoples: (UN document), 60
democratic humility, 5–6
dialogical attribute of pluralism, 81–82
dialogue. *See* interfaith dialogue
"Dialogue Decalogue" (Swidler), 99
dialogue of life, 81, 100, 102
Dies Irae (Catholicism), 219, 221
dignity
   metaphysical conception of, 134
   of the poor, 40–41
the disappeared of Argentina, 183–86
Discalced Carmelite Nuns, Constitution, 42–43
Disputation of Barcelona (1263), 105
Dives in Misericordia (John Paul II), 236
Dominus Iesus (CDF doctrine), 84, 107
doubt, 284
dread, 19, 269
Dublin Zoo, 225–27, 262–67

East of Eden (Steinbeck), 11–12

Eckhardian spirituality, 45
ecumenical secularism, 118
The Education of Little Tree (Carter), 60
egotistical humility, 11
elephants
   the blind men story, 1–2
   forgiveness and, 263–66
empathy
   defined, 58
   in interfaith dialogue, 103
Engaged Buddhism, 51
Enlightenment philosophy
   humility, 137–38
   secularizing effect of, 119, 122, 125
epistemic humility, 5
epistemological humility, 103
Escuela de Mecánica de la Armada (ESMA), 185–86
ethics
   atheist, 140
   and belief, 130–33
   of dialogue, 129
   responsibility, 130
   secular, 78, 127
The Ethics of Memory (Margalit), 157
Eucharist, 219, 220, 222
Europe
   refugee migrants, 149
   religious climate, 120–21
evangelization, 83–84, 107–8. *See also* missionaries
Evicted: Poverty and Profit in the American City (Desmond), 182, 212
evictions from homes, 209–12
exclusivism, disguised as pluralism, 85–88
Exodus (Tanakh), 252
Ezekiel (Prophet), 158, 221, 252

The F Word Exhibition, 231
faith, science and, 12–16
faitheists, 139–140
false humility, 11–12, 44

feminists, 10
Fetullah Gülen movement, 87
Finnegan's Wake (Joyce), 226
The Fire Next Time (Baldwin), 172, 177
For a Song and a Hundred Songs: A Poet's Journey through a Chinese Prison (Liao Yiwu), 182, 187–93
forgetting, 154–56. *See also* memory
forgiveness
    among faiths and cultures, 243–57
    humility and, 226–29, 233–34, 239, 258–62
    levels of, 229–32, 251
    limits of, 226, 237–43
    love and, 259–60
    non-human, 262–64, 265–66
    questions on, 227–28
    restorative justice, 234–37
    of self, 261
    victim centering, 232–33, 235
Forgiveness Project, 231
Four Noble Truths, 53
fragilization, 162
France, secularism, 119, 121
From the Holy Mountain (Dalyrimple), 87

gender
    evictions and, 209–10
    interfaith dialogue and, 101–2
    memory and, 158
    racism and, 160
Genesis (Tanakh), 252
"Genesis: The Source of the Nile" (poem), 219
genocide
    Rwanda, 212–23, 231, 242
    Sri Lanka, 212–15
Ggantija temple, Malta, 149–50
Global Ethic Foundation, 79
Glorious Revolution of 1688, England, 70
God
    debate on need for, 137–38

    forgiveness by, 251–52, 255–57
    human dignity from, 134
    Liao Yiwu on, 190–91
    love for humanity, 270
    postmodernism, 161–62
    presence among the broken, 218
    presence in creation, 120, 130, 145–46
    presence in the world, 120, 130, 145–46
    unforgivable acts and, 240, 241–42, 253. *See also* belief
God is Red: The Secret Story of How Christianity Survived and Flourished in Communist China (Liao Yiwu), 187, 194–95
godless humility, 22–23, 130–33
gorillas, forgiveness and, 263, 265
Gospel in Solentiname (Cardenal), 230
The Gospel of Solentiname (Cardenal), 27
grace, 146
Greece, forgiveness, 244
Guantánamo Bay Prison, 202–8
Guantánamo Diary (Slahi), 182, 203–8

Hagia Sophia, Istanbul, Turkey, 87
Haiti, Rwandans supporting, 222
Hillel (Telushkin), 24
Hinduism
    forgiveness, 246
    humility and, 48–51
    pluralism and, 88
history
    Christianity, 118–22
    ethics, 154–56
    humbling effect, 151–53, 155–56, 158–59, 164–65
    memory's connection with, 153–54
    as pardon, 164
    pluralism, 119–20, 162–63
    postcolonialism, 163–64
    postmodernism, 161–62

poverty, 159–160
reckoning on racism, 177–78
secularism, 118–122. *See also*
testimonies of mass atrocity
A History of the World in 100 Objects
(MacGregor), 99
Hitler's Furies (Lower), 158
Holocaust. *See* Shoah
hope
  inconstant, 104–7
  interreligious, 107–8, 115
housing as fundamental need,
  211–12
"The Human Abstract" (Blake), 9
humanism, 248–250. *See also*
  atheism
humble attribute of pluralism, 72
humble pride, 124, 155
humility
  in acknowledging brokenness,
    126
  atheism, 139–141
  atheist, 134–38
  critics of, 6–11
  democratic, 5–6
  egotistical, 11
  epistemic, 5
  false, 11–12, 44
  forgiveness and, 226–27, 228–
    29, 233–34, 239, 258–262
  godless, 22–23, 130–33
  history's effect on, 151–53, 155–
    56, 158–59, 164–65
  humbling, meaning of, 3–6
  humiliating and, 4–5
  Ignatian, 35–39
  intellectual, 6
  Kantian, 5
  non-human, 267
  prideful, 11, 62–65
  secular, 136–37
  servile, 11
humor, 141
Hutus, in Rwanda, 219–21

Ignatian humility, 35–39
ignorance, intellectual, 7
Iliad (Homer), 244

*The Im-possibility of Interreligious
  Dialogue* (Cornille), 103
imprisonment of African
  Americans, 172–73, 176–77,
  178
inclusive pluralism, 80
India, secularism, 127–28
indigenous faiths, 59–62
indigenous forgiveness, 244–45
Indroit (Catholicism), 219
injustice, rebuking, 73
Insein Prison, Myanmar, 238
intellectual humility, 6
intellectual ignorance, 7
intellectual virtues, 32
interfaith dialogue
  Christianity's appreciation for
    Judaism, 108–14
  gender and, 101–2
  generally, 96–99
  humility and, 102–4
  inconstant hope, 104–7
  interreligious hope, 107–8, 115
  types of, 99–101
The Interior Castle (Teresa of Ávila),
  40
intermonastic dialogue, 101
interreligious hope, 107–8
intrapersonal dialogue, 100
Invisible Man (Ellison), 171
Iraq, Baghdad, torture in, 200
Ireland, secularization, 124
Islam
  Bosnia, 199n78
  five pillars of, 26
  forgiveness, 255–57
  humility, 25–27
  in Malta, 148–51
  The Middle Way, Buddhism, 91
  pluralism and, 79, 88–92
  post-9/11 reaction to, 199–200,
    202, 206–7, 208
  on unbelief, 138

Jainism, 47n4
Jeremiah (Prophet), 158
Jesuit Volunteer Corps (JVC),
  35–37, 39

Jesus Christ
   betrayal of, 220
   as broken, 218
   as ethical guide, 132
   forgiving nature, 253–55
   humility, 160
   as The King, 131
   as Messiah, 111–14
   presence of, 145–46
   second coming, 130
   as Silenus, 141n126
The Jewish Annotated New Testament (Levine and Brettler), 110
Jewish decide, annulled, 110
Jewish-Christian dialogues, 97–98, 107, 109
John (Gospel), 254
John the Baptist, 223
Jonah (Prophet), 252
Joshua (Tanakh), 252
Judaism
   Christianity's appreciation for, 108–11
   conceptions of humility, 8
   forgiveness, 250–53
   on Jesus as Messiah, 111–14
   Jewish Covenant, 85, 106–7, 109
   moderation, 91
   pluralism and, 88–92
   Tanach, 23–25, 110
Judas Iscariot, 220
"The Judgment of the Birds" (Eiseley), 92
June 4th Beijing Massacre, 186–87, 188, 190
just attribute of pluralism, 72–75
Just Mercy (Stevenson), 176–77
justice
   legal, 32
   rebuking injustice, 73
   relational, 77
   restorative, 234–37
   social-justice dialogue, 100

Kantian humility, 5
karma, 133
karma yoga, 49
The King (God), 131

Knights Hospitaller of St. John of Jerusalem, 148–49

Lacrimosa (Catholicism), 221
"Landmines and Vegetables: The Hope and Perils of Recent Jewish Critiques of Christianity" (Admirand), 109–10
The Last of Us (video game), 96
The Laws of Repentance (Maimonides), 252–53
leadership level dialogue, 101
Learned Ignorance (Firestone), 65
legal justice, 32
"Let my rejoicing be in tears" (poem), 42–43
Let Us Now Praise Famous Men (Agee), 11
liberation theology, 74, 112, 159–60, 163
Liberia, civil war atrocities, 240–41
life, dialogue of, 100
Life After Faith: The Case for Secular Humanism (Kitcher), 142–44
The Life of Teresa (Teresa of Ávila), 40
The Lion and the Bird (Dubuc), 96
The Lord of the Flies (Golding), 134
The Lord of the Rings (Tolkien), 96
The Lost History of Christianity (Jenkins), 87
love, 259–260, 270, 272
Luke (Gospel), 223

Machete Season (Hatzfeld), 258
magnanimity, humility balanced by, 31–35
Mahabharata (Hindu literature), 246
Malta, historical context, 148–151
The Many Altars of Modernity (Berger), 125
marginalized
   equality as silencing, 82–83
   women an, 10
Mark (Gospel), 160, 254

Mary, mother of Jesus, 27–28
Mass Effect (video game), 96
"Massacre" (Liao Yiwu), 187
Matthew (Gospel), 131, 160, 254
Mean, as a moral virtue, 58
memory
    of the dead, 156–57
    ethics, 154–56
    history's connection with, 153–54
    theories of, 157–58. See also history; testimonies of mass atrocity
Merovingian Court, 229
Mexico, indigenous people in, 244–45
Middle Ages
    Jewish population in Spain, 269
    Jewish tradition of pluralism developed, 89
    use of "secular," 118
The Middle Way, Buddhism, 53, 91–92
mindfulness, 53
missionaries, 59–62, 83–84, 89, 105
. See also evangelization
monkish virtues, 8–9, 46
moral failure, 199–201, 219–221, 224
moral indifference, 83–84
morality. See ethics
mortality. See death
Moses, Man of the Mountain (Hurston), 24
Moses and Monotheism (Freud), 24
Muhammed (Prophet), 256–57
multiple secularisms, 127
mutual complementarity, 81
"My Dungeon Shook" (Baldwin), 177
Myanmar, Insein Prison, 238

Native Americans, 59–62
nature, pluralism in, 92–94
Navy Petty-Officers School of Mechanics (ESMA), 185–86
Neolithic people, 150
"New Atheism" (Davies), 124

The New Jim Crow (Alexander), 172–73, 177
New York Mets, 116–17, 147
Nichomachean Ethics (Aristotle), 32, 91
Nickel Mines, Pennsylvania (Amish school girls), 200
1984 (Orwell), 202
No Way Out: Precarious Living in the Shadow of Poverty and Drug Dealing (Duck), 175–76
noble eight-fold path, 53
North Korea, prison camps, 238–39
Nostra Aetate (Vatican II document), 105–6
Notes of a Native Son (Baldwin), 172
Notre Dame de l'Atlas (Trappist monastery), 19
Numbers (Tanakh), 252

"Of Studies" (Bacon), 158
On Politics (Ryan), 122
"On Yellow-Crane Tower" (Li Po), 56–57
ontological pluralism, 79, 80
open secularism, 128
"Orthodox Rabbinic Statement on Christianity" (Jewish document), 109
overlapping consensus, 129
The Oxford Handbook of Atheism, 142

panentheisim, defined, 120
pantheism, defined, 120
pardon, history as, 164
Parque de la Memoria, Buenos Aires, 183–85
People's Tribunal on Sri Lanka, 212
Pesahim (Talmud), 252
philosophical level of dialogue, 100–101
pluralism. See religious pluralism
pluriform plurality, 80
"Poet on a Mountaintop" (painting), 56

340 SUBJECT INDEX

Poetry of Witness: The English Tradition 1500-2001 (Wu), 217
police brutality, 174–75, 178
polyabsolutism, 80
poor, option for, 130, 159–60
postcolonialism history, 163–64
postmodernism, 161–62
poverty
    among African Americans, 175–76, 178
    evictions' effect on, 209–12
pride, 33–34, 62–65
prideful humility, 11
priests, in Rwanda, 220–21
primal faiths, 59–62
prisoner violence, 192–94
Psalms, 252
publicness, forms of, 129–30
punishment, 234–36

Qur'an, 90–91, 111n68, 113, 206–7, 256

racism
    author's experience, 165–70
    civil rights rollbacks, 171
    eviction and, 209–12
    gender and, 160
    imprisonment, 172–73, 176–77, 178
    neighborhood effects, 175–76
    persistence of, 170–72
    police brutality, 174–75
    reckoning on, 177–78
raja yoga, 49
Ramayana (Hindu literature), 246
The Ransom of the Soul: Afterlife and Wealth in Early Western Christianity (Brown), 229
rational inquiry, 129
reconciliation. *See* forgiveness
redlining, racism and, 170–71
Reformation, contribution to secularized society, 119
refugees, deaths of, 149
relational justice, 77
relationships, 96–97
relativism versus pluralism, 73
religion
    evolutionary benefits, 133–34
    in public space, 118
religious atheists, 140, 141–44
religious pluralism
    compassion attribute, 75–78
    dialogical attribute, 81–82
    equality and the marginalized, 83–84
    exclusivism, disguised as, 85–88
    generally, 66–72, 94–95
    Hinduism and, 88
    history and, 119–20, 162–63
    humble attribute, 72
    identity and tradition, 84–85
    Islam and, 88–92
    Judaism and, 88–92
    just attribute, 72–75
    kinds of, 125
    of memory, 157–58
    as moral indifference, 83–84
    in nature, 92–94
    pluralist attribute, 78–81
    relativism versus, 73
    role of secularism in, 128–29
religious self-sufficiency, 53
religious-secular dialogue. *See* secular-religious dialogue
ren (benevolence), 58
Republic (Plato), 7
Requiem, Rwanda (Apol), 182, 215–23
Requiem Mass, 218, 219, 221
Resentment's Virtue (Brudholm), 237
responsibility, ethical, 130
restorative justice, 234–37. *See also* forgiveness
"Ruined for life" (JVC slogan), 35
Rūpyāvatī (story of), 52–53
Rwanda
    forgiveness, 231, 242, 258–59
    genocide, 212–23

"A Sacred Obligation" (Christian document), 109
Saga (comic book), 96
Sahih al-Bukhari, 257
Sanctus (Catholicism), 222, 223
Sarajevo, Bosnia (Serbian bombing of 1999), 199n78
science and faith, 12–16
Scripture, on ethics, 131–32
"Sea mi gozo en el llanto" (poem), 42–43
The Season of Trouble: Life Amid the Ruins of Sri Lanka's Civil War (Mohan), 182, 212
Second Ecumenical Council of the Vatican, 31
2 Samuel (Tanakh), 252
Second-Hand Time (Alexievich), 224
secular, defined, 78
A Secular Age (Taylor), 124, 129, 143
Secularism and Freedom of Conscience (Taylor and Maclure), 128–29
secularity and secularism
    defined, 117–18
    ethics, 127
    godless humility, 130–33
    history, 118–22
    inter/intra-religious context, 126–30
    in Ireland, 124
    multiple secularisms, 127
    in pluralism, 128–30. *See also* atheism
secularization thesis, 122–25
secular-religious dialogue
    atheist values, 133–34
    bridge-building, 136
    conflict, 138–39
    on need for God, 137–38
    sacred/secular blending, 125–26, 144–46
    shared platforms, 138–141
self, conquering through humility, 28–31
self-forgiveness, 261
self-sufficiency, religious, 53
September 11th attacks, 200–202

Serbia (Sarajevo bombings of 1999), 199n78
Sermon on the Mount, 27, 50, 108, 220
servile humility, 11
Shoah
    denial among Muslims, 206
    effect on faith, 120, 134–35
    effect on interfaith dialogue, 105
    forgiveness, 241–43, 250
    moral failure in, 125–26
    post-9/11 abuses compared to, 200
    postmodernism, 161
Sikhism, 47n4
Silenus, 141n126
The Silenus (magazine), 17
Sisters of Our Lady of Sion, 109
snakes, role of in ancient texts, 21n1
social-justice dialogue, 100
soft atheism, 143
solidarity with the suffering, 185
Spain, Jewish population in, 269
"*Spe Salvi*" (papal encyclical), 108
Spinney Hill, N.Y., 165–66
Spiritual Exercises (Ignatius), 36–39
Sri Lanka, genocide, 212–15
"The Star Thrower" (Eiseley), 93
Star Wars (film), 96
Sula (Morrison), 170
Summa Theologiae (Aquinas), 31, 91
The Sunflower (Wiesenthal), 241

Talmud, 40, 89, 253
Tamil Tigers, 213
Tamils people, 212–15
Tanach (Hebrew Bible), 23–25, 110, 132
Tao Te Ching (Lao-Tzu), 56
Taoism
    on Confucius, 57–58
    humility and, 54–57
temperance, 33
Teresa of Ávila, 40–46
testimonies of mass atrocity
    about, 182, 224
    Argentina, 183–86
    China, 186–98

testimonies of mass atrocity (*cont.*)
    humbling effect, 184, 185
    Rwanda, 212–23
    Sri Lanka, 212–15
    United States, 198–201, 202–8, 209–12
theist-atheist dialogue. *See* secular-religious dialogue
theological level of dialogue, 100–101
theological virtues, 32
Thomas, of Aquinas, 31–35
Tiananmen Square massacre, Beijing, China, 186–87, 188, 190
Torah, 111
torture. *See* testimonies of mass atrocity
totalitarianism, anti-memory propaganda, 155
Toul Sleng Prison, Cambodia, 237–38
Treatise on Tzedakah (Maimonides), 40
The Trial (Kafka), 202
Truth and Reconciliation Commission (Liberia), 240–41
Turkey, Hagia Sophia, Istanbul, 87
Tutsis, in Rwanda, 216, 219–21

ultra-pluralism, 80
unbelief, attempts to quantify, 123–24. *See also* atheism
unduly humble, 33
unforgivable acts, 227–28, 239–43, 253, 256, 266
The Unintended Reformation (Gregory), 118
United States
    African Americans (*See* African Americans)
    American Revolution, 119
    Enlightenment's philosophy impact, 119
    eviction practices, 209–12
    Native American's treatment, 59–62
    post-9/11 abuses, 198–201, 202–8
    religious climate, 119, 120–21
    universal housing vouchers, 211–12
Universal Pluralism, 79
us/them fallacy, 199–200

Vanity Fair (Thackeray), 11, 258
Vatican Council II, 31
victim-centered forgiveness, 232–33, 235
Voting Rights Act (1965), 171

The Walking Dead, 261–62
War on Drugs, 172–74, 177
water, as metaphor of many possibilities, 55–56
The Way of Perfection (Teresa of Ávila), 40
wealth, distribution of, 47
witness testimony. *See* testimonies of mass atrocity
women
    in the Bible, 27–28
    equality for, 42
    gender discrimination, 54
    marginalized, 10
    in religions, 102
wu-wei (action less action), 55, 57

Yangon, Insein Prison, Myanmar, 238
yoga, 48–49

Zechariah (Biblical figure), 223
The Zohar (kabbalist text), 40
Zoroastrianism, 47n4

www.ingramcontent.com/pod-product-compliance
Lightning Source LLC
Chambersburg PA
CBHW020109010526
44115CB00008B/756